Language and Literacy from an Educational Perspective

Volume II: In Schools

A reader edited by Neil Mercer
at the Open University

OPEN UNIVERSITY PRESS

Milton Keynes · Philadelphia

Open University Press
Open University Educational Enterprises Limited
12 Cofferidge Close
Stony Stratford
Milton Keynes MK11 1BY, England

and

242 Cherry Street
Philadelphia, PA 19106, USA

First Published 1988

British Library Cataloguing in Publication Data

Language and literacy from an educational perspective:
  a reader.
  Vol. 2: In schools
  1. Language arts
  I. Mercer, Neil
  407'1   LB1575.8
  ISBN 0–335–10293–X

  ISBN 0–335–15558–8 Pbk

Library of Congress Cataloging in Publication Data
Main entry under title:
Language and literacy from an educational perspective.
  Contents: ——v. 2. In schools.
  1. Children——Language. 2. Home and school.
3. Language arts (Elementary). 4. Literacy.
I. Mercer, Neil.
LB1139.L3L3224 1987   372.6   87–22052

ISBN 0–335–10293–X

ISBN 0–335–15558–8 (U.S. : pbk.)

Project management: Clarke Williams
Printed in Great Britain

Contents

Section III : Teaching Reading

Section IV : Teaching Writing

Section V : Monitoring and Assessment

Language and Literacy from an Educational Perspective

Volume II

In Schools

E815 central course team

L. John Chapman

Janet Maybin

Neil Mercer

Harold Rosen

Preface

In this 'age of information', the development of children's spoken and written language deserves to be given high educational priority. There are, however, many ways in which this development may be defined, and a wide variety of educational practices claim the justification of helping children achieve an effective command of language. This book consists of a collection of articles which, despite being drawn from very different sources, all deal with aspects of children's experience of oral and written language in school. As such, it represents many of the conflicting views and continuing debates which typify this field of education.

This is the second volume of *Language and Literacy from an Educational Perspective*, and so some of the issues dealt with here assume a theoretical basis in the contents of Volume I (subtitled *Language Studies*). Both volumes were expressly created to serve the needs of E815 *Language and Literacy*, which is one module of the Open University's taught MA in Education. They should therefore provide suitable reading for all postgraduate students of education, and especially those who are also practising teachers.

For the sake of brevity, most of the articles included have been reduced to shorter forms of their originals (editorial cuts are indicated thus: [. . .]). I am very grateful to Harold Rosen, John Chapman and Janet Maybin for their help in preparing this collection of readings.

Neil Mercer

Acknowledgements

All possible care has been taken to trace ownership of the material included in this volume, and Open University Press would like to make grateful acknowledgement for permission to reproduce it here.

1.1 B. Tizard *et al.* 'Language and Social Class: Is Verbal Deprivation a Myth?', *Journal of Child Psychology and Psychiatry*, Pergamon Press, Volume 24, No. 4, pp. 533–542.

1.2 S. Brice-Heath (1985). 'A Search for Shared Backgrounds', *Harvard Educational Review*, Volume 55, No. 4, pp. 443–447.

1.3 S. Brice-Heath (1982). 'What No Bedtime Story Means: Narrative Skills at Home and School', *Language and Society*, Volume 11, pp. 49–76.

1.4 H. Rosen (1985). 'The Voices of Communities and Language in Classrooms: A Review of *Ways With Words*', *Harvard Educational Review*, Volume 55, No. 4, pp. 448–456.

1.5 M. Hoffman (1981). 'Children's Reading and Social Values', *Language in School and Community*, Edward Arnold, pp. 192–214.

1.6 J. French and P. French (1984). 'Gender Imbalances in the Primary Classroom: An Interactional Account', *Educational Research*, NFER Publishing Company Limited, Volume 26, No. 2, pp. 127–136.

1.7 J. Levine (1981). 'Developing Pedagogies for Multilingual Classes', *English in Education*, The National Association for the Teaching of English, Volume 15, No. 3, pp. 25–33.

2.1 W. Mittins (1987). 'But Where's the Bloody Horse?', *NATE News*, The National Association for the Teaching of English, Spring edition, pp. 6–8.

2.2 K. Perera (1987). 'Understanding Language'. This article is reproduced by kind permission of the National Association of Advisers in English. The article is based on a talk given by Katherine Perera at the Association's Annual Conference in York in September 1986.

3.1 D. Pidgeon (1984). 'Theory and Practice in Learning to Read', *Language Awareness and Learning to Read* edited by J. Downing and R. Valtin, Springer-Verlag New York Inc.

3.2 J.M. Morris (1984). 'Focus on Phonics: Phonics 44 for Initial Literacy in English', *Reading*, United Kingdom Reading Association, Volume 18, No. 1, pp. 13–24.

3.3   C.B. Cazden. 'Social Context of Learning to Read', *Theory and Practice of Early Reading* edited by L.B. Resnick and P.A. Weaver. Reprinted by permission of Lawrence Erlbaum Associates, Inc.

3.4   K.S. Goodman and Y.M. Goodman (1977). 'Learning about Psycholinguistic Processes by Analyzing Oral Reading', *Harvard Educational Review*, Volume 47, No. 3, pp. 317–32.

3.5   K. Topping (1986). 'W.H.I.C.H. Parental Involvement in Reading Scheme? A Guide for Practitioners', *Reading*, United Kingdom Reading Association, Volume 20, No. 3, pp. 148–156.

3.6   T. Martin (1986). 'Leslie: A Reading Failure Talks About Failing', *Reading*, United Kingdom Reading Association, Volume 20, No. 1, pp. 43–52.

3.7   R. Moy and M. Raleigh (1980). 'Comprehension: Bringing it Back Alive', *The English Magazine*, The ILEA English Centre, Autumn 1980, pp. 29–37.

4.1   'Writing, Composition and Rhetoric' by Janet Emis. Reprinted with permission of The Free Press, a Division of Macmillan, Inc. from *Encyclopedia of Educational Research*, Fifth Edition, Harold E. Mitzel, Editor in Chief, Volume 4, pages 2021–2036. Copyright © 1982 American Educational Research Association.

4.2   L. Thorogood and B. Raban (1985). 'Fostering Development in the Writing of Eight Year Olds', *Reading*, United Kingdom Reading Association, Volume 19, No. 2.

4.3   A. Freedman and I. Pringle (1984). 'Why Students Can't Write Arguments', *English in Education*, National Association for the Teaching of English, Volume 18, No. 2.

5.1   From *Handbook of Reading Research*. Editor P. David Pearson. Copyright © 1984 by Longman Inc. All rights reserved.

5.2   Gorman, White, Orchard, Tate and Sexton (1979). 'Language Performance in Schools', *APU Primary Survey Report No. 1*, HMSO. Reproduced with the permission of the Controller of Her Majesty's Stationery Office.

5.3   H. Rosen (1982). 'The Language Monitors: A Critique of the APU's Primary Survey Report *Language Performance in Schools*', *The Language Monitors*, Bedford Way Papers 11, Institute of Education, University of London.

5.4   M. MacLure (1987). Commissioned for this collection.

5.5   B. Stierer (1983). 'A Researcher Reading Teachers Reading Children Reading', *Opening Moves* edited by M. Meek, Bedford Way Papers 17, Institute of Education, University of London.

SECTION I

Home, School and Society

Introduction

Some of the most controversial issues in educational research are those to do with the relationship between children's experience of life outside school and the ways they spend their time in the classroom. Often tied to a concern about the relative educational achievement of children from different social backgrounds, much research about these matters has focused on language use. This section begins with a paper by Tizard, Hughes, Carmichael and Pinkerton, who use their own observations of young children at home and in nursery schools to discuss the contentious issue of 'verbal deprivation'.

Much of the vitality in this field of research comes from a healthy disagreement amongst researchers about just what are the key questions which should be addressed, and how can they best be answered. This is well reflected in the next three articles. First there is a critical review by Shirley Brice Heath of Tizard *et al.*'s research, as presented in more detail in the influential book *Young Children Learning* (Tizard and Hughes, 1984). This is followed by one of Heath's own research papers; the reader may thus judge the critic's own performance. This is followed by a critical review of Heath's own influential book *Ways with Words* (which draws on the same research as her paper included here) by Harold Rosen.

A very different perspective on literacy and social values is provided by Mary Hoffman, who examines the *content* of children's reading and considers the implications of this 'reading diet' for their moral education. The article which then follows, by French and French, shows how the cultural values of society may directly influence how teachers and children interact in class. They discuss the well-established finding that, in mixed-sex classrooms, boys typically receive more attention from teachers than girls.

The final article of this section deals very specifically with the needs of children whose out-of-school experience might well be perceived as educationally advantageous, but is all too often defined in terms of 'handicap'. Josie Levine outlines some ways of teaching which may offer most benefit to bilingual children.

Reference

Tizard, B. and Hughes, M. (1984) *Young Children Learning*. Harvard University Press, Cambridge, MA.

1.1 Language and Social Class: Is Verbal Deprivation a Myth?

Barbara Tizard, Martin Hughes, Helen Carmichael and Gill Pinkerton

Source: Edited version of Tizard, B., Hughes, M., Carmichael, H. and Pinkerton, G. (1983) 'Language and social class: is verbal deprivation a myth?' *Journal of Child Psychology and Psychiatry*, Vol. 24, No. 4, pp. 533–542.

Introduction

In 1969, Labov wrote a famous paper, *The Logic of Non-standard English*, in which he argued that "the notion of verbal deprivation is a part of the modern mythology of educational psychology". This myth was said to be composed of a number of propositions, each of which he contested — that urban ghetto children have a verbal deficit, that this deficit is a result of inadequate verbal stimulation in the home and of restriction to a non-standard dialect which does not allow the expression of complex or logical thinking, and that this verbal deficit is a major cause of poor performance at school. Labov contended that, far from receiving inadequate language stimulation at home, ghetto children grow up in a highly verbal culture and, further, that their dialect has the same potentiality for logical thinking as does standard English. Hence he concluded that it cannot be the language deficiencies of the child which are responsible for poor school performance: language compensatory programmes are therefore unnecessary and misleading.

Why, then, has the myth developed? Labov accepted that lower class children may be monosyllabic in conversation with teachers and psychologists, but argued that this apparent verbal deficit is in reality a response to a social situation which they perceive as threatening. He illustrated his point by quoting from an interview transcript in which a black child answered questions briefly, almost monosyllabically. When the same interviewer transformed the social situation by sitting on the floor, sharing round potato crisps, bringing along another child, introducing taboo words and topics, and turning the interview into something more in the nature of a party, the previously non-verbal child began to talk freely. Labov concluded that the social situation is the most important determinant of verbal behaviour, and that an adult must enter into the right social relationship with a child if he wants to assess his language capacity.

At about the same time, Houston (1970) argued that since language learning is a species universal, disadvantaged children cannot be linguistically deprived. The ability to abstract, generalise and categorise is innate, and implicit in the use of language itself. For this reason, much of language is impregnable to environmental variations. Like Labov, Houston believed that the notion of linguistic deprivation arose because disadvantaged children have two 'registers' or styles of language for different situations. Teachers and psychologists usually hear only the limited school register, deployed by the child in alien and potentially threatening settings. In their non-school register the children use language as fluently and for the same purposes as other children. It should be noted that neither Labov nor Houston argued that there were *no* social class differences in children's language — they suggested that lower class children might need help in learning to be explicit and in extending their vocabulary, but not in conceptual and logical thinking.

However, in Britain at least, a belief in working class verbal deprivation is still widely held. Despite the attention paid to social context by linguists in recent years, the influence of situational variables on language is rarely acknowledged within educational psychology. Joan Tough (1977), for example, who has had a major influence on in-service training for primary teachers, cites the following conversation between a teacher and a 5-year-old child, Paul, who is playing with a toy farm, to show "the difficulty that many children have in taking part in conversation".

T: Tell me what is happening, will you?
P: That's a farm.
T: Oh, that's a farm here, is it? Who lives in the farm, I wonder?
P: Them lot. (points)
T: Oh, who are they?
P: The people.
T: What sort of people live in a farm?
(P Shrugs)
T: What do we call the man who lives in a farm, do you know?
P: Farmer.

At no point does Tough consider the possibility that Paul's limited contribution to this conversation reflects his social unease or defensiveness, rather than his limited grasp of language, or suggest that the teacher might learn from listening to his conversation in an out-of-school setting or by transforming the social situation between teacher and child. Similarly, a recent influential government report states that "many young children do not have the opportunity to develop at home the more complex forms of language which school education demands of them" (Bullock Report, 1975). This is said to be because "the context in which they use language and the nature of exchange at home does not call for the higher degree of complexity . . . what is needed is to create the context and conditions in which the ability can develop".

Arguing from the same premise, Joan Tough states that whilst most children experience a good deal of language aimed at controlling their behaviour, some rarely hear language used for explanations, reflecting on the reasons for behaviour, examining interesting features of the world around them, etc. Hence she urges the teacher to foster more complex uses of language by asking children such questions as "What happened at your party yesterday?" "What are you going to do next?" or "Why does a fort need high walls?"

Neither the Bullock Report nor Joan Tough commit themselves about the proportion of children whose homes are language-deficient: rather, they invoke, without defining it, the concept of 'disadvantage'. In our discussions with teachers we have found that they often believe that most children in working class areas are in need of special language help. For example, in another study we found that the most frequently mentioned aim of nursery education listed by teachers was 'enriching language', often in relation to the deficiencies of the home (Tizard *et al.*, 1981). These beliefs are not usually based on any first-hand evidence of the language used in working class homes. Tough, for example, quotes conversations overheard in launderettes and on buses, and it is probably true that most people have heard very controlling conversations from working class mothers in public places. But it cannot be assumed that in the privacy of the home these families do not use language for other purposes. Indeed, the supposition seems inherently implausible — it is difficult to imagine a culture or subculture in which the nature of social exchange does not call for recall, anticipation and reasoning. It seems much more likely that working class mothers also have different speech registers and that in a public situation, where they feel open to criticism, they talk differently to their children than they do at home.

We were able to test some of the hypotheses discussed above in a study of the conversations of 4-year-old girls at school and at home. That is, we were able to see whether children used a more limited speech register in talking to their teachers than to their mothers, whether the working class children used language for complex thinking purposes and whether these usages appeared in the language directed to them by their mothers. We were also able to look for social class differences in children's and mother's talk, and to see whether there was evidence that the teachers were compensating for the mothers' linguistic deficiencies. Other findings from this study have been reported elsewhere (Tizard *et al.*, 1980, 1982, 1983). Some are basic to the interpretation of the present study; there were three times as many adult–child conversations at home as at school, and these conversations were twice as long at home as at school; further, there were no social class differences in either of these quantitative measures.

Method

Subjects

The subjects were 30 girls, aged between 3 years 9 months and 4 years 3 months (mean age 3 years 11 months, S.D. 1.8 months). Half the girls were working class; that is, their fathers were manual workers and their mothers had left school at the minimum school-leaving age with no educational qualification. The other girls were middle class; that is, their fathers were in professional or managerial positions and their mothers had either attended university or colleges of education or had qualified to do so. The other criteria were that the children should attend morning nursery school and spend their afternoons at home with their mothers, that they should have not more than one or two sibs, that they should come from intact two-parent families and that the language used at home should be English. Three of the 30 girls were only children. Six mothers in both social classes worked or studied part-time, in the morning or evening. Of the working class fathers, two-thirds were skilled manual workers, e.g. electricians and fitters; the rest were semi-skilled or unskilled.

The working class children lived in small, two-parent families, the majority in Council housing, and appeared to be well cared for, much loved and plentifully supplied with toys. Nursery schooling in Britain, although free, is not compulsory, and the children were therefore not a random selection of 4-year-olds. However, when we asked the mothers why they had sent their children to nursery school, none of the working class mothers gave 'educational' reasons — they usually answered that the child needed company, that she got bored at home and that the school was just down the road. These answers suggest that the children were probably typical of the majority of working class children who attend half-day nursery school. Their I.Q.s were within the expected range. The mean Stanford Binet I.Q. of the working class girls was 106.4, S.D. 13.2., and of the middle class girls, 122.3, S.D. 11.3.

The children were drawn from nine different schools; in each school, children from both social classes were selected. In schools where more than two children from each social class fulfilled our criteria, the study children were selected by tossing a coin. All the parents of the children who fulfilled our criteria agreed to take part in the project; that is, we were not studying a self-selected group. Two very timid children could not be persuaded to wear the special dress required and were replaced by children from the same schools who met our criteria.

Schools
All nine schools were run by the local authorities for children aged three and four years. The children were in classes of 20–25 children, staffed by a trained teacher and one or two assistants, usually helped by one or two students. Most of the morning was spent in free play with a wide variety of equipment. The staff role was primarily to suggest, and sometimes to demonstrate, ways of using play material, and to help the children's language by informal conversation. Some of the schools also had a group story or music session for the whole class, but we excluded these sessions from our study.

Recording method
The children wore a sleeveless dress, fitted with a tiny microphone and radio-transmitter. The transmitter had a range of about 100 yards, so that the

child could move freely about house and garden. An observer followed the children fairly closely, in order to record a detailed context of the conversations (*cf.* Hughes *et al.*, 1979).

Recording times

Since our pilot study had suggested that the first day of observation tends to be atypical (Hughes *et at.*, 1979), we observed in the homes for two consecutive afternoons from 1 to 3.30 p.m. but used only the data from the second day. In the schools, we observed for three consecutive mornings from about 9 to 11.30 a.m. and used only the data from the second and third days. It was necessary to record for an extra day at school because of the smaller number of adult–child conversations at school (Tizard *et al.*, 1980).

Complex cognitive uses of language

Each turn of both adult and child talk was scrutinised to see whether it used language in any of the ways listed below. The codes were derived largely from Joan Tough's classification of the cognitive uses of language, omitting those uses which she describes as universal and including those which she argues are unfamiliar to disadvantaged children (Tough, 1976). The only questions coded were YES/NO questions and tag questions — the others were the subject of a separate analysis (Tizard *et al.*, 1983). Repetitions of a remark were not coded; more than one code could be applied to a turn if it included more than one instance of a complex use of language.

1. Comparisons, similarities and differences, e.g. "You're too big for that lorry".
2. Recall of events, e.g. "Last week we went to granny's, didn't we?".
3. Future plans, e.g. "We'll go swimming tomorrow".
4. Linking at least two events in time by the use of such words as "while", "when", "until" and "then", e.g. "We can't go shopping till Daddy gets home".
5. Describing purposes of objects, e.g. "The elastic is for making a mask".
6. Giving reasons, explanations, purposes or results of actions, e.g. "The cat's run away 'cos you pulled her tail" (explanations which took the form of assertions, authority statements, or the expression of wishes, e.g. "Because it is/I want to/I say so", were excluded).
7. Conditionals concerned with hypothetical events, e.g. "If it stops raining we can go in the garden".
8. Generalisations and definitions, e.g. "Pigs don't fly, birds do".
9. Reasoning and inference, e.g. "If you eat your sweets, you can't save them".
10. Projecting into self or other's thought or feelings, e.g. "I expect Joan is feeling very sad now".
11. Problem solving, i.e. a creative insight into the situation, e.g. C. "We haven't got enough lolly sticks to make it". M. "Well, we'll break them in two, then" (M's turn coded 11).

The speech forms did not have to be grammatically correct but the use of language had to be explicit.

Results

Reliabilities
Exact agreement between two coders on the use of individual language codes in 30 conversations was 72%. If the turns where both coders agreed that no code was required are included, the agreement was 92%.

Cognitive uses of language: adults
Expressed as hourly rates, mothers used language for complex purposes significantly more often than did teachers, and middle class mothers did so significantly more often than did working class mothers (Table 1). There was also a significant social class difference in the teachers' talk, with more complex uses being addressed to middle class children than to working class children. This was true both for all the codes summed together and for each code considered separately. The higher rates for mothers were, of course, associated with the fact that much more mother–child talk occurred per hour than teacher–child talk (Tizard *et al.*, 1980). Whilst hourly rates represent the input to the child, the proportion of complex language usages in a speaker's talk represents her characteristic style. Table 1 shows that the teachers' talk was more densely packed with complex language usage than was the mothers. This was true for all the codes summed together and for each code considered separately. Both at home and at school, complex uses of language formed a smaller proportion of the talk addressed to working class children than to middle class children.

Table 1. Adult's total complex uses of language

| | Hourly rates | | Percentage of total turns | |
	School mean	Home mean	School mean	Home mean
Working class	11.4	38.4	14.3	8.8
Middle class	17.4	51.5	17.2	11.6
School vs home	$F = 79.4***$		School vs home $F = 21.4***$	
Class	$F = 5.0*$		Class $F = 5.2*$	
No significant interaction			No significant interaction	

$***P < 0.001$; $**P < 0.01$; $*P < 0.05$

Cognitive uses of language: children
In terms of hourly rates, children used language for complex purposes much more often at home than at school, and in both settings middle class children used language for these purposes significantly more often than working class children (Table 2). However, the effect of setting was more marked for the working class children, as is shown by the significant interaction between class and setting. This was also true when uses of language were considered as a proportion of the children's total talk. Indeed, in terms of *proportion* of total

talk, there was no difference in the middle class children's use of language at home and at school, but for working class children there was a significant difference.

Table 2. Children's total complex uses of language

| | Hourly rates | | Percentage of total turns | |
	School mean	Home mean	School mean	Home mean
Working class	2.2	17.1	2.4	3.8
Middle class	5.0	20.1	4.6	4.4
School vs home $F = 110.1***$			School vs home $F = 6.2***$	
Class $F = 6.3*$			Class $F = 9.7**$	
Interaction $F = 5.5*$			Interaction $F = 6.2*$	

$***P<0.001; **P<0.01; *P<0.05$

Range of language use: adults and children

Table 3 shows that for both adults and children there was a wider range of language usage (that is, a greater number of codes were used) at home than at school. This finding was no doubt associated with the greater amount of adult–child talk at home. There was a significant social class difference between children in the range of language usage but not between mothers.

Table 3. Range of language usage (means)

| | At home | | At school | |
	Mothers	Children	Teachers	Children
Middle class	8.7	7.8	7.9	5.7
Working class	8.3	6.7	7.2	3.3
Adults: home vs school, $F = 8.1**$;		Class	$F = 2.1$, N.S.	
Children: home vs school, $F = 38.0***$;		Class	$F = 10.8*$	

$***P<0.001; **P<0.01; *P<0.05$

Correlations

1. *Home vs school.* There were no significant correlations between the hourly rate or proportion of complex uses of language addressed to the same child at home and at school or spoken by the same child at home and at school.

2. *Adults' use vs children's use.* There were significant correlations between the hourly rate with which the mother and child, but not teacher and child, addressed language for complex purposes to each other (working class at home: $r = 0.76$. $P<0.001$; middle class at home: $r = 0.72$, $P<0.01$).

3. *With other aspects of language.* There were significant Pearson correlation coefficients between the hourly rate of the adults' cognitive demands to the child (*cf.* Tizard *et al.*, 1982) and the hourly rate with which the adult used language for complex purposes in talking to her (to both working class and middle class at school: $r = 0.6$, $P < 0.05$; to working class at home: $r = 0.8$, $P < 0.001$; to middle class at home: $r = 0.6$, $P < 0.05$). For the working class children only, there was a relationship between the hourly rate of the mothers' complex use of language and the hourly rate of the child's "why" and "how" questions ($r = 0.06$, $P < 0.06$).

Discussion

Our evidence certainly supports Labov's and Houston's contention that setting has a marked effect on the language style of working class children. Working class girls displayed a smaller range of complex language usages in talking to their teachers than to their mothers, and their talk to teachers contained a smaller proportion of these usages. In five hours at school, 4 of the 15 working class girls made either no use of language for complex purposes in talking to teachers or only one use, yet in half that time at home they made respectively 31, 28, 50 and 7 such uses. For one of these children, the longest conversation with a teacher was as follows:

T: That's beautiful (looking at C's drawing).
    What's this? (points at figure).
C: A dog.
T: A dog?
C: But he hasn't got no legs.
T: Just didn't want any legs, did he? What's that bit there?
C: I dunno.
T: Will you write your name on it?
(C: Doesn't reply. T writes C's name on drawing).

At home, the same child took a much more active part in initiating and sustaining conversations. She also showed command of most of our coded complex uses of language; she used several in the following conversation, which took place whilst she was making a pool of water in the earth in her garden:

C: Is it leaking?
M: Looks like it.
C: Why is it?
    (M. No reply.)
C: Is it, does it leak now?
M: Yes, it's all soaking in the ground.
C: Oh well, we better put some stones in then. Better get a little chunk of dirt so it won't go down. That one won't do, this is better. There. That'll save it. Now it won't go away, will it?

The inhibiting effect of the teachers on the working class girls was also apparent in other aspects of their language, reported elsewhere (Tizard *et al.*, 1980, 1983). This effect is all the more striking in that, while Labov was describing 8-year-old urban ghetto boys, alienated from somewhat punitive schools, our observations were made on girls aged not quite four, attending nursery schools and classes with a free play regimen. We can only speculate about why the working class girls were more affected by the nursery school setting than were the middle class girls. For the middle class girls, there were certainly more points of resemblance between home and school (e.g. in the play equipment, and the teachers' accent and speech style); the middle class mothers were more confident in their relations with the teachers; and more of the middle class children had previously attended playgroups.

A second contention of Labov's and Houston's was also confirmed: that in their own milieu, working class children display all the essential verbal cognitive skills. During the course of 2½ hours at home all but one of the working class girls in our study made comparisons, recalled past events and discussed future plans, and all but two linked events in time and used if-then constructions. Similarly, during the afternoon *all* the working class mothers made comparisons, offered explanations, used if-then constructions and linked events in time, and all but one used language for recall and to discuss the future.

Nevertheless, in the case of both mothers and children there were social class differences in the frequency of these usages. The less frequent use of language for complex purposes by working class mothers seemed to be linked with their tendency to express their meaning more implicitly. Of course, much meaning in everyday spoken discourse *is* implicit, and all the mothers in our study used many implicit meanings. The middle class mothers used them less frequently, perhaps because their prolonged education had social-ised them to a greater extent into explicit usages or because they more often thought it important to be sure that their child grasped their explanations.

But all the mothers became explicit at times. One working class mother frequently gave very implicit explanations, for example: M. "Don't play with the baby now" (the baby was eating his dinner). C. "Why?" M. "He might get a lump". Later in the afternoon she became very explicit about an issue which she clearly wanted her daughter to understand: C. "I'll save these and eat them, right?" (a packet of sweets) M. "You can't save them *and* eat them. You either save them and *don't* eat them, or you eat them. So what do you want to do? Save them? Or eat them?" C. "Save them and get another packet". M. "Where you gonna get the money for the next packet?"

It was certainly not the case that these children were more often exposed to complex usages of language at school. True, the teachers' talk was more densely packed with such usages than was that of either group of mothers, although the range they used was slightly smaller, but because each child was spoken to much less often by her teacher than her mother, she was less likely to hear language used for complex purposes at school than at home. Thus, although the recording time at school was twice as long as at home, at school fewer working class children heard language used to make comparisons and if-then constructions, recall, discuss future plans, make generalisations, draw inferences or project into others' feelings and thought than at home. Further, despite the teachers' compensatory intentions, they did in fact address significantly fewer of these usages to working class than to middle class children.

Arguably, the amount of talk at home may have been more enhanced by the presence of the observer than was the case of school. Nevertheless, it seems reasonable to expect that the home, with an adult–child ratio of 1–2 or 1–3, will generate more adult–child talk than school, with its adult–child ratio of 1–10 or 1–15. Not only is the adult–child ratio at home better than in any school, but in the close parent–child relationship the child is more likely to talk freely. Further, far from it being the case that "the nature of the exchange (at home) does not call for the higher degree of complexity" (Bullock Report, 1975), the very texture of family life requires such usages. Disputes between children, and between parents and children, frequent shopping expeditions and weekend visits to and from relatives are all likely to require language to be used to compare, recall, explain, plan and predict. It is in the nursery, where the 'here and now' of the play environment dominates and where the child is not close enough to her teacher to want to confide in her, that the more primitive uses of language will suffice the child.

It may be argued that our findings are not in conflict with the widely held belief that lower class children have a language deficit, because our sample was not drawn from the lower working class — only one-third had fathers in semi-skilled or unskilled occupations, while the rest were skilled manual workers. In this respect, however, our study did not differ markedly from most British studies of disadvantaged children, since children with fathers in social classes 4 and 5 never consitute a majority in any school, even in deprived areas (*cf.* Barnes and Lucas (1975) for an exposition of this point). Thus in Bernstein's (1970) major empirical study, 42% of the children had fathers in semi-skilled or unskilled manual jobs (Brandis and Henderson, 1970); in the West Riding Educational Priority Area Project the proportion was 44% (Smith, 1975); and in the N.F.E.R. compensatory pre-school project, 30% (Woodhead, 1976). Further, the mothers in our sample had a uniformly low educational level — all had left school at the earliest possible age, with no public examination successes. There is thus no reason to believe that our sample differed drastically from other British area- or school-based studies of working class children.

We did, with this sample, find social class differences in language usage; in this paper we show that the working class children less frequently used language for complex purposes, and other differences are recorded elsewhere. To describe such a difference as a 'verbal deficit' is, however, likely to be seriously misleading, suggesting as it does a lack of basic skills. Bernstein (1970), to whom this view is often attributed, explicitly rejects the notion of verbal deficit. Further, although it is generally assumed that such language differences are the *cause* of social class differences in educational achievement, this has yet to be established. The relationship could be correlational, levels of educational achievement being related to other factors, e.g. parental expectations of and reinforcement for academic work, teachers' expectations, and children's interest in sedentary activities.

Despite the widespread belief, enshrined in the Bullock Report, that working class children benefit from nursery school attendance because of the teacher's "measured attention to the child's language needs" (p. 54), the evidence suggests that they are much more likely to receive this from their mothers. Of course, there will be some children of whom this is not true. It seems likely that they would require an intensive compensatory education programme, with a very much higher adult–child ratio than is provided in British nursery schools.

None of this implies that children do not generally benefit from nursery school attendance. Apart from social gains, nursery school offers opportunities for physical, musical and creative activities, and acts as a valuable half-way post between home and school. Our findings, reported here and elsewhere, suggest, however, that in the majority of cases the child's basic verbal-cognitive skills are developed at home.

Summary

A study was made of complex usages of language in the spontaneous conversation of 30 4-year-old girls, their mothers and their teachers, at home and at school. There were significant social class differences in frequency, but almost all the usages appeared in the talk of almost of all the mothers and children at least once. The working class girls' language style changed more between home and school than did that of the middle class girls. The teachers' talk contained a higher proportion of these usages than the mothers', but the overall input to the children was less at school. The findings are discussed in relation to Labov's argument that verbal deprivation is a myth.

Acknowledgements

We would like to acknowledge the cooperation of the teachers, parents and children in the study, and the statistical help of Ian Plewis and Charles Owen.

References

Barnes, J. and Lucas, M. (1975) Positive discrimination in education: individuals, groups and institutions. In J. Barnes (ed.) *Educational Priority, Vol. 3. Curriculum Innovation in London's EPAs* (Edited by Barnes, J.), pp. 237–279. H.M.S.O., London.
Bernstein, B. (1970) Education cannot compensate for society. *New Soc.* **15**, 26th February, 344–347.

Brandis, W. and Henderson, B. (1970) *Social Class: Language and Communication.* Routledge & Kegan Paul, London.

Bullock Report (1975) *A Language for Life.* D.E.S. H.M.S.O., London.

Houston, S. (1970) A re-examination of some assumptions about the language of the disadvantaged child. *Child Dev.* **41,** 947–963.

Hughes, M., Carmichael, H., Pinkerton, G. and Tizard, B. (1979) Recording children's conversations at home and a nursery school: a technique and some methodological considerations. *J. Child Psychol: Psychiat.* **20,** 225–232.

Labov, W. (1969) The logic of non-standard English. *Georgetown Monogr. Ling.* **22,** 11–31.

Smith, G. (ed.) (1975) *Educational Priority. The West Riding Project.* H.M.S.O., London.

Tizard, B., Carmichael, H., Hughes, M. and Pinkerton, G. (1980) Four year olds talking to mothers and teachers. In *Language and Language Disorders in Childhood* (Edited by Hersov, L. A., Berger, M. and Nichol, A. R.), Ch. 3, pp. 49–76. Pergamon Press, Oxford.

Tizard, B., Mortimore, J. and Burchell, B. (1981) *Involving Parents in Nursery and Infant Schools.* Grant McIntyre, London.

Tizard, B., Hughes, M., Carmichael, H. and Pinkerton, G. (1982) Adults' cognitive demands at home and at nursery school. *J. Child Psychol. Psychiat* **23,** 105–116.

Tizard, B., Hughes, M., Carmichael, H. and Pinkerton, G. (1983) Children's questions and adults' answers. *J. Child Psychol. Psychiat.* **24,** 269–281.

Tough, J. (1976) *Listening to Children Talking.* Ward Lock Educational, London.

Tough, J. (1977) *Talking and Learning: A Guide to Fostering Communication Skills in Nursery and Infant Schools.* Ward Lock Educational, London.

Woodhead, M. (ed.) (1976) *An Experiment in Nursery Education.* N.F.E.R., Slough.

1.2 A Search for Shared Backgrounds: A Review of *Young Children Learning*

Shirley Brice Heath

Source: Edited version of Heath, S.B. (1985) 'A search for backgrounds'. *Harvard Educational Review*, **55**, No. 4, 443–447.

In a recent critique of contemporary moral philosophy Alasdair MacIntyre suggests that social scientists characteristically adopt an extremely tolerant attitude toward counterexamples of generalizations, and such generalizations persist in social science publications.[1] Norms of social science research do not require the statement of either the precise conditions under which generalizations stand or a well-defined set of conditions under which conclusions are not likely to hold. Hence other researchers have no guidelines by which to apply generalizations beyond the limits of the observations reported in specific situations; each individual research study in social science tends therefore to stand alone, and cumulative knowledge applicable to situations across settings is hard to come by. *Young Children Learning*, written by two psychologists, exemplifies these characteristics of social science research in both its content and the way in which the authors put forth the book's findings.

British educational psychologists Barbara Tizard and Martin Hughes tape-recorded (over an unspecified period of time) 30 four-year-old girls — 15 from the working class and 15 from the middle class — at home with their mothers and in nursery school. They classified, quantified, and compared the types of talk in each setting and across socioeconomic classes; they have since 1979 reported these results in the *Journal of Child Psychology and Psychiatry* [The article included in this reader — *Ed.*] and also in their appendix to *Young Children Learning*. They felt, however, that quantification of their findings had not adequately captured the richness of the data, and this book is their effort to display qualitatively what the children were learning at home, how social class differences affected what and how the children learned at home, and what the main differences were between the teaching done by mothers and that done by nursery school teachers. Throughout the book, anecdotes and transcripts of the thirty children demonstrate their intricate verbal efforts to accumulate, test, and create knowledge with their mothers. Differences between working class and middle class mothers' verbal interactions with their children are relatively minor. In nursery school, children of both classes exhibit few of the verbal talents they develop at home for testing, disputing, creating, and sorting information.

The authors assert that their work challenges previous findings that working class mothers do not use comparisons, explanations, and conditional statements as frequently or as effectively as middle class mothers do in their talk to young children. Though Tizard and Hughes found differences in the proportion and rate of language for "complex purposes" between working class and middle class homes, they conclude that each class had within itself wide variations and that considerable overlap exists between the two social classes. Citing William Labov's now famous article, *The Logic of Non-standard English*, they reassert the importance of the social situation of language use for assessing lower class children's cognitive and linguistic abilities.[2] They argue, therefore, that data collected on mothers talking to their children in laboratory settings will not accurately reflect language patterns of the home, and that educators have little data on which to base their view that professionals in formal school settings provide a more "educational" environment for young children than parents do.

Educational and developmental psychologists who still study children and their mothers in non-naturalistic settings may find the conclusions of Tizard and Hughes surprising. However, the growing number of cognitive psychologists, linguists, and anthropologists who have in the past several years examined children's language in social interactions in homes, communities, and schools will find little to dispute in their assertions.[3] They will, no doubt, wonder why Tizard and Hughes seem unaware that a considerable number of other scholars share their premises and have reached similar conclusions over the past five years. *Young Children Learning* constitutes evidence that social scientists tolerate counterevidence. Moreover, the barriers between disciplines, such as linguistics, anthropology, and social psychology, block comparative considerations of conclusions regarding the same phenomenon and result in uninformed presentation of old discoveries as though they were original. For example, the report of Tizard and Hughes's research is curiously and selectively ahistorical. Though a quotation from Jerome Bruner opens the book, neither he nor the stream of scholars who have followed his approaches to studying child development in different social and cultural settings are mentioned again.[4]

What is equally curious is the failure of Tizard and Hughes to acknowledge the theories of L. S. Vygotsky. The authors seem unaware of this Soviet psychologist's theories of learning and language development, yet their chapter on "the puzzling mind of the four-year-old" proposes "passages of intellectual search" which closely parallel Vygotsky's "independent problem-solving."[5] Much of the book focuses on the social interactions which sustain learning. The authors document repeatedly the constructivist approach children take in dialogues with adults who guide them beyond their current conceptual development through "intellectual scaffolding" (p. 131), a term which scholars following both Bruner and Vygotsky have used to describe the routines and question–answer sequences in which parents and children habitually participate. The authors repeatedly criticize Jean Piaget's limited views of young children's intellectual abilities, but they show little awareness, except for an acknowledgement of Margaret Donaldson's research,[6] of the past decade's substantial amount of research on the active role children take in their own learning. In their very sparse notes, they cite only four items (aside from their own research reports and that of one other author published in the same series as *Young Children Learning*) published since 1980. They mention only briefly the extensive research on children's language carried out in Bristol, England, by Gordon Wells.[7] Moreover, some social science researchers, including psychologists, now accept as common-place research techniques the authors defend as though they were new: tape-recording children in their homes, carrying out research through participant-observation in homes and communities, and comparing language uses in homes and schools.

This book also assumes tolerance by social scientists for generalizations which do not specify adequately the scope or conditions under which their research findings might hold. Tizard and Hughes do not indicate where and when they carried out their study. [. . .] We never learn more specifics of the study's location(s); we are left to wonder, rural or urban, same or different regions of the country? For the time span covered, readers are left with only hints. We learn that, at the time of the study, only 6 per cent of British women whose youngest child was under five worked full time, and that fewer than 10 per cent of British children lived in homes where the primary language was not English, or in single-parent families or families with more than three children, but we are not told how common these conditions are in Britain today. Moreover, American researchers will recognize immediately that the pool of subjects differs sharply from a major portion of homes in the United States — homes in which both parents work full time, single-parent homes, and language minority families. Among these, there are few shared backgrounds with the subjects of the British study.

Young Children Learning illustrates the powerful, independent learning strategies of young children of any class or sociological background. Children and adults co-construct and negotiate knowledge; children facilitate their language learning by initiating and sustaining conversations. The greater the shared background between adult and child, the greater the possibility for extended discourse. Children work hard to make sense of the environment around them, and they use language to ask the experts around them to confirm, deny, or supplement their hypotheses. Children across classes and sociological backgrounds have numerous preschool experiences with lit-eracy. Routines, disputes, negotiation of who is in control, games of naming and matching, and imaginative play promote children's language learning and exploration of concepts. Adults scaffold children's learning by prescribing tasks and allowing the child gradually to assume a bigger part in the performance of the task. In such interactions, adults base their expecta-tions on what they believe the child can currently do and what the child will next be able to do or learn to do. Much of children's learning is facilitated by persistent explorations with analogies and by their ability to express verbally their curiosity about associations between two objects, labels, people or events. Adults help such intellectual explorations by asking clarification questions and remembering and relating children's past experiences to matters of their current attention.

Young Children Learning echoes the findings of the parade of studies of classroom language which have come since the publication of James Britton's *Language and Learning* in 1970.[8] The language of the majority of classrooms is impoverished, limited, and unfulfilling in comparison to that of other settings. In classrooms, the communicative role of language is diminished as language becomes the object of instruction — segmented, decontextualized, stripped of affect, and reinforced by testing procedures which rarely offer children the opportunity to do more than fill in blanks or add partial phrases.

Though the authors give almost no attention to the formal and functional features of language per se, child language researchers will find in *Young Children Learning* abundant data on several topics of current interest: children's attention to homophones, cognitive exploration through play, and ability to sustain conversation. Especially important is the detail the authors amass to show the extent to which children work verbally to create and confirm shared background experiences with their mothers.

The children's homes are rich with such shared experiences, ranging from routine family events to television programs. Children use mothers (and presumably other adult members of the households) to confirm, deny, and supplement the hypotheses and rules the children generate to make sense of the world. The children's limited uses of language for these purposes at school suggest that they recognize that, in contrast to their mothers, the nursery school teachers (and presumably teachers in general) share with them relatively few experiences around which they can build conversations.

The data of Tizard and Hughes support the conclusion that the verbal environment of nursery schools is relatively deprived because teachers have sought few ways of creating a shared background among and with students. In school, teachers ask questions of children, but many of these are questions for which teachers know the answers, and children respond minimally or not at all. In contrast to the sometimes rapid-fire questions they generated at home, most of these four-year-olds asked very few questions at school. In short, the "width of their curriculum" (p. 148) at home insured for these children opportunities to initiate and to sustain communication structured by their own needs, curiosity, and negotiation of attention, playtime with mothers, and preferred treats or toys. Moreover, mealtimes provided intellectual nourishment as well as nutritional and social benefits. In both working class and middle class homes, mothers took time during meals to ask their children about experiences which the mothers had not shared: television viewing, school activities, or the activities of friends. When mothers were engaged in house work or play with their children, the youngsters asked them questions about their current activities or future plans.

Young Children Learning thus joins the growing mass of research which maintains that patterns of language use in communities of not only different social classes but also different cultural groups are tightly interrelated with families' use of time, problem-solving techniques, varieties of experiences shared with children, and opportunities for children to participate in activities beyond the family. Middle class families seem to provide two types of language use found less frequently in working class homes: a focus on labels, attributes, and language as such (for example, What's this? What color is this? What's this called?), and attention to children's imaginative play, recalling of past events or forecasting of events to come.

The practical implications of these findings for nursery school teachers remain unexplored in *Young Children Learning*. The failure to suggest some recommendations for formal schooling seems especially curious, since many features of the book suggest that the authors did not intend it primarily for a research audience. The sparse citations, absence of an effort to link the findings under discussion to the work of other researchers, and simplified explanations of terms such as "egocentric" and "cognitive demands" suggest that the authors (and publisher) intended a lay readership. But these readers are left to translate the findings given here through their own creative interpretation if they are to derive classroom practices or principles.

It is difficult to disagree with the substantive findings of this book. It is splendid to have reported for analysis and interpretation the actual data recorded in working class and middle class homes. It is good to hear mother's responses to interviewers' questions about their views of their children's play, questions, and nursery schools, and to share in their perception of what they are teaching their children. *Young Children Learning* is a useful addition to research on children's learning in homes and schools. It must be faulted, however, for failing to specify clearly enough the conditions of the research, for not referring adequately to related research literature, and for not taking responsibility for suggesting educational implications, presumably the author's underlying concern. [. . .]

Notes

1 MacIntyre, *After Virtue* (Notre Dame, IN: University of Notre Dame Press, 1985).
2 Labov, "The Logic of Non-standard English," in *Georgetown University Round Table on Languages and Linguistics*, ed. James E. Alatis (Washington, DC: Georgetown University Press, 1969).
3 See Peggy J. Miller, *Amy, Wendy, and Beth: Language Learning in South Baltimore* (Austin: University of Texas Press, 1982); Shirley Brice Heath, *Ways with Words: Language, Life, and Work in Communities and Classrooms* (Cambridge: Cambridge University Press, 1983); Elinor Ochs and Bambi B. Schieffelin, *Acquiring Conversational Competence* (London: Routledge & Kegan Paul, 1983); E. Tory Higgins, Diane N. Ruble, and Willard W. Hartup, eds., *Social and Social Development: A Sociological Perspective* (Cambridge: Cambridge University Press, 1983); and Bambi B. Schieffelin, "Language Acquisition and Socialization: Three Developmental Stories and their Implications," in *Culture Theory: Essays on Mind, Self and Emotion*, ed. Richard Shweder and Robert LeVine (New York: Cambridge University Press, 1984), pp. 216–252.
4 Bruner, *The Relevance of Education* (New York: Vintage Press, 1973).

5 Vygotsky, *Mind in Society: The Development of Higher Psychological Processes*, trans. Michael Cole, Vera John-Steiner, Sylvia Scribner, and Ellen Souberman (Cambridge, Mass.: Harvard University Press, 1978).

6 Donaldson, *Children's Minds* (London: Croom Helm, 1978).

7 Wells, *Learning through Interaction: The Study of Language Development* (Cambridge: Cambridge University Press, 1981).

8 Britton, *Language and Learning* (Harmondsworth, Eng.: Penguin Books, 1970).

1.3 What No Bedtime Story Means: Narrative Skills At Home And School

Shirley Brice Heath

Source: Edited version of Heath, S. B. (1982) 'What no bedtime story means: narrative skill at home and school'. *Language and Society* 11, 49–76.

In the preface to *S/Z* Roland Barthes' work on ways in which readers read, Richard Howard writes: "We require an education in literature . . . in order to discover that *what we have assumed* — with the complicity of our teachers — *was nature is in fact culture, that what was given is no more than a way of taking*" (emphasis not in the original; Howard 1974:ix).[1] This statement reminds us that the *culture* children learn as they grow up is, in fact, "ways of taking" meaning from the environment around them. The means of making sense from books and relating their contents to knowledge about the real world is but one "way of taking" that is often interpreted as "natural" rather than learned. The quote also reminds us that teachers (and researchers alike) have not recognized that ways of taking from books are as much a part of learned behavior as are ways of eating, sitting, playing games, and building houses.

As school-oriented parents and their children interact in the pre-school years, adults give their children, through modeling and specific instruction, ways of taking from books which seem natural in school and in numerous institutional settings such as banks, post offices, businesses, or government offices. These *mainstream* ways exist in societies around the world that rely on formal educational systems to prepare children for participation in settings involving literacy. In some communities these ways of schools and institutions are very similar to the ways learned at home; in other communities the ways of school are merely an overlay on the home-taught ways and may be in conflict with them.[2]

Yet little is actually known about what goes on in story-reading and other literacy-related interactions between adults and preschoolers in communities around the world. Specifically, though there are numerous diary accounts and experimental studies of the preschool reading experiences of mainstream middle-class children, we know little about the specific literacy features of the environment upon which the school expects to draw. Just how does what is frequently termed "the literate tradition" envelope the child in knowledge about interrelationships between oral and written language, between knowing something and knowing ways of labelling and displaying it? We have even less information about the variety of ways children from *non-mainstream* homes learn about reading, writing, and using oral language to display knowledge in their preschool environment. The general view has been that whatever it is that mainstream school-oriented homes have, these other homes do not have it; thus these children are not from the literate tradition and are not likely to succeed in school.

A key concept for the empirical study of ways of taking meaning from written sources across communities is that of *literacy events;* occasions in which written language is integral to the nature of participants' interactions and their interpretive processes and strategies. Familiar literacy events for mainstream preschoolers are bedtime stories, reading cereal boxes, stop signs, and television ads, and interpreting instructions for commercial games and toys. In such literacy events, participants follow socially established rules for verbalizing what they know from and about the written material. Each community has rules for socially interacting and sharing knowledge in literacy events.

This paper briefly summarizes the ways of taking from printed stories families teach their preschoolers in a cluster of mainstream school-oriented neighborhoods of a city in the Southeastern region of the United States. We then describe two quite different ways of taking used in the homes of two English-speaking communities in the same region that do not follow the school-expected patterns of bookreading and reinforcement of these patterns in oral storytelling. Two assumptions underlie this paper and are treated in detail in the ethnography of these communities (Heath 1983): (1) Each community's ways of taking from the printed word and using this knowledge are interdependent with the ways children learn to talk in their social interactions with caregivers. (2) There is little or no validity to the time-honored dichotomy of "the literate tradition" and "the oral tradition." This paper suggests a frame of reference for both the community patterns and the paths of development children in different communities follow in their literacy orientations.

Mainstream school-oriented bookreading

Children growing up in mainstream communities are expected to develop habits and values which attest to their membership in a "literate society." Children learn certain customs, beliefs, and skills in early enculturation experiences with written materials: the bedtime story is a major literacy event which helps set patterns of behavior that recur repeatedly through the life of mainstream children and adults.

In both popular and scholarly literature, the "bedtime story" is widely accepted as a given — a natural way for parents to interact with their child at bedtime. Commercial publishing houses, television advertising, and children's magazines make much of this familiar ritual, and many of their sales pitches are based on the assumption that in spite of the intrusion of television into many patterns of interaction between parents and children, this ritual remains. Few parents are fully conscious of what bedtime storyreading means as preparation for the kinds of learning and displays of knowledge expected in school. Ninio and Bruner (1978), in their longitudinal study of one main-stream middle class mother–infant dyad in joint picture-book reading, strongly suggest a universal role of bookreading in the achievement of label-ling by children.

In a series of "reading cycles," mother and child alternate turns in a dialogue: the mother directs the child's attention to the book and/or asks what-questions and/or labels items on the page. The items to which the what-questions are directed and labels given are two-dimensional representa-tions of three-dimensional objects, so that the child has to resolve the conflict between perceiving these as two-dimensional objects and as representations of a three-dimensional visual setting. The child does so "by assigning a privileged, autonomous status to picture as visual objects" (1978: 5). The arbitrariness of the picture, its decontextualization, and its existence as some-thing which cannot be grasped and manipulated like its "real" counterparts is learned through the routines of structured interactional dialogue in which mother and child take turns playing a labelling game. In a "scaffolding" dialogue (cf. Cazden 1979), the mother points and asks "What is x?" and the child vocalizes and/or gives a nonverbal signal of attention. The mother then provides verbal feedback and a label. Before the age of two, the child is socialized into the "initiation–reply–evaluation sequences" repeatedly described as the central structural feature of classroom lessons (e.g., Sinclair and Coulthard 1975; Griffin and Humphrey 1978; Mehan 1979). Teachers ask their students questions which have answers prespecified in the mind of the teacher. Students respond, and teachers provide feedback, usually in the form of an evaluation. Training in ways of responding to this pattern begins very early in the labelling activities of mainstream parents and children.

Maintown ways

This patterning of "incipient literacy" (Scollon and Scollon 1979) is similar in many ways to that of the families of fifteen primary-level school teachers in Maintown, a cluster of middle-class neighborhoods in a city of the Piedmont Carolinas. These families (all of whom identify themselves as "typical," "middle-class," or "mainstream,") had preschool children, and the mother in each family was either teaching in local public schools at the time of the study (early 1970s), or had taught in the academic year preceding participa-tion in the study. Through a research dyad approach, using teacher-mothers as researchers with the ethnographer, the teacher-mothers audio-recorded their children's interactions in their primary network — mothers, fathers, grandparents, maids, siblings, and frequent visitors to the home. Children were expected to learn the following rules in literacy events in these nuclear households:

1. As early as six months of age, children *give attention to books and information derived from books.* The rooms contain bookcases and are decorated with murals, bedspreads, mobiles, and stuffed animals which represent characters found in books. Even when these characters have their origin in television programs, adults also provide books which either repeat or extend the characters' activities on television.

2. Children, from the age of six months, *acknowledge questions about books.* Adults expand nonverbal responses and vocalizations from infants into fully formed grammatical sentences. When children begin to verbalize about the contents of books, adults extend their questions from simple requests for labels (What's that? Who's that?) to ask about the attributes of these items (What does the doggie say? What color is the ball?)

3. From the time they start to talk, children *respond to conversational allusions to the content of books; they act as question-answerers who have a knowledge of books.* For example, a fuzzy black dog on the street is likened by an adult to Blackie in a child's book: "Look, there's a Blackie. Do you think *he's* looking for a boy?". Adults strive to maintain with children a running commentary on any event or object which can be book-related, thus modelling for them the extension of familiar items and events from books to new situational contexts.

4. Beyond two years of age, children *use their knowledge of what books do to legitimate their departures from "truth."* Adults encourage and reward "book talk," even when it is not directly relevant to an ongoing conversation. Children are allowed to suspend reality, to tell stories which are not true, to ascribe fiction-like features to everyday objects.

5. Preschool children *accept book and book-related activities as entertainment.* When preschoolers are "captive audiences" (e.g. waiting in a doctor's office, putting a toy together, or preparing for bed), adults reach for books. If there are no books present, they talk about other objects as though they were pictures in books. For example, adults point to items, and ask children to name, describe, and compare them to familiar objects in their environment. Adults often ask children to state their likes or dislikes, their view of events, and so forth, at the end of the captive audience period. These affective questions often take place while the next activity is already underway (e.g. moving toward the doctor's office, putting the new toy away, or being tucked into bed), and adults do not insist on answers.

6. Preschoolers *announce their own factual and fictive narratives* unless they are given in response to direct adult elicitation. Adults judge as most acceptable those narratives which open by orienting the listener to setting and main character. Narratives which are fictional are usually marked by formulaic openings, a particular prosody, or the borrowing of episodes in story books.

7. When children are about three years old, adults discourage the highly interactive participative role in bookreading children have hitherto played and children *listen and wait as an audience.* No longer does either adult or child repeatedly break into the story with questions and comments. Instead, children must listen, store what they hear, and on cue from the adult, answer a question. Thus, children begin to formulate "practice" questions as they wait for the break and the expected formulaic-type questions from the adult. It is at this stage that children often choose to "read" to adults rather than to be read to.

A pervasive pattern of all these features is the authority which books and book-related activities have in the lives of both the preschoolers and members of their primary network. Any initiation of a literacy event by a preschooler makes an interruption, an untruth, a diverting of attention from the matter at hand (whether it be an uneaten plate of food, a messy room, or an avoidance of going to bed) acceptable. Adults jump at openings their children give them for pursuing talk about books and reading.

In this study, writing was found to be somewhat less acceptable as an "anytime activity," since adults have rigid rules about times, places, and materials for writing. The only restrictions on bookreading concern taking good care of books: they should not be wet, torn, drawn on, or lost. In their talk to children about books, and in their explanations of why they buy children's books, adults link school success to "learning to love books," "learning what books can do for you," and "learning to entertain yourself and to work independently." Many of the adults also openly expressed a fascination with children's books "nowadays." They generally judged them as more diverse, wide-ranging, challenging, and exciting than books they had as children.

The mainstream pattern.   A close look at the way bedtime story routines in Maintown taught children how to take meaning from books raise a heavy sense of the familiar in all of us who have acquired mainstream habits and values. Throughout a lifetime, any school-successful individual moves through the same processes described above thousands of times. Reading for comprehension involves an internal replaying of the same types of questions adults ask children of bedtime stories. We seek *what-explanations*, asking what the topic is, establishing it as predictable and recognizing it in new situational contexts by classifying and categorizing it in our mind with other phenomena. The what-explanation is replayed in learning to pick out topic sentences, write outlines, and answer standardized tests which ask for the correct titles to stories, and so on. In learning to read in school, children move through a sequence of skills designed to teach what-explanations. There is a tight linear order of instruction which recapitulates the bedtime story pattern of breaking down the story into small bits of information and teaching children to handle sets of related skills in isolated sequential hierarchies.

In each individual reading episode in the primary years of schooling, children must move through what-explanations before they can provide *reason-explanations* or *affective commentaries*. Questions about why a particular event occurred or why a specific action was right or wrong come at the end of primary-level reading lessons, just as they come at the end of bedtime stories. Throughout the primary grade levels, what-explanations predominate, reason-explanations come with increasing frequency in the upper grades, and affective comments most often come in the extra-credit portions of the reading workbook or at the end of the list of suggested activities in text books across grade levels. This sequence characterizes the total school career. High school freshmen who are judged poor in compositional and reading skills spend most of their time on what-explanations and practice in advanced versions of bedtime story questions and answers. They are given little or no chance to use reason-giving explanations or assessments of the actions of stories. Reason-explanations result in configurational rather than hierarchical skills, are not predictable, and thus do not present content with a high degree of redundancy. Reason-giving explanations tend to rely on detailed knowledge of a specific domain. This detail is often unpredictable to teachers, and is not as highly valued as is knowledge which covers a particular area of knowledge with less detail but offers opportunity for extending the knowledge to larger and related concerns. For example, a primary-level student whose father owns a turkey farm may respond with reason-explanations to a story about a turkey. His knowledge is intensive and covers details perhaps not known to the teacher and not judged as relevant to the story. The knowledge is unpredictable and questions about it do not continue to repeat the common core of content knowledge of the story. Thus such configured knowledge is encouraged only for the "extras" of reading — an extra-credit oral report or a creative picture and story about turkeys. This kind of knowledge is allowed to be used once the hierarchical what-explanations have been mastered and displayed in a particular situation and, in the course of one's academic career, only when one has shown full mastery of the hierarchical skills and subsets of related skills which underlie what-explanations. Thus, reliable and successful participation in the ways of taking from books that teachers view as natural must, in the usual school way of doing things, precede other ways of taking from books.

[. . .]

Close analyses of how mainstream school-oriented children come to learn to take from books at home suggest that such children learn not only how to take meaning from books, but also how to talk about it. In doing the latter, they repeatedly practice routines which parallel those of classroom interaction. By the time they enter school, they have had continuous experience as information-givers; they have learned how to perform in those interactions which surround literate sources throughout school. They have had years of practice in interaction situations that are the heart of reading — both learning to read and reading to learn in school. They have developed habits of performing which enable them to run through the hierarchy of preferred knowledge about a literate source and the appropriate sequence of skills to be displayed in showing knowledge of a subject. They have developed ways of decontextualizing and surrounding with explanatory prose the knowledge gained from selective attention to objects.

They have learned to listen, waiting for the appropriate cue which signals it is their turn to show off this knowledge. They have learned the rules for getting certain services from parents (or teachers) in the reading interaction (Merritt 1979). In nursery school, they continue to practice these interaction patterns in a group rather than in a dyadic situation. There they learn additional signals and behaviors necessary for getting a turn in a group, and responding to a central reader and to a set of centrally defined reading tasks. In short, most of their waking hours during the preschool years have enculturated them into: (1) all those habits associated with what-explanations, (2) selective attention to items of the written text, *and* (3) appropriate interactional styles for orally displaying all the know-how of their literate orientation to the environment. This learning has been finely tuned and its habits are highly interdependent. Patterns of behaviors learned in one setting or at one stage reappear again and again as these children learn to use oral and written language in literacy events and to bring their knowledge to bear in school-acceptable ways.

Alternative patterns of literacy events

But what corresponds to the mainstream pattern of learning in communities that do not have this finely tuned, consistent, repetitive, and continuous pattern of training? Are there ways of behaving which achieve other social and cognitive aims in other sociocultural groups?

The data below are summarized from an ethnography of two communities — Roadville and Trackton — located only a few miles from Maintown's neighborhoods in the Piedmont Carolinas. Roadville is a white working-class community of families steeped for four generations in the life of the textile mill. Trackton is a working-class black community whose older generations have been brought up on the land, either farming their own land or working for other landowners. However, in the past decade, they have found work in the textile mills. Children of both communities are unsuccessful in school; yet both communities place a high value on success in school, believing earnestly in the personal and vocational rewards school can bring and urging their children "to get ahead" by doing well in school. Both Roadville and Trackton are literate communities in the sense that the residents of each are able to read printed and written materials in their daily lives, and on occasion they produce written messages as part of the total pattern of communication in the community. In both communities, children go to school with certain expectancies of print and, in Trackton especially, children have a keen sense that reading is something one does to learn something one needs to know (Heath 1980). In both groups, residents turn from spoken to written uses of language and vice versa as the occasion demands, and the two modes of expression seem to supplement and reinforce each other. Nonetheless there are radical differences between the two communities in the ways in which children and adults interact in the preschool years; each of the two communities also differs from Maintown. Roadville and Trackton view children's learning of language from two radically different perspectives: in Trackton, children "learn to talk," in Roadville, adults "teach them how to talk."

Roadville

In Roadville, babies are brought home from the hospital to rooms decorated with colorful, mechanical, musical, and literacy-based stimuli. The walls are decorated with pictures based on nursery rhymes, and from an early age, children are held and prompted to "see" the wall decorations. Adults recite nursery rhymes as they twirl the mobile made of nursery-rhyme characters. The items of the child's environment promote exploration of colors, shapes, and textures: a stuffed ball with sections of fabrics of different colors and textures is in the crib; stuffed animals vary in texture, size, and shape. Neighbors, friends from church, and relatives come to visit and talk to the baby, and about him to those who will listen. The baby is fictionalized in the talk to him: "But this baby wants to go to sleep, doesn't he? Yes, see those little eyes gettin' heavy." As the child grows older, adults pounce on word-like sounds and turn them into "words," repeating the "words," and expanding them into well-formed sentences. Before they can talk, children are introduced to visitors and prompted to provide all the expected politeness formulas, such as "Bye-bye," "Thank you," and so forth. As soon as they can talk, children are reminded about these formulas, and book or television characters known to be "polite" are involved as reinforcement.

In each Roadville home, preschoolers first have cloth books, featuring a single object on each page. They later acquire books which provide sounds, smells, and different textures or opportunities for practicing small motor skills (closing zippers, buttoning buttons, etc.). A typical collection for a two-year-old consisted of a dozen or so books — eight featured either the alphabet or numbers, others were books of nursery rhymes, simplified Bible stories, or "real-life" stories about boys and girls (usually taking care of their pets or exploring a particular feature of their environment). Books based on Sesame Street characters were favorite gifts for three- and four-year-olds.

Reading and reading-related activities occur most frequently before naps or at bedtime in the evening. Occasionally an adult or older child will read to a fussy child while the mother prepares dinner or changes a bed. On weekends, fathers sometimes read with their children for brief periods of time, but they generally prefer to play games or play with the children's toys in their interactions.

Bookreading time focuses on letters of the alphabet, numbers, names of basic items pictured in books, and simplified retellings of stories in the words of the adult. If the content or story plot seems too complicated for the child, the adult tells the story in short, simple sentences, frequently laced with requests that the child give what-explanations.

In Roadville's literacy events, the rules for cooperative discourse around print are repeatedly practiced, coached, and rewarded in the preschool years. Adults in Roadville believe that instilling in children the proper use of words and understanding of the meaning of the written word are important for both their educational and religious success. Adults repeat aspects of the learning of literacy events they have known as children. In the words of one Roadville parent: "It was then that I began to learn . . . when my daddy kept insisting I *read* it, *say* it right. It was then that I *did* right, in his view."

The path of development for such performance can be described in three overlapping stages. In the first, children are introduced to discrete bits and pieces of books — separate items, letters of the alphabet, shapes, colors, and commonly represented items in books for children (apple, baby, ball, etc.). The latter are usually decontextualized, not pictured in their ordinary contexts, and they are represented in two-dimensional flat line drawings. During this stage, children must participate as predictable information-givers and respond to questions that ask for specific and discrete bits of information about the written matter. In these literacy events, specific features of the two-dimensional items in books which are different from their "real" counterparts are not pointed out. A ball in a book is flat; a duck in a book is yellow and fluffy; trucks, cars, dogs, and trees talk in books. No mention is made of the fact that such features do not fit these objects in reality. Children are not encouraged to move their understanding of books into other situational contexts or to apply it in their general knowledge of the world about them.

In the second stage, adults demand an acceptance of the power of print to entertain, inform, and instruct. When [children can] no longer participate by contributing their knowledge at any point in the literacy event, they learn to recognize bookreading as a performance. The adult exhibits the book to [the child; the child is] to be entertained, to learn from the information conveyed in the material, and to remember the book's content for the sequential followup questioning, as opposed to ongoing cooperative participatory questions.

In the third stage, [children are] introduced to preschool workbooks which provided story information and are asked questions or provided exercises and games based on the content of the stories or pictures. Follow-the-number coloring books and preschool "push-out and paste" workbooks on shapes, colors, and letters of the alphabet reinforce repeatedly that the written word can be taken apart into small pieces and one item linked to another by following rules. [Children are given] practice in the linear, sequential nature of books: begin at the beginning, stay in the lines for coloring, draw straight lines to link one item to another, write your answers on lines, keep your letters straight, match the cutout letter to diagrams of letter shapes.

The differences between Roadville and Maintown are substantial. Roadville adults do not extend either the content or the habits of literacy events beyond bookreading. They do not, upon seeing an item or event in the real world, remind children of a similar event in a book and launch a running commentary on similarities and differences. When a game is played or a chore done, adults do not use literate sources. Mothers cook without written recipes most of the time; if they use a recipe from a written source, they do so usually only after confirmation and alteration by friends who have tried the recipe. Directions to games are read, but not carefully followed, and they are not talked about in a series of questions and answers which try to establish their meaning. Instead, in the putting together of toys or the playing of games, the abilities or preferences of one party prevail. For example, if an adult knows how to put a toy together, he does so; he does not talk about the process, refer to the written material and "translate" for the child, or try to sequence steps so the child can do it.[3]

Adults at tasks do not provide a running verbal commentary on what they are doing. They do not draw the attention of the child to specific features of the sequences of skills or the attributes of items. They do not ask questions of the child, except questions which are directive or scolding in nature. [. . .] Explanations which move beyond the listing of names of items and their features are rarely offered by adults. Children do not ask questions of the type "But I don't understand. What is that?" They appear willing to keep trying, and if there is ambiguity in a set of commands, they ask a question such as "You want me to do this?" (demonstrating their current efforts), or they try to find a way of diverting attention from the task at hand.

[. . .]

Roadville parents provide their children with books; they read to them and ask questions about the books' contents. They choose books which emphasize nursery rhymes, alphabet learning, animals, and simplified Bible stories, and they require their children to repeat from these books and to answer formulaic questions about their contents. Roadville adults also ask questions about oral stories which have a point relevant to some marked behavior of a child. They use proverbs and summary statements to remind their children of stories and to call on them for simple comparisons of the stories' contents to their own situations. Roadville parents coach children in their telling of a story, forcing them to tell about an incident as it has been pre-composed or pre-scripted in the head of the adult. Thus, in Roadville, children come to know a story as either an accounting from a book, or a factual account of a real event in which some type of marked behavior occurred and there is a lesson to be learned. Any fictionalized account of a real event is viewed as a *lie*; reality is better than fiction. Roadville's church and community life admit no story other than that which meets the definition internal to the group. Thus children cannot decontextualize their knowledge or fictionalize events known to them and shift them about into other frames.

When these children go to school they perform well in the initial stages of each of the three early grades. They often know portions of the alphabet, some colors and numbers, can recognize their names, and tell some their address and their parents' names. They will sit still and listen to a story, and they know how to answer questions asking for what-explanations. They do well in reading workbook exercises which ask for identification of specific portions of words, items from the story, or the linking of two items, letters, or parts of words on the same page. When the teacher reaches the end of story-reading or the reading circle and asks questions such as "What did you like about the story?", relatively few Roadville children answer. If asked questions such as "What would you have done if you had been Billy [a story's main character]?", Roadville children most frequently say "I don't know" or shrug their shoulders.

Near the end of each year, and increasingly as they move through the early primary grades, Roadville children can handle successfully the initial stages of lessons. But when they move ahead to extra-credit items or to activities considered more advanced and requiring more independence, they are stumped. They turn frequently to teachers asking "Do you want me to do this? What do I do here?" If asked to write a creative story or tell it into a tape recorder, they retell stories from books; they do not create their own. They rarely provide emotional or personal commentary on their accounting of real events or book stories. They are rarely able to take knowledge learned in one context and shift it to another; they do not compare two items or events and point out similarities and differences. They find it difficult either to hold one feature of an event constant and shift all others or to hold all features constant but one. For example, they are puzzled by questions such as "What would have happened if Billy had not told the policemen what happened?" They do not know how to move events or items out of a given frame. To a question such as "What habits of the Hopi Indians might they be able to take with them when they move to a city?", they provide lists of features of life of the Hopi on the reservation. They do not take these items, consider their appropriateness in an urban setting, and evaluate the hypothetical outcome. In general, they find this type of question impossible to answer, and they do not know how to ask teachers to help them take apart the questions to figure out the answers. Thus their initial successes in reading, being good students, following orders, and adhering to school norms of participating in lessons begin to fall away rapidly about the time they enter the fourth grade. As the importance and frequency of questions and reading habits with which they are familiar decline in the higher grades, they have no way of keeping up or of seeking help in learning what it is they do not even know they don't know.

Trackton
Babies in Trackton come home from the hospital to an environment which is almost entirely human. There are no cribs, car beds, or car sets, and only an occasional high chair or infant seat. Infants are held during their waking hours, occasionally while they sleep, and they usually sleep in the bed with parents until they are about two years of age. They are held, their faces fondled, their cheeks pinched, and they eat and sleep in the midst of human talk and noise from the television, stereo, and radio. Encapsuled in an almost totally human world, they are in the midst of constant human communication, verbal and nonverbal. They literally feel the body signals of shifts in emotion of those who hold them almost continuously; they are talked about and kept in the midst of talk about topics that range over any subject. As children make cooing or babbling sounds, adults refer to this as "noise," and no attempt is made to interpret these sounds as words or communicative attempts on the part of the baby. Adults believe they should not have to depend on their babies to tell them what they need or when they are uncomfortable; adults know, children only "come to know."

When a child can crawl and move about on his own, he plays with the household objects deemed safe for him — pot lids, spoons, plastic food containers. Only at Christmastime are there special toys for very young children; these are usually trucks, balls, doll babies, or plastic cars, but rarely blocks, puzzles, or books. As children become completely mobile, they demand ride toys or electronic and mechanical toys they see on television. They never request nor do they receive manipulative toys, such as puzzles, blocks, take-apart toys or literacy-based items, such as books or letter games.

Adults read newspapers, mail, calendars, circulars (political and civic-events related), school materials sent home to parents, brochures advertising new cars, television sets, or other products, and the Bible and other church-related materials. There are no reading materials especially for children (with the exception of children's Sunday School materials), and adults do not sit and read to children. Since children are usually left to sleep whenever and wherever they fall asleep, there is no bedtime or naptime as such. At night, they are put to bed when adults go to bed or whenever the person holding them gets tired. Thus, going to bed is not framed in any special routine. Sometimes in a play activity during the day, an older sibling will read to a younger child, but the latter soon loses interest and squirms away to play. Older children often try to "play school" with younger children, reading to them from books and trying to ask questions about what they have read. Adults look on these efforts with amusement and do not try to convince the small child to sit still and listen.

Signs from very young children of attention to the nonverbal behaviors of others are rewarded by extra fondling, laughter, and cuddling from adults. For example, when an infant shows signs of recognizing a family member's voice on the phone by bouncing up and down in the arms of the adult who is talking on the phone, adults comment on this to others present and kiss and nudge the child. Yet when children utter sounds or combinations of sounds which could be interpreted as words, adults pay no attention. Often by the time they are twelve months old, children approximate words or phrases of adults' speech; adults respond by laughing or giving special attention to the child and crediting him with "sounding like" the person being imitated. When children learn to walk and imitate the walk of members of the community, they are rewarded by comments on their activities: "He walks just like Toby when he's tuckered out."

Children between the ages of twelve and twenty-four months often imitate the tune or "general Gestalt" (Peters 1977) of complete utterances they hear around them. They pick up and repeat chunks (usually the ends) of phrasal and clausal utterances of speakers around them. They seem to remember fragments of speech and repeat these without active production. In this first stage of language learning, the repetition stage, they imitate the intonation contours and general shaping of the utterances they repeat. Lem 1;2 in the following example illustrates this pattern.

Mother: [talking to neighbor on porch while Lem plays with a truck on the porch nearby] But they won't call back, won't happen =
Lem: = call back
Neighbor: Sam's going over there Saturday, he'll pick up a form =
Lem: = pick up on, pick up on [Lem here appears to have heard *form* as *on*]

The adults pay no attention to Lem's "talk," and their talk, in fact, often overlaps his repetitions.

In the second stage, repetition with variation, Trackton children manipulate pieces of conversation they pick up. They incorporate chunks of language from others into their own ongoing dialogue, applying productive rules, inserting new nouns and verbs for those used in the adults' chunks.

They also play with rhyming patterns and varying intonation contours.

Mother: She went to the doctor again.
Lem (2;2): [in a sing-song fashion] went to de doctor, doctor, tractor, dis
           my tractor, doctor on a tractor, went to de doctor.

Lem creates a monologue, incorporating the conversation about him into his
own talk as he plays. Adults pay no attention to his chatter unless it gets so
noisy as to interfere with their talk.

In the third stage, participation, children begin to enter the ongoing conversations about them. They do so by attracting the adult's attention with a
tug on the arm or pant leg, and they help make themselves understood by
providing nonverbal reinforcements to help recreate a scene they want the
listener to remember. For example, if adults are talking, and a child inter-
rupts with seemingly unintelligible utterances, the child will make gestures,
extra sounds, or act out some outstanding features of the scene he is trying to
get the adult to remember. Children try to create a context, a scene, for the
understanding of their utterance.

This third stage illustrates a pattern in the children's response to their
environment and their ways of letting others know their knowledge of the
environment. Once they are in the third stage, their communicative efforts
are accepted by community members, and adults respond directly to the
child, instead of talking to others about the child's activities as they have done
in the past. Children continue to practice for conversational participation by
playing, when alone, both parts of dialogues, imitating gestures as well as
intonation patterns of adults. By 2;6 all children in the community can imitate
the walk and talk of others in the community, or frequent visitors such as the
man who comes around to read the gas meters. They can feign anger, sadness,
fussing, remorse, silliness, or any of a wide range of expressive behaviors.
They often use the same chunks of language for varying effects, depending on
nonverbal support to give the language different meanings or case it in a
different key (Hymes 1974). Girls between three and four years of age take
part in extraordinarily complex stepping and clapping patterns and simple
repetitions of hand clap games played by older girls. From the time they are
old enough to stand alone, they are encouraged in their participation by
siblings and older children in the community. These games require anticipation and recognition of cues for upcoming behaviors, and the young girls
learn to watch for these cues and to come in with the appropriate words and
movements at the right time.

Preschool children are not asked for what-explanations of their environment. Instead, they are asked a preponderance of analogical questions which
call for non-specific comparisons of one item, event, or person with another:
"What's that like?" Other types of questions ask for specific information
known to the child but not the adults: "Where'd you get that from?" "What
do you want?" "How come you did that?" (Heath 1982). Adults explain their
use of these types of questions by expressing their sense of children: they are
"comers," coming into their learning by experiencing what knowing about

things means. As one parent of a two-year-old boy put it: "Ain't no use me tellin' 'im: learn this, learn that, what's this, what's that? He just gotta learn, gotta know; he see one thing one place one time, he know how it go, see sump'n like it again, maybe it be the same, maybe it won't." Children are expected to learn how to know when the form belies the meaning, and to know contexts of items and to use their understanding of these contexts to draw parallels between items and events. Parents do not believe they have a tutoring role in this learning; they provide the experiences on which the child draws and reward signs of their successfully coming to know.

Trackton children's early stories illustrate how they respond to adult views of them as "comers." The children learn to tell stories by drawing heavily on their abilities to render a context, to set a stage, and to call on the audience's power to join in the imaginative creation of story. Between the ages of two and four years, the children, in a monologue-like fashion, tell stories about things in their lives, events they see and hear, and situations in which they have been involved. They produce these spontaneously during play with other children or in the presence of adults. Sometimes they make an effort to attract the attention of listeners before they begin the story, but often they do not. Lem, playing off the edge of the porch, when he was about two and a half years of age, heard a bell in the distance. He stopped, looked at Nellie and Benjy, his older siblings, who were nearby and said:

> Way
> Far
> Now
> It a church bell
> Ringin'
> Dey singin'
> Ringin'
> You hear it?
> I hear it
> Far
> Now

Lem had been taken to church the previous Sunday and had been much impressed by the church bell. He had sat on his mother's lap and joined in the singing, rocking to and fro on her lap, and clapping his hands. His story, which is like a poem in its imagery and line-like prosody, is in response to the current stimulus of a distant bell. As he tells the story, he sways back and forth.

This story, somewhat longer than those usually reported from other social groups for children as young as Lem,[4] has some features which have come to characterize fully-developed narratives or stories. It recapitulates in its verbal outline the sequence of events being recalled by the storyteller. At church, the bell rang while the people sang. In the line "It a church bell," Lem provides his story's topic, and a brief summary of what is to come. This line serves a function similar to the formulae often used by older children to open a story: "This is a story about (a church bell)," Lem gives only the slightest hint of story setting or orientation to the listener; where and when the story took place are capsuled in "Way, Far." Preschoolers in Trackton almost never hear "Once upon a time there was a——" stories, and they rarely provide definitive orientations for their stories. They seem to assume listeners "Know" the situation in which the narrative takes place. Similarly, preschoolers in Trackton do not close off their stories with formulaic endings. Lem poetically balances his opening and closing in an inclusio, beginning "Way, Far, Now." and ending "Far, Now.". The effect is one of closure, but there is no clearcut announcement of closure. Throughout the presentation of action and result of action in their stories, Trackton preschoolers invite the audience to respond or evaluate the story's actions. Lem asks "You hear it?" which may refer either to the current simulus or to yesterday's bell, since Lem does not productively use past tense endings for any verbs at this stage in his language development.

Preschool storytellers have several ways of inviting audience evaluation and interest. They may themselves express an emotional response to the story's actions; they may have another character or narrator in the story do so often using alliterative language play; or they may detail actions and results through direct discourse or sound effects and gestures. All these methods of calling attention to the story and its telling distinguish the speech event as a story, an occasion for audience and storyteller to interact pleasantly, and not simply to hear an ordinary recounting of events or actions.

Trackton children must be aggressive in inserting their stories into an ongoing stream of discourse. Storytelling is highly competitive. Everyone in a conversation may want to tell a story, so only the most aggressive wins out. The content ranges widely, and there is "truth" only in the universals of human experience. Fact is often hard to find, though it is usually the seed of the story Trackton stories often have no point — no obvious beginning or ending; they go on as long as the audience enjoys and tolerates the storyteller's entertainment.

Trackton adults do not separate out the elements of the environment around their children to tune their attentions selectively. They do not simplify their language, focus on single-word utterances by young children, label items or features of objects in either books or the environment at large. Instead, children are continuously contextualized, presented with almost continuous communication. From this ongoing, multiple-channeled stream of stimuli, they must themselves select, practice, and determine rules of production and structuring. For language, they do so by first repeating, catching chunks of sounds, intonation contours, and practicing these without specific reinforcement or evaluation. But practice material and models are continuously available. Next the children seem to begin to sort out the productive rules for speech and practice what they hear about them with variation. Finally, they work their way into conversations, hooking their meanings for listeners into a familiar context by recreating scenes through gestures, special sound effects, etc. These characteristics continue in their story-poems and their participation in jump-rope rhymes. Because adults do not select out, name, and describe features of the environment for the young, children must perceive situations, determine how units of the situations are related to each other, recognize these relations in other situations, and reason through what it will take to show their correlation of one situation with another. The children can answer questions such as "What's that like?" ("It's like Doug's car") but they can rarely name the specific feature or features which make two items or events alike. For example, in the case of saying a car seen on the street is "like Doug's car," a child may be basing the analogy on the fact that this car has a flat tyre and Doug's also had one last week. But the child does not name (and is not asked to name) what is alike between the two cars.

Children seem to develop connections between situations or items not by specification of labels and features in the situations, but by configuration links. Recognition of similar general shapes or patterns of links seen in one situation and connected to another, seem to be the means by which children set scenes in their nonverbal representations of individuals, and later in their verbal chunking, then segmentation and production of rules for putting together isolated units. They do not decontextualize; instead they heavily contextualize nonverbal and verbal language. They fictionalize their "true stories," but they do so by asking the audience to identify with the story through making parallels from their own experiences. When adults read, they often do so in a group. One person, reading aloud, for example, from a brochure on a new car decodes the text, displays illustrations and photographs, and listeners relate the text's meaning to their experiences asking questions and expressing opinions. Finally, the group as a whole synthesizes the written text and the negotiated oral discourse to construct a meaning for the brochure (Heath 1982).

When Trackton children go to school, they face unfamiliar types of questions which ask for what-explanations. They are asked as individuals to identify items by name, and to label features such as shape, color, size, number. The stimuli to which they are to give these responses are two-dimensional flat representations which are often highly stylized and bear little resemblance to the "real" items. Trackton children generally score in the lowest percentile range on the Metropolitan Reading Readiness tests. They do not sit at their desks and complete reading workbook pages: neither do they tolerate questions about reading materials which are structured along the usual lesson format. Their contributions are in the form of "I had a duck at my house one time." "Why'd he do that?" or they imitate the sound effects teachers may produce in stories they read to the children. By the end of the first three primary grades, their general language arts scores have been consistently low, except for those few who have begun to adapt to and adopt some of the behaviors they have had to learn in school. But the majority not only fail to learn the content of lessons, they also do not adopt the social interactional rules for school literacy events. Print in isolation bears little authority in their world. The kinds of questions asked of reading books are unfamiliar. The children's abilities to metaphorically link two events or situations and to recreate scenes are not tapped in the school; in fact, *these abilities often cause difficulties*, because they enable children to see parallels teachers did not intend, and indeed, may not recognize until the children point them out (Heath 1978).

By the end of the lessons or by the time in their total school career when reason-explanations and affective statements call for the creative comparison of two or more situations, it is too late for many Trackton children. They have not picked up along the way the composition and comprehension skills they need to translate their analogical skills into a channel teachers can accept. They seem not to know how to take meaning from reading; they do not observe the rules of linearity in writing, and their expression of themselves on paper is very limited. Orally taped stories are often much better, but these rarely count as much as written compositions. Thus, Trackton children continue to collect very low or failing grades, and many decide by the end of the sixth grade to stop trying and turn their attention to the heavy peer socialization which usually begins in these years.

From community to classroom

A recent review of trends in research on learning pointed out that "learning to read through using and learning from language has been less sytematically studied than the decoding process" (Glaser 1979: 7). Put another way, how children learn to use language to read to learn has been less systematically studied than decoding skills. Learning how to take meaning from writing before one learns to read involves repeated practice in using and learning from language through appropriate participation in literacy events such as exhibitor/questioner and spectator/respondent dyads (Scollon and Scollon 1979) or group negotiation of the meaning of a written text. Children have to learn to select, hold, and retrieve content from books and other written or printed texts in accordance with their community's rules or "ways of taking," and the children's learning follows community paths of language social- ization. In each society, certain kinds of childhood participation in literacy events may precede others, as the developmental sequence builds toward the whole complex of home and community behaviors characteristic of the soci- ety. The ways of taking employed in the school may in turn build directly on the preschool development, may require substantial adaptation on the preschool development, may require substantial adaptation on the part of the children, or may even run directly counter to aspects of the community's pattern.

[. . .]

In the early reading stages, and in later requirements for reading to learn at more advanced stages, children from the three communities respond differ- ently, because they have learned different methods and degrees of taking from books. In comparison to Maintown children, the habits Roadville chil- dren learned in bookreading and toy-related episodes have not continued for them through other activities and types of reinforcement in their environment. They have had less exposure to both the content of books and ways of learning from books than have mainstream children. Thus their need in schools is not necessarily for an intensification of presentation of labels, a slowing down of the sequence of introducing what-explanations in connection with bookreading. Instead they need *extension of these habits to other domains* and to opportunities for practicing habits such as producing running commentaries, creating exhibitor/questioner and spectator/respondent roles. Perhaps most important, Roadville children need to have articulated for them *distinctions in discourse strategies and structures.* Narratives of real events have certain strategies and structures; imaginary tales, flights of fantasy, and affective expressions have others. Their community's view of narrative discourse style is very narrow and demand a passive role in both creation of and response to the account of events. Moreover, these children have *to be reintroduced in a participant frame of reference to a book.* Though initially they were participants in bookreading, they have been trained into passive roles since the age of three years, and they must learn once again to be active information-givers, taking from books and linking that knowledge to other aspects of their environment.

Trackton students present an additional set of alternatives for procedures in the early primary grades. Since they usually have few of the expected "natural" skills of taking meaning from books, they must not only learn these, but also *retain their analogical reasoning practices* for use in some of the later stages of learning to read. They must *learn to adapt the creativity in language, metaphor, fictionalization, recreation of scenes and exploration of functions and settings of items they bring to school.* These children already use narrative skills highly rewarded in the upper primary grades. They distinguish a fictionalized story from a real-life narrative. They know that telling a story can be in many ways related to play; it suspends reality, and frames an old event in a new context; it calls on audience participation to recognize the setting and participants. They must now *learn as individuals to recount factual events in a straightforward way* and *recognize appropriate occasions for reason-explanations and affective expressions.* Trackton children seem to have skipped learning to label, list features, and give what-explanations. Thus they need to *have the mainstream or school habits presented in familiar activities with explanations related to their own habits of taking meaning* from the environment. Such "simple," "natural" things as distinctions between two-dimensional and three-dimensional objects may need to be explained to help Trackton children learn the stylization and decontextualization which characterizes books.

To lay out in more specific detail how Roadville and Trackton's ways of knowing can be used along with those of mainstreamers goes beyond the scope of this paper. However, it must be admitted that a range of alternatives to ways of learning and displaying knowledge characterizes all highly school-successful adults in the advanced stages of their careers. Knowing more about how these alternatives are learned at early ages in different sociocultural conditions can help the school to provide opportunities for *all* students to avail themselves of these alternatives early in their school careers. [. . .]

Notes

1 First presented at the Terman Conference on Teaching at Stanford University, 1980, this paper has benefitted from cooperation with M. Cochran-Smith of the University of Pennsylvania. She shares an appreciation of the relevance of Roland Barthes' work for studies of the socialization of young children into literacy; her research (1981) on the story-reading practices of a mainstream school-oriented nursery school provides a much needed detailed account of early school orientation to literacy.

2 Terms such as *mainstream* or *middle-class* cultures or social groups are frequently used in both popular and scholarly writings without careful definition. Moreover, numerous studies of behavioral phenomena (for example, mother–child interactions in language learning) either do not specify that the subjects being described are drawn from main-stream groups or do not recognize the importance of this limitation. As a result, findings from this group are often regarded as universal. For a discussion of this problem, see Chanan and Gilchrist 1974. Payne and Bennett 1977. In general, the literature character-izes this group as school-oriented, aspiring toward upward mobility through formal insti-tutions, and providing enculturation which positively values routines of promptness, linearity (in habits ranging from furniture arrangement to entrance into a movie theatre), and evaluative and judgmental responses to behaviors which deviate from their norms.

   In the United States, mainstream families tend to locate in neighborhoods and suburbs around cities. Their social interactions center not in their immediate neighborhoods, but around voluntary associations across the city. Thus a cluster of mainstream families (and not a community — which usually implies a specific geographic territory as the locus of a majority of social interactions) is the unit of comparison used here with the Trackton and Roadville communities.

3 Behind this discussion are findings from cross-cultural psychologists who have studied the links between verbalization of task and demonstration of skills in a hierarchical sequence, e.g. Childs and Greenfield 1980; see Goody 1979 on the use of questions in learning tasks unrelated to a familiarity with books.

4 Cf. Umiker-Sebeok's (1979) descriptions of stories of mainstream middle class children, ages 3–5 and Sutton-Smith 1981.

References

Basso, K. (1974) The ethnography of writing. In R. Bauman and J. Sherzer (eds), *Explorations in the ethnography of speaking*. Cambridge University Press.

Cazden, C. B. (1979) Peekaboo as an instructional model; Discourse development at home and at school. *Papers and Reports in Child Language Development* **17,** 1–29.

Chanan, G. and Gilchrist, L. (1974) *What school is for*. New York: Praeger.

Childs, C. P. and Greenfield, P. M. (1980) Informal modes of learning and teaching. In N. Warren (ed.), *Advances in cross-cultural psychology,* vol. 2 Academic Press, London.

Cochran-Smith, M. (1981) The making of a reader. Ph.D. dissertation. University of Pennsylvania.

Cohen, R. (1968) The relation between socio-conceptual styles and orientation to school requirements. *Sociology of Education* **41,** 201–20.

——. (1969) Conceptual styles, culture conflict, and nonverbal tests of intelligence. *American Anthropologist* **71** (5), 828–56.

——. (1971) The influence of conceptual rule-sets on measures of learning ability. In C. L. Brace, G. Gamble, and J. Bond (eds). *Race and intelligence.* (Anthropological Studies, No. 8, American Anthropological Association), 41–57.

Glaser, R (1979), Trends and research questions in psychological research on learning and schooling. *Educational Researcher* **8** (10), 6–13.

Goody, E. (1979) Towards a theory of questions. In E. N. Goody (ed), *Questions and politeness: Strategies in social interaction.* Cambridge University Press.

Griffin, P. and Humphrey, F. (1978) Task and talk. In *The study of children's functional language and education in the early years.* Final report to the Carnegie Corporation of New York, Arlington, Va.: Center for Applied Linguistics.

Heath, S. (1978) *Teacher talk: Language in the classroom.* (Language in Education 9.) Arlington, Va.: Center for Applied Linguistics.

——. (1980) The functions and uses of literacy. *Journal of Communication* **30** (1), 123–33.

——. (1982) Questioning at home and at school: A comparative study. In G. Spindler (ed.), *Doing ethnography: Educational anthropology in action.* New York: Holt, Rinehart & Winston.

——. (1982). Protean shapes: Ever-shifting oral and literate traditions. In D. Tannen (ed.). *Spoken and written language: Exploring orality and literacy.* Norwood, N. J.: Ablex.

——. (1983). *Ways with words: language, life and work in communities and classrooms.* Cambridge: Cambridge University Press.

Howard, R. (1974) A note on S/Z. In R. Barthes, *Introduction to S/Z.* Trans. Richard Miller. New York: Hill and Wang.

Hymes, D. H. (1973) On the origins and foundations of inequality among speakers. In E. Haugen and M. Bloomfield (eds.). *Language as a human problem.* New York: W. W. Norton & Co.

——. (1974) Models of the interaction of language and social life. In J. J. Gumperz & D. Hymes (eds.). *Directions in sociolinguistics.* New York: Holt, Rinehart and Winston.

Kagan, J., Sigel, I. and Moss, H. (1963) Psychological significance of styles of conceptualization. In J. Wright and J. Kagan (eds.). *Basic cognitive processes in children.* (Monographs of the society for research in child development.) **28** (2), 73–112.

Mehan, H. (1979) *Learning lessons.* Cambridge, Mass.: Harvard University Press.

Merritt, M. (1979) Service-like events during individual work time and their contribution to the nature of the rules for communication. NIE Report EP 78–0436.

Ninio. A. and Bruner, J. (1978) The achievement and antecedents of labelling. *Journal of Child Language* **5**, 1–15.

Payne, C. and Bennett, C. (1977) "Middle class aura" in public schools. *The Teacher Educator* **13** (1), 16–26.

Peters, A. (1977) Language learning strategies. *Language* **53**, 560–73.

Scollon, R. and Scollon, S. (1979) The literate two-year old: The fictionalization of self. *Working Papers in Sociolinguistics.* Austin, TX: Southwest Regional Laboratory.

Sinclair, J. M. and Coulthard, R. M. (1975) *Toward an analysis of discourse.* New York: Oxford University Press.

Sutton-Smith, B. (1981) *The folkstories of children.* Philadelphia: University of Pennsylvania Press.

Umiker-Sebeok, J. D. (1979). Preschool children's intraconversational narratives. *Journal of Child Language* **6** (1), 91–110.

Witkin, H., Faterson, F., Goodenough, R. and Birnbaum, J. (1966) Cognitive patterning in mildly retarded boys. *Child Development* **37** (2), 301–16.

1.4 The Voices of Communities and Language in Classrooms: A Review of *Ways With Words*

H. Rosen

Source: Extracts from Rosen, H. (1985) 'The voices of communities and language in classrooms'. *Harvard Educational Review* **55**, No. 4, 448–456.

[. . .]

The reputation of Shirley Brice Heath's book will have marched triumphantly ahead of this review, not, I hasten to add, because of a voguish novelty in its content, not because it is ethnography-on-the-doorstep, but rather because it represents a unique blend of cultural-linguistic analysis with a resolute intention to intervene positively in the world she describes. We have not been short of analyses in the human sciences which purport to offer, and on occasion actually provide, illumination to teachers. Heath's huge endeavor to present the texture and meaning of the daily goings-on and of the talk, as we say, of "ordinary folk" is complemented by a readiness, notoriously rare, to work alongside teachers in the construction of programs and practices. These are then informed by an awareness of the language and culture she has come to know as "ethnographer learning." For all her expertise she stays a learner, offering the teachers and students ways of understanding but also learning from them.

Trackton and Roadville are the two small communities at the heart of Heath's study. They are, you might say, exotic little places as remote — culturally speaking — from the lives of most contemporary city dwellers or farming communities as the Trobriand Islands described by Bronislaw Malinowski.[1] Why, then, should we follow with the closest attention the inhabitants' daily doings on porches or in the plaza, and eavesdrop on their chatter? We must admit that we often have a voyeuristic taste for scenes from the lives of those who in space, time, or culture seem distantly bizarre. There are academic studies which pander, wittingly or unwittingly, to these desires in peeping-Tom mainstreamers. Heath's book, however, is never in danger of being one. Heath proposes that (a) there are more Roadvilles and Tracktons than we recognise and know about, even if they are a stone's throw away, and (b) that schools which address themselves to formulating a culture-sensitive curriculum must be, in a sense, ethnographic centers. Her book, then, is no travelogue for the fireside but a sharp challenge to everyone concerned with schooling, teachers in particular.

Heath is a rare figure, an academic who does not see her role as a chastener of the ignorant. We do not have to hear yet again how teachers have got it all wrong, are victims of their cultural prejudices, and are irredeemably class-bound, linguistically naive, and politically impotent. She operates amongst them as a colleague who shares their dilemmas and strategies. It can be put very simply: she is not seeking the accolades of the academy but intends, when her ethnography is put to work, to help students to learn.

Back then to Roadville and Trackton in the Piedmont Carolinas.

[. . .]

In an uncompromising prologue, Heath lays out the context and theoretical starting-points of her study. The context was the concern felt by "black and white teachers, parents, and mill personnel," about communication, the "effects of the preschool home and community environment on the learning of those language structures and uses which were needed in classrooms and job settings" (p. 2). At this point, let me pause to say that the citation of the "concern" felt by certain significant people does not make clear whether Heath subscribed to that view or is merely tendering it for the record. I had the same difficulty at certain critical points in the text. The concern of millowners baffles me, too, for right down at the end of the book we are told that the mill offers "almost no opportunities to write, few chances to read, and almost no occasions when their uses of oral language are critical for success" (p. 365).

Heath sets out, nevertheless, to satisfy a "need for a full description of the primary face-to-face interactions of children from community cultures other than [the] mainstream one" (p. 3) which would meet the above concerns and in the end "help working-class black and white children learn more effectively" (p. 4). At this stage in the text certain terms begin to glow provocatively. I take it that here "working class" is being contrasted with "mainstream." What then does "mainstream" imply? Middle class? There is the suggestion here of a norm. Sure enough, tucked away in the notes to a later chapter is an attempt to face up to the difficulty (p. 391, n. 2), but it raises more questions than it answers: What are the *fundamental* determinants of class? How do the practices of everyday life relate to them? Who are the "middle class" and to what extent is it a homogeneous stratum? Yet her allegiance is clear and explains how it was that she became, through her collaboration with teachers, an "associate, colleague, aide, and sometime-coauthor of curricular materials" (p. 4).

[. . .]

Rich and intimate as it is, Heath's description cannot be total; telling how it is means telling how it seems through a prism which foregrounds the significant and does not register what seems insignificant. Consider this: "Any reader who tries to explain the community contrast in this book on the basis of race will miss the central point of the focus of culture as learned behavior and on language habits as part of that shared learning. Children in Roadville and Trackton came to have different ways of communicating, because their communities had different social legacies" (p. 11).

I was distressed by this evasion, especially as it runs counter to some of the deepest *implicit* awarenesses of the book. A second reading (my first was almost uncritically rapturous) revealed a persistent refusal to confront the issue of race. I do not trust Heath's apparent naivete; at best it is an astute calculation of political possibilities. Throughout the text we are made aware that Roadville is white and Trackton is black. Why bother? Yes, indeed, communities have different social legacies. A major component of this legacy must be the experience of racism and *its continued existence.* Why has Heath chosen to warn us off? Black English is the expression and negotiation of black experience. Racism does no more than lurk in the shadows of this text, raising questions which are not posed by Heath. The historical chapter firmly announces, "The Civil Rights Movement forced the breaking of the color barrier on hiring, and blacks began to assume production line jobs in the mills" (p. 27). In the rest of the book there is scarcely a whiff of the continuation of that struggle. Are Trackton people so "lumpen" that none of their "ways with words" are affected? One way of cleansing the book of such awkward considerations is to avoid (a) analyzing talk in black and white encounters and (b) probing further the implications of what momentarily pops up in the text. From the description of Gateway, homogeneously "mainstream," there peeps out the existence of black suburbs. Suddenly we hear someone in Roadville declaring, "When the niggers (pause) uh, the blacks, you know, started comin' in, I knew that wasn't for me. I wasn't ever gonna work for no nigger" (p. 39). These almost subliminal moments make one aware of a kind of self-denying ordinance or self-censorship operating in the ethnography.

By the same token, Heath's history tells how "workers began to show signs of an independent and unbiddable spirit when strikes claimed the lives of some of their leaders" (p. 25). Does nothing of that remain in either Roadville or Trackton? Apparently not. In speaking of Trackton, Heath writes that "they do not themselves take part in any aspect of the political process . . ." (p. 62). Of white Roadville no such comment is made, though it seems to apply equally. For them "the sun shines on the chimneys of the mill" (p. 47). On the job in both Roadville and Trackton, "workers look for no reasons for the task, nor do they give their opinion of the role of their task in the whole. . . . The topics of their talk rarely include their work" (p. 365). I find it odd, but it is perhaps true. Are they unionized or not? Do they never talk about their working conditions and attempt to change them? Is it all harmony, or resignation? Do blacks and whites occupy the same kinds of posts, and is this never a theme of anyone's conversation? What is the significance of the fact that "most households [in Trackton] have a double portrait of Coretta and Martin Luther King" (p. 55)?

Gateway's townspeople, we are told, are mainstreamers divided into two groups — "old-timers" and "newcomers." From thousands of miles away I remain skeptical. I cannot believe they are all economically and professionally successful, that there are no sharp divisions and clashes based on ethnicity and class. Nor can I envisage a town of 50,000 inhabitants without its "lower orders" — garage mechanics, truck drivers, workers in small enterprises, street cleaners, hospital employees, school ancillary staff, minor government employees, and so forth.

I have a feeling that there is a calculated strategy behind this, for, as I have indicated, Heath is highly conscious of these matters and how they have been debated. Yet she treads very warily round them. The reason eludes me. The book is far, far richer ethnographically than, for example, Paul Willis's *Learning to Labour*,[2] but far weaker politically. However, nothing I have said would lead anyone to be in doubt about the unique qualities of this book. Indeed, I suspect that it is constructed in order to provoke my kind of response.

Let us now see how Heath imposed order on what must have been one of the most daunting piles of accumulated material ever to have confronted a researcher at the moment of writing-up.

[. . .]

I shall single out one central aspect of oral traditions — narrative — and let is stand as a paradigm for all that is best in this book. Since I hold that narrative is a touchstone of oral tradition, I believe that Heath's account should become a point of reference for all discussion of spontaneous oral story telling.[3] Moreover, Heath's work on literacy in the community was being cited widely before the appearance of this book.[4]

In Roadville there are criteria for story telling which establish a clear framework, firmly excluding some possibilities and making very clear the principles of inclusion. Stories must be accounts of actual events, free from hyperbole, "an expression of social unity, a commitment to maintenance of the norms of the church and of the roles within the mill community's life" (p. 150). Above all, they require a moral or summary message. The induction of children into story telling constitutes a dramatic apprenticeship to this tradition: "Children in Roadville are not allowed to tell stories, unless an adult announces that something which happened to a child makes a good story and invites a retelling. When children are asked to retell such events, they are expected to tell non-fictive stories which 'stick to the truth' " (p. 158).

Fictive stories are lies. Roadville stories are moral episodes, and the monitoring of their narrations ensures that the model is thoroughly learned.

Sue: Why did you drop your eggs? What did Aunt Sue tell you 'bout climbing on that thing?
Wendy: We better be careful.
Sue: No, 'bout eggs 'n climbing?
Wendy: We better not climb with our eggs, else 'n we'd drop 'em. (p. 158)

To turn to Trackton's stories is to enter another narrative universe. In Trackton, "Good story-tellers . . . may base their stories on an actual event, but they creatively fictionalize the details surrounding the real event, and the outcome of the story may not even resemble what indeed happened" (p. 166).

Stories do not contain didactic highlighting to guide or control moral conduct. The stories must be dramatic, and therefore storytellers frequently resort to dialogue, which in itself opens up a source of mimicry, humor, narrative point. The free expression of feeling generates word-play and word-artistry which Heath is quick to pounce on (see twelve-year-old Terry's tale on p. 181 in which fantasy and reality are inextricably interwined). She sums up her detailed examination and comparison with a bold contrast: "In short, for Roadville, Trackton's stories would be lies; for Trackton, Roadville's stories would not even count as stories" (p. 189). All this is laid out beautifully and delicately for us: the participants, the settings, the microdramas of the tellings and their subtexts. To all this are added some very detailed inspections of the storyteller's art in both communities, rounded off with a more general and distanced view. However, to demur a little again, there is no attempt to tell us *why* such divergent cultural practices have arisen, nor to see their roots in the social and economic experience of the narrator. Black and white again?

Part 2 is the knight's move, for it contains an account of the collaboration between the author and the schools, a maneuver of high risk not only in its execution but even more in its being recorded here in cold print. The project, as I have indicated, is "to make accessible to teachers an understanding of the differences in language and culture their students bring to their classrooms" (p. 265), and then to engage in the development of programs and practices in the light of that understanding. The goal is success in school for everyone. [. . .]

Picking her way judiciously through the innovations, Heath makes very clear that the teachers did not see themselves as launching basic changes in content, nor abandoning established classroom methods (basal readers, for example). The criteria for "school success" in the end remain unchanged, and the core of mainstream values is not tampered with: "students learned to share the goals and methods of the classroom" (p. 340). There is not a hint that black and white students in the Carolinas studying in the same class-rooms might raise some tricky issues in history and social studies and in the job-getting aspects of some of their work. What Heath has chosen to do is to present all that seems most positive in the teachers' work and to imply that ethnicity did not affect the basic processes. Yet, the introduction of teachers — and, later, students — to ethnographic ways of studying surreptitiously their own and their community's practices does in fact erode the old curriculum. New *ways* of learning constitute new learning. How else can one begin? As Heath observes, "Students now provided information for the teacher to question — the reverse of the usual classroom practice of the teacher presenting the information and questioning students on their knowledge" (p. 342). Furthermore, she offers: "Critical in the thinking of these teachers was that their approach was not a remedial one designed for poor learners. Instead, they felt that the attention given to different ways of talking and knowing, and the manipulation of contexts and language benefited all students" (p. 355).

The principles do not in themselves constitute a complete apparatus for changing the role of language in the curriculum, but they have a huge potential if pushed to their logical conclusion. They could be extended into a critical examination of the language of textbooks or the ways in which communities are linked to and shaped by influential forces in society, including the ways in which language is used in the media, by politicians and others, to affect daily lives. Finally, there is the question of how Roadville and Trackton students are to develop their own voices so that they can articulate a critical view of society and act more powerfully in it. Ethnography cannot by itself achieve these ends. To assert this is not to diminish the courageous work of the teachers; it is only to sketch out its essentially initiatory character and its vulnerability.

And vulnerable it proved to be. In a sad but all too familiar phrase, we learn that "in the Piedmont of today, the methods used by these teachers have all but disappeared" (p. 356). The bureaucracy of tests has taken over and, as one teacher says, "there's no joy left in teaching now" (p. 359). This defeat is known on both sides of the Atlantic. To reverse it requires acting outside the classroom.

Heath writes in her last pages of "a recognition and a drive to use language as a source of power," but an indication of limits she sets herself is registered in the way that the sentence tails off into a circumscribed notion of power and its source: "for access to and maintenance of expanded types and places of work" (p. 363). The source of the power is much more than the job market.

In the end, teachers can defend successfully the enclaves they have constructed only if they have won the parents and community to their methods and can invoke their support in sustaining them. And those are "ways with words" which have to be learned too. They constitute the language of political participation. If all of us do not learn this way with words, we shall go on placing wreaths on the tombstones of projects all over the world, overcome with sadness and impotence.

Whatever we do or fail to do in resisting the conversion of our schools into brutally frank machines for social control, in the end thousands of teachers must encounter millions of students daily in classrooms. Heath's book suggests to us a new way of looking at that encounter. Ethnographers are the heroes of her text. There are other kinds of heroes whom we need to acknowledge, but that should not prevent us from saluting the ethnographers — and Shirley Brice Heath in particular.

Notes

1 Malinowski, *Coral Gardens and Their Magic*, vol. 2 (London: Allen & Unwin, 1935).
2 Willis, *Learning to Labour* (Westmead, Eng.: Saxon House, 1977).
3 See Rosen, *Stories and Meanings* (Sheffield, Eng.: National Association for the Teaching of English, 1984).
4 See, for example, "Protean Shapes in Literacy Events," in *Spoken and Written Language: Exploring Orality and Literacy*, ed. Deborah Tannen (Norwood, NJ: Ablex, 1982).

1.5 Children's Reading and Social Values

Mary Hoffman

Source: Edited version of Hoffman, M. (1981) 'Children's reading and social values'. In Mercer, N. (ed.) *Language in school and community*. London, Edward Arnold.

> The advance of children's literature from its dismal pre-war condition is . . . as a response to curious and wonderful convulsions in the literary, moral and social landscapes, (Blishen, 1975, p. 9)

Of recent years, the content of children's reading, in and out of school, has caused much concern, first among teachers, parents and librarians and later among publishers and critics; it has now even reached children's writers themselves, even if only as a subject for controversy, disagreement and alarmist threats of a New Censorship.

And yet some of the best writers for children, with that streak of anarchy which characterizes the creative process, were among the first to reject the literary *status quo* of the inter-war years and establish a more vigorous ethos. Geoffrey Trease's (1975) imaginary 'do's' and 'don'ts' for British authors of the 1920s and 1930s, include 'A "loyal native" is a man, dark of skin and doglike in devotion, who helps the British to govern his country. A "treacherous native" is one who does not. Similarly, in history, the common people sub-divide into simple peasants, faithful retainers and howling mobs . . . Girls *could* be introduced as characters into the boys' adventure story, but only as second-class citizens.' (p. 14). In other words, race, class and sex were not only areas of inequitable treatment in the run-of-the-mill children's story, they were also presented within a framework of social values which had already begun to disintegrate. This is a characteristic to which I shall return.

The rise of children's books as a subject for serious criticism

Another aspect of children's literature earlier this century, deplored by Trease and many others, was that it was accorded little or no literary status and was not subjected to any sustained criticism. Which was the result of which is not an answerable question. Both have now changed, at least within a small circle of readers, writers and reviewers (who are often the same people). Many journals about children's literature are now available, the TES and TLS publish four Children's Book 'Extras' a year and many national daily newspapers boast a Children's Books Editor. For the last ten years the National Book League has run a popular annual touring exhibition of *Children's Books of the Year* and has for many years stimulated and encouraged activities within a national programme for Children's Book Week.

So, on the literary and critical front, children's books have — if not come of age — at least been allowed to come down from the nursery, and be inspected by the grown-ups. Controversies there are, particularly wherever one set of practitioners e.g. teachers, comes up against another set, e.g. writers. Critics tend to be either those who evaluate books according to literary criteria or those whose prime concern is socio-cultural content. But there is now an indisputable children's book world, in which serious people take seriously what children read.

Children's voluntary reading

But what about the children themselves? What *do* they read from choice and what relation does it have to the self-congratulatory or self-scrutinizing world of these serious people? Whitehead *et al.* (1977) in their final report on the Schools Council research project into Children's Reading Habits, 10–15, questioned a very large (N = 7,839) representative sample of school children about their recent voluntary reading of books and periodicals. One of the most striking of their findings, across three age groups, is the number of children who claimed to have read *no books at all* in the preceding four weeks. This ranged from 9.4 per cent of the 10 + girls in the sample to 40 per cent of the 14 + boys. The average number of books read over four weeks by all ages, boys and girls, was 2.39.

Because of the unprecedented scope of the Whitehead research, it is worth looking further at its results, in terms of what kinds of reading constitute that just over half a book per week. Seventy seven per cent of all book reading was of narrative material (fiction and non-fiction). The researchers also subclassified narrative books, subjectively and by consensus, into 'juvenile' and 'adult', 'quality' and 'non-quality'. Using these definitions, they report that over the whole sample there was twice as much non-quality juvenile narrative being read (33.4 per cent) as quality juvenile narrative (17 per cent). The most widely read book at age 10 + was *Black Beauty,* and at 12 + was *Little Women*. At 14 + there was an incongruous tie for top place between *Little Women* and *Skinhead*. It must be remembered that these most widely read books represent tiny percentages of the age group, ranging from the 4.5 per cent of ten-year-olds who read *Black Beauty* to the 1.7 per cent of fourteen-year-olds who read Louisa Alcott and Richard Allen. *Little Women,* it should be noted, which was the fourth most-read book in the 10 + category, as well as heading the other two lists, was read by fewer than ten boys in each age group.

The authors comment on 'the overwhelmingly nineteenth-century flavour' (Whitehead op. cit. p. 133) of the 10 + list and describe the 12 + nominations as 'similarly redolent of the past'. This is a point I shall return to later. The children in the sample were also asked to name their favourite writers and here there is a further surprise. Enid Blyton, firmly categorized by the team as a writer of 'non-quality juvenile narrative', heads all lists. She was chosen by a remarkable 20 per cent of the whole sample (with no less than half of the 10 + girls naming her), although Louisa May Alcott, the author of the ubiquitous *Little Women* was given a derisory 43 mentions by nearly 8,000 children.

It is important to remember that the Whitehead research, although published in 1977, was based on data collected in March 1971. It also tells us nothing about the reading of the under-tens, which was not within its brief. So there are dangers in extrapolating to the reading of present day children; a decade is a long time in education. In the context of the discussion, however, the three main points to remember about what 10–15 year-olds were reading ten years ago are:

1. It was very little and a quarter of the children read nothing at all
2. It was mainly narrative and, at the lower ages, mainly nineteenth century
3. It was mainly 'non-quality'.

These aspects, together with the tremendous range of books mentioned (7,839 children yielded 7,557 titles) form the background to the picture of the content of children's voluntary reading which I want to consider here. Though the particular titles will have changed over the last ten years, it is perhaps less likely that a new overall trend will have emerged. I shall also consider the content of children's compulsory reading in school. Because of the nature of the social values inherent in the material I shall treat reading in and out of school together, in relation to different areas of social importance.

Reading and social values

I'm here using the term 'social value' to refer to any belief held by an individual which affects his or her actions in relation to others. Cumulatively, within a society, those individual beliefs also make up the social values of the community to which the individuals belong. In some cases it is the sharing of these social values, as much as geography or income, which constitutes a recognizable community. Any writer, both as an individual and as a member of a community, holds social values and is bound to demonstrate them in what he or she writes, whether fiction or non-fiction. Only such materials as tube maps may be outside that scheme. It is also to be hoped that more idiosyncratic values and opinions will also find their way into the writing of any individual. No one in the children's book world is advocating, even if it were possible, either the blankness of writing which would share the value-free nature of the tube map or the blandness which stems from writing, without any personal involvement, within a framework of received social values.

Children's books and class

The concern in the UK with the content of children's books began with an uneasiness about the limited treatment of social class. Trease (op. cit.) and other historical novelists, such as Rosemary Sutcliffe, were concerned to rid historical fiction of its 'gadzookery' and engage more closely with social and political realities. *Bows Against the Barons* and *Comrades for the Charter* (both 1934) were Trease's unglamorous but invigorating treatments of the Robin Hood story and the conditions out of which the chartist movement grew, starting a line of children's fiction that continued with such books as Frederick Grice's *Bonny Pit Laddie* (1960) and Susan Price's *Twopence a Tub* (1974).

Reading schemes and class

By the mid-1960s there was a growing feeling of dissatisfaction with the picture of life shown in the primers through which most small children were being taught to read. The two-parent, two-child, one-dog and at least one-car family living in a suburban house with a well tended garden has become a standard target for criticism now, because of its remoteness from the more complex and shifting family and economic patterns of most British children. Yet, until the advent of *Nippers* (1968) and *Breakthrough to Literacy* (1970), the Janet and John ambience had held the stage for over 20 years. The objections to that ambience are manifold and more complicated than its simple dismissal as 'middle class' can reveal.

Firstly, the presentation of social values in reading schemes is seen as particularly important because this is the material through which the majority of children have been, and still are, introduced to reading as an activity. This argument assumes both that attitudes are formed or at least affected by what we read and that the first books encountered are likely to be particularly influential. The objections to reading primers are thus poised on an axis between what attitudes it is considered harmful or life-enhancing to convey and what is motivating for children to read in their first encounters with print. These objections, although linked, are different. One is critic-centred; the other child-centred. Taken together they imply that early reading materials shoud be subjected to a closer scrutiny than any others, as indeed they have been. Later, I shall look at them from the point of their implicit racial and sex-role attitudes.

But to continue with class. There is a further question as to whether that suburban idyll of *Janet and John, Ladybird Keywords* and the like, reflects a recognizable social milieu for *any* reader. It is rather, in an admittedly limited and unimaginative form, a romantic idealization of a particular way of life, with all unpleasantness smoothed away. The dog has no teeth, the siblings no rivalry, the house has no connection with main drainage. Perhaps this is not so important as the cruder surface props of dress, decor and diet which may enable children of similar surroundings to feel 'That's me!' as Berg (1972) claims 'every middle class child has done practically since babyhood'. I doubt it, since even in their revised editions Ladybird families do not seem part of the last quarter of the twentieth century when, for example, 'middle class' mothers are as likely to work outside the home as anyone else.

Linked with this second objection is a third, based on language and literary values. The controlled vocabulary and syntax of this kind of primer leads to the often-parodied type of 'look, look John, see the little red car' inanity which bears no relation to the language experience of any child.

These three objections are often confused. Often when the social values of such reading schemes are criticized, whether on grounds of attitudes to class, race, or sex-roles, other will reply that these criticism are irrelevant because of the low literary quality of the books overall. This of course is to ignore the fact of the enormous number of children who have cut their literary teeth on them. *Janet and John* was in use in 81 per cent of primary schools in the Home Counties and Midlands in 1968 according to Goodacre (1969). Grundin (1980) questioned a random sample of 631 headteachers of infant schools over Great Britain in 1978 and found that 27.7 per cent still use *Ladybird* as the principal scheme and a further 26.6 per cent use it regularly to supplement the main scheme.

When Leila Berg wrote the first *Nippers* books in the late 1960s, they were disliked by many teachers because their social milieu was intentionally working class. Typical of the many abusive reactions were 'I feel the subject matter is very poor and low-class, and in several cases ungrammatical. Perhaps they would be suitable for children in slum schools or from deprived backgrounds, but even so they tend to show a side of life from which we are trying to lead the children away.' (quoted in Dixon, 1977 p. 88). It is necessary to remind the reader here that the subject matter was not drugs or abortion but a family having a take-away supper of fish and chips. *The Nippers* and *Little Nippers*, several of which are now available as trade books as well as in schools, have sold millions of copies and have brought a new vitality to the world of reading primers but they have in their turn been criticized for creating a new set of social sterotypes, this time working class ones.

Fiction and class
Similarly, some works of children's fiction, such as *The Family from One End Street*, and *Magnolia Buildings* which were greeted as new and revolutionary for being about families where Dad was a dustman or railway man, now reveal a condescending tone and a dated and inaccurate view of working-class language — plenty of 'cor!' with or without 'blimey!', and everything 'flippin'' and 'bloomin''. [. . .]

Children's books and race

Concern about attitudes to race in children's reading, both in and out of school, has also grown over the last decade. It has developed out of the wider movement against racial prejudice in education generally. Teachers Against Racism (TAR) was formed in 1971 and later became subsumed under the *National Association for Multiracial Education* (NAME). The Commission for Racial Equality has education officers, including one with a special brief for looking at children's books. In 1979 a new quarterly magazine *Dragon's Teeth* was launched by the National Committee on Racism in Children's Books, one of whose aims is to 'campaign against racial bias in children's books'.

Fiction and race

Many writers have given detailed criticisms of the racial bias in specific children's titles. (See Milner, 1975; Children's Rights Workshop, 1975; Zimet, 1976; Dixon, 1977). The most common targets in fiction have been the 'Biggles' books of W. E. Johns, several titles by Enid Blyton, particularly *The Three Golliwogs* (re-issued 1973) and *The Little Black Doll* (1937), several titles in Hugh Lofting's Dr Dolittle series, particularly *The Story of Dr Dolittle* (1920) and Helen Bannerman's *The Story of Little Black Sambo* (1899). This list at first appears an assembly of rather elderly Aunt Sallies. But we should look again at Whitehead's (1977) survey results before dismissing these books as rendered harmless by age or neglect. (No one, now, I think would make the other possible defence that their degree of artistic achievement mitigates their racist bias.)

Blyton was declared 'most popular writer' by 20 per cent of Whitehead's sample. She is a writer whose popularity is linked with her prolific output; when one title has been enjoyed, there is always another for the reader to move on to. The titles particularly singled out for criticism, which blatantly equate blackness with wickedness, ugliness and inferiority, are as likely to be read as other less racially offensive of her stories, simply because they carry her name. *Five Fall into Adventure* (1950, re-issued 1968), in which a girl is frightened by a 'dreadful face' at the window — 'It looked very dark — perhaps it was a black man's face!' (p. 30) was in fact mentioned by more than ten children as having been read in the previous four weeks, as one of 19 *Famous Five* titles thus listed.

Three *Biggles* titles were listed by more than ten children, and W. E. Johns was named favourite writer by 96 children (all boys); 241 of his books were read over the four-week period. The *Dr Dolittle* books were also listed among the more popular, although Hugh Lofting himself received no mentions.

As for *The Story of Little Black Sambo* in spite of its age Dixon (1977) mentions its successful (over ¼ million) sales and the controversy that arose when Bridget Harris of TAR outlined its racist content in *The Times* newspaper in 1972. Currently, there is a 'revised and updated' pamphlet *Children and Books* available from the National Confederation of Parent-Teacher Associations, which lists *Little Black Sambo* as 'a lovely book for babies' (reported in Children's Book Bulletin No. 3, Spring 1980 pp. 13–14). The term 'sambo', like 'Golliwog', 'Wog', and 'Nigger', has been used as a term of racialist abuse for a long time in this country, (Blyton's *'Three Golliwogs'* were originally named, Golly, Woggie and Nigger) an uncomfortable reality surpressed not only by those who felt that Bannerman's book 'did them no harm' but also by Robertson's Foods Ltd., the jam manufacturers, who are celebrating their Golliwog symbol's fiftieth anniversary at the time of writing (1980). Their marketing director refers to 'Golly' (sic) as 'a warm and sympathetic symbol' but Murray (1980) affirms 'black people have said that Golly is offensive to them as members of a racial group'. Yet, in 1979, a brand new reincarnation of this racist symbol surfaced in an expensive illustrated children's book *Here Comes Golly!* by Giles Brandreth.

Another book, mentioned in the Whitehead research is *Skinhead* by Richard Allen. Remember that it was jointly most popular book for the 14 + age group with *Little Women*. Attitudes held in this book and its sequels have been analysed by Salter (1972). Joe Hawkins, hero of *Skinhead* is an overt racist: ' "Spades" or "wogs" don't count. They were imposters on the face of a London which should always be white. . .'. Salter convincingly argues that Allen is also 'Peter Cave', author of *Mama*, a book in which a 14-year-old Pakistani boy is scalped by Hell's Angels after mama has said 'Turn the little bastard into curry if you want to.'

Some higher-quality children's books which have also been criticized for racial stereotyping are *Sounder* and *The Cay* (both 1969) and *Charlie and the Chocolate Factory* (1964). The two former were award-winning American books about blacks and the objections to their content and treatment of race, brought in the new perspective of white writers being unqualified to write about the black experience. 'Authenticity in this case hinges upon life experience' (Schwartz, 1970). The objections to the original (1964) edition of *Charlie and the Chocolate Factory*, in which Willy Wonka's nauseous and sometimes dangerous confections were made and tested by dispensible black pygmies from Africa resulted in editorial change to the 1973 version. However, although the little workers are now white, they are still called Oompa-Loompas and sing a song containing the lines

. . . and cannibals crowding 'round the pot,
stirring away at something hot.

The belief in the cannibalism of 'primitive', particularly Black, civilizations is as long-established calumny, which has been described as 'a subtle form of racism' (Arens, 1979). Yet even in a recent maths textbook *O and B Maths Bank 2*, there appear 'two pairs of cannibals, each with white men in their pots'. (Children's Book Bulletin, No. 4 1980 p. 11).

As with the class argument above, there is now a backlash of adverse criticism against books which were initially postively received. *The Trouble with Donovan Croft* (1974) is one such example. Donovan Croft is a West Indian boy who has been temporarily fostered by a white family while his mother has gone to Jamaica to look after a sick relative. The 'trouble' with him is that he doesn't understand that the separation is temporary — no one seems to have explained it to him — and as a result, he withdraws into himself and refuses to speak. This book won the Other Award in 1976 instituted by the Children's Rights Workshop to commend non-biased books of literary merit. Now, however, a practising teacher writes 'under no circumstances should the book be used as a token West Indian story. . . . Donovan and his father come across very much as English with black skin.' (Griffin, 1980). The criteria for assessing the treatment of race in children's fiction are becoming stricter and it is difficult to find a single book on one of the many recommended 'multi-ethnic' or 'multi-cultural' reading lists which has not also been criticized in some more radical forum.

Reading schemes and race

As far as reading schemes are concerned, for a long time they were racially prejudiced simply through omission, in that they contained no non-white characters at all. In the United States, multi-ethnic basal readers were not produced until the latter half of the 1960s (Zimet, 1976, p. 61). The *Nippers* and *Breakthrough* series mentioned above, which began to be published in the UK at about this time, do contain some blacks and the *Sparks* (1972) scheme is intentionally multi-racial. Nelson also publish a scheme called *New West Indian Readers*, and the *Terraced House Books, All Sorts, Dominoes* and *Ladybird Sunstart* books all feature at least some titles with multi-racial settings. If anything in contemporary publishing could be described as a boom industry, it would be the production of more multi-cultural early reading books. So far, however, there has been no sustained analysis of what the actual content of these apparently more culturally diverse materials convey about social values in relation to race. The newer schemes are not in use in many schools. 1.9 per cent use *Sparks* as the main scheme and 3.2 per cent use *Dominoes* (Grundin, 1980). With the current limitations on spending, it is likely that the old uni-racial schemes will continue to be widely used.

Textbooks and race

Another area of school reading which has received more attention from the point of view of social values and race is the ethno-centrism, specifically the eurocentrism of textbooks used in geography and history. Preiswork and Perrot (1978), in their analysis of 30 history textbooks in common use in western schools found that 'a critical approach to the European system of values is non-existent'. When it comes to taking 'O' level exams, the content of the syllabus may reveal an overwhelming bias towards the empire-building and colonizing role of the British, with little attention to the effects of this role on the countries they colonized.

[. . .]

Cultural bias may be present in a whole range of assumptions about how school subjects are taught and assessed, as the 'discontinuity' argument discussed elsewhere in this book has shown. Taylor (1980) in marking English language 'O' level exams, discovered that the content of topics set for essays would discriminate against a child without an English background. The four essay topics on the paper he marked were based on fox-hunting, a traffic jam, a blizzard and a record-club's advertisement. As Taylor points out, 'an essay cannot be written in a vacuum, there must be a subject and a subject of which the candidate is previously aware. This implies a shared background of experience among the candidates, from which titles may be drawn and in our multi-cultural society this background is less solid and more varied than it has been previously.'

Clearly the arguments about race and children's reading are complex. What most of the researchers in this area would agree is that the issues, where presented to children at all, take no account of that complexity. Children's own views about race have been documented by Milner (1975), Zimet (1976) and Jeffcoate (1977 and 1979) among others. It has been demonstrated (Litcher and Johnson, 1967; Fisher, 1965) that reading stories which show minority characters in a favourable light, particularly when combined with discussion, does effect a significantly positive shift in attitudes of the dominant group.

[. . .]

Children's books and sex-roles

Stereotyping, the simplified assignment of characters to a category to the point where distortion occurs, has received a great deal of attention in relation to sex-roles. The 'traditional' assignment of sex-roles in the UK, in which men work and provide for their families and women do not work outside the home but service their husbands' and families' needs, is often symbolized in children's books by the apron, on the one hand, and the pipe and newspaper on the other. In the case of children, the traditional image is put across, whether consciously or unconsciously, through the active and aggressive behaviour of boys and the passive and quiescent behaviour of girls. My contention is not that such traditional roles are wrong, for any individual child or adult, but that the range of behaviour of both sexes is much more varied and interesting than the images conveyed in children's reading.

Reading schemes
Unlike racism, sexism (a word created analogically to mean adverse discrimination on the grounds of gender) has been well studied in relation to reading schemes. One of the earliest American sources (Women on Words and Images, 1972) put the case against the reading-primer view of sex-roles forcefully and polemically: 'The authors of this study assume that there are ways in which we can make better use of the talents and energies of our female population beyond directing them into the kitchen and the obstetrics ward. In the coming years there must be a drive in all educational fields to improve motivational incentives for this underrated, under-encouraged, 50 per cent of the population. Grade-school readers are a top priority area for change, since they influence children at their most vulnerable and malleable stage of development.' (Introduction pp. 3–4). At the same time, in this country, Cannon (1972) was concluding that *Ladybird Keywords* dealt with 'precisely the dif-

ference between boys' and girls' roles and mothers' and fathers' roles'. Rathbone (1970) had already found that even the newer reading schemes continued to present stereotyped sex-roles. *'Things I can do'* (Breakthrough) depicts a variety of children's activities. The text reads: 'I can be good'. To illustrate goodness a little girl is shown sweeping the floor. 'I can be bad' is illustrated by two boys having a fight. Looking on is a prim little girl in a pink dress.

Lobban (1974) coded the content of six British reading schemes published between 1958 and 1970 and updated her study (1975) to include two more published in the early 1970s. She concluded: 'virtually none of the readers presented non sex-typed models, activities or goals to suggest new non-stereotyped behaviours to the children ... children need preparation for present day and future reality but these reading schemes prepare them for a reality of 20 years ago.' (Lobban, 1975, p. 209) [. . .]

Schoolbooks and sex-roles

Other literature encountered in school conveys the same message. Austerfield and Turner (1972) speculate that the relatively low number of girls taking science subjects at GCE 'O' level and 'A' level, is at least partly accounted for by the presentation of sex roles in junior science textbooks. Adult males are portrayed in a wide range of occupations and are shown as sources of information. Women are confined to their nurturant roles and take no interest in explanations or activities in these books. The experiments are likewise conducted by boys while girls look on. Stroking kittens or blowing bubbles are the nearest the girls get to carrying out any activities of their own. Davey (1979) who carried out a survey of the past and present reading habits of women engineers, found that a third of her two control groups (non-technicians) considered that science-linked categories of books were intended for boys only and only a very small number of these girls still read such books. Over half the girl technicians, however, did read them, even though 13 per cent of them agreed about their intended male audience. In other words, the girls in Davey's survey who read more science-based literature, about how things work and how to do things, and who took up careers in engineering did so in the belief that they were acting atypically for their sex and crossing recognized gender-boundaries.

American maths textbooks have been analysed by Federbruch (1976) who found that boys were frequently shown in illustrations helping the girls to understand mathematical problems, whose range for females did not extend further than the challenge of adding up a shopping bill. 'The expressions on girls' and women's faces are sometimes the model of bewilderment as they struggle to find a way to put order into a seemingly chaotic or even simple numerical situation.' (p. 180).

My own survey of sex-education books (Hoffman, 1975) revealed sexist views of female sexuality and a distorted view of marriage in which girls would have to unlearn the modesty and passivity into which they had been socialized, in order to satisfy their husband's sexual requirements ... 'for a full and happy married life, [a girl] must learn to respond in the bedroom while she maintains a ladylike appearance the rest of the time.' (Pomeroy, 1969).

History textbooks, as with race, may present a partial view of the role of women. 'History has been selected by males and women have been left out. Men have defined what is important in their terms and so they have looked at part civilizations and seen only wars and male politics and antics.' (Spender, 1979). A quick scan through most school history textbooks will confirm the impression that women, with a few notable exceptions such as the wives of Henry VI, Queens Elizabeth, Anne and Victoria, did not exist in this country until the Suffragettes [sic] at the beginning of this century. How the suffragists are treated is also a matter where the historians' own social values are clearly demonstrated. For an excellent comparative exercise on the treatment of Emily Davison's death at the Derby in 1913, using primary and secondary sources, see The Schools Council's History 13–16 Project, Book 4, *Problems of Evidence* (1976).

Those women who lived before 1900 and were not of royal or aristocratic birth, or were not public practitioners of the private servicing and nurturant role, such as Florence Nightingale and Elizabeth Fry, go unrecorded. As Virginia Woolf had already noticed 50 years ago, 'The history of England is the history of the male line, not of the female . . . of our mothers, our grandmothers our great grandmothers, what remains? Nothing but a tradition. One was beautiful, one was red haired, one was kissed by a Queen. We know nothing of them except their names, and the dates of their marriages, and the number of children they bore.' (Woolf, 1929). History, as we know it, 'is about chaps'.

This dismissal or omission of women overlaps with another social value, of course. Because the 'chaps' that history is about are the kings and king-makers, the makers and breakers of treaties, the warmongers and the 'discoverers' of non-European countries. If women are absent so are most men of the largest social class; after the villeins of medieval history, they are nameless cannon-fodder or workhands until the industrial revolution when they re-emerge as machine-breakers and chartists. Yet when ordinary men and women *can* be rediscovered and exhumed from documents of the past, as by Ladurie (1978), their lives are found fascinating and their chronicle becomes a best seller.

Fiction and sex roles

Children's fiction, in the picture books of the early years, has largely reflected the same stereotyped sex-roles as portrayed in the reading scheme. Girls are in the minority as characters, particularly main characters. Brennan (1973) examined over 200 picture books and found only 46 heroines. Moon (1974), who analysed 200 fiction books from pre-reading texts to books with readability levels of 8.5, found 115 stories with male central characters and only 27 with female central characters. Twice as many men as women were present in the books. Weitzman *et al.* (1974) read 'several hundred picture books' before concentrating on an analysis of 18 winners and runners-up for the Caldecott Medal given by the American Library Association for the most distinguished picture book of the year. (The UK equivalent is the Library Association's Kate Greenaway Award), and concluded 'through picture books, girls are taught to have low aspirations because there are so few opportunities portrayed as available to them. The world of picture books never tells little girls that as women they might find fulfillment outside their homes or through intellectual pursuits. . . . The simplified and stereotyped images in these books present such a narrow view of reality that they must violate the child's own knowledge of a rich and complex world.' (pp. 25 and 27–8).

For a description of the sex-roles in older fiction see Dixon (1977). He devotes much space to Louisa M. Alcott's books which he takes as being deliberately about the learning of appropriate sex-roles by boys and girls, particularly girls. (cf. Cannon's comment on reading schemes above). Dixon describes four themes which recur 'physical movement and deportment; speech; role-enforcement and dress and, lastly . . . the reward for conformity, the gilt on the cage.' (Vol. 1. p. 10). It is interesting to see that Dixon also indicts Alcott as a deliberate propagandist. 'There are too many sly digs at feminism, scattered throughout the books, for us to excuse Alcott of unawareness.' (p. 11). *Little Women*, you will remember, was listed among the five most widely read books for each of Whitehead *et al.*'s (1977) three age groups. These researchers themselves refer to the 'moral wholesomeness' of *Little Women* and say 'we can be glad that it continues to retain a justified popularity'. I find Whitehead *et al.*'s *own* social values easier to endorse when they turn to *Skinhead*, which I have already discussed in relation to race. Girls and women are treated solely as sex-objects in this book. One quotation, from a rape scene, will suffice to illustrate the social values as far as relations between the sexes are concerned: ' "Me next mate", [Tony] yelled, watching Billy penetrate the half-stupefied girl hippie. Her jeans lay on the beach her thighs pimpled with cold, her buttocks bruised by the relentless rocks . . .' (quoted in Whitehead op. cit. p. 247).

[. . .]

Comics

It is necessary to make a special mention, albeit a brief one, of comics in relation to social values. All reviews of this topic mention Orwell's (1940) essay on Boys' Weeklies and often refer to it as 'seminal'. It is perhaps this phrase which has earned it its place in the literature: '[Children are] absorbing a set of beliefs that would be regarded as hopelessly out of date in the Central Office of the Conservative Party.' In other words if children's reading in general shows a framework of social values which has begun to disintegrate or no longer exists, then children's comics are at the very furthest extreme of this distant approximation to contemporary culture. And it is the very worst aspects of departed systems that comics perpetrate. Cannon (1972) believed that comics for young girls 'articulate the conflict between the masculine independence a girl may have a child, and the increasing pressures to be feminine as adolescence looms nearer.' This conflict is usually presented in the context of 'posh' boarding schools — a very remote ethos for most comic-readers.

Johnson (1966) found that boys' comics were still teaching xenophobia towards Britain's world war II enemies and nicknames like Kraut, Hun, Nip and Jap were being kept alive for a generation of children whose own parents were themselves children during the last war. Walt Disney's comics, which form 10 per cent of the net annual profits of the Walt Disney organization (Tisdall, 1977) have been used to convey anti-Allende or anti-Vietcong messages. According to Tisdall in Chile in 1971 Donald Duck cried 'Restore the King!' in a special campaign, through the comics, to undermine Allende's government. It should go without saying that, although the kinds of propaganda here are anti-Marxist or anti-Soviet, the objections are to the use of comics for *any* kind of political propaganda.

The attitudes to social class in children's comics are very musty — everyone is familiar with Lord Snooty and his chums — but have recently received a new twist with the story of 'The House that Jackie Bought' in the weekly comic *Tracy*. As outlined by Edwards (1980), Jackie is the daughter of a family harrassed by their neighbours because they have bought their own council house. Called 'Miss Toffee-Nose' and 'Miss Snobby Snout' by the other people on the estate, Jackie is subjected to a campaign of threats and physical violence. Clearly there is some form of propaganda going on here but whether it is intended to discourage or encourage the purchase of council houses it would take a subtle sociologist to decipher!

This content, which may seem laughable rather than amusing, matters when viewed in the context of the heavy comic reading of children. Whitehead *et al.* (op. cit.) discovered that an average of 2.3 comics were regularly read by the children in their sample. 76.4 per cent of periodical reading by boys at 10 + , for example, was of comics and 86.2 per cent of girls' periodical reading at 10 + . So a large number of these vehicles for propaganda and outworn social values are being read by children every week.

Censorship

It is impossible to talk about social values in children's reading for long without someone saying 'what about free speech?' or 'surely you aren't advocating censorship?' Shackford (1970) discussing *The Story of Dr Doolittle*, which has been criticized as racist (see above) asks 'Is it not possible to develop in children a critical judgement that will make it unnecessary to remove from the shelves such problematical classics?' (p. 163). In this country, King (1980) a children's writer, says 'There are people setting up a whole range of taboos on the subject of *race* . . . [this philosophy] is being used to persuade librarians not to buy [certain books], to persuade teachers not to use them, and to frighten writers off writing them.'

In the ten years or so that I have been involved with groups studying the socio-cultural content of children's books and seeking to present those views at conferences, seminars and meetings, I have never come across a list of proscribed books. On the contrary, as the next section will show, lists of *recommended* books have proliferated. The editors of Children's Book Bulletin give a lucid definition of real censorship involving the seizure or banning of printed works and distinguish it from the practice of what King characterizes as New Prudery and they themselves call 'new criticism': 'The first seeks to control and *restrict* what is available. The second, by pointing out omissions and distortions and posing alternative seeks to *increase* the range of options available to children in their literature' (Stones and Mann, 1980).

Alternative approaches to children's books

If you don't ban books whose social values are dissonant with your own, what do you do? [. . .]

The provision of many alternative books does seem a good idea and there are now many lists of recommended non-sexist books and books for the multi-cultural society. (See bibliography.) Many publishing houses now provide their own lists and it is worth writing to ask for them. Some publishers have also produced guidelines for writers and editors. Scott Foresman and McGraw Hill did this in the States in relation to sexist language and images, in the early 1970s and provoked much adverse criticism over here. However, *Women in the Publishing Industry Group* in the UK drew up their own Non-Sexist Code of Practice for Book Publishing in 1976 and the EPC currently have a working party on sexism in children's books. There are also checklists and guidelines for assessing the racist or sexist content of books, produced by Centre for Urban Educational Studies, Equal Opportunities Commission, NUT, NUS and others.

Reading and social values in the context of language, school and community

Recently there has been a call for researchers and other educators to provide data that the reading of sex-biased material has any effect on the reader (Tibbetts, 1978). This is a much larger question in relation to the power and influence of reading on human belief and behaviour as a whole. Kimmel (1970) says 'it has begun to seem as if the belief that a child's attitudes can be affected by his reading is considered almost as an act of faith among teachers, librarians, parents and publishers.' These authors find the kind of evidence cited in, e.g. Zimet (1976) insufficient, though Tibbetts herself does not refer to that evidence. She also has to admit that her argument implies: 'By the same token, no one can demonstrate that sexist reading material is *not* damaging.' (p. 168).

As a writer on this topic, and a literature graduate I cannot, nor would wish to, claim impartiality on this issue. I believe that great literature and badly written rubbish can both change people's lives. To go further, I think that the written word is the most powerful moulder of beliefs and values that many of us encounter, often outweighing even personal experience. The confident and tough schoolgirl who once bellowed at me in a classroom 'When I go out with my bloke, I want to be treated *fragile!*', the small daughter of a friend who, asked to draw a doctor at school, drew a man, though the only two doctors she had ever encountered were both women, have both acquired sex-role images from outside their own nature and experience and I believe books to have played a part in that acquisition. I do not, of course, offer that belief to Tibbetts or anyone else as 'evidence'.

The social values conveyed in children's reading are a part of the social values inherent in wider language use. One of the worse epithets you can use to anyone involves women's sexual anatomy. 'Effeminate' used of a man and 'mannish' of a woman are derogatory terms, with childhood equivalents in 'sissy' and 'tomboy'. Women and men are even supposed to use language differently (see e.g. Lakoff, 1975). Blackness and whiteness have a long history of polarized usage in association with moral qualities. Class-based words such as 'peasant' are used derogatively by some; in the same way some others now use 'middle class', even 'very middle class' as a boo-word. 'Spastic' and 'brain damaged' are used colloquially to mean 'feeble' or 'disoriented'. 'It's a bit Irish', 'French leave', 'to Welsh on an agreement' — the English language is peppered with assumptions about groups of people. A language preserves in a fossilized form the social values of those who speak it.

The social values conveyed in school reading materials will be seen against a background of the social values held within the school itself. Reading does not take place within a vacuum, any more than writing does. Children read 'we dress up as doctors and nurses' (Breakthrough *Dressing Up*) and see an illustration of two girls dressing up as nurses only. They see female teachers doing dinner duty and performing all sorts of nurturant extra-curricular tasks. They see that Headteachers in mixed secondary schools are usually male and deputies female. They see themselves sexually segregated for activities, on the register and in the dinner queue. The boys hear themselves asked to lift and move heavy furniture; the girls hear requests for help with watering plants or cleaning up after cookery. The boys are punished and rewarded in different ways from girls and have different standards of work-presentation and behaviour accepted. The girls are comforted when they are hurt, the boys encouraged to grin and bear it.

All those things happen in some schools; some happen in all schools. An equivalent background could be constructed to social values connected with race and class. The social values in reading materials will converge with or diverge from the background model and teachers should examine this divergence or convergence. The book within the language, the language within the school, the school within the community, each goes to make up a larger whole of values to which the developing child is exposed. The values of the larger society, as conveyed through the mass media, are reflected in the social and moral climate of the school, its language and its reading. The values expressed by the writer can be part of a movement to change that climate and that society.

In all the areas of children's reading examined in this chapter but particularly fiction, we have seen the same pattern emerging. First there develops a restlessness with the monotony of the social values expressed in a given area, usually characterized by the initial omission of a particular group of people — the working class, Blacks, interesting girls. Then in the next phase, a few pioneering books attempt to change the ethos and in their wake, many titles appear which do at least feature those missing persons. Next there is a backlash of more sophisticated criticism which objects to a new kind of stereotyped being developed. The fourth phase, in which the social values expressed again no longer constitute the content of a book but are part of its treatment, is yet to come.

References

Arens, W. (1979) Eating people isn't right. *New Scientist*, 20 September. (See also Arens, W. *The Man-Eating Myth*, Oxford: OUP 1979).

Austerfield, V. and Turner, J. (1972) What are little girls made of? *Spare Rib*, 3 September.

Berg, L. (1972) Language of *Nippers*. (letter) *Times Educational Supplement*, 15 December.

Blishen, E. (ed.) (1975) *The Thorny Paradise: Writers on Writing for Children*. Harmondsworth: Kestrel.

Brennan, D. (1973) Sugar and Spice and all things. . . . *Shrew* 5, 4 October.

Cannon, C. (1972a) Female from Birth. *Times Educational Supplement*, 14 January.

— (1972b) The Crazy Comic Conflict, *Spare Rib* 5, November, pp. 36–7.

Children's Rights Workshop (eds.) (1975) *Racist and Sexist Images in Children's Books*. London: Writers and Readers Publishing Cooperative.

— (1976) *Sexism in Children's Books*. London: Writers and Readers Publishing Cooperative.

Davey, A. (1979) *Ballet Shoes or Building Sites?* Birmingham: Birmingham Library School Cooperative.

Dixon, B. (1977) *Catching Them Young* (2 vols.). London: Pluto Press.

Edwards, R. (1980) The trials of Miss Snobby Snout. *New Statesman*, 11 July.

Federbrush, M. (1976) The sex problems of school maths books. In Stacey, J. *et al.*, *And Jill Came Tumbling After: Sexism in American Education*. New York: Dell.

Fisher, F. L. (1965) The influences of reading and discussion on the attitudes of fifth graders towards American Indians. Unpublished doctoral dissertation, University of California, Berkeley.

Goodacre, E. (1969) Published Reading schemes. *Educational Research* 12 (1), pp. 30–35.

Griffin, C. (1980) Worthy intentions; but whose image? *The English Magazine* 3, Spring, pp. 17–18.

Grundin, H. 1980: Reading schemes in the Infant School. *Reading* 14 (1), pp. 5–13.

Hoffman, M. (1975) Assumptions in sex education books. *Educational Review* 27 (3), pp. 211–20.

Jeffcoate, R. (1977) Children's racial ideas and feelings. *English in Education*, Spring.

—— (1979) *Positive Image: Towards a Multi-Racial Curriculum*. London: Writers and Readers Publishing Cooperative/Chameleon Press.

Johnson, N. B. (1966) What do children learn from war comics? *New Society*, 7 July.

Kimmel, E. A. (1970) Can children's books change children's values? *Educational Leadership* **28** (2), pp. 133–61.

King, C. (1980) Blatantly racist children's books. *The Author* **xci** (2), Summer, pp. 90–92.

Litcher, J. and Johnson, D. W. (1969) Changes in attitudes towards Negroes of white elementary school students after use of multi-ethnic readers. *Journal of Educational Psychology* **60**, pp. 148–52.

Ladurie, E. Le Roy (1978) *Montaillou*, Paris: Editions Gallimard. (Also Harmondsworth, Penguin 1980).

Lakoff, R. (1975) *Language and Women's Place*. New York: Harper & Row.

Lobban, G. (1974) Presentation of sex-roles in reading schemes. *Forum for the Discussion of New Trends in Education* **16** (2), Spring, pp. 57–60 (Reprinted in Children's Rights Workshop (1976)).

—— (1975) Sex-roles in Reading Schemes. *Educational Review* **27** (3), June, pp. 202–9.

Milner, D. (1975) *Children and Race*. Harmondsworth: Penguin.

Moon, C. (1974) Sex-role stereotyping in books for young readers. Unpublished Dip. Ed. Thesis, University of Bristol Library.

Murray, E. (1980) What's wrong with golly? *Dragon's Teeth* **2** (2).

Orwell, G. (1940) Boy's Weeklies. In *Inside The Whale & Other Essays*. London: Secker & Warburg (also Penguin 1969).

Preiswerk, R. and Perrot, D. (1978) *Ethnocentricism and history: Africa, Asia, and Indian American in western text books*. New York: NOK Publishers International.

Rathbone, F. (1970) 'Girls are always afraid', said Bill. unpublished paper. An abbreviated version appears in *Shrew* **5** (4).

Salter, D. (1972) The hard core of children's fiction. *Children's Literature in Education* **8,** pp. 39–55.

Schwartz, A. V. (1970) *Sounder:* a black or a white tale? *Interracial Books for Children* **3** (1) (reprinted in Children's Rights Workshop (1975).

Shackford, J. W. (1970) Dealing with Dr Dolittle: A new approach to the '-isms.' *Language Arts* **55,** pp. 180–7.

Spender, D. (1979) Education or indoctrination? Paper for the Working Party on Sexism of the National Association for Teachers of English.

Stones, R. and Mann, A. (1980) Censorship or selection? *Children's Books Bulletin* **3,** Spring.

Taylor, R. (1980) It's not what you say it's the way that you say it . . . cultural bias in Ordinary level English Language examinations. *New Approaches in Multi-Cultural Education* **8** (2), pp. 5–6.

Tibbetts, S. L. (1978) Wanted: data to prove that sexist reading material has an impact on the reader. *The Reading Teacher* **32** (2), pp. 165–9.

Tisdall, C. (1977) Imperialist mousepiece. *Guardian* 25 January.

Trease, G. (1975) The revolution in children's literature, in Blishen (1975).

Weitzman, L. *et al.* (1972) Sex-role socialisation in picture books for pre-school children. (reprinted in Children's Rights Workshop (1976) q.v.).

Whitehead, F. *et al.* (1977) *Children and their books*. London: Macmillan Education for the Schools Council.

Women on Words and Images (1972) *Dick and Jane as Victims*. Princeton, NJ: National Organization of Women.

Woolf, V. (1929) Women and Fiction. *The Forum*, March; reprinted in Woolf, L. (ed.) (1972) *Virginia Woolf; Collected Essays, Vol. III*. London: Chatto & Windus.

Zimet, S. G. (1976) *Print and Prejudice*. London: Hodder & Stoughton.

Children's books and textbooks mentioned in this chapter

All Sorts Readers, J. Marshall. London: Warne (1969)

Black Beauty, A. Sewell. London: Jarrold & Sons (1877)

Boot Boys, Richard Allen. London: NEL (1972)

Bonny Pit Laddie, Frederick Grice. Oxford: OUP (1960)

Bows Against the Barons, Geoffrey Trease. (1934) (Reissued Leicester: Hodder & Stoughton Children's Books)

Breakthrough to Literacy, D. Mackay *et al*. Harlow: Longman (1970)

Charlie and the Chocolate Factory, R. Dahl. New York: Knopf (1964) (also revised edition Puffin 1973)

Comrades for the Charter, Geoffrey Trease. (1934) (Reissued Leicester, Hodder & Stoughton Children's Books)

Dominoes, D. Glynn. Edinburgh: Oliver & Boyd (1972)

Five Fall into Adventure, E. Blyton. Leicester: Brockhampton (1950) (reissued 1968)

Girls and Sex, W. B. Pomeroy. Delacorte Press (1969) (also Penguin)

Here Comes Golly!, G. Brandreth. London: Pelham Books (1979)

Janet and John, M. O'Donnell and R. Munro. Welwyn: Nisbet (1949)

Ladybird Key Words, W. Murray. Loughborough: Ladybird (1963)

Ladybird Sunstart, W. Murray. Loughborough: Ladybird (1974)

Little Black Sambo, H. Bannerman. London: Chatto & Windus (1899)

Little Women, L. M. Alcott. Boston: Robert Bros (1868)

Magnolia Buildings, E. Stucley. London: Bodley Head (1960)

Mama, P. Cave. London: NEL (1971)

New West Indian Readers, C. Borely *et al*. London: Nelson (1969)

Nippers, L. Berg *et al*. London: Macmillan (1968)

O and B Maths Bank 2, K. J. Dallison and J. P. Rigby. Edinburgh: Oliver and Boyd (1978)

Schools Council History 13–16 Project (Book 4 *Problems of Evidence*), A Boddington *et al*. Edinburgh: Homes McDougall (1976)

Skinhead, R. Allen. London: NEL (1970)

Sounder, W. H. Armstrong. New York: Harper & Row (1969)

Sparks, R. M. Fisher *et al*. Glasgow: Blackie (1972)

Suedehead, R. Allen. London: NEL (1971)

Terraced House Books, P. Heaslip. London: Methuen (1979)

The Cay, T. Taylor. New York: Doubleday (1969)

The Family from One End Street, E. Garnett. London: Frederick Muller (1937)

The Little Black Doll, E. Blyton (1937) Manchester: World Distributors (reissued 1965)

The Story of Dr Dolittle, H. Lofting. London: Cape (1920)

The Voyages of Dr Dolittle, H. Lofting. London: Cape (1922)

The Three Golliwogs, E. Blyton. London: Pan (reissued 1973)

The Trouble with Donovan Croft, B. Ashley. Oxford: OUP (1974) (also Puffin, 1977)

Turn of the Century, R. Hoare. London: Macdonald Education (1975)

Twopence a Tub, S. Price. London: Faber (1974)

World Problems, B. Ferris and P. Toyne. Amersham: Hulton (1970)

World Problems, M. Long and B. S. Roberson, London: Hodder & Stoughton (1969/1977)

1.6 Gender Imbalances in the Primary Classroom: An Interactional Account

Jane French and Peter French

Source: Edited version of French, J. and French, P. (1984) 'Gender imbalances in the primary classroom: an interactional account'. *Educational Research,* **26**, No. 2, 127–136.

Introduction[1]

It is now well established that in mixed sex classrooms male pupils receive more teacher attention than do females. Brophy and Good, for example, have observed that 'boys have more interactions with the teacher than girls and appear to be generally more salient in the teacher's perceptual field' (1970, p. 373). Stanworth (1981) and Spender (1982) have also noted an imbalance in this respect and, although their formulation is more tentative, Galton, Simon and Croll's conclusion is in essence the same: 'There does appear to be a slight tendency for . . . boys to receive more contact than girls' (1980, p. 66).

The present study reveals imbalances in teacher–pupil contact which, in broad terms, are compatible with these observations. However, rather than simply reporting the occurrence of the imbalances and thereby giving yet more voice to an already well documented trend, it takes the gender-differentiated distribution of teacher attention as a starting point for further analysis and investigates its grounds. As Spender points out: 'While it has been known for a long time that boys get so much more attention from teachers than do girls . . . few attempts have been made to explain this phenomenon' (1982, p. 54). The principal aim of this study is to provide the basis for such an explanation through an examination of classroom interaction.

The database

The data to be considered comprise a verbatim transcription of a fourth-year junior school lesson (pupils aged 10 to 11 years). The lesson is one from an extended series that one of us (JF) observed and recorded as part of an ethnographic study of gender differentiation in primary classrooms. The grounds for selecting this particular lesson for analysis will be discussed later in the article. The lesson is organized as a teacher–class discussion of the topic

'What I do on Mondays and what I would like to do on Mondays'. In an earlier lesson pupils had addressed this topic in writing, but their essay answers proved unsatisfactory to the teacher. The present lesson therefore covers a number of points which, the teacher explains, he would like to have seen included. After the lesson, pupils make a second attempt at the essay. The class contained 29 pupils, 16 girls and 13 boys. The teacher was male.

Analysis

(i) Distribution of interaction turns between boys and girls
We begin the analysis with a numerical breakdown of the interaction turns that occurred during the lesson.[3]

Table 1

Turns taken by teacher	81
Turns taken by pupils as 'chorus'	33
Turns taken by unidentified pupils	8
Turns taken by boys (13 out of 29 pupils)	50
Turns taken by girls (16 out of 29 pupils)	16
Total	188

Table 1 indicates that, when taken as categories, 'boys' took more turns than did 'girls': 50 instances of turn-taking are clearly attributable to boys as against only 16 girls. When one considers that girls are in a (16:13) majority in the class, the proportions of the imbalance become all the more apparent.

Although, as Spender suggests, few studies have tried directly to account for distributions of this type, statements are now emerging from feminist research which could at least throw some light on the present patterning. These statements tend to be of two types. The first concern teachers' attitudes. We have in mind here proposals expressed in, for example, Clarricoates (1978, 1980) and Stanworth (1981) that teachers have a general and overall preference for male pupils. Given that in teacher–class discussions it is the responsibility of the teacher to allocate turns to pupils (cf. McHoul, 1978; Edwards, 1981), then a preference for interacting with boys might give rise to the sort of pattern represented in Table 1. On the basis of such an analysis, the responsibility for gender imbalances rests largely with the teacher. They may be seen to result from his/her being socially and psychologically predisposed to solicit contributions to the lesson from boys (by, for example, directing questions to them) at the expense of involving girls.

Whilst the data under consideration do not directly contradict this explanation, there are further aspects of the lesson to be discussed in Section (iii) which suggest that it may lead us to underestimate the part played by pupils themselves in achieving the gender-based imbalance.

The second type of statement that feminist researchers have advanced which may be relevant to the interpretation of the present turn distribution deals in more directly interactional categories. Here we have in mind the proposals that boys are more likely than girls to, for example, ask questions, to 'volunteer' information and to make heavier demands on the teacher's time (Stanworth, 1981). Contained in these proposals there is, we think, a very promising basis for explaining gender-differentiated rates of pupil participation. However, it is clear to us that if one is to gain any adequate understanding of gender-differentiated patterns, then these notions must be qualified, clarified and refined in various respects. It is this task that we see ourselves as addressing in the sections of analysis below.

(ii) Detailed breakdown of interaction turns

Table 2

Male speakers	(turns)	Female speakers	(turns)
Tom	17	Marie	5
Matthew	10	Rachel	3
Andrew	10	Angela	2
Simon	5	Sharon	2
Peter	3	Anne	1
Wayne	3	Claire	1
Jason	1	Laura	1
Warren	1	Rowena	1
Thomas	0	Anna	0
Andrew C.	0	Debbie	0
Allan	0	Gina	0
Martin	0	Helen	0
Paul	0	Jenny	0
		Joanne	0
		Linda	0
		Lorraine	0

It is clear from Table 2 that it is not the boys generally who monopolize the interactional space of the lesson. Indeed, some boys take fewer or no more turns than most girls. The distributional imbalance between boys and girls is manifestly due to a particular, small subset of boys taking a disproportionately high number of turns (Tom 17, Matthew 10, Andrew 10 and Simon 5). Some interactional processes through which these boys come to take such a large number of turns will become clear from a consideration of the extracts of talk represented below.

(iii) Interaction examined

Extract 2 follows immediately upon Extract 1. Prior to their beginning, the teacher had posed the generally addressed question: *anybody get up earlier than eight o'clock?* At the start of Extract 1, Tom is sitting with his hand raised.

Extract 1 (conventions of transcription appear at the end of the article)

1.	T.	what time do you get up Tom?	
2.		(0.7)	
3.	Tom	half past four	
4.	T.	what?	
5.	Tom	half past four	
6.	T.	what do you get up at that time for)?	
7.	Ps	((exclamations etc.))	
8.	Tom	(no:) I've got to feed the a-animals	
9.		and (clean all the aviary)	
10.	T.	what?	
11.	Tom	I've got to clean the (aviary) and feed	
12.		all the animals and (.) all that	
13.	T.	what animals?	
14.	Ps	all the [animals	((various pupils call out — difficult to distinguish individuals))
15.		[he's got a (hamster)	
16.	T.	(I think) half past four perhaps is a little bit early I mean that's	
17.		half way through the night Tom	
18.		(1.9)	
19.	T.	what animals have you got?	
20.	Tom	erm =	
21.	T.	= you've got your parakeet	
22.	Tom	two cats (.) two dogs (.) hams-no	
23.		hamster (.) two rabbits	
24.	Wayne	birds	
25.	Tome	erm (1.0) parrot (1.0) that's all (.)	

26.		I've got about (0.5) two rabbits (.)
27.		(I've) got about (.) fifty three birds something like that
28.	T.	what (.) have you got them in an aviary have you (.)
29.		(have you to them in the garden)?
30.	tom	yeah
31.	T.	well it must take a long time to
32.		feed so you'll have to get up a bit before eight o'clock that's true (.)
33.		what happens on a Saturday then?
34.	Tom	I cleans 'em all out
35.	T.	yeah but what time do you get up on a Saturday then
36.		you've still got to feed them
37.		(0.5)
38.	Tom	I gets up about (.) half past eight
39.		(1.0)
40.	T.	half past eight (.) what time do you get up early? ((to Rachel))

Extract 2

1.	T.	what time do you get up early? ((to Rachel))
2.	Rachel	quarter to eight
3.	T.	quarter to eight (.) what about you Laura?
4.	Laura	half past seven
5.	T.	half past seven ((nods to Jason))
6.	Jason	quarter to eight

7. T.   quarter   to   eight
            ((points to Rowena))
8. Rowena seven o'clock
9. T.   seven o'clock

In the first extract, Tom takes ten turns at talking, nine in response to the teacher and one prompted by Wayne. In contrast to this, in Extract 2 four pupils take one turn each. Each pupil is selected to speak by the teacher and produces an answer to the question *what time do you get up early?* The teacher then acknowledges the answer and passes on to the next pupil. This pattern of interaction — i.e. of pupils being given a single rather than several successive turns at answering — has been reported widely in studies of classroom discourse (cf. Mehan, 1979; MacLure and French, 1981). In respect of Extract 1, it seems clear that the teacher allocates Tom an extended series of turns on the basis of what he (Tom) has to say. The teacher's further questions are occasioned by the type of answer Tom has given to the first question. Tom's claim that he gets up at half past four is out of the ordinary and newsworthy when compared with what everyone knows about weekday getting up times. It is the sort of claim one might wish to investigate further. However, when the teacher does investigate further (*what do you get up at that time for?*), the other answers produced by Tom are no less extraordinary, and thus in turn warrant investigation. For example, the claim at line 26-7 that he keeps *about fifty-three birds* occasions yet another question from the teacher: *what(.) have you got them in an aviary have you?* Returning briefly to Extract 2, it can be seen that the getting-up times claimed by pupils there (e.g. *quarter to eight, even o'clock*) do accord with everyday expectations and are treated as warranting nothing more than an acknowledging repetition.

To move to a more general level of analysis, it is clear that the turns in Tom's series do not have a purely 'voluntary' basis, but are answer turns which have been solicited by the teacher's questions. However, it is also clear that at least some of the teacher's questions do not have a purely voluntary basis either: they are responses to the newsworthy, or extraordinary, answers Tom has produced in the previous turn. Thus teacher and pupil are seen as acting collaboratively, each simultaneously producing and inviting further talk in response to constraints provided by the other. In view of this, we would suggest that the sort of model which best explains turn distribution in this instance is not one which implies responsibility to lie unilaterally with the teacher, but an *interactional* one which emphasizes the collaborative aspects of classroom behaviour.

The analysis we have advanced in respect of Tom's achieving an extended series of turns rests heavily upon the proposal that pupils' answers making newsworthy claims occasion requests for further information. This proposal finds some additional justification in Extracts 3 and 4:

72 *Jane French and Peter French*

Extract 3

1.	T.	what about you Peter
2.	Peter	half past six
3.	T.	why do you got up at that time?
4.	Peter	my mum gets up early
5.	T.	does she? (0.5) what time does she go to work?
6.	Peter	eight o'clock
7.		That's early (0.5) what about you Matthew?

Extract 4

1.	T.	what about you Matthew?
2.	Matthew	half past five to six o'clock got
3.		to feed my horses and dogs and all that
4.	T.	do you do that before you come to school everyday =
5.	Matthew	yeah
6.	T.	= do you? (.) oh well people obviously (go) — some
7.		people then have got to get up er at er (1.0) well
8.		before it's light

Whilst the claims to getting up times made by pupils here (*quarter to seven, half past six*) are not as far removed from everyday expectations as was Tom's, the teacher nevertheless explores them further. What is more, there is evidence that pupils themselves may look upon these types of claim as requiring explanation. In Extract 4, for example, Matthew, who it will be recalled is a member of the subset of boys taking a large number of turns, appends to his answer (*half past five to six o'clock*) the justification *got to feed my horses and dogs*. The knowledge that self-reports of unusual practices are to be accounted for may provide a powerful resource for pupils who wish to talk more about themselves.

Claims like those produced by Tom and Matthew in Extracts 1 and 4 give pupils prominence within the classroom setting; they mark them out as different from their peers. Tom's activity in Extract 5 also has this effect;

Extract 5

1.	T.	put your hand up all those people who like
2.		coming to school on Tuesday (2.0) ((most pupils' hands are raised))
4.	T.	put your hands down (0.5) put your hands up
5.		all those people who don't like coming to
6.		school on Tuesdays
→ 7.		(2.5) ((Tom's hand goes up, alone))
8.	P's	((laughter))
9.	P1	⌐it's swimming Tom
10.	P2	⌐it's swimming
11.	Tom	we don't do owt on Tuesdays
12.	Ps	we do we do ((several pupils calling out at once))
13.	Tom	(I) do now
14.	Ps	((laughter))
15.	T.	so Mondays then (.) Monday's a pretty hard day then
16.		really isn't it?

The teacher's request for a show of hands at lines 4–6 (*put your hands up all those people who don't like coming to school on Tuesdays*) must be interpreted against the background information that Tuesday is the day that the class goes to the swimming baths. Given what we know about the likes and dislikes of children of this age, there is an expected outcome to this request, i.e. that pupils will not raise their hands. Only Tom raises his hand. Interestingly, in this case it is the other pupils rather than the teacher who take Tom up on his response. In answering them, Tom achieves two further turns at speaking. In some respects the pattern here is very similar to that in Extract 1. Tom's extra turns are produced in response to the talk of others, but again this talk was in turn generated by the unusual or 'out of line' character of his previous activity. [. . .]

Not all the additional turns taken by the highly participating boys identified in Table 2 can be accounted for by reference to the sorts of practices so far described. A further tendency appearing in the data was for these boys to make unsolicited comments on the lesson's topic. The type of turn we have in mind here is illustrated in Extract 8, where Simon addresses Claire's answer to the teacher's question:

Extract 8 ((question: *which bits of maths do you like doing?*))

1.	T.	What about you Claire?
2.	Claire	er I like in the Fletcher books where you've got
3.		to do something
→4.	Simon	ugh that's horrible
5.	T.	what about you? ((to next pupil))

As previous studies of classrooms have pointed out, teacher–class lessons are guided by certain normative 'rules' of participation whereby pupils' rights to speak are governed by the teacher (cf. McHoul, 1978; Edwards, 1980, 1981). Unsolicited contributions from pupils are sanctionable events. It is the prerogative of the teacher to decide whether they be let pass (as in Extracts 8 and 9), suppressed (as in 10) or accepted, endorsed and developed (as in Extract 11):

Extract 9

1.	T.	perhaps some people might think that er em (1.0)
2.		they should never be — there should not be any
3.		Mondays
4.	Ps	((talking among themselves, laughing))
5.	Andrew	Sir if there weren't any Mondays Tuesday would be
6.		like a Monday it would be exactly the ⌜same
→7.	T.	⌞perhaps then we
8.		should go straight from Sunday to Tuesday

9.	Ps	yes
10.	Andrew	'cos Tuesday'd be a Monday it'd be exactly the same
11.	Ps	(talking among themselves)
12.	T.	right now then before you start . . .

Extract 10

1.	T.	right put your hands down ⌐(0.4) if I (***) =
2.	Tom	⌐ I'd rather (***)
3.	T.	= Marie and Nina?
4.	Marie	only sometimes
5.	T.	not on Mondays though (.) we're talking about Mondays
6.		in particular aren't we?
7.		(1.0)
8.	Andrew	Sir I like coming to school on Tuesdays Wednesdays
9.		and Fridays
10.	Wayne	Tuesday's swimming
11.	Pl	Sir I like- ((at this point several pupils begin to call out and it is impossible to distinguish individuals))
→12.	T.	alright now look if you want anything (.) sh sh if you
13.		want to say anything now you've got to put your hand up
14.		otherwise we'll have twenty nine people trying to talk
15.		all at once and (that'll never do)

Extract 11 (T. speaking of importance of English, i.e. end of
Extract 7)

1.	T.	is it an important thing to have to do?
2.	Ps	yes
3.	Andrew	you wouldn't have any General Knowledge without English
4.	T.	pardon?
5.	Andrew	you wouldn't have any General Knowledge without English
6.	T.	(well you wouldn't have much chance (.) I know (.)
7.		in the evenings — there's three evenings a week for example
8.		when I — when I take classes for adults (1.0) in
9.		the evenings I take classes for adults who can't read
10.		and write . . .

However, even though the decision to pass over or endorse unsolicited contributions lies ultimately with the teacher, it is nonetheless a decision that
pupils can influence to some extent. If we consider the character of, for
example, Andrew's comment in Extract 11, we can see that his utterance, *you
wouldn't have any General Knowledge without English*, expresses the sort of
view a teacher might be expected to endorse and develop. It may well be that
when pupils produce comments of this type, the teacher can allow concerns
of pedagogy to override those of interactional protocol. The capacity to gauge
the concerns of teachers may again constitute an important interactional
resource for pupils who wish their voices to be heard and their comments to
be addressed by the teacher.

Discussion and conclusion

In this final section, we shall be concerned to do three things. The first is to provide an account of the grounds upon which our data were selected and the generality of the patterns they express. The second is to give some more explicit consideration to whether or not one may look upon the pupil activities discussed here as tactical, goal-oriented behaviour. And the third is to develop some policy implications from the findings we have presented.

(i) Selection of data and generality of findings

As mentioned at the outset, the lesson examined here is only one from a large number of lessons that were observed and recorded as part of an ethnographic project. Our reasons for having selected this particular lesson are essentially practical. A great many of the recordings are characterized by small subsets of boys 'dominating' the proceedings, and the activities by which they achieve their prominence are aligned with those examined here. In most cases, though, the uneven distribution of turns is not quite so marked, and the activities are rather less frequent in occurrence. Because they are so richly represented in the present lesson, it provides us with a focal point for the presentation and discussion of patterns which, we would claim, are widely distributed across primary classrooms.

(ii) Intentional status of pupil activities

A large part of our analysis concerns the ways in which pupils, through making newsworthy claims or taking up unusual positions, secure the extended attention of the teacher (and/or other pupils). The question we have so far side-stepped is whether one can say that they produce these claims with the specific aim of gaining attention. The issue of intentionality is one of dogged debate within the social sciences (cf. Coulter, 1974, 1979), and the present context is not the place to resurrect the well-known arguments in any detail. Suffice it to say that the making of statements about the motivational states of actors is never unproblematic. However, the impression that we gain in many instances in our data is that pupils are actively seeking attention. The basis of this impression lies in the fact that certain pupils take up unusual positions on issues of classroom discussion so frequently and consistently that their behaviour argues for more than coincidence. [. . .]

(iii) Policy implications

Our suggestion here has been that gender imbalances in teacher attention and turn distribution among pupils may be in part attributable to subsets of boys engaging in strategies to secure that attention. Rather than attempting an exhaustive account of these strategies, we have provided only a broad outline of some of the more obvious examplars. The analysis should be received, then, as a beginning, not as an end, to investigation of this area. Even at this early stage, however, we would see the sort of approach adopted here as bearing relevance to those who are concerned about the remediation of gender imbalances at the level of classroom practice.

Feminist work in pursuit of this goal has already pointed, though in general rather than detailed terms, to the tendency for boys to demand more of the teacher and hence receive more than their share of attention (cf. Clarricoates, 1978, 1980; Spender, 1982). Whilst existing analyses have therefore acknowledged that pupils may play a part in the shaping of classroom events, rather more emphasis has, in our view, been placed upon teachers being socially and psychologically predisposed to favour boys. As we have already noted, we do not oppose this claim. However, we would suggest that the redress of imbalances in teacher attention does not necessarily follow from the remediation of male-biased attitudes in teachers, unless they also become sensitive to the interactional methods used by pupils in securing attention and conversational engagement. Although there is occasionally evidence that teachers are aware of pupils' behaviour in this respect it may well be that in a great many instances pupil strategies remain invisible to them. Teachers' immersion in the immediate concerned of 'getting through' lessons may leave them unaware of the activities performed by boys in monopolizing the interaction.

This view finds support in a recent report by Spender. Even though she consciously tried to distribute her attention evenly between boys and girls when teaching a class, she nevertheless found that 'out of 10 taped lessons (in secondary school and college) the maximum time I spent interacting with girls was 42% and on average 38%, and the minimum time with boys was 58%. It is nothing short of a substantial shock to appreciate the discrepancy between what I *thought* I was doing and what I actually *was* doing' (Spender 1982, p. 56; original emphasis). We think that one would be safe in assuming that Spender's lack of success could not be attributed to her having a male-biased outlook. It seems clear to us that much would be gained from developing, in the context of teacher education programmes, an interaction-based approach to this issue which sought to increase teachers' knowledge and awareness of what may be involved-through the use of classroom recordings.

Appendix Conventions of transcription

The system used here is simplified version of that developed by Gail Jefferson for use in Conversation Analysis.

1. Participants' identities appear
   on the left, as in a play script.
   The teacher is identified as T.
   Pupils' names appear where
   they are known. Where a
   pupil's identity is not known

he/she appears as P1, P2 etc. Where pupils speak collectively they are identified as Ps.

2. Participants' speech appears to the right of their identities, again as in a play script.

3. Speech enclosed in single parentheses indicates that the transcriber thinks that this is what was said but is not 100 per cent sure, e.g. (What do you get up at that time for)?

4. Asterisks enclosed in parentheses indicate that a speaker said something but that the transcriber was unable to decipher it properly. The asterisks represent the number of syllables heard, e.g. (***).

5. Empty parentheses indicate that a speaker said something but that the transcriber was unable to hear even how many syllables were uttered.

6. Words enclosed in double parentheses represent a description of some relevant activity, e.g. ((shrugs)), ((various pupils call out)).

7. A colon following a syllable indicates that the syllable was pronounced in a long, drawn-out style, e.g. no:

8. Pauses between utterances are timed in seconds and tenths of seconds, e.g. (1.5) represents a pause of one and half seconds. A full stop between parentheses indicates an immeasurably brief pause.

9. An equals sign may be used to indicate 'latched' speech, i.e. where a second speaker comes in immediately the first speaker has stopped speaking, e.g.

> T.　　　what animals have
> 　　　　you got?
> Tom　　erm =
> T.　　　= you've got your
> 　　　　parakeet

Equals signs may also be used
to indicate that a speaker is
continuing with his/her turn
when it has perhaps been
interrupted by a second
speaker, e.g.

> T.　　　do you do that
> 　　　　before you come to
> 　　　　school everyday =
> Matthew yeah
> T.　　　= do you? (.) oh well
> 　　　　then . . .

10. Dashes may be used to indicate
that a speaker hesitates or
stammers over a word, e.g.

> T.　　　in the evenings —
> 　　　　there's three even-
> 　　　　ings a week for
> 　　　　example when I —
> 　　　　when I . . .

11. Where participants' speech
overlaps, a square bracket
indicates the onset of overlap,
e.g.

> Andrew　it would be exactly
> 　　　　⌈the same
> T.　　　⌊perhaps then

Notes

1　Thanks are owing to the staff and pupils of the primary school near Bristol who participated in the study. Their names and initials have been changed for the usual reasons.

　　'An initial investigation into the strategies used by boys and girls when initiating exchanges with the teacher', was first presented at the BERA Annual Conference, Cardiff, 1980. Thanks are due to Sandra Acker, Tony Edwards, Martyn Hammersley, Alison Kelly and Rod Watson, who all commented on the earlier draft.

2　Counting of pupil turns is, of course, only one of several measures that we could have employed (e.g. pupil contributions could have been subjected to word counts). The only advantage that turn-counting has it that it allows us — with the aid of notes made *in situ* — to include pupils' non-verbal turns, which word count measures would miss.

　　We acknowledge that turn counting is not unproblematic, but have tried to adhere to the following general guidelines: only talk and activities directed into the official proceedings of the lesson have been counted — asides from one pupil to another and 'background talk' have been excluded from the figures. Non-verbal activities have been counted where they are integral to the enactment of the interaction (e.g. a nod from a pupil in response to a teacher's question). Where they are concurrent with verbal turns (e.g. a pupil nodding at the same time as answering 'yes'), they do not appear in the figures.

References

Brophy, J. E. and Good, T. L. (1970) Teachers' communications of differential expectations for children's classroom performance: some behavioural data', *J. Educ. Psychol.* **61**, 5, 365–74.

Clarricoates, K. (1978) 'Dinosaurs in the classroom: a re-examination of some aspects of the "hidden" curriculum in primary schools', *Women's Studies International Quarterly* **I**, 353–64.

Clarricoates, K. (1980) 'The importance of being Ernest . . . Emma . . . Tom . . . Jane. The perception and categorization of gender conformity and gender deviation in primary schools.' In: Deem, R. (ed.).

Coulter, J. (1974) *Approaches to Insanity.* London: Robertson.

Coulter, J. (1979) *The Social Construction of Mind: Studies in Ethnomethodology and Linguistic Philosophy.* London: Macmillan.

Deem, R. (ed.) (1980) *Schooling for Women's Work.* London: Routledge & Kegan Paul.

Edwards, A. D. (1980) 'Patterns of power and authority in classroom talk.' In Woods, P. (ed.).

Edwards, A. D. (1981) 'Analysing classroom talk.' In French, P. and MacLure, M. (eds).

French, P. and MacLure, M. (eds) (1981) *Adult-Child Conversation.* London: Croom Helm.

Galton, M., Simon, B. and Croll, S. (1980) *Inside the Primary Classroom.* London: Routledge & Kegan Paul.

McHoul, A. (1978) 'The organisation of turns at formal talk in the classroom'. *Language in Society,* **7**, 183–213.

MacLure, M. and French, P. (1981) 'A comparison of talk at home and at school'. In Wells, G. (ed.).

Mehan, H. (1979) *Learning Lessons: Social Organisation in the Classroom.* Cambridge, Mass.: Harvard University Press.

Spender, D. (1982) *Invisible Women: The Schooling Scandal.* London: Writers and Readers Publishing Cooperative Society with Chameleon Editorial Group.

Stanworth, M. (1981) *Gender and Schooling: A Study of Sexual Divisions in the Classroom.* London: Women's Research and Resources Centre.

Wells, G. (ed.) (1981) *Learning Through Interaction: the study of language development.* Cambridge: Cambridge University Press.

Woods, P. (ed.) (1980) *Teacher Strategies: explorations in the sociology of the school.* London: Croom Helm.

1.7 Developing Pedagogies for Multilingual Classes

Josie Levine

Source: Edited version of Levine, J. (1981) 'Developing pedagogies for multilingual classes'. *English in Education*, **15**, No. 3, 25–33.

Second-language learners are 'ordinary'[1] learners

The teaching of English as a Second Language to children in this country, in so far as a tradition is established, has been in the hands of a band of dedicated, specialist teachers who, until quite recently, have worked within a withdrawal system of one kind or another — which one, depending on what was regarded as a favourable *administrative* solution to the 'problem' of 'non-English speakers' in 'our' schools.

Throughout this history there has always been a minority view among specialist language teachers that the needs of 'second-language learners' would be served best by being part of a 'normal' class, following the 'normal' curriculum[2] — given, of course, that the 'normal' class and the 'normal' curriculum in any individual case was actually worth joining. This group of people would say that the difficulty has been to persuade other specialists, administrators and 'ordinary' class and subject teachers that joining in was best.

Over the years a rationale for this has grown — along with that or mixed ability grouping — that goes beyond language learning into the whole development of children: linguistic, cognitive, social, attitudinal: one which does not isolate each of these for separate treatment. (You could say the same, for example, about the teaching of reading, where, if it is taught as if it were possible to learn it as an accretion of separate hierarchically arranged units, learners are deprived of the opportunity of effectively bringing to the task their natural competences. As a result of undergoing such treatment, they can come to view themselves as being without the skill or wit to learn.)

The argument for 'whole' reading and for mixed ability has been developed outside the teaching of English as a Second Language, but individuals in both groups have been — perhaps unknown to each other — developing in their own ways similar attitudes towards anti-racist teaching and the role of language in learning to the point where they could both say that the best way to develop skills and fluency in language, the best ways to promote intergroup understandings and sharing of power is to learn how to do it as one goes along in real life situations (and that includes school) — but with the right kinds of support.[3]

For very good reasons this view is gaining ground both within and without the specialist language teaching lobby. Teachers do not like the racist, anti-social, anti-educational implications of leaving this particular group of learners (those who are developing as bi-linguals) to manage as best they can on the periphery of the class. Nor do they like the isolationist implications of withdrawal. So, even while recognising that the past is ever with us ('I wish I could do something to help them but what can one do when there's twenty-eight others in the class', 'You teach them English then I'll teach in my subject'. 'How can they go into ordinary classes and do ordinary curriculum work unless they have a good grounding in vocabulary and structure?') more and more specialist teachers want to work in 'ordinary' classes alongside children doing 'ordinary' work, and 'ordinary' class teachers want to know how to work with 'second-language learners' in their classes.

Interesting work is being undertaken as a result of this mutual concern. A most fruitful working party convened under the aegis of ILEA English Centre is to publish its findings soon.[4] Jean Bleach describing the work of second-language learners in her mixed ability secondary English classroom[5] and Hilary Hester with the work done on her Second Language Learners in Primary Classrooms Project (SLIPP)[6] are beginning to show ways in which certain kinds of structuring of lessons support developing bi-linguals in their cognitive and social learning and also in development of their use of English for school purposes. Nancy Lee's small study in a withdrawal situation of the deliberate use of home-language as an aid to school learning begins to suggest that far from being a hindrance to developing a use of English, the use of home-languages may be a positive help.[7] Maurice Oliphant, in a special language centre, has successfully undertaken poetry sessions which combine works in several tongues with literary and personal comment on them in English. Such work could as easily obtain in and enrich 'ordinary' English lessons.[8] [. . .]

The 'solution' of withdrawal being no longer the only one we can allow ourselves, the question I want to address myself to in this article is, 'What do I need to know about second-language learning that will help me teach my subject better?' or to rephrase it entirely, 'What are the tools of hospitality?'

Hospitality to diversity: some general tactics

(a) Joining in

Let me take a small point first — one which arises over and over again in the course of any day in any secondary school where there are children studying in a language which is not their mother-tongue. It is, like all the topics discussed here, related to the business of finding ways of making meaningful what is often only a hollow phrase: being hospitable to diversity. For the children it is the problem of how to get into the discourse, or — put another way — how to fulfil the demands of any particular teacher and subject classroom; but, in addition, it is also now to take on the ambience of the class s/he has joined. Developing bi-lingual speakers who are learning to use English often know what they are required to do, but do not know how to do it, nor how to put into words questions they know they want to ask or knowledge that they know they have. The uncertainties and diffidence created by this can permanently damage their ability and willingness to learn and to join in the community of school. Furthermore, in addition to communicating with a teacher, at the very least, they must be able to ask a neighbour what to do. For second-language learners and others who are entering a strange environment, such small things can make the difference between feeling welcomed (and, therefore, able to accept the invitation to work together) and feeling rejected. Many of them, after all, are bemused by their lack of success in English schools, coming as they may have done from successful school careers elsewhere.

(b) Tunes in the head[9]

In secondary schools, second-language learners are probably not exposed to enough spoken discourse — including being read to — for them to be able to internalise well enough tunes and rhythms of English. In any case, certainly not as well as they might in more propitious circumstances. Even in English lessons, this is probably the case. But, if second-language learners are to develop their 'own voice', speak, listen, read and write fluently then they must, at least, have as much opportunity to hear the English of others as they are given opportunity to read and write for themselves.

Reading to the children takes on new meaning in multilingual classes. It is a most satisfying form of offering literary models.

(c) Monitoring learners' devices

[. . .] To write fluently is difficult with limited vocabulary and structure available to you. It is additionally so when you are aware that you are likely to get the grammar of the language wrong. If you are the sort of person who is meticulous about 'getting it right', then you are likely to be paralysed by a writing task. Kun Sung, then a fourth year boy, exactly this meticulous kind of person, taught me how to help others like him at a similar stage in writing in English. The previous year he had had some special English tuition at the local language centre. In addition, because of his English lessons in Hong Kong he was no stranger to exercises of the filling-in-blank variety. He was extremely imaginative about their use. He wrote and left blanks where he did not know what to write or where he was unsure about usage. Then he would say, 'Miss, come and help me.' It was my task — not his — but in consultation with him, to fill in the blanks!

In transforming the exercise, he made it possible for himself to be both ambitious about vocabulary and also cautious in those areas where he had uncertainties (in his case, and it will come as no surprise, about verb forms). However, in both ambitious and cautious ways he was helping himself to learn, using what he knew about language skills as they had come to him through his first language (in this case, a sense of fluency), and what he had met as language learning techniques as they had come to him from learning English.

Of course, it doesn't require only an adult to help in this kind of thing. A pupil-colleague could just as easily have collaborated with him. Once, however, the adult understands what kinds of processes are at work, it is easy to hand over some of the responsibility to the children themselves. A balance must be maintained, though, since the new users of English will need to show his/her teacher how s/he's getting on.

(d) Support with comprehension

Certain kinds of understanding can often be promoted by visual clues, for example using film or video recordings where available of plays, novels or short stories being read in class. This way an overall understanding can be achieved. The children need time to assimilate all the many kinds of details that are coming at them, so another strategy is, as often as possible,[10] to go over again, with those who need it, the content and the assignment — perhaps taking each further back than in the general lesson. (See the section on task setting.) Encourage the children to ask the questions, help them to frame their responses. Only that way will you get to know what support they need. Only that way will they get the practice that they need in construing, considering, testing out their own thoughts, understanding those of other people, and in appropriately expressing it all. Again, show them how to do all this. Because reading round and asking 'comprehension' questions as a check to their understanding of what has been read seems only to make children anxious, once again it is worth encouraging them in initiating collaboration in their learning. Whether reading aloud or reading silently is their own best way of understanding a text, they are bound to encounter vocabulary, phrases and whole chunks of text that they *know* they don't understand. Again, phrases are needed and again, choose phrases that are appropriate for the children's situation. Mine, offered here, are only rough examples of kinds. 'What does it mean when . . .' 'What does this word/bit mean?' 'Why does X do Y?' or to a pupil-colleague 'What do you make of this (bit)?'.

Once these interchanges are established, then helpful questioning that can lead young readers into deeper understanding of a text can be seen for what it really is — and not as part of an interrogation.

Hospitality to diversity: forethought, afterthought and action

The above matters of joining in, tunes in the head, monitoring learners' devices, support with comprehension, I have written about from the point of view of inviting people into the teaching-learning context. I see them as examples of the invitational mode in pedagogy, things that one can do then and there out of *ordinary* hospitality. In this section, I want to look, by brief example, at two aspects of our *professional* hospitality: how we make clear to ourselves what the demands of our lessons are and how we might analyse reponses to them. The first of the these is Task Analysis and the second is Error Analysis.[11] Both of these contribute to the manner in which we achieve a fruitful match[12] between our pupils, ourselves and the materials/content/ methods we work with in our classrooms.

(a) Task analysis

Much work in specialist second-language teaching focuses on linguistic data directed at vocabulary, structure and function — although the best of it won't begin with the planning of the work at these levels. The authors of *Scope, Stage 2*,[13] for instance planned the materials as if they were planning classroom work where language use was recognised as important for other learning. What they did was:

— choose the topic
— gather the subject matter
— decide appropriate activities and organisations for the learning to take place
— allow to emerge, from the subject matter and activities, the language functions necessary for understanding and exploring the topic
— choose, for the benefit of second-language learners, structures and vocabulary which would enable them to perform the functions
— create material which is core, and other which provides extensive practice of language in use
— suggest ways in which specialist language practice can be provided
— see that there was a range of styles, register and language-linked learning skills demanded of learners, *and also* that they should be supported in their learning of them.

Such support will attend, among other things, to what makes an assignment more or less difficult for an individual, and it will be not only linguistic criteria. Any one of the following may play a part:

— how much is to be done
— how much help is given
— what kind of activity is to be undertaken
— how complex the presentation is to be
— whether new vocabulary items are present
— the nature of the subject content
— structural variety.

A simplification of one may make a whole task more accessible. But that is just for note here, since the aspect of Task Analysis that I want to highlight is at the level of language-linked learning (e.g. extracting information from texts, relating text to diagrams) rather than that of language items (e.g. vocabulary associated with a subject, use of linking words in an extended piece of writing). The rest have to do with fostering communication and commitment among those in the classroom — eminently worth considering after an event for future action.

However, such things as the elements of learning that are language-linked can be analysed prior to the event and need to be where multilingual classes are concerned. For many children the instruction 'Get into groups and discuss X' will be enough opportunity to bring their own learning strategies to bear. For more inexperienced others, opportunity only is not enough. They need something more. But do we always know what?

For example, take this common task in English: read a short story/poem, talk about it in small groups, write about it for homework (alternatively, the 'end product' might be to prepare a report of the discussion to present to the rest of the class).

The language linked elements entailed would include:

(a) getting started
   — reading the text
   — reading comprehension
   — reading aloud (possibly)
(b) collecting information
   — picking out ideas in the text
   — note taking
   — forming own ideas and responses however tentatively
   — matching ideas in the text to own thoughts and experiences
   — stating all of these, and
   — stating the relationships made between them
(c) conducting discussion
   — listening comprehension
   — expressing own ideas
   — agreeing with others' opinions and statements
   — disagreeing
   — questioning
   — responding to questions
   — interrupting
   — remaining silent
(d) (i) collecting opinions together — if joint report is to be made
   — listening comprehension
   — organising strategies appropriate to the nature of the discussion
   — note taking
(d) (ii) preparation for writing — if individual work to be done
   — musing
   — organising strategies
   — taking decisions about the view to be expressed in the writing
(e) (i) reporting back
   — organising strategies
   — using notes
   — speaking extended logical text in an appropriate style for retaining listeners' attention
(e) (ii) writing own piece
   — organising strategies
   — being prepared to 'accept' new ideas that come by virtue of doing own writing
   — writing extended logical text in an appropriate style.

The list is not ordered entirely hierarchically, although, obviously, some sub-headings must necessarily come before others in the process of performing the task. Also obvious is how many interlinked processes are called into play. Task Analysis, which should never be taken to be suggesting offering pupils less than a whole activity, gives clues to where support might be offered *within* the whole activity.

Linked with this particular type of task is the question of accessibility of a single text to a whole mixed ability group or class. One solution to this is offering specially prepared texts. It is one which is often relevant. Another is to follow Stenhouse[14] and allow to all children what is offered as a right to 'clever' children and advanced students: the opportunity of engaging with something that is too hard for them! University students do this all the time, getting to know their material through engaging in discussions about it.

(b) Error Analysis

Error Analysis is a technique developed in Applied Linguistics for the observation of second-language learning development.[15] It can apply to both spoken discourse and written text although in its earliest, narrowest formulation it was applied to the omission, addition, selection and ordering of grammatical and lexical items in speech or writing. It is not such an unpromisingly negative a technique as it sounds. A distinction is made between lapses, mistakes and errors. Lapses are slips of the tongue or pen, mistakes are the selection of the wrong style for a particular situation, errors in second-language learners are 'Those features of the learner's utterances which differ from those of any native speaker'.[16] None of these are to be regarded as morally reprehensible since everyone makes lapses, and the words 'mistake' and 'error', although here they apply to someone doing something which breaks a rule, it is a rule which is not yet known to them.

A second important point to take on is that a second-language learner who does not make many mistakes may be being over cautious and allowing him/herself to do only what s/he knows s/he can do.

A third point is that some errors will be systematic and others apparently made at random. I was interested to note recently that the English verb forms of a Cantonese speaking boy were wrong but that he had a system, always 'correctly' expressed within itself, of indicating past perfect, present perfect, past and present aspects of verbs. He knew the distinctions, merely had not yet acquired the forms.

Within language we can say that errors and mistakes are caused by lack of experience in the formulation of appropriacy rules of phrases, sentences, discourse; of reference ('brother' for the relationship we would choose to define as 'cousin'); of style ('No miss, you fuck off, you wrong!' for 'I'm really sorry to have to tell you, but it isn't true, what you're saying').

However, one major source of error in language use stems from outside language itself: it can often be traced to the way in which we teach. Consequently, now, when I'm looking at children's work, some of the criteria which I bring to bear in assessing it are extra-linguistic.

— what was the teaching context?
— how much help did the pupil get?

— was the task realistic?
— what thought processes and cultural experiences did they demand?
— to what extent were pupil's and teacher's intentions matching?
— did the pupil have to move more towards the teacher, than the teacher made moves towards the pupil?
— is the pupil taking risks?
— is s/he prepared to be adventurous?
— is s/he demonstrating a personal tone of voice?
— is s/he aware of the shaping and patterning of certain literary styles?
— at what point is the pupil in the move towards full form of expression?
— can one catch the tone, intention and shaping of a piece of work by reading it aloud?

In a practical error analysis session held in January 1980,[17] the following general points were made. These taken together with those made above, I want to suggest, are a rich enough set of suggestions, questions and comments to begin thinking about and creating good learning environments for multilingual classes.

— Either directly or indirectly children are using models to work from. Part of what we need to intuit is what these models are. A child writing as s/he spekas may be demonstrating *in*experience in aspects of written language, but s/he is also demonstrating both initiative (the degree to which s/he is able to risk) and the manner of his/her process of the move towards standard written English.
— We should read children's work from the point of view of their intentions, pick up also their 'tone of voice' otherwise the generative aspect of an error can be missed.
— Evidence of progressive states of inter-language cannot be deduced from one piece of work.
— There is a need to know the setting of a piece of work. Sometimes errors can be induced by the models presented or the direct teaching undertaken.
— There is always a chance that the teacher will assume incorrectly what the learner's intentions are, mistake his or her meanings and therefore make inappropriate corrections. Often they can be nothing more than imposing the teacher's style on the child.
— The quantity and type of correction will vary considerably and depend at least on the individual child's approach to learning and on the distance or closeness of the pupil's relationship with the teacher.
— Wherever possible, negotiation over a child's writing should take place *with* the pupil.

Notes

1 Many words and phrases, such as 'ordinary', 'problem', 'non-English speakers', 'our', 'normal', have been used in the past, without inverted commas to suggest that developing bilinguals were somehow not ordinary, nor normal, but were deficient, problematic and not part of us.
2 See Schools Council, *Scope, Stage 2: a language development course*, Longman (1972).
3 (i) See Levine, J. and McLeod, A. 'Children from families of overseas origin'. In Rosen, H. (ed.), *Language and Literacy in our schools,* NFER/ULIE (1975).
(ii) All London Teachers Against Racism (ALTARF) *Teaching and Racism,* a document published from 116b Talbot Road, London W11.
(iii) All London Teachers Against Racism (ALTARF) *Race in the classroom: teaching against racism in the Primary School,* a document published from 66 Littleton Street, London SW18.

4 It is possible that the document will be on sale from Mike Raleigh, ILEA English Centre, Ebery Teachers' Centre, Sutherland Street, London SW1. It is worth enquiring anyway.

5 See Bleach, J. 'No turning back from awareness: mixed ability and English teaching'. Unpublished dissertation for MA, University of London Institute of Education (1979).

6 Video cassettes showing the work of the Project are available. They are programmes 2 and 3, 'Working Together' and 'Supporting Understanding' of a four-programme series, *Language in the multiethnic primary school* sponsored jointly by the DES, the Outer London Boroughs and the ILEA. Programme 1 is a general programme, 'Linguistic Diversity', Programme 4 focuses on dialect speakers of English, 'The way we speak'. All are available for sale from Central Film Library, Government Building, Brownyard Avenue, Acton W3 8JB, and to those inside the ILEA on loan (£3 for each cassette) from Centre for Learning Resources, 275 Kennington Lane, London SE11.

7 See Lee, S. H. 'What are the language demands of the school on second language learners such as the Chinese and how could teachers help pupils to meet these demands, unpublished dissertation for MA, University of London Institute of Education (1978).

8 See Maurice Oliphant 'Mother Tongue in Practice'. In *Issues in race and education*, no. 29, Sept. (1980). Bi-termly paper published by members of London branches of National Association for Multiracial Education (NAME) and ALTARF. Available from 11 Carleton Gardens, Brecknock Road, London N19.

9 See Bleach, J., ibid.

10 One of the ways in which such time can be offered them is by working with student-teachers in the classroom.

11 See reference section for readings in this area.

12 See Schools Council Progress in Learning Science Project, *Match and mismatch: Raising Questions, Match and mismatch: finding answers*, Oliver & Boyd (1977).

13 See *Scope, Stage 2*, ibid.

14 See Stenhouse in Ruddick, J. (ed.) *Learning to teach through discussion*, University of East Anglia.

15 See reference section for readings in this area.

16 Corder, Pit, *Introduction to Applied Linguistics*, Penguin, p. 260.

17 Language in Inner City schools Conference, *Linguistic Diversity and Standard Written English*, Report on Day conference, 26 Jan. (1980). The extracts taken from the Report of Group A: Second-language teachers and learners in normal classrooms.

References

Corder, Pit, *Introduction to applied linguistics*, Penguin.

Richards, Jack, *Error Analysis*, Longman.

Richmond, John, (1979) Dialect Features in mainstream school writing, in *NAME* Journal, Autumn.

Selinker, Larry, Article in *International Review of applied linguistics* (IRAL), 1972.

SECTION II

Language Awareness

Introduction

As this book goes to press, deliberations have begun within a Committee of Enquiry (established by the Secretary of State for Education) which is expected to provide a 'model of the English language, whether spoken or written', which is relevant to the needs of all teachers and children in British schools. As the most recent manifestation of the age-old and widespread debate about the 'standards' of competence in language and literacy achieved by children through schooling, the establishment of the Kingman Committee has once again highlighted the extent of disagreement which exists amongst concerned parties (both within and beyond the education system) about two fundamental, closely-related issues. First, what constitutes 'competence' in spoken and written language; by whose standards is this judged? And, second, what is most useful and appropriate for children to learn about their native language, if this is to be of benefit to them in their wider life experience?

This second point then raises a further issue, and one no less contentious; what do *teachers* need to know about language to be able to teach children properly?

The two readings in this section are intended to contextualize and clarify these issues. The first, by Bill Mittins, discusses some problems of definition in relation to recent government policy statements about English language education. The second, Katharine Perera sets out her views, as a linguist and former English teacher, about what the study of the English language can usefully offer teachers and children.

2.1 'But Where's the Bloody Horse?'

Bill Mittins

Source: Extracts from Mittins, W. (1987) 'But Where's the Bloody Horse?'. *NATE News*, Durham, National Association for the Teaching of English, Spring edition, pp. 6–8.

[. . .]

We are often told that English is not a subject with a matter of its own. It is a predicament or a 'disaster area' — which is not much advance on William L'Isle of Wilburgham's remark in 1638:

> Tell me not it (i.e. English) is a mingle-mangle; for so are all.

Of course, English *literature* is more like a subject. There are still those who, supported by what Robert Witkin describes as 'the entirely dubious and patronizing assumption that works of literature have civilizing influences per se', insist on the centrality in English of literature. The promise of a manageable, coherent literature-centred English was always weakened by the difficulty of defining or circumscribing 'English literature'. By what criteria is literature to be distinguished from non-literature, and how is 'English' to be interpreted? The 'exposure theory' that competence in English language will be acquired by reading literature (however broadly understood) has not survived a growing school population in an increasingly sophisticated world.

[. . .]

English was once derided as an easy language. Bishop Lowth was not the only eighteenth-century grammarian to press for the revival of inflectional endings because the reliance on small words, especially prepositions, made English — by comparison with Latin, a superior language — *too* easy. Today, on the other hand, writers emphasize the remarkable complexity of the English language. One of the earliest paragraphs in *English from 5 to 16*[1] (1.4) sympathizes with 'all who teach English' because the growth of their pupils' command of language 'is a complex matter because language is complex. It is the principal means by which we think, define what we experience and feel, and interpret the world in which we live.' This truth is not novel; sadly, nor is the speed with which the Inspectors abandon important generalities about the total phenomenon and plunge into bits and pieces catalogued as 'objectives'.

Their very next paragraph (1.5) names the conventional four modes of language — speaking, listening, reading, writing. Then (1.6) the interrelation of these four modes is equated with the Bullock Report's[2] organic whole comprising a rather different four — writing, talk, reading, plus *experience.* This is not simply a slip of the pen. Whatever the vague term 'experience' means, it is not of the same semantic order as the other three *verbal* modes. The confusion is increased later in the same section of *English from 5 to 16* when, preserving the cherished 'four', the Inspectors add to the three 'aims' for speaking, reading and writing a 'fourth aim', again of a different order — the notorious '*about* language' which 'applies over *all* the modes of language'.

The fault in both four-fold classifications is what used to be condemned as 'cross-division'. The transference to the English language from classical Latin of categories appropriate, not to a living, analytical, positional language, but to a dead inflexional language which had survived solely in unchanging written form, was most conspicuous in a taxonomy — the oddly-named 'parts of speech' — accepted by compilers of school grammars as a basis for the teaching of English (i.e. of what one critic cynically described as 'school-mastered English').

The prerequisite for classifying is definition. In order to define, the various and many components comprising the various and many classifications have used phonological, inflexional, grammatical (morphological and syntactic) and semantic criteria. Since these criteria themselves need classification according to criteria which need classification and so on, the dangers of embarking on an infinite regression are obvious. Teachers and school grammarians therefore call a halt and accept an *ad hoc* arbitrary list. It is depressing in these circumstances to hear of schools, even primary schools, still claiming to teach parts of speech and to see how school inspectors include the main parts of speech in their 'about language' objectives. If the seven classes classified by them as 'main' are really distinguishable by a single kind of criterion, these parts might conceivably be learned, at least by older and abler students. But the various kinds of criteria used have been variously invoked in support of various classifications. In the simpler terminology of traditional school-grammar books, some parts of speech are defined semantically (nouns name, adjectives describe), some syntactically (conjunctions join, prepositions introduce noun phrases), some functionally (pronouns replace nouns, interjections express noises), some formally (adverbs end with — *ly*), some by a mixture of some or all of these things. This 'mixed' pseudo-classification is not found satisfactory or successful by most teachers. To make it worse for schools, the experts in the twentieth-century 'explosion' in linguistics, assigning priorities to the relevant criteria, have usually stressed the more easily observable, formal (audible, readable) criteria, neglecting or reducing or even banning semantic criteria. More recently, however, semantics — the study of the elusive dimension of meaning — has reclaimed a place in language theory. In that words have dual characteristics — form and meaning — this renewed interest in the nature of meaning should make language-study more useful and more relevant to the teaching of English and indeed of all subjects.

Wallace Chafe, one of the American exponents of a grammar that recognizes the importance of semantics (he wrote *Meaning and the Structure of*

Language, 1970), famously remarked that 'Language is without doubt an extraordinarily complicated elephant'. It is so complicated that all its aspects — from phonological to semantic — are inseparably intertwined.

Starting with any one aspect inevitably leads into involvement in all the others. Since meaning is central, not just to language, but to the whole school curriculum, any attempt to provide English with a coherent framework that sorts out and tidies up the 'mingle-mangle' of the miscellany characterizing school English might start with meaning. That territory is formidably difficult, but not more so than 'grammar' (whatever that is) has proved to be for centuries.

Teachers are always being urged to 'start where they [i.e. the learners] are', thence moving on from the familiar to the novel. That age-old principle was followed by the primary-school teacher who, it is said, asked a young child: "What's wrong with saying 'The cow and the horse *is* in the same field?' " The immediate answer was: "They ought to be in different fields." For the learner, meaning was much more important than the verbal form (phonic or graphic) of the code used. Too often teachers nevertheless follow academic linguists by giving priority to form. There are many understandable reasons for this. One reason is the comparative manageableness of form by contrast with the elusiveness of meaning. Language resists semantic systematization even more than 'formal' pigeon-holing. That resistance is embedded in the facts of change; formal change of pronunciation or spelling is a good deal easier to deal with than changes of meaning. Red pencil is simpler than marginal 'It all depends . . .' Add to this the circumstance that the relationship between form and meaning, itself arbitrary, moves sometimes in harness (e.g. 'disc' becomes 'disk' in computerese), but more often independently (e.g. the change of form from 'grammar' to 'glamour' hardly matches the change of meaning), and system is further defied.

Nevertheless, traditional formal language-study (loosely called 'grammar') is discredited. The alternative of 'incidental' language-teaching ("We deal with points of grammar, figures of speech, punctuation, and so on, as and when they arise") is at best hazardous, at worst ineffective. If teachers of English — encouraged in principle by *English from 5 to 16* — concede that some kind of language-study is needed, then NATE ought to investigate the possibility of devising a system that makes feasible greater competence than the results of the 'uneasy agnosticism' of which teachers of English have been accused.

For various reasons, teachers of English (many of whom have not themselves studied language beyond 'O' Level) have not always achieved a coherent and systematic view of modern language. Therefore, before trying to outline a study-course for learners, it is necessary to plan a language-programme for teachers, allowing that teachers should know more than learners and should not overtly use all their knowledge. This is not to deny that many are knowledgeable about many aspects of English, its history, early language development, etymology, vocabulary, the manifold fallacies and

myths that beset English, etc. Most of the two-thirds with 'discernible qualifications' satisfying Bullock are well-informed in literature. But where,
underpinning *all* these and other aspects, is the coherent view of English as a
whole? Where, in fact, is that 'bloody horse'?

A rough set of agenda notes for discussion of a meaning-based language-
study course for teachers might be:

> Segmentation (slicing up the 'big, booming, buzzing confusion' of experience)
> Classifying and defining (accepting that all distinctions are fuzzy)
> Referential and emotive meaning; denotation and connotation

Words and meanings

> Polysemy
> Approximate (more or less) meaning
> Oblique meaning; euphemism
> Deceptive meaning; irony, lies, propaganda, advertising
> Obscure meaning; doublespeak, gobbledygook
> Ambiguity, disambiguation
> Meaning and context
> Nature of verbal meaning
>> Modes; speech, writing
>> Analogy; figurative language, metaphor, simile
>> Units; morpheme, word, phrase, sentence, paraphrase
>> Word order; resources of word arrangement
>> Register.

More controversial considerations include metalanguage. Items in the
'About Language' sections of *English from 5 to 16* indicate that a clearer
consensus about the meaning of certain terms is needed before discussion can
profitably proceed. In particular:

page 9
> 'vowels and consonants' (what about semi-vowels? what about *schwa*?)
> 'statements, questions, commands and exclamations' (does this classification survive
> Austin's argument on illocution, perlocution, etc.?)
> 'word order determines meaning' (always? influence rather than determine?)
> 'past, present or future tense' (confusion between grammatical tense and semantic time?)

page 12:
> 'form, content and style' (is even a working definition of 'style' possible?)
> 'sentence, clause and phrase' (which of the 200 + descriptions of sentence? how differ-
> entiate clause from phrase?)   .
> 'simile, metaphor and cliche' (are these 'stylistic effects'?)

There is, of course, much else clamouring for admission to any English
language debate — standard English, RP, dialect, second/foreign language,
attitudes towards varieties of English language and to foreign languages and
to language as such, the status and prestige granted to certain languages,
multi-cultural English, gender in language, etc. But the foundations need to
be laid in clarifying the nature of language. For this purpose, it is time to get

beyond Roy Campbell's 'snaffle and bit' stage and to find and ride the 'bloody horse'. Analogously, we should get beyond pigeon-hole categories (from parts of speech to 'skills') and focus on meaning. Years ago, R.B. McKerrow argued that "The natural way to approach the grammer of English is from the 'meaning' end". And much later Roman Jakobson dared to state the glaringly obvious: 'Language without meaning is meaningless'.

Notes

1   DES (Department of Education and Science) (1985) *English from 5 to 16: curriculum matters 1*. London: HMSO.
2   DES (1975) *A Language for Life* (The Bullock Report). London: HMSO.

2.2 Understanding Language

Katharine Perera

Source: Edited version of Perera, K. (1987) 'Understanding language'. One of a series of occasional papers published by the National Association of Advisers in English. It is based on a talk given by the author to the NAAE annual conference, September 1986.

Knowledge about language

In the discussion document *English from 5 to 16* (DES, 1985), four aims of English teaching are outlined. The first three relate to speaking, reading and writing; the fourth aim, applying to all the language modes, is: 'to teach pupils *about* language, so that they achieve a working knowledge of its structure and of the variety of ways in which meaning is made, so that they have a vocabulary for discussing it, so that they can use it with greater awareness, and because it is interesting' (p. 3). This aim is translated into twenty age-related objectives; for example, eleven-year-olds are said to need to know 'the difference between vowels and consonants' (p. 9) and sixteen-year-olds 'the functions and names of all the main parts of speech' (p. 12).

In the public discussion that followed the publication of *English from 5 to 16*, nothing caused more disagreement, or more criticism, than the twenty objectives relating to knowledge about language. In their subsequent report, *The Responses to Curriculum Matters 1*, HMI acknowledge that there was, 'widespread and vigorous rejection of grammatical analysis and of teaching the terminology listed in the objectives' (DES, 1986 p. 16). They suggest, with notable circumspection, that 'there may be some grounds for believing that there may be wide accord with the aim, though there is little agreement, as yet, about alternative objectives' (p. 16).

I believe that one reason why reference to 'knowledge about language' provokes so much disagreement is that such knowledge can be of at least three different kinds, and it is not always clear which kind is being referred to. Firstly, there is the implicit knowledge that all native speakers have. This enables us to say that, 'Yesterday our team won the match' is a possible sentence, whereas *'Yesterday our team wins the match' is not; or that, 'She has bought a red car' is all right but *'She has bought a car red' is not. The fact that we can confidently recognize the ungrammaticality of these sentences shows that we know which verb tense is appropriate with a given adverb, and what the order of adjectives and nouns should be. The important point, though, is that such knowledge does not depend on having the technical terminology for describing the language: speakers who reject *'Yesterday our team wins the match' have an implicit knowledge of English verb tenses even if they cannot identify the verb in the sentence or say what tense it is. This example concerns the grammar of English, but it would be equally possible to illustrate the point with reference to the vocabulary or sound system of the language. Secondly, there is explicit knowledge about the nature and functions of language: an understanding of how it is acquired, used and abused; of how and why it varies and changes; of how it can enchant or offend, manipulate or persuade or alienate. Thirdly, there is explicit knowledge of the structure of language — knowledge which includes the technical terminology necessary to described the production and organization of speech sounds, the relationships of meaning between different words, and the grammatical structures of the language.

The three kinds of knowledge about language are not rigidly separated from each other: our implicit knowledge of our mother tongue informs any study we make of it; an understanding of the way the language has changed over the centuries is bound to involve discussion of sounds, word meanings and grammatical structures, and so on. Nevertheless, lessons that are designed to develop an understanding of the nature and functions of language (sometimes referred to as 'language awareness' courses) will differ appreciably in their approach, methodology and terminology from lessons that aim to establish a systematic description of the phonology, semantics and grammar of English. For example, on the first type of course, secondary pupils could be led to an awareness that, while rhyme depends on a patterning of vowel sounds, alliteration arises from the repetition of consonant sounds. But it would only be on the second type of course that *definitions* of the terms 'vowel' and 'consonant' would be needed.

Another reason for some of the hostility from English teachers towards 'knowledge about language', I think, is that it is not always made clear that there is a difference between what teachers need to know about the language and what they need to teach. Therefore, the purpose of this paper is to try to outline what I believe all primary teachers and secondary English teachers need to know about language, and to suggest briefly what aspects of that knowledge might be of benefit to their pupils. I shall be concerned with an understanding of the nature and functions of language (the second of the three kinds of knowledge I identified earlier), but first I should like to digress to make a point about the academic study of language structure.

In *English from 5 to 16*, it is stated that, 'Learning *about* language is necessary as a means to increasing one's ability to use and respond to it; it is not an end in itself' (p. 14). This idea that teaching children about their own language is justified only if it leads to some kind of improvement in their linguistic behaviour is very widespread — and I find it rather odd. Language is an integral and fascinating part of our environment — every bit as important as the electric bell or fold mountains or the Spinning Jenny — and yet we require it to justify its place in the curriculum by demonstrating its practical usefulness. That seems, as Bloor (1979) has suggested, like telling biology teachers that they should not teach their pupils about the digestive system unless they can prove that doing so enables them to digest their food better.

When language study as an academic subject is well taught by knowledgeable teachers it can be very appealing to pupils; experience of the new Joint

Matriculation Board 'A' level in English Language convinces me of that. One of the more surprising effects of this 'A' level course has been that it has given students a sense of pride in their own language. Apparently, many of them had felt that English was in some way inferior to French or German, believing that it lacked — in the words of one of them — 'verbs and grammar and that'. I understand that it has been a source of considerable satisfaction to discover that English does indeed have a grammar.

However, I do believe that the academic study of language, as an end in itself, requires (like any other academic subject) teachers who are specifically trained to teach it. I also think that it should be an optional subject, not an obligatory one, and that it is best suited to the upper years of the secondary school. So it is not that type of language study that I am focusing on in this paper; rather, it is the kind of language teaching that is part of the work of any primary teacher or secondary English teacher, as they strive to help their pupils increase their ability to use and respond to their mother tongue.

Language acquisition before five

An important starting point for primary teachers is an awareness of how much language children have already acquired by the time they start school. By the age of five or so, most English-speaking children already have a vocabulary of at least 2,000 words and have mastered many hundreds of grammatical constructions. As Tough (1977) has shown, they can use all this language for a number of purposes — to get what they want, to control other people's behaviour, to describe what they are doing, to recall what they have done, to make up stories, and so on. Yet, despite all this learning, it is occasionally suggested that some children from English-speaking homes come to school with little or no language. In *The Responses to Curriculum Matters 1*, it is reported that 'Some teachers in urban primary schools challenged the statement that "before starting school most children already have considerable experience in and command of at least spoken English" . . . referring to widespread disadvantage among indigenous children, which they felt had been underestimated' (DES, 1986 p. 4). While it would be absurd to suggest that all children will have developed language to the same extent by the time they start school, it is nevertheless worth emphasizing that the acquisition of language is so much a part of normal human development that the virtual absence of language in a five-year-old would be a sign that something was seriously wrong, with the child being in need of specialist help.

There are a number of reasons, I think, why we may underestimate the amount of language that five-year-olds have learnt. In the new and strange world of the school, some children do not find it easy to respond to the kinds of topic or to the style of conversation initiated by unfamiliar adults. In their puzzlement, they may react with non-verbal responses, such as nodding their heads, or crawling under the table. [. . .] Another factor that can lead to an underestimate of children's language ability is that, even when they are able to talk to their teachers, their speech can still sound very childish. Finally, there may be a mismatch between the kind of language that the child uses at home and the kind that is generally required and accepted in school. [. . .]

Varieties of English — accent, dialect and standard English

Accent is an aspect of pronunciation. English can be spoken with an accent that reveals the speaker's geographical origins, as a Scottish or Yorkshire or Liverpool accent does, or with an accent that is not restricted to any region (but does reveal something about social class). The most common regionless accent is called Received Pronunciation — RP, for short. (It is worth noting that RP speakers are sometimes described as 'not having an accent'. In fact, from a linguist's point of view this is an impossibility, since any pronunciation entails an accent of some kind. In everyday use, however, the term 'accent' most often means 'regional accent'.) More than ten years ago, the Bullock Report (DES 1975 p. 143) declared firmly, and I thought uncontroversially, 'We believe that a child's accent should be accepted, and that to attempt to suppress it is irrational and neither humane nor necessary'. Yet only recently I heard a tape recording of some eleven-year-olds in a remedial class in Northumberland who were being asked to tell the teacher about a book they had been looking at. One of them said — in the accent of the region — 'It's aboot [about] tigers.' To which his teacher replied, 'Not a *boot*, Nigel; a boot is something you wear on your foot.' [. . .]

In contrast with *accent*, the terms *dialect* and *standard* refer to the grammatical structure and the vocabulary of the language. Very broadly, we can say that dialects of English show variation from one region to another whereas standard English is uniform (in grammar and to a lesser extent in vocabulary) throughout the English-speaking world. In fact, there are a number of standard Englishes with slight differences between them. For example, some American standard English speakers say, 'He dove into the water' where British standard English speakers say, 'He dived into the water'; and Scottish standard English has, 'These shoes need mended' in contrast with English standard English, 'These shoes need mending'. Nevertheless, if we restrict ourselves to the English spoken in England and Wales, it is true to say that there is one virtually uniform standard variety (bearing in mind that this refers only to grammar and vocabulary, not to pronunciation) and many dialectal varieties, which are associated both with different regions of the country and with social class.

A regional dialect will always be spoken in a regional accent; but standard English can be spoken either in RP or in a regional accent; indeed, very many people in England and Wales speak standard English with a regional accent. So sentences (1) and (2) — in the regional dialects of south-east and south-west England respectively — will normally be pronounced in the appropriate regional accent. They will sound odd if spoken in RP, by a BBC newsreader for example:

(1) It ain't 'alf 'ot mum.
(2) Give 'em what they likes to eat.

In contrast, the standard English sentence at (3) can be pronounced in a Liverpool or Cockney or Birmingham accent, as well as in RP, and it will still be standard English:

(3) The weather was terrible yesterday.

The diagram below presents a simplified version of the relationship between standard English English and socio/regional varieties:

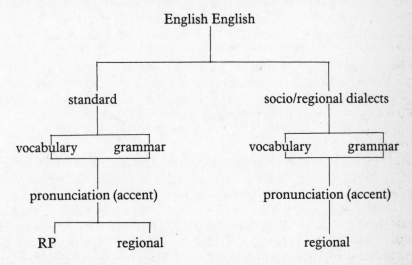

Each variety, whether standard or regional, has its characteristic grammar and vocabulary. What the diagram cannot show, however, is that whatever the differences between them (and within England and Wales they are only slight), all of the varieties have a great deal in common, which is why we are able to group them under the general heading 'English', rather than classifying them as separate languages.

Vocabulary in standard English covers the whole range from slang and colloquialisms to formal and literary expressions, so if a pupil says, 'I've lost my flipping book' (or worse), it may not be elegant but it is, nonetheless, standard English, since it is not restricted in its currency to any one area of Britain. However, in the sentence, 'It's backendish today, isn't it?' — the regional dialect word 'backendish' probably does not convey the meaning that the weather feels distinctly autumnal to people south of Yorkshire. As far as language in schools is concerned, dialect vocabulary should not present any problems because it is no longer extensive — and in any case is not widely used by younger speakers. It can, of course, be studied as an interesting aspect of the language — particularly since examples of dialect vocabulary from grandparents' speech will serve to illustrate one of the ways in which the language has changed over the last fifty years or so.

We have already seen that standard English can be spoken with either a regional or a regionless pronunciation; so long as speech is comprehensible to the listeners, there is no reason why schools should attempt to alter their pupils' accents. What does matter, though, is grammar: what is at issue is whether children who habitually speak one of the regional varieties of English can also use the grammar of standard English when it is appropriate. In order to consider this question carefully, it is necessary first of all to discuss what is meant by the term *grammar*.

The word 'grammar' is used with a number of different meanings. Linguists use it, first, to refer to the ways in which words are combined to make sentences. In this sense, all adult native speakers of English know the grammar of their language because they are capable of combining words to make an infinite variety of sentences that can be understood by other English speakers, even if they have never been heard before. Linguists use it, secondly, to label the body of statements they write about the language as they attempt to make explicit this implicit knowledge that native speakers have. For example, because (4) is a possible sentence in English —

(4) The cat chased the rat

— and because thousands more sentences could be constructed on the same pattern, linguists state that one sentence type in English is Subject-Verb-Object. And that statement becomes a part of a descriptive grammar of English. By extension, 'grammar' then comes to mean the reference work in which such statements are collected, e.g. *A Comprehensive Grammar of the English Language*, by Quirk *et al.* (1985). In addition, linguists describe the grammar of the different regional and social class varieties of English. Linguists consider grammatical any systematic, rule-governed form of linguistic behaviour shared by a speech community. So example (5), by a Liverpool speaker, is not *un*grammatical but it follows a *different* grammar from the standard — which makes no distinction between singular and plural forms of the second person pronoun:

(5) What are yous doing?

It would be ungrammatical if it was random, idiosyncratic and could not be described by any general rule. So (6) is ungrammatical because there is no group of native English speakers who regularly use that form:

(6) *What are doing you?

This use of the term 'grammar' to refer to non-standard varieties of the language is the one that differs most sharply from its everyday use because, popularly, 'grammar' is often restricted to descriptions of the standard language and carries with it strong associations of correctness. For example, one of the definitions given in Collins (1979) Dictionary is, 'the use of language with regard to its correctness or social propriety'. The big problem, of course, is that what I have called *different* grammar is to some extent socially stigmatized: there is no denying that people who cannot speak and write standard grammar when the situation requires it can be at a considerable social disadvantage. So my own view is that schools *do* need to teach standard grammar to those pupils who use a socio/regional variety, but that we need to recognize that it is being taught for social rather than for strictly linguistic reasons. That is, non-standard grammar is not intrinsically less comprehensible than standard grammar but it does lack its high prestige and wide social acceptability. I have emphasized this point because I believe that if we can think objectively and clearly about what is a very emotive issue, we stand more chance of teaching the standard language in ways that are likely to be effective and do as little\damage as possible to pupils' self-esteem. What is at issue, then, is not *whether* the grammar of standard English is taught but in what terms. We have to remember that language is an integral part of being human, not an optional extra skill like riding a bicycle or playing the flute. So an attack on a person's language becomes an attack on the person himself. Furthermore, language is so closely bound up with home and family, with community and friends, that its emotional roots are strong and deep. This means that handling the standard/non-standard issue in children's speech and writing requires both social sensitivity and an understanding of the nature of linguistic differences. I am ashamed to recall the number of times, when I was an English teacher, that I said, 'You can't say that', when the pupil manifestly could and did. A variant of this, used by some teachers is the indignant 'I *beg* your pardon', which the child quickly learns does *not* mean, 'I didn't hear that — please say it again' but rather, 'I heard what you said and I don't ever want to hear it again.'

If teachers are to teach standard English effectively, they need a precise knowledge of the language forms that are characteristic of their region and of how they differ from the standard. For example, in the variety of English spoken in a number of areas, including Merseyside, the past tense of the verb *to see* is *seen* rather than standard *saw*, so we find this pattern:

Merseyside English	*Standard English*
I seen it	I saw it
I've seen it	I've seen it

If pupils are told, 'You mustn't write *seen*; use *saw*', they may well produce not only 'I saw it' but also *'I've saw it', because they have *over*corrected their language and produced a form that is genuinely ungrammatical, not used by speakers of either the Merseyside or the standard variety of English. So any guidance about the use of standard English needs to be carefully given. It is sometimes suggested that pupils who, having been told what the standard forms are, continue to use their regional forms, are being lazy or careless or uncooperative. In order to understand the difficulties such pupils face in changing their grammar, speakers of standard British English could try changing the following sentences into standard American English:

(7a)   I've got a new car recently.
(8a)   We've got off at the wrong stop.
(9a)   They'd got into trouble.
(10a) She got very wet last night.
(11a) He's got blue eyes.

We are all aware that Americans use *gotten* where we use *got*, but not perhaps of the precise linguistic contexts where the different form will occur:

(7b)   I've gotten a new car recently.
(8b)   We've gotten off at the wrong stop.
(9b)   They'd gotten into trouble.
(10b) She got very wet last night.
(11b) He's got blue eyes.

Simply replacing all instances of *got* with *gotten* does not produce correct standard American English because (i) *gotten* is only used after a part of *have* and so does not appear in (10); and (ii) it is not used when *got* means 'have' or 'possess', as in (11). I find that, because I am not a native speaker of American English, I have to check a grammar book (e.g. Trudgill and Hannah, 1982) for these examples: my own ear does not tell me whether they are right or not. That is just the position in which non-standard speakers find themselves, because they cannot necessarily tell whether a particular form is right or wrong; which I think is why some children find the linguistic demands of the school so baffling and apparently inconsistent.

Having said that I believe it is necessary for the school to teach standard English, that raises the questions of the best age to begin this teaching and the most effective methodology for doing it. There is a very wide range of opinions about age, with some people (e.g. Edwards, 1979) suggesting that standard English should be taught as soon as children start school and others (e.g. Richmond, 1979) thinking that about fourteen is early enough. My own view is that, although even infant children are aware of different styles of language, there is a lot to be said for delaying until the third or fourth year of the junior school, the kind of explicit teaching of standard English that will mean some children having to alter their own language patterns. There are a number of reasons for this choice. I do not think it is a good idea for teachers to focus on linguistic differences until most children have acquired a basic level of competence in reading and writing: the acquisition of literacy is so demanding that it seems unreasonable to expect children to become self-aware with regard to their own language use at the same time. But there are advantages in beginning to think about what can be an unsettling topic while children are still in the relatively secure environment of a primary school, where they spend the whole day with one teacher, who knows them very well. Besides, research by Reid (1978) and Cheshire (1982), for example, suggests that at least some children are already altering their grammar to suit different situations by the age of eleven, and it seems worth capitalizing on this.

Whatever age is chosen, I am sure that it is best to start with the language variety that the children themselves use and encourage them to think about some of the different varieties that they encounter. Once they have recognized that local forms are important because of the sense of group identity that they foster, and that the standard form is useful because of its wider currency, then it is possible to explain why standard English is the form most commonly used in writing. After that, teachers can encourage their pupils to use standard English in those pieces of writing where it is clearly appropriate. The question of which variety of English is used in oral work in the classroom is perhaps more contentious. My own feeling is that it is probably unwise for primary teachers to interrupt pupils' speech in order to alter any non-standard grammar in their spoken language. The need for a speech style with wide social acceptability usually does not become apparent until the later years of compulsory schooling. By the age of fourteen or fifteen, pupils have had many years' exposure to standard English through their listening, reading and writing and will have developed some familiarity with its forms. Furthermore, they will by then be approaching the age when they will be faced with rather formal speech situations, such as job interviews. Perhaps at that stage it will be appropriate for teachers to establish the expectation in some classroom oral work that standard English is to be used. Clearly, the whole issue, including age, methodology and terminology, should be a carefully thought-out part of any school language policy and should be discussed by teachers in secondary schools with those in their feeder primary schools.

Language varieties and multi-culturalism

We tend to take language for granted because we use it unthinkingly all the time. One way of coming to a richer and fuller understanding of our own language is by being aware of how it differs from others'. As well as regional differences (illustrated by sets of words like *alley, jigger, ginnel, snicket* etc.), we can consider generational differences — for example, the fact that elderly women frequently use the word *frock* where younger women are more likely to say *dress*. Then there are the differences between various English-speaking countries: the Scots say *outwith* where the English say *outside*; Americans say *faucet* where the British say *tap*; and in the Caribbean, *day-clean, pannier* and *overstand* are used where *daybreak, basket* and *understand* occur in Britain. Schools that have pupils with a range of different mother tongues, and indeed writing systems, are in an excellent position to explore and exemplify the richness and variety of human language. Such an undertaking could 'raise the social status of pupils who could speak other languages, including members of ethnic minorities, since they could be used as "experts" on their own languages; and the explicit consideration of these languages would raise the social status of the languages themselves' (CLIE, 1984 p. 9). The study of some of the differences within and between languages is one way in which the ideals of multi-culturalism could become a living reality in the classroom.

Spoken and written language

Another way of thinking about the variety within language is to consider the differences between the spoken and written forms. This is particularly important because, in school, the written language has a central place. This does not mean only that children have to learn how to write letters and words and how to recognize them on the page — and that alone is hard enough; it also means that they have to become familiar with the grammatical structures that are characteristic of the written language, because writing is not simply the language of speech written down.

There are two important points to be made that concern the nature of speech on the one hand, and the nature of writing on the other. First, there is a fairly widely-held but mistaken view that speech is some kind of careless or sloppy version of writing. This view leads people to make judgments of speech that are inappropriate because they derive from the written standard. I remember once pointing out to a friend that the expressions *an ice cream* and *a nice cream* are indistinguishable in speech. Her response was that if only we all spoke more carefully there would be no problem. In fact, only a foreigner — or a talking robot — would pronounce the two phrases differently. The suggestion arises from a mistaken understanding of the relationship between speech and writing. As far as the grammer of the language is concerned, an example that illustrates an important difference between the two modes is the positioning of the word *only* in a sentence like this:

(12a) I only eat fish on Fridays.

Some prescriptive grammarians would say that, for this sentence to have its most likely meaning, it should be:

(12b) I eat fish only on Fridays.

But the point is that, in speech, the voice gives extra emphasis to whichever part of the sentence *only* refers to, so *only* can stay in its most natural place next to the verb without any risk of misunderstanding. This use of the voice to indicate the relationship between parts of a sentence is, clearly, impossible in writing, where — although common sense usually makes the meaning clear — the placement of *only* can occasionally cause ambiguity, as in (13):

(13)   The problem will only be alleviated by a new computer.

This can mean either that a new computer will make the problem better without solving it completely, or that only a computer will have any effect. A careful writer would rewrite the sentence to ensure that the reader did not have to puzzle out which of the two meanings was intended, but speakers do not have to pretend they are writers and recast the sentence, since they are able to say either:

(13a) The problem will only be ALLEVIATED by a new computer.
or:
(13b) The problem will only be alleviated by a new COMPUTER.

Therefore, although there are sometimes grounds for criticizing the placement of *only* in writing, it is quite mistaken to apply this criticism to the spoken language.

Secondly, it is necessary to realize that written language is not merely a transcription of speech; so learning to read and write means not just learning to make and decode letter shapes but also acquiring new forms of language. Some difficulties in reading spring from the language itself rather than from the written code, because there are some grammatical constructions which are common in writing but which occur very rarely in speech (we can probably say they never occur in the speech of young children). Therefore, when children meet them in their reading they are not able to bring the experience of their oral language to bear on them. The following sentence from a junior school geography textbook illustrates the point:

(14) The watering time allowed each farmer depends on the size of his land.

A non-finite clause, like *allowed each farmer*, after the subject of the sentence is very rare in speech. Much more common is to have the main finite verb immediately after the subject. As *allowed* can be either a non-finite verb, as it is in (14), or a finite verb, young readers are likely to interpret the sentence as:

(14a) The watering time allowed each farmer to depend on the size of his land.

This does not make very much sense — but then some pupils seem to have lost any expectation that their textbooks should make sense. The sentence could be made more readily understandable, while retaining a formal written style, by making the non-finite clause finite:

(14b) The watering time *that is allowed to each farmer* depends on the size of his land.

It is not only reading difficulties that can have their source in the structures of the written language but also writing difficulties, since some errors in writing are signs of growth as children attempt new constructions that they have met in their reading. Of course, there are errors in children's work that are caused by haste or carelessness or a failure to reread while composing — there are errors of that kind in our own writing, come to that. But mistakes made on a new construction are of a different kind. They indicate that the young writer is experimenting with the language and is prepared to risk the unfamiliar, rather than clinging to the predictable and safe patterns learned in early childhood. A common error of this kind occurs in sentences like these:

(15) This is the book *from which I got the idea from.*
(16) My favourite possession is my bicycle *in which I received three months ago.*
(17) We have many clubs like the stamp club *of which I belong.*

My reading of hundreds of pieces of children's writing suggests to me that, at about the age of twelve, a few children are seduced by this construction with a preposition at the beginning of a relative clause. I expect that they have just started meeting it in their textbooks (it rarely occurs in fiction written for children) and they think it is very grown-up. Some use the preposition twice, as in (15); some use a preposition where none is required, as in (16); and some, like the writer of (17), use the wrong preposition altogether. Perhaps he had in mind both 'the club to which I belong' and 'the club of which I am a member' and confused the two.

Another kind of tangle that young writers can get into occurs when they try to include one relative clause within another, as this fifteen-year-old does:

> (18)   I think that the 'easy going' parents *that the writer of the particular passage that I read* are few and far between.

(DES, 1983 p. 17)

It is all too easy for hard-pressed teachers to put a line through something like this and write, 'Use simpler sentences'. More helpful, though admittedly much more time-consuming, is to show the writer how to unravel the different pieces of information that have been woven into the sentence:

> I read the particular passage.
> The writer of the particular passage —— 'easy going' parents.
> 'Easy going' parents are few and far between.

Such unravelling makes it clear to the writer that something like 'describes' or 'refers to' has been left out. It also reveals to the teacher just how complicated the structure is that the pupil has attempted.

Therefore, I think it is worth teachers being aware of differences between speech and writing, partly so that they do not make judgments about speech that are appropriate only to writing, and partly so that they are aware of some of the linguistic difficulties that pupils encounter as they attempt to master a formal written style.

I can now add written language to the diagram of varieties of English:

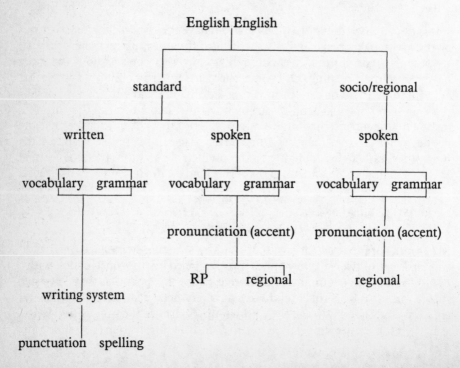

The picture that this diagram presents is over-simplified, since it is possible to have a written representation of socio/regional varieties of English: some novelists, poets and playwrights do manage to write in dialect. Nevertheless, it is generally true that standard English is expected in writing. Once again the diagram misleads by failing to show how much the different varieties have in common, but it does usefully highlight the fact that, just as there are written constructions that rarely occur in speech, so there are vocabulary items and grammatical structures that are a normal part of standard spoken English without being acceptable in written English. Sentences like (19) and (20) can be considered as part of the grammar of spoken but not written English:

(19) It was really good that film.
(20) The woman who was serving on the cheese counter — she said there was no demand for Gorgonzola.

The diagram also draws attention to the fact that spelling and punctuation are conventions of the writing system and not part of the grammar of the language itself. I do not think that making these distinctions is merely splitting hairs. An examination of some of the indignant letters to the press that castigate 'bad grammar' reveals that many complainants use the phrase as an umbrella term to cover a wide variety of linguistic irritants, such as dropped h's, colloquial vocabulary, swearing, Americanisms, split infinitives, spelling mistakes and the misuse of commas. Where there are problems in language use, it is worth being able to diagnose them precisely, so that we can work out the most appropriate and beneficial remedy. It is common, for example, to hear the lament that pupils cannot write in sentences. This sounds like a grammatical problem. In fact, it very often turns out to be the case that the writer has used fully grammatical sentences but has failed to demarcate them with full stops: it is not the grammar that is wrong but the punctuation. The answer is not to teach definitions of the sentence (when the pupil has already demonstrated implicit knowledge of sentence structure) but to show how, by making sentence boundaries visible on the page, full stops provide valuable guidance for the reader.

Varieties of written language

Even within the written language there is considerable variety. Most obviously, there are some important linguistic differences between the language of fiction and of non-fiction. This means that even when pupils can read stories comfortably, they may not be able to cope with their subject textbooks; and even if they can write a very satisfactory imagined tale or factual account, they may not be able to produce writing in science or geography that is acceptable to subject specialists in the secondary school. This raises two large questions: first, at what age and educational level should pupils be expected to read and produce the kind of impersonal formal language that characterizes the writing of adult academics? And second, whose responsibility is it to teach this type of language — the English teacher's or the subject teacher's? Learning to read and write academic prose is so difficult that I believe English teachers have a role to play, either in direct teaching or as consultants to their colleagues in the subject areas. In particular, I think that English teachers could be encouraged to read good non-fiction aloud to their pupils — not textbooks, but biographies, travel books and so on — so that some of its characteristic grammatical structures and patterns of discourse organization are acquired easily and pleasantly, as we first acquired the patterns of the spoken language.

Language acquisition after five

I have already emphasized how much language children have acquired by the time they start school. Now I should like to consider some aspects of language that remain to be learnt after the age of five.

The fact that some of the structures characteristically used in writing are different from those used in speech helps to explain why children are still acquiring the grammar of the language during the school years, since, understandably, they do not generally master the constructions of the written language until they themselves are fluent readers. It is necessary to make this point because during the past twenty years or so it has been something of a commonplace to assert that language acquisition is virtually complete by the age of five or six. For example, Slobin (1971 p. 40), the eminent psycholinguist, has written:

> A little child masters the exceedingly complex structure of his native language in the course of a short three or four years.

Similarly, the de Villiers (1979 p. 12) explain:

> Our story will end at school age because by the age of six the child's language is in many respects like an adult's.

This emphasis on the rapidity of the young child's language learning is valuable and important because it gives due weight to the extent of the five-year-old's linguistic competence. Nevertheless, there is now a considerable body of research which reveals how much of the structure of the language is still being acquired during the school years. (There is a brief overview of this research in Perera (1984).) A few examples must serve to illustrate the later stages of language acquisition.

It is often the case that negative sentences are rather harder to comprehend — even for adults — than the corresponding positive sentences. For example, in a study of the wording of questions in chemistry exams (Johnstone, 1978), six thousand fifteen-year-old Scottish pupils were given either the positive or negative version of this multiple choice question:

(21) Which one of the following could/could not be the atomic weight of the element?

When the question was positive, the number of correct answers was 12% higher than when it was negative. Clearly, there is no difference in the chemistry: it is the form of the language itself that increases the difficulty of the task. Given the fact that negatives are often intrinsically harder to understand, there are some negative constructions that are more difficult than others. One problematic type is the so-called concealed negative; that is, a sentence with a negative meaning but without an overt negative word like *not*, *no* or *never*, e.g.

(22) Tom's mother was anything but pleased.

Reid (1972) found that more than half the seven-year-olds she tested thought that this meant that Tom's mother was pleased. [. . .]

Another grammatical structure which can cause comprehension problems for children up to the age of eleven or so is the passive sentence. If a passive occurs in an everyday setting where the subject matter is familiar, then it is likely that there will be sufficient non-linguistic clues to guide the child to the right interpretation. For example, although there is a passive verb phrase in the sentence, 'The dog was run over by the bus', young children will not make the mistake of interpreting it as if it were an active sentence — 'The dog ran over the bus' — because their knowledge of the world tells them that buses run over dogs, rather than the other way round. Trouble may arise, however, if a potentially difficult construction occurs in an academic context where the vocabulary and subject matter are unfamiliar. Then the likelihood of misunderstanding becomes much greater. I found this sentence in a textbook being used by ten-year-olds:

(22) The herds are preyed on by carnivores.

I gave the children this sentence with alternatives (a) and (b) beneath it and asked them to tick the one that meant the same as the original:

(22a) The herds prey on the carnivores.
(22b) The carnivores prey on the herds.

Since 57% of them wrongly chose (a), it suggests that even at the age of ten, some children are over-influenced by word order when the vocabulary does not provide enough meaning clues to guide them. If school textbooks contain not only demanding concepts and recondite vocabulary but also grammatical constructions that may, unbeknown to the teacher, impede comprehension, then it is no wonder that many pupils are unable to extend their knowledge of a subject by means of their own private reading.

We can also find evidence of children's continuing language acquisition in some of the errors they make in their speech and writing. (It is necessary to be cautious in referring to 'speech errors'. Some forms will be dialectal, others slips of the tongue like those that adults make in spontaneous speech. We can

only consider forms as possible evidence of incomplete language development when they are used several times by children but generally not by
adults.) Children up to the age of twelve or so commonly make grammatical
mistakes when they are talking about hypothetical possibilities. Some leave
out obligatory *could* (or *would*), like this ten-year-old:

(23) Int: Why would you like to be an air hostess?
     R: 'Cos I go all over the world in a plane.

                                                      (Perera, 1984 p. 111)

A different kind of error comes from twelve-year-old Heidi who, when asked
why she would like to be a teacher, gives a less than noble reason:

(24) Int: Why would you like to be a teacher?
     Heidi: If I have children you'll have the same time off as the children . . . if I'm a
             hairdresser you won't have so much time off.

                                          (Fawcett and Perkins, 1980: IV p. 124)

Here she switches between the pronoun *I* and the generic pronoun *you*. If it
had happened only once, it could have been a simple slip of the tongue, but
the fact that she does it twice suggests that she finds it hard to know whether
her hypothetical future should be talked about in personal or general terms.
Since this construction causes problems in speech, we cannot be surprised
when errors appear in writing, as in this piece by a ten-year-old:

(25) We have a nice headmaster who hardly ever grumbles at us. I don't blame him if
     he did.

                                                      (Harpin, 1976 p. 28)

Further studies that provide evidence of difficulty in writing are ones in
which pupils are asked to join sentences using certain connectives — such as
consequently in this extract from an essay by a college student:

(26) He would like to go on a vacation. Consequently, he cannot afford it.

                                                      (Henderson, 1979 p. 72)

Other connectives that may be wrongly used even by young adults are *likewise, moreover, hence* and *besides*.

I believe it is helpful to be aware of these relatively late acquisitions so that
we can recognize when pupils are struggling at the edge of their linguistic
competence. I remember that, when I was an English teacher and I was
marking a piece of work in which the writer had become enmeshed in grammatical complexity, I used to say, 'Read it aloud to me and see if it *sounds*
right.' I now realize that although such advice is helpful if the error arises
from a careless slip, such as leaving words out, it is of no use if the pupil has
attempted a construction that is still in the process of being acquired, because
he or she will not know how the sentence should sound.

These late-acquired constructions are much more common in written than
in spoken language, so children are not likely to come across them very often
until they are reading both fluently and extensively. This, of course, is why
they are generally not acquired until pupils are nine or so. There is a particu-

lar problem for children who do not read with ease because they are losing an important stimulus to their own language development. Here we find powerful justification for reading aloud to children, not just in the early years of the primary school but right through the juniors and into the secondary school as well. When I was a child, I listened to stories on the radio on Children's Hour — stories that I could understand and enjoy when they were well read but which probably would have been too difficult for me to read by myself. At school I was fortunate to have some gifted teachers who loved reading aloud and shared their favourite authors with us. For today's children, although there are good stories read well by television presenters, it is worth noting that dramatized versions of the classics do not have the same language-enhancing function because the only langauge that is used is dialogue; the novelist's descriptions of settings, characters and feelings are interpreted by the designer, the actors and the director, and presented visually rather than through language. As far as reading aloud in schools is concerned, I have the impression that some teachers and headteachers are vaguely uneasy about it, feeling that perhaps it is timewasting to be reading to children who should be doing 'real work'. [. . .] In fact, we can be confident that in reading aloud from really fine books — books that would be too difficult for the pupils to read by themselves — we are helping them to develop an ear for the language in a way that no textbook exercises can.

Emphasizing the fact that language is acquired through reading and writing, as well as through talking and listening, highlights their importance as language-learning, language-enhancing activities. I believe that this is important because there is a tendency in some circles to adopt a rather utilitarian approach to reading and writing: to suggest, for example, that pupils need to learn to read and write sufficiently to enable them to cope with the literacy demands of the adult world — to read safety warnings, for example, or to fill in a job application — but that higher levels of literacy for all are unnecessary in a world blessed with cinemas and televisions, telephones and tape recorders. It is not unusual to hear parents or politicians complaining that children spend too much time in school writing stories and poems: 'What use is that going to be to them? Once they leave school they won't be writing poems. Anyway, how many poets does this country need?' I am convinced that such an attitude reflects a profound misunderstanding of the nature of written language. Some of its structures allow us to assemble our thoughts and to link our ideas in ways that are not so readily available in the language that is typical of everyday spontaneous speech, so acquiring them helps us to become more effective language users. Quite apart from all the humanistic reasons for pupils writing stories and poems, there are sound linguistic reasons, because the activity gives them the opportunity to experiment with language, trying out forms they would otherwise never use. Once mastered through writing, these structures are available for use in speech if the occasion demands it, thereby increasing the power and flexibility of the oral repertoire. Therefore, if we want children to develop their language competence to the full, we can argue against the utilitarians for the central place of a wide range of styles of writing in the language curriculum. This is simply the good practice that able English teachers have always followed; but — as with reading aloud — it is both necessary and reassuring to be able to provide justification for it.

An ear for language

English teachers want to help their pupils to become more competent language users and they are particularly concerned about their performance in writing. It is not surprising, therefore, that they sometimes offer rules which they believe will lead to an improvement in children's written work. Some of the ones most frequently heard are: 'Never begin a sentence with *and*'; 'Don't use a comma before *and*'; 'Don't end a sentence with a preposition'. There is probably a greater tendency to inculcate such rules when teachers are put on the defensive by one of the periodic bouts of public anxiety over 'declining standards' of English in schools. It is easy to see what causes some of the rules to gain their currency. When young children first start composing their own stories, they may join all the sentences with *and* in an immature attempt to establish a sense of continuity within the text. A particular problem with *and* is that it has many meanings: it can express a temporal or causal link between ideas, for example, as well as simple addition. This makes it an easy, multi-purpose connective for the writer, but something of a nuisance for the reader, who has to work out what the relationship between the ideas is. A considerate writer tries to make the reader's task easier by using the most precise connective available. So teachers are right to wean their pupils away from an over-dependence on *and*. Even so, this does not mean that writers should never begin a sentence with *and*: highly respected authors do just that when it will make their point for them. For this reason it is essential to recognize that language is too complex to be handled by a series of prescriptons, or, more often, proscriptions. A more valid alternative is to provide guidelines rather than rules; saying, for example, 'Think carefully about . . .' rather than, 'Never . . .'.

It is important that an awareness by teachers of the simplistic nature of some of the commonest statements about language should not be misinterpreted by the public as a belief that 'anything goes', or that there are no standards. There is a real danger that when teachers try to move away from a prescriptive approach to language teaching, they give the false impression that they believe there is no such thing as bad grammar, or that grammatical mistakes do not matter. It is all too easy for the denial of simple formulaic judgments to make it sound as if precision and care in language use are not important. It might help if, when they jettison unreliable negative commandments, English teachers offer in their place some of the positive guidelines that can usefully be given to young writers; for example, 'Try to put the most important idea at the end of the sentence'; 'Vary the way you start your sentences'; 'Try to put yourself in the position of your reader'. It is also necessary to explain that any sensitive approach to language teaching has to be based on how language is actually used in a range of different circumstances. As an example we can consider another very familiar prescription — and one with a great deal of validity: 'All sentences must have verbs'. It is true that most written sentences do have verbs but an occasional carefully-placed verbless sentence can be highly effective. In a study by Cazden, Cordeiro and Giacobbe (1985 p. 114) there is mention of a piece of writing by a six-year-old American boy, who had described a holiday camp where he was given sausages for breakfast every morning. He hated sausages. His story ended with his happy homecoming: 'We are having pancakes for breakfast. Without sausages.' This forceful climactic ending would be spoilt if his teacher insisted that all his sentences had to have verbs.

If we replace prescriptive rules with guidelines, if we favour positive approaches rather than concentrating on prohibitions, and if we encourage a flexibility of language use in response to different situations, then we shall be on the right lines. But ultimately, it is our ear that tells us whether something is right or not, and all the guidelines in the style books can be broken on occasion by great writers to achieve the effects they want. By the same token, a piece of writing can still be bad even if it does not violate any of the cherished prescriptions. There may be no split infinitives or final prepositions and yet the language can still be pompous or turgid or pretentious. it is noticeable how often respected commentators on English refer to the ear. For example, Gowers (1986 p. 106), in the revised edition of his *Complete Plain Words*, writes:

> Do not hesitate to end a sentence with a preposition if your ear tells you that that is where the preposition goes best.

This raises the question of how we develop an ear for the language. It can only be through reading or listening to works in a wide variety of styles written by really fine authors — historians, biographers and explorers as well as dramatists, novelists and poets.

This brings me to what I see as the paradox of English teaching. Because it does not require a great body of technical knowledge, it seems simple. (I do not believe it is necessary, for example, that all English teachers should be familiar with all the models of grammatical description put forward by linguists, or that they should know a long list of technical names in order to be able to talk about language.) Yet teaching English is peculiarly difficult precisely because there is not a clearcut body of knowledge to be imparted, and success depends on the teachers' own sensitivity to language and on their skill as language users. They need to be able to recognize good writing and to discriminate between the good and the bad; they need to be able to write well themselves, otherwise how can they help their pupils to improve their written work? Simply being a native speaker of English does not equip someone to teach it. The notion that it is reasonable to expect secondary teachers of any subject to fill up their timetables by doing a few periods of English with the younger age groups is one that needs to be firmly rebutted. One of the more startling findings of the Bullock Report (DES 1975 p. 227) was that 'a third of those involved in secondary English teaching have no discernible qualification for the role'. The Report concluded, 'There can be no other secondary school subject which is staffed by such a large proportion of people without appropriate qualifications. Nor can there be any subject which "borrows" so many teachers from other areas of the curriculum and assumes they can fill the role with little or no preparation.'

Pupils' knowledge about language

What pupils need to know in order to help them become more skilful in their own handling of language and more sensitive to others' use of it obviously depends to some extent on their age and ability. I am sure that, at some stage, they should understand that language is systematically organized in terms of sounds, meanings and grammatical structures. I also believe that they need to be able to make explicit their implicit awareness that language is not monolithic: rather, that there are many different varieties that are appropriate for different purposes, people and places. These varieties may be characterized by their pronunciation, vocabulary or grammar — or, indeed, by all three. Related to this is the inescapable fact that any living language changes over time, so there is always the possibility of linguistic misunderstanding across generations.

Further, I think it is valuable for pupils to think explicitly about the differences between speech and writing; about how and why writing was invented and what its uses are, so they come to realize that the written language is the indispensable basis of our civilization. They need to understand that, in writing, almost the whole burden of communication has to be borne by the language. This is quite different from speech, where intonation, gesture, expression and so on contribute to the speaker's meaning. Such a realization helps to explain why the choice of vocabulary, the construction of sentences and the overall organization of the dicourse require much more careful attention in writing than they do in speech. If young writers gradually develop an awareness of the needs of their readers, then they can come to see that punctuation is not an irritating, arbitrary irrelevance but rather a means by which they can convey some of those aspects of meaning that would be conveyed by their voice in speech.

I should like to see pupils learning to consider the ways in which language can be used to persuade, to manipulate, to insult and to wound: the sad fact that as well as being a channel of communication it can also be a divisive barrier. There is material all around us that can be used to illustrate these ideas. During August 1986, for example, there was extensive correspondence in the *Guardian* over whether the word *cripple* is a neutral way of describing a particular kind of disability or whether it is a demeaning pejorative term. More cheerfully, I believe that pupils can be taught to see language as an agent of humour, fantasy, imagination, and enchantment, and as a source of delight in riddles, jokes and puns, in stories, plays and poems.

This is by no means an exhaustive list of what pupils can learn about the nature and functions of language. I have concentrated on those aspects that seem to me most likely to lead to a greater sensitivity in using and responding to language.

So far, I have not said anything about the kind of terminology that is needed if there is to be explicit discussion of these aspects of language in the classroom. It is the question of terminology that generally causes the most disquiet among English teachers when knowledge about language is discussed. Indeed, many are afraid that such knowledge really means labelling the parts of speech. It is no wonder, then, that they express hostility to the whole idea of language study since, in the past, there were pupils who could use their language competently and yet who were made to feel that they 'couldn't do English' because they could not label prepositions or whatever.

It is obviously helpful if primary teachers and secondary English teachers have sufficient command of the technical terms to be able to read books written for teachers about children's language. Furthermore, it is almost certainly easier for teachers to identify their pupils' linguistic strengths and weaknesses if they have the vocabulary for describing them. Those upper secondary pupils who undertake an academic study of language structure will also need to master the terminology of the subject. But for other pupils, I believe that the terminology that is needed to talk about the nature and functions of language is, in the first instance, just as much as is required to be able to think and talk about the kind of topics I have outlined. What form it takes is not of the greatest importance, so long as there is agreement among teachers working in the same school. It can be as formal or as informal as they find helpful. I am sure that we should think of the technical terms simply as a descriptive convenience, not as an end in themselves. Words like *verb* and *noun* provide an economical way of referring to whole classes of words that share certain gramatical characteristics; words like *subject* and *object* make it possible to talk about relationships between different parts of a sentence; words like *intonation* and *stress* enable us to say something about the tunes and rhythms of language. Many teachers will find the economy of such labelling useful and will use the terms when they talk about language, in the same way that they use words like *sentence, phrase* and *word*. That does not mean that their pupils need to do labelling exercises or be tested on their knowledge of the terms. The particular danger of having objectives for English teaching that specify that certain technical terms should be understood by a given age is that the labelling activity may assume an unwarranted importance, with the understanding that should precede the labels taking a poor second place. It is worth making the point that although in one sense educated adults all know what a word like *sentence* means, there is no denying that linguists find it exceptionally difficult to produce a watertight definition of such a common term.

I can best express my feelings about labelling activities by quoting the first verse of a poem by Henry Reed, about soldiers doing rifle drill. It is called *Naming of Parts*.

Today we have naming of parts. Yesterday
We had daily cleaning. And tomorrow morning,
We shall have what to do after firing. But today,
Today we have naming of parts. Japonica
Glistens like coral in all of the neighbouring gardens,
And today we have naming of parts.

'Japonica glistens like coral in all of the neighbouring gardens' — for me that stands as a metaphor for the vitality and richness that can be found in language work in the classroom, so long as it is not reduced to a naming of parts.

References

Bloor, T. (1979) Learning about language: the language studies issue in secondary schools. *English in Education*, **13**, 3, 18–22.

Cazden, C. B., Cordeiro, P. and Giacobbe, M. E. (1985) Spontaneous and scientific concepts: young children's learning of punctuation. In G. Wells and J. Nicholls (eds) *Language and Learning: an international perspective*. London: Falmer Press.

Cheshire, J. (1982) Dialect features and linguistic conflict in schools. *Educational Review* **34**, 53–67.

CLIE (Committee for Linguistics in Education) (1984) *Guidelines for Evaluating School Instruction about Language*. University College London: Committee for Linguistics in Education.

Collins (1979) *Collins English Dictionary: 1979 edition*. London: Collins.

DES (Department of Education and Science) (1975) *A Language for Life*. (The Bullock Report). London: HMSO.

—— (1983) *How Well can 15-year-olds Write?* London: HMSO.

—— (1985) *English from 5 to 16: curriculum matters 1*. London: HMSO.

—— (1986) *English from 5 to 16: the responses to curriculum matters 1*. London: HMSO.

de Villiers, P. A. and de Villiers J. G. (1979) *Early Language*. London: Fontana.

Edwards, J. R. (1979) *Language and Disadvantage*. London: Edward Arnold.

Fawcett, R. P. and Perkins, M. R. (1980) *Child Language Transcripts 6–12*, Vols I–IV. Pontypridd: Polytechnic of Wales.

Gowers, E. (1986) *The Complete Plain Words*. (3rd edition, revised by S. Greenbaum and J. Whitcut.) London: HMSO.

Harpin, W. (1976) *The Second 'R'*. London: George Allen & Unwin.

Harris, R. J. (1975) Children's comprehension of complex sentences. *Journal of Experimental Child Psychology* **19**, 420–33.

Henderson, I. (1979) The use of connectives by fluent and not-so-fluent readers. D. Ed thesis, Columbia University Teachers College.

Johnstone, A. (1978) What's in a word? *New Scientist*, 18 May, 432–4.

Perera, K. (1984) *Children's Writing and Reading*. Oxford: Blackwell.

Quirk, R., Greenbaum, S., Leech, G. and Svartvik, J. (1985) *A Comprehensive Grammar of the English Language*. London: Longman.

Reid, E. (1978) Social and stylistic variation in the speech of children: some evidence from Edinburgh. In P. Trudgill (ed.) *Sociolinguistic Patterns in British English*. London: Edward Arnold.

Reid, J. F. (1972) Children's comprehension of syntactic features found in some extension readers. In J. Reid (ed.) *Reading: problems and practices*. London: Ward Lock Educational.

Richmond, J. (1979) Dialect features in children's writing. *Language Development, PE 232, Block 2, Supplementary readings*, 41–55. Milton Keynes: Open University Press.

Slobin, D. I. (1971) *Psycholinguistics*. Glenview, Illinois: Scott, Foresman and Co.

Tough, J. (1977) *The Development of Meaning*. London: George Allen & Unwin.

Trudgill, P. & Hannah, J. (1982) *International English*. London: Edward Arnold.

Wells, G. (1987) *The Meaning Makers: children learning language and using language to learn*. London: Hodder & Stoughton.

SECTION III

Teaching Reading

Introduction

Although most people with an interest in language, literacy and education will have become aware of the existence of different (and apparently competing) approaches to the teaching of reading, it has not always been easy for anyone who was not a 'reading specialist' to understand the nature of the differences, or to judge the viability of different approaches. The first three articles in this section offer some clarification on these matters.

In the first article, Douglas Pidgeon gives a broad, comparative review of the field of teaching reading. This is followed by two articles which offer very different views on the process of learning to read. Joyce Morris describes the rationale underlying the 'Phonics' approach', and gives reasons for the continued importance of this influential method of teaching reading, while Courtney Cazden argues for the importance of analysing the process of learning to read as a social activity rather than as a solitary process whereby an individual acquires cognitive skills.

The fourth article, by Kenneth and Yetta Goodman, is not concerned with particular methods of teaching reading, but instead aims to show how children's 'oral reading' (reading aloud) can be used by researchers and teachers to understand the cognitive processes involved. Their aim is also to show that reading should be seen as an integrated part of more general language processes, and not defined as a separate, unique activity.

During the last ten years, it has become increasingly apparent that 'learning to be literate' does not begin or end in the classroom. One developing area of educational interest in the 1980s is thus the involvement of parents in their children's reading development. In the next article, Keith Topping provides a brief, comparative survey of different ways that parents may help their children to learn to read.

The two articles which end this section are firmly rooted in classroom life. First, Tony Martin offers a unique account of the process of learning to read by 'Leslie', a nine-year-old boy who has been designated a 'reading failure'. And in the final article, Bob Moy and Mike Raleigh provide a stimulating, practical discussion of how 'comprehension work' in schools can be rescued and redesigned to encourage an involvement with texts and so help children become more enthusiastic, critical readers.

3.1 Theory and Practice in Learning to Read

Douglas Pidgeon

Source: Extracts from Pidgeon, D. (1984). In Downing, J. and Valtin, R. (eds) *Language Awareness and Learning to Read*. New York, Springer-Verlag.

Some theoretical considerations

[. . .] Teachers concerned with the task of teaching beginners are not always cognizant of the theory underlying their activities, and indeed some have such little interest they question that it has any relevance at all. The intention, therefore, is first, to take a brief look at different theoretical views; and second, to examine the actual practices found in a sample of reception classes [. . .] It should be made clear at the outset that the concern here is with the process and practice of learning to read and not with the actual exercise of reading once the elements of the task have been mastered. Indeed, the study dealt not only with the early stages of reading but also with what are usually described as prereading activities, it being appreciated that the two are very closely linked.

As will be noted later, the process of learning to read and write bears a similarity to that of learning spoken language. It must be noted, however, that the latter requires no instruction at all — learning to achieve mastery of oral communication, albeit often to only a limited extent, is somehow acquired by the growing child with no direct help — excluding the odd grammatical correction by parents or teachers. On the other hand, seemingly the reverse applies to learning to read and write. Here, with a few exceptions from mostly gifted children, the vast majority do need specific instruction. Under normal circumstances, reading and writing are not just acquired as children mature.

Since the acquisition of spoken language does not require any instruction, the study of its theoretical basis might appear to have little value; yet it is the very complexity of the grammatical structure of language and the fact that young children can apparently work this out for themselves that has led to extensive theoretical speculation. At the same time, one has only to compare the divergent theories of Skinner (1957) and Chomsky (1968), whose names and views are quite unknown to all but a few parents, to illustrate how unnecessary theories are in language acquisition.

Is it necessary, therefore, to have a theoretical framework when it comes to learning to read and write? Does the fact that some kind of instruction is required make all the difference? It might be argued that it all depends upon what is meant by "theory." On the one hand, there are the ideas which over the centuries various people have had about how reading should be taught, and, on the other, as with language acquisition, there are basic theories about how children actually learn, which, of course, may well influence the practical approach taken to initial instruction. Until possibly within the past 20 or so years there is no doubt that the former dominated the reading field. From the 16th century on, nearly every method and approach known today had been suggested at one time or another — alphabetic, whole word, whole sentences, phonic, etc. (Fries, 1963). It was not until the present century, however, that studies of their relative merits were undertaken, with the question of starting with a meaning emphasis approach (whole word) or a code emphasis approach (phonics) given prominence. Chall (1967), reviewing this work, drew two conclusions that bear on this present account: first, that a code emphasis method is one that "views beginning reading as essentially different from mature reading" and, second, that it "produces better results." Chall, however, had serious misgivings about research on beginning reading, expressing the view that too much of it was trying to prove that "one ill-defined method was better than another ill-defined method." She advocated more coordinated studies to give "definite answers" — presumably to produce better defined methods — but she gave no indication as to how these might be formulated. Barton and Wilder (1964), on the other hand, in their extensive review of reading researchers over the period from 1930 to 1960, while also condemning them as being mostly of "poor quality and non-cumulative," did make a plea for the development of a systematic model which "would lead us toward a theory of learning to read." They also noted that the "isolation of the reading field has recently been threatened by invasions from experts in other fields," and mentioned notably linguistics and experimental psychology.

Jenkinson (1969) endorsed the move away from the pragmatic approach to solving reading problems and set out the sources of knowledge required for theory building which included the encompassing of other disciplines. In seeking to explain the failure to evolve theories of reading, she quoted Wiseman's (1966) reminder that the distinguishing mark of a scientific theory was not that it could be proved true but that it must be susceptible to disproof. This is a very important point which has tended to be overlooked in the attempt to evolve theories of both learning to read and language acquisition. The problem as it relates to learning to read will be referred to later, but it can be illustrated by comparing Chomskyian and Skinnerian views of verbal behavior. Chomsky attacks Skinner's hypotheses (Chomsky, 1959, 1971), yet as McLeish and Martin (1975) demonstrate, the latter being behavioral in nature can be put to experimental test, while Chomsky, in order to explain the child's acquisition of grammar, demands the need for an innate linguistic competence and a language-acquisition device, both of which are mentalistic and therefore not readily susceptible to disproof.

It would appear that it is the need for instruction that distinguishes learning to read from acquiring a language, and yet, at the same time, it has been the emphasis on trying to prove which method of instruction is superior which has been the greatest stumbling block to focusing attention on what are now seen as important theoretical issues. Theories of learning to read, like theories of language development, are essentially concerned with the nature of the process: that is to say, some operation is performed by the central nervous system on a given input to produce a particular output and the theory attempts to explain the nature of this operation not only for the furtherance of knowledge but also to serve, at least in the case of reading, as a guide for appropriate practical activities permitting maximum efficiency in the accomplishment of the task. Basically, in reading the input is graphic and the output is meaning, which is internalized but which can be externalized as speech or some other action. It may be noted that, with language development, the only apparent difference is that the input is aural instead of graphic — a fact which appeared to influence the early theoretical ideas. The first incursions of linguists into reading stressed the similarity of the comprehension aspects of both listening and reading, while accepting the different ways in which the physical stimuli — sound and sight — impinged on the central nervous system. The process of learning to read, as Fries put it, was simply "the process of transfer from the auditory signs for language signals which the child has already learned to the new visual signs for the same signals" (Fries, 1963). Somewhat earlier, Bloomfield had made the same point (Bloomfield, 1942), insisting that, in beginning reading, learning the alphabetic code was a necessary prerequisite to discovering meaning. In accordance with his theoretical ideas, he required that a start should be made with regularly spelled words so that the general relationship between letters and sounds should first be discovered.

The practical outcome of this early linguistic influence, which stressed starting with phonics, was to add fuel to those opposing the widely accepted wholeword, meaning-emphasis approach (Flesch, 1955; Daniels and Diack, 1956), and led to an increase in studies comparing the two approaches and, in the course of time, to further debate on the theoretical issues involved. Danks (1980) discussed in some detail the fundamental question of whether the process of comprehension was the same or different for spoken and written language, noting, however, that the strict separation between decoding on the one hand and comprehension on the other may be a "fiction that ultimately cannot be maintained" since the decoding processes for listening and reading being necessarily different may influence the comprehension stages. Danks, stressing the many methodological issues and factors involved, provided no clear answer to the question, but did relate how the answer would influence classroom practices. "If there are no fundamental differences between listening and reading, then a general language experience approach including both listening and reading would be sufficient. If, however, differences between listening and reading appear in one or another comprehension task, then training on that task would be appropriate" (Danks, 1980), whether the task was concerned with vocabulary, syntax, the organization of ideas, or some other aspect.

It is interesting to note that Danks, writing after a decade or so of more theoretically oriented studies in the Chromskyian tradition, does not draw the same conclusion as would Bloomfield and Fries, namely, that if the comprehension of listening and reading were the same, then the practical outcome must be an emphasis on decoding. He did, however, note that educational psychologists as diverse as Thorndike (R.L.) and Goodman espouse the unitary view. The former, analyzing data from several modern empirical studies, produced evidence to support the thesis first advanced by Thorndike (E.L.) (1917) that beyond the first stage of decoding, reading consisted largely of a "thinking" or reasoning component only (Thorndike, 1974). For Goodman, the essence of reading was seeking meaning, and he too maintained that the same process was involved in arriving at meaning whether from an aural or visual input. For him, however, meaning did not exist in the surface structure of language arrived at by precise decoding, but was constructed from past experiences of language. Comprehension was not, therefore, a passive, automatic process as Bloomfield and Fries declared, but was an active process, and learners possessed an innate competence which enabled them to discover the deeper meaning through the use of grammatical and semantic mechanisms (Goodman, 1966, 1970). The influences of Chomsky's theories are clearly seen here and their application to reading has also been expounded by Smith (1971, 1973), who contended that the comprehension of reading, since it depended upon an innate knowledge of "linguistic universals," did not have to be taught but was acquired in the same way as spoken language was acquired. It followed from this that reading instruction per se was unnecessary and Smith, in fact, argued that the function of the teacher was not so much to teach reading as to help the child learn, and reading programs often merely stood in their way — "children learn to read by reading" (Smith, 1973).

The implications of this theoretical approach meant that teaching children *about* reading was quite unnecessary. The essence of reading was a search for the deeper meaning, and learning facts extracted from the surface structure, such as phonic associations, only made the task harder. As Downing (1979) queried, however, even if there was backing for some of the theoretical ideas of Goodman and Smith, did these inevitably give the complete explanation of the reading process and did it follow that what was true for fluent readers necessarily applied to those learning to read? Other writers, notably Eeds-Kniep (1979) and Stott (1981), have attacked the intrusion of psycholinguists, particularly Goodman and Smith, into the field of reading mainly because of their contempt for phonics teaching about which they were "poorly informed" (Scott, 1981).

What is important for this account is the influence of these psycholinguistic theories on classroom teaching. Not merely is phonics disparaged but the approach to reading requires a complete revision. The idea of immersing children in written language much as they are when learning to understand spoken language was put forward in a technique called "assisted reading" by Hoskisson (1975) and was severely criticized by Groff (1979). This technique does not appear to have been widely employed, but, without a doubt, the psycholinguistic invasion has had some effect. Certainly, in Great Britain, starting directly with phonics has gone out of fashion and meaning emphasis approaches of one kind or another for beginning reading appear to have predominated throughout the 1970s.

A further theoretical advance, stemming from the much earlier work of Vygotsky, was developed in the early 1970s which postulated that listening and reading were not parallel processes. Vygotsky distinguished two stages of knowledge acquisition; in the first, a concept evolved spontaneously and unconsciously, and, in the second, it slowly became conscious. Reading was more difficult to acquire than speaking and listening, since it was only a way of representing speech — a spontaneous activity — and, therefore, involved the second stage (Vygotsky, 1934). Mattingly put this a different way, suggesting that acquiring an understanding of spoken language was a primary linguistic activity involving language-acquisition mechanisms, many of which were not accessible to immediate awareness, while reading was a secondary activity, which, in contrast, did necessitate an awareness of certain aspects of language behavior, which he called "linguistic awareness." He contrasted the facility of oral-language learning and the apparent difficulty of learning to read by regarding reading as a "deliberately acquired language-based skill, dependent upon the speaker's awareness of certain aspects of primary linguistic activity" (Mattingly, 1972).

This notion of linguistic awareness, sometimes called metalinguistic knowledge, was elaborated by other writers. Cazden described it as the "ability to make language forms opaque and attend to them in and for themselves," and she noted that it was "less easily and less universally acquired than the language performance of speaking and listening" (Cazden, 1974). Ehri put forward a slightly different idea and drew the distinction between implicit knowledge and metalinguistic awareness, describing the former as that which "governs the child's ability to process and comprehend speech or print," noting that it "emerges earlier and is quite separate from metalinguistic awareness which entails the ability to focus upon, think about, or make judgments about the structures comprising language" (Ehri, 1978). Mattingly himself later described linguistic awareness, which he considered to be prerequisite for learning to read as "the ability of a speaker-hearer to bring to bear rather deliberately the grammatical and, in particular, the phonological knowledge he does have in the course of reading" (Mattingly, 1979a). The proposition that awareness of the grammatical rules underlying language may indeed be prerequisite for the attainment of reading proficiency was stressed by Ryan. For her, metalinguistic knowledge or linguistic awareness "involves the ability to focus attention upon the form of language in and of itself, rather than merely as the vehicle by which meaning is conveyed," and defined it as part "of the general cognitive ability to utilize knowledge deliberately and consciously" (Ryan, 1980).

These theoretical advances still postulated language-acquisition mechanisms which were actively engaged both in learning to speak and in learning to read. But they were no longer the same and, while the former was largely unconscious and therefore mentalistic, the latter involved a conscious knowledge of at least some of the rules of language. Mattingly maintained that possession of this metalinguistic knowledge varied considerably from child to child. For some children — the linguistically aware — their language-acquisition mechanisms continued to function beyond the point necessary for simply processing spoken sentences, and, hence, when it came to reading, the phonological segmentation and the morphological structure of words were intuitively obvious so that the orthography seemed reasonable and no direct obstacles prevented their learning to read. But there were others whose language-acquisition mechanisms ceased operating once they had passed the period of learning to talk and they then atrophied, and the principles by which the orthography transcribed words seemed quite mystifying so that learning to read presented problems. In such cases, the task of the teacher was essentially "to rekindle this awareness by getting the language acquisition machinery started again" (Mattingly, 1979b).

The linguistic awareness theory has been taken one step further by Downing who has drawn on the notion of cognitive confusion advanced by Vernon as a prime cause of reading failure and has expounded what he has called the "cognitive clarity theory" of reading (Downing, 1979). Following an extensive study of reading failure, Vernon had concluded that "the fundamental trouble appears to be a failure in development of [the] reasoning process" (Vernon, 1957 p. 48). She described the cognitively confused child as being "hopelessly uncertain and confused as to why certain successions of printed letters should correspond to certain phonetic sounds in words." Downing perceived the necessity of removing this and other confusions, and he summarized his theory in eight postulates which, put very briefly, claimed that children approach the task of reading instruction "in a normal state of cognitive confusion about the purposes and technical features of language" and that "the learning to read process consists in the rediscovery of (a) the functions and (b) the coding rules of the writing system" (Downing, 1979).

The ideas inherent in the concept of linguistic awareness were in essence still psycholinguistic, although they now contained the need for learners of reading to have conscious views about the nature of the process involved — in direct contrast to the earlier notions of Smith and Goodman. Vernon and Downing, however, were more concerned with the practical aspects of learning to read, and thus Downing's contribution was to reformulate the ideas of linguistic awareness reached by psycholinguistic analysis into a more practically based theory more readily susceptible to disproof.

Existing practices in reception classes

The purpose of this brief account of theoretical developments over the past 20 years or so has been to set the stage for a description of the position adopted in a recently completed study concerned with the development and evaluation of a new reading program. The idea for the study came from a relatively informal survey of just under 120 reception classes in some 50 or so infant schools scattered throughout Great Britain. A judgment sample only was employed which, although it included schools from a broad cross section of socioeconomic backgrounds, was deliberately biased towards those from the lower end of the scale. The visits, mostly carried out over the period 1973–1975, were made by the author who spent some time observing the reading instruction in each class containing children who had just started school, and discussing with the teachers the reasons for the general approach adopted and the specific activities which they employed, dwelling particularly on the theoretical knowledge they possessed of the learning-to-read process. Most of the schools had three intakes each year, in September, January, and after Easter, so that generally one visit was sufficient to cover progress over most of the first year. In about a quarter of the schools, however, two visits were made spread over one year. It should be pointed out that, although the official age of starting school in Britain is five years, a great many schools employed the practice of accepting "rising fives" (children who would only become five some time during the ensuing school year) and thus the age range of the observed pupils on starting school was from four and a half to five and a quarter years.

It is probably no more than a statement of the obvious to say that there appeared to be almost as many variations in teacher practices as there were teachers. What was more relevant, however, was the wide range in the teacher's knowledge and understanding of the processes they were attempting to teach. At the same time, it did seem possible to make certain generalizations. Many of the teachers, for example, seemed appreciative of the fact that prereading activities of one kind or another were necessary before some children should actually be given reading instruction. There was considerable diversity, however, about what prereading activities were imant and where these ended and reading itself began. Many teachers used one or more of the many commercial packages available, covering mostly visual and/or aural discrimination, but very few indeed sought specifically to ensure that all their pupils had acquired an adequate degree of understanding of what the nature of the reading process comprised. While many teachers had a fairly clear idea in their minds what their prereading program was, by no means all of these, and very few of those who had no explicitly planned program of prereading work, could give any theoretical justification for the activities they pursued. Certainly, the line between prereading and reading was very blurred and confused (cf. Standish, 1959). Except for a few instances where a child's linguistic handicap appeared so great that taking any steps toward teaching them to read seemed quite pointless, most teachers, whatever else they did, moved on to teaching reading as quickly as possible. For the most part, this occurred during the first term, sometimes after only a week or two of schooling, although some exceptions were noted. Two teachers or example, in different schools made a deliberate point of not making any formal moves towards teaching reading until the second term, even if, as appeared to be the case, a number of children in the class were more than ready to make a start. In both these instances, however, the prereading activities undertaken included learning phonic associations.

For the most part, formal instruction began with the development of a small sight vocabulary by means of printed notices, flash cards, or simple, amply illustrated books. A fairly common practice was for the teacher, claiming to be using the language experience approach, to write out a short phrase or sentence to be copied under a child's drawing — usually with no previous instruction on how to form the letters. Progression to a specific reading scheme or combination of schemes was made as soon as the teacher felt a child was able to cope; and coping too often meant simply being able to learn the associations between the graphic representations of words and their sound equivalents. Progress invariably was measured by the amount that pupils could remember; that is, they were judged by how far they had moved through the reading scheme, although a great many instances were found where pupils were basically learning words by heart. Phonics, or the associations between specific letters and the sounds they represented, were fairly universally taught as a group exercise and children were encouraged to try "sounding-out" words which they met in their reading as soon as possible. Unfortunately, many pupils failed in this task, sometimes because they were unable to remember a particular association, but more often because they had no clear idea of what they were meant to be doing — it was one thing to learn parrot-fashion the association between, say, the symbol "i" and the sound /i/, but quite another to understand the generalized concept that a series of marks on paper represented or signaled a specific set of sounds. And, without this understanding, the whole exercise of "word building" from a row of marks to a combination of sounds that conveyed meaning was both a mystifying and a meaningless task.

The variation among teachers cannot be emphasized enough. There were some who were fully aware of the implications of the task that confronted the child struggling to say what the teacher wanted, while looking at a row of meaningless marks on paper, but it would be true to say that a great many did not. This survey revealed some interesting facts about the classroom practices of teachers of reading and also about the knowledge, or lack of it, that they possessed to justify their activities. It is intended to report the full results in some detail elsewhere, but some of the more important points are listed below with a few appropriate comments:

1. *Too many assumptions were made about the prior knowledge thought, often erroneously, to be possessed by pupils.* This applied especially to the "technical" language used in teaching reading; words such as "sound," "word," "top," "middle," etc. (Downing, 1970; Downing & Oliver, 1973–1974), but also to many other reading prerequisites such as left-to-right directionality, the orientation of letters, the segmentation of sounds into words, and even the purpose of reading, and the fact that a relationship existed between spoken and written language (Reid, 1966; Downing, 1971–1972; Francis, 1973, 1977).

2. *The learning load was far too great for many pupils.* This was observed both in the instructions given by teachers and in published reading materials. An analysis carried out by Malt (1977) demonstrated that, on average, the first book alone of eight popular

reading schemes introduced the pupil to 26 words and 20 letters and employed 27 phonemes and 34 graphemes. This abundance of learning appeared quite acceptable for beginners who had been well prepared by earlier language experiences, but it led only to confusion for those who had little awareness of what it was they were meant to be doing.

3. *There was an almost universal tendency for teachers to be solely concerned with teaching children to read with very little attention paid to ensuring that they learned how to read.* There is a subtle difference implied here that is related to the theoretical aspects considered earlier. Learning *how* to read involves an understanding of the nature of the process or possessing "linguistic awareness." Learning *to* read could simply mean learning the associations between marks on paper and a particular sound or a row of marks and a given meaning. In practical terms, learning *to* read is a short-term activity with the learner ending up possibly permanently on the infamous plateau so well known by teachers of reading.

4. *The reading ability of pupils was mainly judged by the progress made through a reading scheme.* There were slight variations, of course, especially where some teachers utilized more than one set of reading books; but, almost universally, the criterion of progress was how much individual pupils could read. While there may seem nothing at fault with this procedure and, beyond a certain level of reading ability, it provided a reasonable assessment, it had what appeared to be unacceptable consequences. It meant that many teachers felt under pressure either from parents or colleagues to "get their pupils reading," and this often led to a greater emphasis on associative learning by heart at the expense of the development of any clear understanding of how the reading process really worked. In other words, the pupils were pushed into performing a task which was called "reading" when they still had little idea of the actual nature of the task, including remaining unaware of the connection between what they were doing and understanding and speaking their own language. Diack made the same point when he said "The trial of the teacher's patience comes when she is trying to get the child to understand what the letters are there for. Children will appear to be able to read long before they are actually able to do so in the full sense of the word" (Diack, 1965).

5. *Few teachers made any systematic check with beginners concerning their existing knowledge of the reading process but were inclined to rely on intuition about when and how to begin actual instruction.* Moreover, with many teachers, a certain ridigity was observed in the methods and techniques employed. For example, a particular teaching approach, such as building up a small sight vocabulary before introducing phonics, was adhered to for nearly all pupils irrespective of the wide differences in previous language experiences, motivation, and learning abilities which existed among them.

6. *The time spent actually learning was, on average, a small proportion of the time devoted to instruction.* There was great variation here clearly related both to the skill of the teacher concerned and to the linguistic backgrounds of the pupils. Teachers who were unable to organize their reading instruction well and/or had to deal with large classes of pupils from poor or "different" linguistic backgrounds — the very ones who had the most problems in learning to read — invariably produced the poorest performance. In such classes, the average "efficiency" of instruction was often little more than 10 per cent. That is to say, of the time the teacher devoted to trying to teach reading, the average pupil was concentrating only for a little over 10 per cent of that time on learning some even remotely related aspect of the task. This crude efficiency index increased to around 60 to 70 per cent in some middle class area schools with well-organized teachers, thus emphasising the importance of both motivation and well-organized instruction. In relation to this last point, Southgate, deprecating the "swamp them with books and they will soon learn to read attitude," states "children will fail to learn to read in infant classes unless a good deal of guidance and instruction is undertaken by the

teacher. There are some children who would neither be 'motivated' nor 'ready' by the time they were eight or nine or ten, if someone did not do something about it" (Southgate, 1972, p. 39).

7. *For many pupils the incentive to learn to read was low, leading to frequent lapses of concentration.* This also applied far more to pupils from poor linguistic environments. The difficulty in concentrating seemed to arise mostly from two sources — the fact that for many pupils the learning tasks they met in reading were alien to what their previous backgrounds had either provided or had led them to expect, and also to the fact that in many cases the pupils did not understand what they were being asked to do and hence failed to see how or why they should do it. Although, in general, teachers were very well aware of the importance of their pupils' feelings, learning to read was regarded almost exclusively as a straightforward cognitive task, and sometimes insufficient attention was paid to its affective aspects. The fact that failure could be a *cause* of failure was not always appreciated in the early stages and pupils were often expected to continue, sometimes for weeks and even months on end, with tasks (such as plodding through a reading book) which they did not understand and on which they had little hope of success. There seemed to be an unbroken vicious circle of inability to concentrate, leading to failure which promoted a negative self-image reinforcing the inability to concentrate.

8. *Initial instruction almost universally involved associative learning.* Whatever deeper meaning might be extracted from a line of print by a mature reader, the initial instruction given by the vast majority of teachers consisted of getting pupils to learn that two things were related. Using a whole-word approach, pupils were expected to associate the graphic display of a row of marks on paper with spoken sounds and thus with meaning, while, with phonics, they were taught to associate a particular mark with a specific language sound. This kind of learning could be effected — and very often was — with the learner in complete ignorance of its purpose. Moreover, in the whole word approach, the associations were between an unknown (the graphic representation) and supposed knowns (the phonological and semantic information presumably stored in the pupil's internal lexicon or memory). In phonics, the association was between a graphic representation and a language sound — both unknown for beginners, since, although they might use a particular phoneme attached to others in speech, they invariably had no concept of it existing as an entity in its own right. Of course, given sufficient time and enough repetition, even the slowest learner would acquire a given set of associations, conveying the impression that progress was being made in mastering the reading process. Inevitably, however, the law of diminishing returns would begin to operate and, unless some additional knowledge or understanding was acquired, pupils tended to slow up and even stop their learning — clearly one of the major factors which held them on the infamous plateau (cf. Diack, 1965).

9. *Teaching was invariably from sight to sound.* Whether a whole word or a phonics approach was employed, pupils were presented with a graphic representation and then given the spoken word or sound to be associated with it. At first sight this may seem the natural order of progression since reading is basically a visual activity — at least the input is visual. But knowledge of the spoken language precedes any activity directed at learning to read. Nearly all children, with the possible exception of the congenitally deaf and possibly some non-native speakers who form special cases, learn first to speak their language (however crudely) before learning to read. In other words, meaning is conveyed through the sounds of a language initially, and it would appear to make sense in learning to read as in any other task to move from the known to the unknown, that is, from sound to sight, and not try to operate the other way round (Pidgeon, 1979).

One general point which emerged from this survey was that few of the reception class teachers had very much knowledge of the theories advanced for how children learn to read or understood themselves much about the nature of the learning process involved in the task. The practices they adopted appeared to have been largely based on a combination of what was thought to be appropriate and bits of gleaned knowledge. The same approach was used with each new intake with occasional modifications arising from using new published materials noticed in advertisements or at publishers' exhibitions or recommended by colleagues. None of this is meant to imply that this group of teachers were not fully dedicated to their jobs or did not have the best interests of their pupils at heart.

Nevertheless, despite these generalizations about how teachers decided on their approach, theories about reading had clearly filtered through over time and had exerted an influence. For example, the alphabetic method was rarely seen in any form, and only a small proportion of teachers plunged in at the beginning with direct phonic instruction. In various degrees, it was the ideas of Goodman and Smith that were most in evidence even though few teachers had even heard of their names or appreciated that what they were doing was based largely on their theories. The notion of linguistic awareness, however, was quite unknown, which was not really surprising, since, at the time of the survey, the general implications which arose from it were far from clear.

The main object of the survey had been to review, in general, the relationship between known theory and current teaching practices and, in particular, to attempt to build a theoretical framework from which a new practical program could be constructed. The overall impressions gained from the survey, including the points listed above, were therefore carefully considered, resulting in the emergence of four general principles. These were:

1. There should be a definite sequence in the learning order of basic concepts such that no pupil should be asked to learn a concept which subsumed knowledge of earlier concepts which were possibly not fully understood. This implied not only the introduction of an overall structure in the teaching of reading but that pupils should always have an understanding or awareness of what they were being asked to learn.
2. Some form of continuous feedback to the teacher providing information on the progress being made in the learning sequence of individual pupils was essential. The first principle could not be properly employed unless a constant check was carried out on the developing awareness of each individual pupil.
3. The early learning activities should possess a meaningful structure designed to provide short periods of inherently motivated learning and the avoidance of fragmented imposed instruction which often failed to contribute any significant incentive. To bring this about, the instructional materials must be such as to arouse and sustain interest, thus helping to promote a positive self-image.
4. Some understanding of the structure of spoken language was an essential prerequisite of learning how to read. This, in the practical context of the classroom at a level that was meaningful for young beginners, appeared the appropriate way to ensure the development of linguistic awareness.

Although derived solely from observations of the task of learning to read, it will be noted that the first three of these principles are all found within the general concept of mastery learning (Carroll, 1963; Bloom, 1968, 1971a; Block

1971). The aim of mastery learning is to get all, or nearly all, pupils to a specified criterion level in a particular learning task (in this case, learning to read and write) by providing the optimum time and conditions required by each individual learner to achieve mastery of that task. In practice, this means developing a structured learning sequence — usually a sequential set of objectives to be achieved — and providing appropriate learning activities for each objective together with feedback information indicating whether or not the essential principles have been grasped. The practical application of the model also takes full account of the affective side of learning (Bloom, 1971b, 1976). The important aspect of mastery learning is, of course, the structured learning sequence, and it was to determine what this should contain and how it should be sequenced that resort was made to the theoretical issues discussed earlier and to the fourth principle listed above.

The general position adopted considered the acquisition of a task such as reading to consist essentially of three practical stages. These were: (1) developing an awareness of the nature of the reading process; (2) mastering the essential features of reading and writing; and (3) developing the techniques of fluency so that performance becomes automatic. Although arrived at independently, these stages are not dissimilar to those advanced by Fitts and Posner (1967) relating to all human skill learning. They postulated first the *cognitive* phase in which the learner becomes familiar with the relevant features and nature of the task; second, the *mastering* phase in which the skill is practised until mastered; and third, the *automaticity* phase where further practice is undertaken until the skill is performed without conscious effort.

Unfortunately, the impression gained from the survey was that, with reading, little conscious effort appeared to have been made by teachers to distinguish among the three stages stated above, with the result that not only were many children plunged straight into the practical task of basic learning (stage 2) before they had even the faintest idea of what reading was all about (Reid, 1966; Downing, 1970), but, all too frequently, they were expected to acquire the fluency techniques of stage 3 (e.g. developing a sight vocabulary) when they should have been concentrating on the more important stage 1 aspects of discovering the "how" and "what" of reading. In a sense, such children were placed in the position of trying to decipher a code when they not only had no idea of the key, but they did not even know that it was a code or even what a code was. It should be made clear that these comments do not apply to all children. Those from linguistic backgrounds who are surrounded by books and are read to constantly from a very early age do, as Mattingly puts it, become linguistically aware or, as he states, come "to know the phonology of the language so that the morphophenemic representations of words in [their] personal lexicon(s) match the transcriptions of the orthography" (Mattingly, 1979a). [. . .]

References

Barton, A. H. and Wilder, D. E. Research and practice in the teaching of reading: A progress report, In M. B. Miles (ed.), *Innovation in Education*. New York, NY: Teachers College Press, 1964.

Block, J. H. (ed.) *Mastery Learning: Theory and practice*. New York, NY: Holt, Rinehart, & Winston, 1971.

Bloom, B. S. Learning for mastery. U.C.L.A.-C.S.E.I.P. *Evaluation Comment*, 1968, **1**, 2.

Bloom, B. S. Mastery learning and its implications for curriculum development. In E. W. Eisner (ed.), *Confronting Curriculum Reform*. New York, NY: Little, Brown, 1971 (a).

Bloom, B. S. Affective consequences of school achievement. In J. H. Block (ed.), *Mastery Learning: Theory and practice*. New York, NY: Holt, Rinehart, & Winston, 1971 (b).

Bloom, B. S. *Human Characteristics and School Learning*. New York, NY: McGraw Hill, 1976.

Bloomfield, L. *Language*. New York, NY: Holt, Rinehart, & Winston, 1933.

Bloomfield, L. Linguistics and reading. *Elementary English Review*, 1942, **19**, 125–130 and 183–186.

Carroll, J. B. A model of school learning. *Teachers College Record*, 1963, **64**, 723–733.

Cazden, C. B. Play with language and metalinguistic awareness: One dimension of language experience. *The Urban Review*, 1974, **7**, 28–39.

Chall, J. *Learning to Read: The great debate*. New York, NY: McGraw Hill, 1967.

Chomsky, N. Review of Skinner's "Verbal Behavior." *Language*, 1959, **35**, 26–58.

Chomsky, N. *Language and Mind*. New York, NY: Harcourt, Brace & World, 1968.

Chomsky, N. The case against B. F. Skinner: Review of "Beyond freedom and dignity." *New York Times*, 1971, **17**, 18–24.

Daniels, J. C. and Diack, H. *Progress in Reading*. Nottingham, England: University of Nottingham Institute of Education, 1956.

Danks, J. H. Comprehension in listening and reading: Same or different? In F. B. Murray (ed.), *Reading and Understanding*. Newark, Del.: International Reading Association, 1980.

Diack, H. *In Spite of the Alphabet*. London, England: Chatto & Windus, 1965.

Downing, J. Children's concepts of language in learning to read. *Educational Research*, 1970, **12**, 106–112.

Downing, J. Children's developing concepts of spoken and written language. *Journal of Reading Behavior*, 1971–72, 7, 1–19.

Downing, J. *Reading and Reasoning*. New York: Springer Verlag (also Edinburgh: Chambers), 1979.

Downing, J. and Oliver, D. The child's conception of a word. *Reading Research Quarterly*, 1973–74, **9**, 568–582.

Eeds-Kniep, M. The frenetic fanatic phonic backlash. *Language Arts*, 1979, **56**, 909–917.

Ehri, L. C. Beginning reading from a psycholinguistic perspective: Amalgamation of word identities. In F. B. Murray (ed.), *The Development of the Reading Process*. (International Reading Association Monograph No. 3.) Newark, Del.: International Reading Association, 1978.

Fitts, P. M. and Posner, M. J. *Human performance*. Belmont, Calif.: Brooks-Cole, 1967.

Flesch, R. *Why Johnny Can't Read and What You Can Do About It*. New York, NY: Harper & Brothers, 1955.

Francis, H. Children's experience of reading and notions of units in language. *British Journal of Educational Psychology*, 1973, **43**, 17–23.

Francis, H. Children's strategies in learning to read. *British Journal of Educational Psychology*, 1977, **47**, 117–125.

Fries, C. C. *Linguistics and Reading*. New York, NY: Holt, Rinehart, & Winston, 1963.

Goodman, K. S. A psycholinguistic view of reading comprehension. In G. B. Schick and

M. M. May (eds), *New Frontiers in College-Adult Reading*. Milwaukee, Wis.: National Reading Conference, 1966.

Goodman, K. S. Reading: a psycholinguistic guessing game. In H. Singer and R. B. Ruddell (eds), *Theoretical Models and Processes of Reading*. Newark, Del.: International Reading Conference, 1970.

Groff, P. A critique of teaching reading as a whole task venture. *The Reading Teacher*, 1979, **32**, 647–652.

Hoskisson, K. The many facets of assisted reading. *Elementary English*, 1975, **52**, 312–315.

Jenkinson, M. D. Sources of knowledge for theories of reading. *Journal of Reading Behavior*, 1969, **1**, 11–29.

Malt, L. G. A skills analyst takes a look at reading schemes. *Reading*, 1977, **11**(2), 12–28.

Mattingly, I. G. Reading, the linguistic process, and linguistic awareness. In J. F. Kavanagh & I. G. Mattingly (eds.), *Language by Ear and by Eye*. Cambridge, Mass.: MIT Press, 1972.

Mattingly, I. G. Reading, linguistic awareness and language acquisition. Paper presented at the University of Victoria/IRA Research Seminar on Linguistic Awareness and Learning to Read, Victoria, B.C., 1979 (a).

Mattingly, I. G. The psycholinguistic basis of linguistic awareness. In M. L. Kamil & A. J. Moe (eds.), *Reading Research: Studies and applications*. Clemson, SC: National Reading Conference, 1979 (b).

McLeish, J., & Martin, J. Verbal behaviour: A review and experimental analysis. *Journal of Genetic Psychology*, 1975, **93**, 3–66.

Pidgeon, D. A. Why put the cart before the horse? In D. Thackray (ed.), *Growth in Reading*. London: Ward Lock, 1979.

Reid, J. F. Learning to think about reading. *Educational Research*, 1966, **9**, 56–62.

Ryan, E. B. Metalinguistic development and reading. In L. H. Waterhouse, K. M. Fischer, & E. B. Ryan (eds.), *Language Awareness and Reading*. Newark, Del.: International Reading Association, 1980.

Skinner, B. F. *Verbal Behavior*. New York, NY: Appleton-Century-Crofts, 1957.

Smith, F. *Understanding Reading*. New York, NY: Holt, Rinehart, & Winston, 1971.

Smith, F. *Psycholinguistics and Reading*. New York, NY: Holt, Rinehart, Winston, 1973.

Southgate, V. *Beginning Reading*. London, England: University of London Press, 1972.

Standish, E. J. Readiness to read. *Educational Research*, 1959, **2**, 29–38.

Stott, D. H. Teaching reading: The psycholinguistic invasion. *Reading*, 1981, **15**(3), 19–25.

Thorndike, E. L. Reading as reasoning: A study of mistakes in paragraph reading. *Journal of Educational Psychology*, 1917, **8**, 323–332.

Thorndike, R. L. Reading as reasoning. *Reading Research Quarterly*, 1974, **9**, 135–147.

Vernon, M. D. *Backwardness in Reading*. Cambridge: Cambridge University Press, 1957.

Vygotsky, L. S. *Thought and Language*. Cambridge, Mass.: MIT Press, 1962. (Originally published in Russian, 1934.)

Wiseman, S. (1966) Curriculum evaluation. *Mimeograph*, 21.

3.2 Focus on Phonics: Phonics 44 for Initial Literacy in English

Joyce M. Morris

Source: Edited version of Morris, J. M. (1984) 'Focus on phonics: Phonics 44 for initial literacy in English'. *Reading*, **81**, No. 1, 13–24.

Teaching beginners to read and write English is a complex task even when the learners are native speakers of the language. Phonics is but one approach to this task. Nevertheless, it is a very important one because of the nature of the writing system.

The writing system and the rationale for phonics

Briefly, English orthography is a system of systems and therefore 'poly-systemic'. Basically it is 'alphabetic' in that the orthographic symbols (graphemes), whether single alphabet letters or letter combinations, represent the sounds of speech (phonemes). In this respect, it is very different from the Chinese 'logographic' system in which each orthographic symbol (character) represents one or more words (morphemes). However, the English writing system is also based on morphological principles, and its patterns of word-formation include derivation, inflection and compounding.

Therein lies the linguistic part of the rationale for a phonics approach to initial literacy with its highlighting of sound-symbol correspondence and word structure. Therein lies part of the mystery of why the so-called 'Chinese' method of 'look and say' continues to be dominant in English-speaking countries and, no doubt, contributes to the problem of functional illiteracy among their respective populations. Certainly, in many British primary schools, predominantly look-say, basal schemes form the 'core' of the reading programme for the under-nines. This would suggest, amongst other things, that phonics for initial literacy is still widely regarded as an 'optional extra', and the overwhelming research evidence in favour of phonics is being disregarded. If this is so, it could put many children at risk of not achieving their potential for literacy. [. . .] it could even be tragic for 'teacher-dependent' children who do not have favourable home circumstances and, generally, do not belong to that privileged minority to which most professional teachers originally belong; that is, children who are highly-motivated, verbally-gifted and therefore largely able to discover for themselves from their print environment how the traditional orthography of English works.

[. . .] The purpose of this article is to focus attention on one example of the new 'linguistics-informed' type of phonics which it is hoped will be the pattern for the future. This is the system, now called 'Phonics 44', which was originally devised to meet needs revealed by school-based research and the detailed analysis of classroom materials for UNESCO and other bodies. Accordingly, a brief consideration of the system's origins provides a base from which to outline some of its salient features.

Origins of Phonics 44

Twenty-five years ago, at the National Foundation for Educational Research (NFER), the writer had accumulated from professional research (and other reputable sources) sufficient information to suggest how the problem of functional illiteracy in Britain could at least be reduced if not eradicated altogether. Clearly, reforms in teacher education were necessary to ensure that every probationer would be adequately equipped academically and practically to teach reading and related language skills. Amongst other things, there was also a need to improve diagnostic procedures and to provide better literacy materials for the classroom, especially of a linguistics-informed and generally research-based kind.

For various reasons, and with only a few notable exceptions, the proposed changes were received in influential circles either apathetically or with active opposition. One training college principal, for example, declared vehemently to his colleagues in the writer's presence that only over his dead body would courses in the teaching of reading be introduced into his college. (Mercifully for future generations he departed this life soon afterwards.) Paradoxically, these unfavourable attitudes, coupled with growing parental concern about literacy standards during the early 1960s, made it somewhat easier for experiments with the initial teaching alphabet to go ahead. In turn, the widespread publicity engendered by i.t.a. experimentation not only increased interest in the sound-symbol relationships of traditional orthography but helped to establish the United Kingdom Reading Association.

During this eventful period, the writer became even more convinced that a significant contribution to initial literacy could be made by developing a new kind of phonics based on linguistic scholarship. Indeed, it seemed reasonable to suppose that such a development might eventually help to bring about some of the necessary reforms broadly indicated above. Professor D.B. Fry, Head of the Department of Phonetics and Linguistics at University College, London, was sympathetic to these ideas and particularly keen to see linguistic knowledge put to practical use in helping children to become literate. He therefore encouraged the writer to complete the detailed linguistic analyses required as a basis for the 'new' phonics, and provided relevant literature of significance from his own special fields of experimental phonetics, the deaf world and music. In this context, it is significant that it was his junior colleague Dr (later Professor) M.A.K. Halliday who subsequently (1964 to 1970) directed at University College, London, the 'Schools Council's Programme in Linguistics and English Teaching' which, amongst other things, produced *Breakthrough to Literacy* (Mackay, Thompson and Schaub, 1970).

[. . .] In 1970, up-to-date findings were used as the phonics component in a BBC television series for younger children called *Words and Pictures* (Morris, 1971). Finally, with the support of Professor Fry as linguistics consultant, the fully-fledged system, now called 'Phonics 44', was incorporated in *Language in Action* (Morris, 1974).

Sadly, Professor Fry died on 21 March 1983, shortly after he had given his blessing to the writer's proposals for disseminating information about Phonics 44 which would highlight the system's advantages for the acquisition of initial literacy and for the training of teachers. These proposals included the numbering of speech sounds so that the content of the system could be more readily understood by the many teachers whose training, regrettably, has not given them a knowledge of phonetics. The somewhat 'unorthodox' numbering also helps to make explicit the primary problem of English orthography which was the starting point of the linguistic analyses leading to Phonics 44. As such, and because a clear understanding of the primary orthographic problem is essential for teaching beginners to read and write English, it is summarized below.

Aspects of the primary orthographic problem

Although, as already stated, English orthography is basically 'alphabetic', it does not conform to the alphabetic principle which assumes that each speech sound (phoneme) of oral language should have its own graphic representation. This is the primary problem and it has four main aspects.

Dialect differences

The number and specificity of speech sounds in anyone's phoneme inventory depends on his/her particular English dialect. This means that there is individual variation with regard to what the writing system represents in terms of sound-symbol correspondence. It also means that teachers of initial literacy and authors of literacy materials (especially phonic resources) need to be consciously aware of educationally significant dialect differences (which include vocabulary and grammar), such as the difference between English accents which are 'rhotic' or 'r-ful' and those which are 'non-rhotic' or 'r-less'. (Rhotic accents actually pronounce the sound /r/ corresponding to letter *r* in words like *farm*.)

British RP, the basic pronunciation model

As in the case of Phonics 44, the starting point for research into sound-symbol correspondence in British English is naturally the 'standard' accent known as Received Pronunciation. This is because British RP, for short, in the words of yet another authority at University College, London (Gimson, 1981), is a 'basic model which has considerable prestige and is already taught throughout the world'. Moreover, it continued to be the basic model for the fourteenth edition of the world-renowned *Everyman's English Pronouncing Dictionary* (Jones, 1977) which was revised and edited by Professor Gimson, and who explains in his Introduction that RP is an accent which 'remains generally acceptable and intelligible within Britain' largely because the whole population has been exposed to its use in broadcasting for over 50 years.

The basic model serves to illustrate the second main aspect of the primary orthographic problem. British RP has a full phoneme inventory of 24 consonant sounds and 20 vowel sounds (12 monophthongs and eight diphthongs). This makes a total of 44 speech sounds to be represented in the writing system by 26 alphabet letters: a tall order, as clearly illustrated below.

ENGLISH WORDS

SPOKEN	WRITTEN
24 consonant sounds	21 consonant letters
20 vowel sounds	5 vowel letters
44 speech sounds	26 alphabet letters

The consonant sound/letter mismatch

As will be seen, there is a closer match between the numbers of consonant sounds and consonant letters than between the numbers of vowel sounds and vowel letters. This would correctly suggest that the consonant sound/letter mismatch is comparatively easier for learners to cope with. However, it is not as easy as would appear at first sight because, individually, in words, the 21 consonant letters represent only 18 of the 24 consonant sounds. (Letters *c, q* and *x* are 'redundant' insofar as they duplicate the sound-symbol role of letters *k* and *s* in words such as *c*at, *c*ity; che*q*ue; bo*x*.) Accordingly, the six remaining consonant sounds (numbers 19 to 24 inclusive in the Phonics 44 system) are represented by consonant digraphs and other letter combinations of which only *some* examples are given below owing to limitations of space. (Wherever appropriate in what follows, phonetic symbols between slant lines provide for accurate identification of the speech sound(s) in question.)

Consonant sound			Key-word
19	/ʃ/	as in	*sh*op
20	/tʃ/	as in	*ch*impanzce
21	/ð/	as in	*th*e
22	/θ/	as in	*th*umb
23	/ŋ/	as in	ki*ng*
24	/ʒ/	as in	televi*si*on

The vowel sound/letter mismatch

Because there are 20 vowel sounds and only five vowel letters, the representation of vowel sounds in English orthography is a main source of difficulty for beginners learning to read and to spell. The situation is made even more difficult when, as is often the case, especially in the professional literature and phonic resources for the classroom, no clear distinction is made between vowel *sounds* and vowel *letters*. Moreover, the resulting confusion naturally leads back to folk lore about the irregularities of English spelling with its apparent support for the prolonged use of 'look and say'.

The first five vowel sounds in the Phonics 44 system are usually represented in writing by the single vowel letters *a, e, i, o, u,* as in the alphabet key-words *a*pple, *e*gg, *i*nk, *o*range, *u*mbrella. In contrast, the sixth vowel phoneme has the most numerous and varied graphic correspondence of all. This is not surprising because it is the 'schwa' or weak stress vowel/ə/ (as in the key-words *a*nother caterpill*a*r) and therefore has the highest frequency in speech and print.

In the main, and as will be seen below, 'regular' sound-symbol correspondences for the remaining 14 vowel sounds are also varied but in a patterned manner. The thirteenth vowel sound /ɔ:/ is, in a sense, a 'rogue' vowel in that it has two distinct sets of grapheme correspondences, i.e. symbols containing letter *a* and letter *o* respectively. As such, and as the research of Dr Margaret Peters (1970) has shown, it remains a source of spelling difficulty even for upper juniors. For instance, more than half of the whole age-group of 967 ten year olds in one Local Education Authority could not spell the word 'saucer' and, between them, they offered 209 alternative spellings.

Vowel sound			Key-word(s)
7	/eɪ/	as in	*a*pe, ra*i*n, pl*a*y
8	/iː/	as in	*e*ve, *ee*l, s*ea*l
9	/aɪ/	as in	*i*ce, p*ie*, h*igh*
10	/əʊ/	as in	*o*de, *oa*k, t*oe*
11	/uː/	as in	h*oo*p, bl*ue*, l*u*te
12	/ʊ/	as in	h*oo*k
13	/ɔ/:	as in	b*a*ll, w*a*lk, s*aw*, c*au*se, c*or*n, m*ore*
14	/ɑː/	as in	st*ar*
15	/ɜː/	as in	b*ir*d, h*er*mit, p*ur*ple
16	/aʊ/:	as in	m*ou*th, cl*ow*n
17	/ɔɪ/	as in	c*oi*, b*oy*
18	/eə/	as in	squ*are*, ch*air*
19	/ɪə/	as in	*ear*, d*eer*, h*ere*
20	/ʊə/	as in	g*our*d, p*oor*, c*ure*

Linguistic analyses for Phonics 44

Having identified important aspects of the primary orthographic problem in the 1950s, the writer set out to discover how, and with what frequency, the 44 speech sounds of British RP are represented by alphabet letters singly and in combination (clusters). Early work began with the analysis of the 3000 words most frequently in print, with sound values, etc., as given in the eleventh edition of *Everyman's English Pronouncing Dictionary* (Jones, 1956). It continued with the analysis of the speaking, reading and writing vocabularies of children reported, respectively, by Burroughs (1957), by McNally and Murray (1962), and by Edwards and Gibbon (1964). [. . .] Areas of research covered in this way include:

1. the phonemic system in children's speech as the basis for all higher order linguistic structures
2. the relative frequency of the alphabet letters in sample texts
3. the perception by children of alphabet letters in various contexts
4. the different and/or complementary roles of letters in words
5. the spelling patterns of English and their vertical processing
6. the dynamics of word play in children's language and in children's literature.

The linguistic structure of Phonics 44

[. . .]

The sound-symbol base
What then is the linguistic structure of Phonics 44? First of all, its name and sound-symbol base reflect the relationships found, in number and frequency, between the 44 phonemes of British RP and the graphemes representing them in traditional orthography. From the main vocabulary analyses these total 396 but, according to the criteria established, less than 10 per cent are classed as 'divergencies' or 'irregular' spellings. Moreover, this small percentage includes comparatively few words like the word 'one' which are 'hopelessly' irregular, whilst most of the rest fall into divergent *groups* such as the groups of words containing vowel diagraphs *ea* and *ow*, corresponding respectively to the vowel sounds in 'bread' and 'snow' rather than to those in 'seal' and 'clown'. In short, Phonics 44 supports the contention of a number of linguists that 'English spelling is a reasonably reliable system based on both sound-to-spelling correspondence and on morphological principles.'

The didactic sequence at alphabet level
Children usually begin to learn about sound–symbol correspondence in an informal manner using alphabet books in which each letter in initial word position is presented in sequence. Research at a more formal alphabet level indicated that the didactic sequence for Phonics 44 should be based on a

division of the letters (except *x*) into three groups, with the repetition of some letters for specific and mainly contrastive purposes. Here it should be noted that, although Phonics 44 provides the basic linguistic structure for an economical, didactic 'programme' as in *Language in Action* (Morris, 1974), the approach throughout is mainly one of differentiation rather than single sequence. For example, within the three groups of letters shown below, the suggested order of introduction for each letter-sound correspondence in initial word position is not a matter of single sequence. Letters are presented together to highlight contrastive features with regard to capital and lower-case forms, associated letters like *Ss/Zz* and letters which, perceptually, are particularly confusing as in Group 2.

> *Group 1* Tt; Yy; Hh; Ww; Rr; Gg/Jj; Ss/Zz; Cc/Kk/Ss.
> *Group 2* BD/bd; PQ/pq; MN/mn; VW/vw; EF/ef; IL/il; UN/un.
> *Group 3* Aa; Ee; Ii; Oo; Uu.

The 11 different letters in Group 1 play several different and/or complementary roles in traditional orthography including, notably, their contribution to letter clusters such as the digraphs *sh*, *ch* and *th* for consonant sounds 19, 20 and 21 respectively. However, it is important that children first appreciate how single letters correspond to phonemes at the beginning of words before proceeding to learn the function of letter clusters in initial, medial and final word position. It should also be noted that because of the duplicate role of letter *c*, the 11 consonant letters in Group 1 correspond to only 10 different consonant sounds in initial word position, whereas Groups 2 and 3 together introduce a further 14 letters corresponding to 13 different sounds, thereby covering the alphabet in terms of individual sound-symbol correspondence, and leaving the six remaining consonant sounds (numbers 19 to 24 inclusive) to be highlighted in the spelling pattern progression outlined below.

The vowel-centred, vertically-organized, spelling pattern progression

Phonics 44 is a graphic processing system which is vowel-centred because, as already indicated, the vowel representations are a main source of difficulty for beginners learning to read and to spell English words. The vowel phoneme-grapheme sequence is based on frequency of use in words, and as indicated by the numbers given to the vowel sounds. Thus the twentieth and last vowel in the system, as in the word 'gourd', is the least frequent sound in spoken English and, naturally, words in which it is represented are also relatively infrequent in print.

Contrary to popular belief, English orthography is highly patterned. Consequently, Phonics 44 is also a vertically-organized system of spelling pattern progression which begins with the division of monosyllables into major sets as follows:

Set A (vowels 1 to 5)   Words in which the vowel letter corresponds to a so-called 'short' vowel sound; e.g. *cat, hen, pig, dog, sun.*

Set B (vowels 7 to 10)   Words in which marker, modifying or magic *e* signals that the preceding vowel letter corresponds to a so-called 'long' vowel sound; e.g. *ape, eve, ice, ode.*

Set BB (vowels 7 to 10)   Words in which vowel digraphs correspond to the same so-called 'long' vowel sounds; e.g. *rain, play; eel, seal; pie, high; oak, toe.*

Set C (vowels 11 to 20)   Words in which the rest of the vowel phonemes (10) are represented in different ways; e.g. *hoop, blue, lute; hook; ball, walk, saw, cause, corn, more; star; bird, hermit, purple; mouth, clown; coil, boy; square, chair; ear, deer, here; gourd, poor, cure.*

Within each of the above sets of spelling patterns, the vertical processing system develops monosyllabic words with consonant clusters of various kinds including letter combinations for the six remaining consonant sounds from the alphabet level. For example, the sequence in Set A is as follows:

1. double letters or their equivalents; e.g. pu*ff*, ba*ck*
2. consonant clusters which occur both at the beginning and at the end of words; e.g. *sk*ip, ri*sk*; *sp*ot, li*sp*; *st*op, lo*st*
3. other consonant clusters of two or three letters which occur at the beginning or at the end of words; e.g. *cl*ub, u*st*, *scr*ap, *str*ap, ste*ps*, sta*nds*, bli*nks*
4. consonant digraphs which occur both at the beginning and at the end of words; e.g. *sh*ip, fi*sh*; *ch*op, mu*ch*; *th*en, wi*th*; *th*in, mo*th*.

Next, within each of the major sets of spelling patterns, disyllabic words are introduced; for instance, present tense forms of verbs such as *skipping* (Set A), *making* (Set B), *painting* (Set BB) and *shouting* (Set C). Also introduced are disyllabic words containing the 'schwa' or weak stress vowel (number 6) in, for example, comparative adjectives such as *redder* (Set A), *nicer* (Set B), *fainter* (Set BB) and *louder* (Set C). Here it should be remembered that, in many verbal contexts, the 'schwa' vowel is also represented in monosyllables as in the very frequent word *the*.

The system also allows for the sequential introduction of words containing the so-called 'silent' letters, in addition to 'silent' marker *e* words. Thus words such as *knit* and *thumb* (Set A) are followed by *knave* (Set B).

Some advantages of Phonics 44

There are many advantages of Phonics 44, and some of them are particularly important. In the first place, the system dispels the age-old myth that English spelling is hopelessly chaotic and, therefore, persistent reading and/or spelling problems are inevitable for a sizeable proportion of the population in all English-speaking countries. Second, it works on the principle of economy in teaching and learning and therefore saves time for both teacher and learner. Third, as incorporated in *Language in Action* (Morris, 1974), the system encourages more rapid progress towards independence in reading and spelling. (Look-say, basal schemes tend to encourage the development of 'primer parrots', not independent readers able relatively soon to move away from schemes to the individual reading books of children's literature.) Fourth, it also acts in the classroom as an on-the-spot diagnostic instrument in that the learner's true progress is indicated by the ability to read and spell words at the various processing stages.

   Probably most important of all, Phonics 44 is based on the systematic study of the English language in spoken and written form and, as such, is a linguistics-informed system. This means that teachers using it gain in professionalism and, hence, are better equipped to evaluate critically the phonic resources available and, in general, to help children with the fundamental task of 'internalizing a model of the orthography'.

Future prospects

It is hoped that Phonics 44 will help to start a peaceful 'revolution' in which knowledgeable teachers will demand from publishers that all phonic resources for the classroom are linguistics-informed and in general research-based. Many have already requested that the system be incorporated in materials for remedial reading and spelling. Others have asked for a separate, detailed 'Guide to Phonics 44' in addition to the tape/slide presentation which is to be published early this year by the Centre for the Teaching of Reading, University of Reading (Morris, 1984). In short, there is a great deal of interest in the system both at home and abroad, which augurs well for a future in which all teachers of initial literacy in English will teach according to the specificity of the language and, hence, will bring nearer the day when functional illiteracy is no longer a national problem in English-speaking countries.

References

Burroughs. G. E. R. (1957) *A Study of the Vocabulary of Young Children*. Edinburgh: Oliver & Boyd.

Edwards, R. P. A. and Gibbon, V. (1964) *Words Your Children Use*. London: Burke.

Gimson, A. C. (1981) *An Introduction to the Pronunciation of English*. Third Edition. London: Edward Arnold.

Jones, D. (1956) *Everyman's English Pronouncing Dictionary*. Eleventh Edition. London: J. M. Dent.

Jones, D. (1977) *Everyman's English Pronouncing Dictionary*. Fourteenth Edition, extensively revised and edited by A. C. Gimson. London: J. M. Dent.

Mackay, D., Thompson, B and Schaub, P. (1970) *Breakthrough to Literacy*. London: Longman.

McNally, J. and Murray, W. (1962) *Key Words to Literacy and the Teaching of Reading*. London: Schoolmaster Publishing Co.

Morris, J. M. (1971) Television and reading. In J. E. Merritt (ed.) *Reading and the Curriculum*. London: Ward Lock Educational.

Morris, J. M. (1974) *Language in Action*. London & Basingstoke: Macmillan Education.

Morris, J. M. (1984) *PHONICS 44*. Centre for the Teaching of Reading, University of Reading School of Education, 29 Eastern Avenue, Reading, Berkshire.

Peters, M. L. (1970) *Success in Spelling*. Cambridge Institute of Education, Shaftesbury Road, Cambridge.

3.3 Social Context of Learning to Read

Courtney B. Cazden

Source: This is an expanded version of a paper by the same title which appears in L.B. Resnick and P.A. Weaver (Eds.) (1981), *Theory and Practice of Early Reading*. Reprinted by permission of Lawrence Erlbaum Associates, Inc.

To adults, reading is a solitary activity, a kind of internal language process that contrasts with interpersonal talk. The contrast is not complete: We read song sheets aloud and together; we exchange notes during a lecture, thus using reading as well as writing for immediate interactional ends; and we listen alone to talk on the radio or TV, thus making a solitary activity of the comprehension of speech. But usually we talk with others and read alone.

Not so with children, especially children just learning to read in the primary grades. Learning to read, like mature reading later on, is certainly a cognitive process; but it is also a very social activity, deeply embedded in interactions with teacher and peers. Hopefully, as we understand those interactions more fully, we will be able to design more effective environments for helping children learn. This paper reviews research on children learning to read in classroom interactions in four parts: influences on time engaged in reading; differences in the focus of instruction; the complexities of reading group lessons; and peer interactions in the older grades.

Influences on Time Engaged in Reading

One obvious way in which classroom interactions affect learning is through their effect on how much time children actually spend engaged in reading tasks. Three descriptions by Piestrup (1973), McDermott (1978), and Au (in press, in preparation), are sociolinguistic and ethnographic analyses of audio- or videotaped lessons. Two descriptions by Hess and Takanishi (1974) and Cazden (1973) are more traditional studies in which observers did on-the-spot coding.

Piestrup's research (1973) is on sources of interference between the language of black children and their teachers. In an analysis of 104 reading instruction episodes audiotaped in 14 first grade classrooms with predominantly black children, Piestrup identified two kinds of interference which she labelled structural and functional. Whether the mismatch is only a temporary misunderstanding or a more serious barrier depends on the teacher's understanding of the problem and her response to it. In the following episode about a workbook lesson, the teacher explicitly and effectively dealt with a structural (dialect) conflict:

T   ". . . how would you harm the colt?"

C_1 Tear it.

T   Huh?

C_1 Tear it.

T   Th — th — Oh! Do you, do you know what a colt is, now?

C_1 Oh, kill it, kill it!

T   No, what's a colt?

C_1 Somethin' you wear.

T   There's an "l" in it. "Coat" is c-o-a-th — don't laugh, that's all right. "Colt" is very hard for city children, because they haven't been out on the farm, and they don't know about it. It's a baby, a baby colt.

C_3 A baby colt.

C_1 Oh yeah!

T   Remember the story? An' it's a c-o-l-t. "Coat" is c-o-a-t, and there's no "l" in it, but listen to — Keisha — co*l*t, co*l*t, co*l*t. Now do you know what a colt is?

C_4 Yeah, I know.

T   What is it?

C_2 A baby horse.

T   Yes, uh-huh, how could you harm a baby horse?

(Piestrup, 1973, pp. 3–5)

Interference is termed functional rather than structural when the mismatch comes from the functions language is used for rather than from structural features of the language itself. In the following excerpt from oral reading, the children shift away from discussion of remote content to verbal play; the teacher is ignored and fails to get their attention back to the reading task:

T   "Off"

C_1 "Off to the —

T   OK. It says "wood."

C_1 — wood.

T   We would say woods — this book was written in England.

C_1 Now, I'm through. I ain't gonna read this page again.

T   OK. Well, we're gonna turn the page and we're just gonna read the next page.

C_1 Uh uh! Darren 'sposed to be first.

T   Well, I'm waiting for Darren to come back. Come on, Darren.

C_2 He just playin' aroun' _____ (not clear).

C_1 He crack his knuckles, in the buckles.

C_3 Uh-uh.

T   OK, Zip and Wendy ran to the woods, and here's the —

C_1 I got a tow truck. My mama bought me one.

T   — father.

C_1 An' I got me a car to hook it on. It got a hook —

(Piestrup, 1973, pp. 6–7)

The two teachers out of the group of fourteen who were able to accommodate most effectively to both structural and functional sources of interference, termed "Black Artful" by Piestrup, had teaching episodes that were both lively and focused on reading, and their children had the highest reading scores at the end of first grade. Piestrup concludes that "the ways teachers communicate in the classroom are crucial to children's success in learning to read" (p. 170).

McDermott (1978) has done an intensive microanalysis, frame by frame, of videotapes of two 30-minute reading groups (top group and bottom group) in one first grade classroom. During those 30-minutes around the reading table, children in the top group spend three times as much time on task as children in the bottom group, and McDermott has tried to understand how this happens. First, the procedure for allocating turns to read is different in the two groups. In the top group, the number of pages in the story is allocated equally among the children, and each child reads his share in order around the table. In the bottom group, there's no fixed order and each turn is negotiated according to who requests a turn and who the teacher thinks can read the page in question. Interruptions are more frequent in the bottom group (40 vs. 2 for the top group) and more disruptive because continuation of reading is more dependent on the teacher for assigning the next turn. Some of these interruptions are even initiated by the teacher herself:

> On one occasion, for example, she organizes the children to call for a turn to read their new books. "Raise your hands if you can read page 4." The children straighten themselves up in their chairs, form neat lines along the sides of the reading table, and either raise their hands for a turn or at least look at their books or the teacher. As their hands reach their highest point, the teacher looks away from the reading group to the back of the room. She yells at one child in the top group, and then another child in the top group. The three children in the bottom group who raised their hands, lower them to the table. Another little boy who didn't have his hand raised thrusts his chair back away from the reading table and the teacher and balances it on its two back legs. The other two children in the group simply look down at their books. The teacher returns and says, "Nobody can read page 4? Why not?" Eventually the children recover, and someone gets a turn. But it all takes time.
>
> (McDermott, 1978)

How does this contrast come about? Possibly the teacher has been told somewhere that calling on children in a random order helps keep the attention of potentially more disorderly children. More importantly, McDermott (1978) suggests:

> What is driving this whole system? I don't think it is the negative expectations of the teacher. Rather, the children in the bottom group represent pedagogical and interactional problems for the teacher. Pedagogically, there is no doubt that it is easier for the teacher to practice reading with the children in the top group than to struggle with the process of teaching decoding to the children in the bottom group. And interactionally, there is the pressure of the competition between the groups and the scarred identities of the children in the bottom group. Even within the bottom group we hear claims of one child against another. ("Oh, you can't read." "Better than you.") Or we can point to a child in the bottom group who constantly calls for turns to read while, at

the same time, appears to struggle to make sure that she does not get eye contact with the teacher.

In response to all these problems, the teacher and the children in the bottom group make adaptations. In response to all these pressures they struggle to solve the pedagogical and interactional problems of coming to school not knowing how to read, of having a teacher who expects them to know how to read, of having a teacher who doesn't know how to overcome that they do not know how to read while she has twenty other children walking around the room, and of overcoming the pressure of having the other children taunt them for their performances. In response to all this, they make very specific adaptations. One adaptation is to make sure that no one child is isolated to read something too difficult. So the teacher uses the two different turn taking systems with the different groups, and this adaptation has the consequences already explicated.

McDermott (1978) concludes:

Success in learning is best predicted by the time a child spends on a task; some may learn faster than others, but with time, almost any child can learn what has to be learned in school, if there are the proper organizational constraints for getting the child on task for the necessary amount of time. The question of why some children achieve more than others has been transformed into a question about the environments in terms of which some children get consistently organized to attend to school tasks in classrooms while others do not. . . .

Certain children, who, for whatever reasons come to school behind their peers in the development of classroom skills, constitute both pedagogical and interactional problems for most teachers. Most teachers say of them that they are harder to teach; part of that reaction is that they need more of the teacher's time if they are to catch up with their peers. In addition, they must learn under the pressure of knowing that they are behind, generally in a classroom which allocates status in part on the basis of the children's intellectual ranking in the classroom. . . .

Thus, the small differences between children in the early years of school expand quickly to the drastic forms of differential performance which become obvious in later years. At the root of these differences is not so much the extreme complexity of the school tasks, nor the differences in the learning potentials of the different children, but the differential environments we offer the children for getting organized and on task so that learning can take place.

I think we have to acknowledge that what McDermott has exposed would be found elsewhere if we dared to take as close a look.

Fortunately, we have reports of one success story too. The Kamehameha Early Education Program (KEEP) is in a privately supported school for ethnically Hawaiian children, whose reading achievement in regular classrooms traditionally has been very low. In 1976 a new reading program was introduced at KEEP, and reading scores of the first grade children increased from an average of the 19th percentile in the preceding three years to the 69th percentile (Jordan, Weisner, Tharp, & Au, 1978).

According to Au (in press), the new reading lessons have three component parts, which she labels ETR, for *E*xperience, *T*ext and *R*elationships: The teacher begins by evoking comments from the children about their *experiences* that relate to the story (which is usually from a basal reader); she then assigns a page or two of *text* to be read silently and questions the children about the text; finally, she draws out *relationships* between the text and their experiences.

So far, except for the careful attention to evoking the children's personal experiences to engage their attention and provide schemata for comprehension, this sequence does not sound different enough to account for such striking gains. Au believes that the success lies not only in the cultural congruence of the content but, as with Piestrup's Black Artful teachers, in the cultural congruence of the context as well. Briefly, the rapid interactions between teacher and children, and the cooperative interaction among the children who build on one another's responses, produce lesson talk with striking similarities to "talk-story," a form of collaborative narrative of personal experience that is a special speech event in Hawaiian culture [. . .] Quantitatively, the children are certainly more engaged in reading tasks in the new program; but qualitatively the focus of their attention has been changed as well.

Hess and Takanishi (1974) observed student "engagement" in eight 30-minute observations in 39 elementary school classrooms in low-income communities to find out what teachers did to "turn on" their students to academic work in mathematics and language arts. Overall, they found that student engagement was strongly and consistently related to teacher behavior, but not to classroom architecture, nor to student characteristics such as sex and ethnicity. Two demonstrations of intra-teacher consistency in their data are impressive. First, two teachers were observed during two consecutive years. Although they had completely different classes and reported that they felt large differences between the two years, the mean level of engagement in their classes remained almost identical. Second, during the second year of the study, an entire school being observed moved from a self-contained classroom building to one with open-space architecture. The overall level of engagement across these very different physical environments was identical (82 and 83 percent), and the rank order of teachers in terms of percent engagement in their classrooms was .85.

Contrary to expectations, Hess and Takanishi found that these levels of student engagement were not consistently related across teachers to "specific teacher strategies" such as the frequency of specific questions or of feedback; instead they were strongly related to more "global instructional strategies" such as instructional group size (more engagement in small groups), and direction of student attention (more engagement when directed toward the teacher than toward other students or materials alone). The authors conclude with a recommendation that teacher-training programs concentrate on skills in classroom social organization rather than on more specific teaching behaviors. This is an important caution for competency-based training as it is usually conducted .[. . .]

Differences in the Focus of Instruction

Time on task is a powerful variable, but it is not the only one. One more qualitative variable is where the attention of children and teacher is focused during reading instruction. We know that learning to read requires mastering a complex set of concepts and skills at many levels of a hierarchical system. Analytically, we can separate a series of nested units — from the meaningless sounds symbolized by letters, to larger and larger meaningful units of words, phrases, clauses, paragraphs and stories; and we can isolate the conventions of punctuation, capitalization and layout on a page that support the communication of meaning (remember that the division of print into lines is one visual feature that does not carry meaning except in poetry and that children must therefore learn to ignore). But such analytical separation says nothing about how children should be helped; it does not determine in what order their attention should be focused on different units in the hierarchy, nor how an eventual integration can best be achieved.

The simplest contrast in focus is between decoding skills and meaning. We know we cannot tell what actually happens from the manuals on a teacher's desk or the methods she professes to use. For example, in one of the first grade reading studies supported by the Office of Education Cooperative Research Project, Chall and Feldman (1966) went behind "method A vs. method B" comparisons to examine what teachers actually did to implement those methods. Observational studies of teachers showed no significant relationship between the ranking of the teacher's professed method emphasis (whether "sound-symbol" or "meaning") and the method emphasis observed in her classroom (p. 573).

If attention to phonic skills and to meaning is included in reading group lessons, then that combination can create problems of shifting focus and complex interactions that will be discussed further below. Here I want to report research that describes classrooms in which these foci are separated — by children, by type of instructional event, or by language.

Separation of Focus by Children
In the classroom studied by McDermott, the focus differed from one group in the classroom to another.

> [In the top group] occasionally, the children create problems by word calling instead of reading for meaning, and the teacher's main pedagogical task is to convince the children that there is living language complete with propositions with illocutionary force on the page. Thus, one child reads, "But Ricky said his mother . . ." in a dull monotone, and the teacher corrects her, "Let's read it this way, 'But Ricky, said his mother'."
>
> With the bottom group, the teacher has rather different problems. Accordingly, the teacher and the children constitute rather different environments for each other in the different groups. The children in the bottom group do not read as well as the children in the top group, and the teacher attends less to the language on the book's pages and more to the phonics skills needed to interpret any given word in the text. Thus, there

are many more stopping places in the children's reading, and the story line which is to hold the lesson together is seldom alluded to and never developed. (McDermott, 1978)

This same contrast between focus on meaning for better readers and focus on phonic skills for poorer readers is found in two other studies by Gumperz (1972) and Allington (1978). Gumperz reports observations in a first grade classroom in a racially integrated California district:

> We observed a reading session with a slow reading group of three children, and seven fast readers. . . . With the slow readers she [the teacher] concentrated on the alphabet, on the spelling of individual words. . . . She addressed the children in what white listeners would identify as pedagogical style. Her enunciation was deliberate and slow. Each word was clearly articulated with even stress and pitch. . . . Pronunciation errors were corrected whenever they occurred, even if the reading task had to be interrupted. The children seemed distracted and inattentive. . . .

> With the advanced group on the other hand reading became much more of a group activity and the atmosphere was more relaxed. Words were treated in context, as a part of a story. . . . There was no correction of pronunciation, although some deviant forms were also heard. The children actually enjoyed competing with each other in reading and the teacher responded by dropping her pedagogical monotone in favor of more animated natural speech. (Gumperz, 1972)

Allington's study (1978) suggests that this contrasting focus is not just a chance characteristic of two classrooms that happened to be studied by McDermott and Gumperz. Allington audiotaped oral reading segments of reading lessons with the best and the poorest readers in 20 primary classrooms in three school districts. He analyzed how the teachers responded to children's oral reading errors and found dramatic differences between the two reading groups across the 20 classrooms, differences which fit exactly the pictures described more qualitatively by McDermott and Gumperz. First, there was a difference in the rate of teacher corrections of the errors (68 percent of poor readers' errors were corrected, but only 24 percent of good readers' errors). Second, there were differences in the timing of the correction: teachers were more likely to interrupt poor readers at the point of error (88 percent of poor readers' errors vs. only 70 percent of good readers' errors) rather than waiting for the next phrase or clause boundary. Finally, there were differences in the cues provided by the teachers to help the children read the right word: for the poor readers, the cues were more apt to be graphemic/phonemic (26 percent vs. only 17 percent of the cues for good readers), while the cues for good readers were more apt to be semantic/syntactic (31 percent vs. 14 percent for poor readers).

The critical question raised by these reports is whether such differentiated teacher behavior is helpful or not. Marie Clay speaks from New Zealand of the goals of education as helping children become "self-improving systems" (personal communication). In other words, the goal is not to create children who never make mistakes, but rather children who have the capacity to notice their own mistakes and have strategies for correcting them. She has found that children in the first grade who do the most self-correcting are the children who become the better readers in late grades (Clay, 1973). Does being interrupted make self-correction more or less likely to develop? And if a cue from the teacher is needed, what kind of a cue should it be?

Allington's paper is titled, "Are good and poor readers taught differently? Is that why poor readers are poor readers?" The implication is clear that he believes it is possible (as do I) that these teacher behaviors to low group children may increase their problems in the long run. Prompt interruptions seem too much like a "law and order" approach to errors, as if the teacher is acting out of fear that the errors, like the children themselves, may get out of control. But just because it is the long run that counts, we need longitudinal studies that follow teacher behaviors and children's progress over time. (I am grateful to Rebecca Barr for this caution.) Only then can we separate constructive individualization from destructive bias.

Separation of Focus by Instructional Event

A very different kind of separation of foci of attention is by instructional events distributed throughout the school day. As part of a larger study of children's functional language competence in kindergarten and the primary grades conducted at the Center for Applied Linguistics, Griffin (1977) has described the set of events in which reading happens in one first grade classroom. These include: reading a recipe for hot cross buns that leads to a discussion of the meaning of "lukewarm" and experiments with feeling lukewarm milk later in the day; and story time when the teacher reads aloud, stopping frequently for talk about what is going to happen next. Griffin notices that comprehension skills of vocabulary and prediction were built in such nonreading group times of the day; whereas in the reading groups themselves, phonics was the overriding concern. This separation was so consistent that definite expectations about appropriate responses had been learned by the children. If the teacher shifted momentarily to a meaning cue during a reading group, the children were apt to respond with a phonic-based response anyway. For example:

> One child was reading, in a very halting style: "The pigeon flies far. . . ." He paused. The teacher repeated the sentence in a more fluent style with correct intonation and then gave the child a prompt: "The pigeon flies far. . . . Think. Think, what it would say! The pigeon flies far. . . ." A second child chimes in saying, " 'A' says it name. *Away*." (Griffin, 1977, p. 381)

In considering the merits of such a separation by instructional events, we must remember that it can only work in classrooms where there is a rich set of nonreading group events in which reading takes place. One tragic result of the pressures of the back-to-basic movements may be less time available for experiences like reading recipes and hearing stories in which vocabulary building and comprehension education can so meaningfully occur.

Separation of Focus by Language

In the most extreme case, a focus on meaning and a focus on phonics may be separated in a single classroom not only by reading events, but by languages as well. While this review does not attempt to cover research on learning to read in two languages, my own observations in a bilingual first grade classroom in Chicago are relevant here.[1] In the fall, the teacher's reading instruction was in Spanish only, using a traditional syllabic approach (ma me mi mo mu). Around Christmas, when she felt that the children's oral English had developed sufficiently, the teacher started a phonic-based reading program in English. As she described that attempt afterward, it just didn't work; the children resisted and she finally stoped. About that time, in a graduate class she was taking, she read Sylvia Ashton-Warner's *Teacher* and felt immediately that those ideas fit her philosophy and her children. The result was that by February, when I visited again, instruction in Spanish reading via syllables coexisted, for all children, with instruction in English reading via "key words." Moreover, the teacher was consistent in the cues she gave the children in the two contexts. In Spanish she focused their attention on the syllabic components on which they had had extensive practice:

Fe li pe   to ma   u na   fo to.

In English, she helped with a meaning cue: when a child couldn't read *butter* on his key word card, she asked, "What do you put on your toast?"

At first thought, such separation may seem detrimental to learning. Intuitively, it seems harder for children to get decoding and meaning cues together in a single mental act if they are taught separately in different parts of the school day, or even in different languages. On the other hand, maybe a clear and consistent focus of attention is helpful, especially for beginning readers, as long as both are included somehow, for all the children.

The Complexities of Reading Group Lessons

[. . .]

Reading groups as traditionally enacted in primary school classrooms are inherently complex in content and interactional structure because learning to read requires so many different kinds of learnings. We need interactional analyses of alternative organizations of reading events in which these learnings are separated or combined.

Heap (1978, 1979) is studying the "social organization of reading activities" in 20 classrooms. He has finished only one year of a five-year project, and so only preliminary reports are available. In these reports, he has identified three "social organizational problems" in primary grade reading instruction; two will be familiar to teachers, and all three raise important questions about the relationship between social organization and individual cognition.

The two familiar problems are problems in evaluating a child's response. On the one hand, a child's correct answer in a reading group lesson may be an artefact of other resources that the group provides. As Heap describes a specific example, "As a task organized to make reading skills observable and evaluable, the reading lesson provided an unforeseen resource, reading aloud, for a participant to continue to participate in the task" (Heap, 1979, p. 4) by answering comprehension questions even though her book had been closed. On the other hand, a child's reading errors may be due to obstacles created by that same reading group organization — for example, anxiety about the social performance of reading aloud in front of peers.

The third organizational problem is more complex. Here is Heap's example, from the comprehension section of a second grade reading group lesson after the first part of "Rumpelstiltskin" had been read:

Teacher	Now. Who helped Mineen?
Child	Rumpelstiltskin.
Teacher	Yeah the little man. We don't know his name is Rumpelstiltskin yet do we? The little man. Okay, what was the first thing the prince said — sorry, that the girl gave to Rumpelstiltskin, to the little man. We better call him the little man because we don't know really he's Rumpelstiltskin yet (Heap, 1978, p. 2).

The story was titled "Rumpelstiltskin"; the teacher had written that name on the board as a new vocabulary word at the beginning of the lesson; and she knew that several of the children had seen a movie version of the story the previous year. Yet she still corrected the child, and self-corrected herself, from saying "Rumpelstiltskin" to the vaguer "little man." As Heap says, it is only true that "we don't know his name is Rumpelstiltskin yet" in a very special sense: within the limits of and the terms of a convention, a game, that disengages reading and answering questions about that reading from everything else the child knows, from everything outside the boundary of the text itself.

These "organizational problems" that Heap has described are not unique to reading groups. Any exercise of any cognitive process — for us, as for children — takes place in some context: of particular task format, physical conditions, social organization, conventional rules, etc.; and characteristics of that context will contribute either supports or obstacles to the cognitive tasks performed within it. Cognition is always in some context; and it can't be taught or evaluated apart from some particular context either. (I am indebted to Michael Cole for many conversations on this point.) Because of the importance of reading groups as a context for both instruction and evaluation in the primary grades, we need to examine that context — and the "games" we play within it — with particular care. Yet because reading groups are so traditional and so familiar, that examination is especially hard for participants to do for themselves. To complete the circle back to the first study by Hess and Takanishi reported at the beginning of this review, classroom teaching must be considered as a complex orchestration of social life in which diverse individual cognitive processes can most effectively be developed, and we need to understand teaching from both the social and the cognitive points of view.

Peer Group Interaction in the Older Grades

This review has focused on learning to read in the primary grades — partly because of my own interests and experiences as a teacher (Cazden, 1976) and researcher with younger children, partly because most of the recent sociolinguistic and ethnographic research has focused on the primary grades as the place where children are first inducted into the school "culture" and where their academic "identities" are first formed. I assume that classroom interactions are not less important for reading instructions in the intermediate and secondary grades, but that the relevance takes different forms. One important form is the relationship between the instructional process and interactions among peers.

Consider the implications of just one study: Labov's research on the relationships among the incidence of nonstandard Black English (BE) dialect features, peer group membership, and reading failure (Labov & Robins, 1969; Labov, in press). Labov and his colleagues analyzed the incidence of BE features in the speech of black adolescents in fourth through tenth grade, identified the speakers as either central or peripheral members of peer group in the street culture by sociometric interviews and participant observation, and then correlated these data with performance on standardized reading tests.

One linguistic indicator of BE dialect is saying *have* for *has* in the third singular present. Labov (in press) reports the frequency of the standard form *has*, and then comments on the group differences:

> . . . club members used only 19 percent of the *has* form; the lames [isolates from the street culture] used 60 percent; and white working-class adolescents 100 percent. . . . These [dialect] differences are slight: they are small differences in the probability of a rule being applied. They reflect patterns of communication and ideology, but in no way could they be conceived of as the causes of differences in reading achievement.

Differences in reading achievement existed. All 46 club members, core participants in the street culture, reached a virtual plateau in reading achievement at the fifth grade level, while the 32 lames continued to progress, one-third of them at or above grade level. According to Labov, the dialect differences are not in themselves the cause of these reading problems; they are rather the indicators of group membership and of a value system that accompanies such membership that is in conflict with the school.

Support for Labov's argument comes from the co-occurrence of events around the fifth grade watershed year. This is the time when peer group formation differentiates members and lames in life on the street outside of school, and also differentiates their reading achievement within. More generally, fifth grade is the point at which, across the country, poor children's reading scores decline relative to their richer peers:

> A new state report [by the state legislative analyst's office] says the achievement gap between richer and poorer children in the California schools appears to be widening. . . . [this decline] seems to be part of a national trend, with the decline beginning around the fifth grade and increasing later. (*Palo Alto Times*, 11/3/78)

While these reading achievement data are usually interpreted in terms of the changing character of reading texts and tasks in the intermediate grades, it seems probable that, for some students, value conflicts accentuate the problem.

The connection between this research and the focus of this review comes in Labov's (in press) discussion of possible remedies.

> The techniques of learning and studying imposed by our schools are avowedly individualistic and competitive. Each student is expected to learn by himself, and as I noted at the outset, interaction in the classroom is fundamentally confined to dealing directly with the teacher. . . .
>
> The skills that are highly developed in vernacular culture depend upon a different strategy. Sports, formal and informal, depend upon close cooperation of groups. The same holds for music. . . . Individuals practice by themselves, but the major steps in learning are done in tempo with the group. . . .
>
> If we continue to repress vernacular culture, and try to extract one or two individuals from their cultural context, we will continue the pattern of massive educational failure that we now observe in the schools. The other route is to understand the interests and concerns of the youth who come to school and use that understanding in a positive way (Labov, in press)

This "positive way" will have to make possible less individualistic ways of learning to read, so that the power of group interactions can be used directly as contexts for learning. (See Steinberg & Cazden, in press, for one report of peer teaching in an intermediate grade.) Unfortunately, in discussions of teaching, the term "classroom interaction" has become limited to interactions in which the teacher is involved. We need to expand its meaning back to include all interactions in which learning takes place — not only with the teacher, but among students as well.

Notes

1. These observations are part of a research project on "The social and cultural organization of interaction in classrooms of bilingual children," supported by NIE grant 780099 to Frederick Erickson and Courtney B. Cazden.

References

Allington, E.L. *Are good and poor readers taught differently? Is that why poor readers are poor readers?* Paper presented at the annual meeting of the American Educational Research Association, Toronto, March 1978.

Au, K.H. Etr: Start with the experiences of the minority culture child. *The Reading Teacher*, in press.

Cazden, C.B. How knowledge about language helps the classroom teacher — or does it: A personal account. *The Urban Review*, 1976, *9*, 74–90.

Chall, J., & Feldman, S. *A study in depth of first grade reading: Analysis of the interactions of proposed methods, teacher implementation and child background.* Cooperative Research Project No. 2728, U.S. Office of Education, 1966.

Clay, M.M. *Reading: The patterning of complex behavior.* Auckland, N.Z.: Heinemann, 1973.

Griffin, P. How and when does reading occur in the classroom? *Theory into Practice,* 1977, *16,* 376–383.

Gumperz, J.J. Verbal strategies in multilingual communication. In *Georgetown University Round Table on Languages and Linguistics 1970.* Washington, D.C.: Georgetown University Press, 1972.

Heap, J.L. *Rumpelstiltskin: The organization of preference in a reading lesson.* Paper presented at the annual meeting of the Canadian Sociology and Anthropology Association, London, Ont., June 1978.

Heap, J.L. *The social organization of reading evaluation: Reasons for eclecticism.* Toronto: Ontario Institute for Studies in Education, April 1979.

Hess, R.D., & Takanishi, R. *The relationship of teacher behavior and school characteristics to student engagement* (Tech. Rep. No. 42). Stanford, Calif.: Stanford Center for Research and Development in Teaching, 1974.

Jordan, C., Weisner, T., Tharp, R.G., & Au, K.H. *A multidisciplinary approach to research in education: The Kamehameha Early Education Program* (Tech. Rep. No. 81). Honolulu: The Kamehameha Schools, 1978.

Labov, W., & Robins, C. A note on the relation of reading failure to peer-group status in urban ghettos. *The Teachers College Record,* 1969, *70,* 395–405.

Labov, W. Competing value systems in the inner-city schools. In P. Gilmore & A. Glatthorn (Eds.), *Ethnography and education: Children in and out of school.* Philadelphia: University of Pennsylvania Press, in press.

McDermott, R.P. Pirandello in the classroom: On the possibility of equal educational opportunity in American culture. In M.C. Reynolds (Ed.), *Futures of exceptional children: Emerging structures.* Reston, Va.: Council for Exceptional Children, 1978.

Piestrup, A.M. *Black dialect interference and accommodation of reading instruction in first grade* (Monographs of the Language-Behavior Research Laboratory No. 4). Berkeley: University of California, 1973.

Steinberg, Z., & Cazden, C.B. Children as teachers — of peers and ourselves. *Theory into Practice,* in press.

3.4 Learning About Psycholinguistic Processes by Analyzing Oral Reading

Kenneth S. Goodman and
Yetta M. Goodman

Source: Extracts from Goodman, K. S and Goodman, Y. M. (1977). 'Learning about psycholinguistic processes by analyzing oral reading' *Harvard Educational Review* **47**, No. 3, 317–32.

Over the past dozen years we have studied the reading process by analyzing the miscues (or unexpected responses) of subjects reading written texts. We prefer to use the word *miscue* because the term *error* has a negative connotation and history in education. Our analysis of oral reading miscues began with the foundational assumption that reading is a language process. Everything we have observed among readers from beginners to those with great proficiency supports the validity of this assumption. This analysis of miscues has been in turn the base for our development of a theory and model of the reading process.

In this paper we will argue that the analysis of oral reading offers unique opportunities for the study of linguistic and psycholinguistic processes and phenomena. We will support this contention by citing some concepts and principles that have grown out of our research.

We believe that reading is as much a language process as listening is. In a literate society there are four language processes: two are oral (speaking and listening), and two are written (writing and reading). Two are productive and two receptive. In the study and observation of productive language, we may analyze what subjects say or write; however, except for an occasional slip of the tongue, typographical error, or regression to rephrase, speech and writing offer no direct insight into the underlying process of what the speaker or writer intended to say. The study of receptive language — listening and reading — is even more difficult. Either we analyze postlistening or postreading performance, or we contrive controlled-language tasks to elicit reactions for analysis.

Reading aloud, on the other hand, involves the oral response of the reader, which can be compared to the written text. Oral readers are engaged in comprehending written language while they produce oral responses. Because an oral response is generated while meaning is being constructed, it not only is a form of linguistic performance but also provides a powerful means of examining process and underlying competence.

Consider how Peggy, a nine-year-old from Toronto, reads aloud. Peggy was chosen by her teacher as an example of a pupil reading substantially below grade level. The story she read was considered to be beyond her current instructional level. Peggy read the story hesitantly, although in places she read with appropriate expression. Below are the first fourteen sentences (S1–S14) from 'The man who kept house' (1964, pp. 282–3). In this and other excerpts from the story the printed text is on the left; on the right is the transcript of Peggy's oral reading.

text	*transcript*
(S1a) Once upon a time there was a woodman who thought that no one worked as hard as he did.	(S1b) Once upon a time there was a woodman. He threw . . . who thought that no one worked as hard as he did.
(S2a) One evening when he came home from work, he said to his wife. 'What do you do all day while I am away cutting wood?'	(S2b) One evening when he . . . when he came home from work, he said to his wife, 'I want you do all day . . . what do you do all day when I am always cutting wood?'
(S3a) 'I keep house,' replied the wife, 'and keeping house is hard work.'	(S3b) 'I keep . . . I keep house,' replied the wife, 'and keeping . . . and keeping . . . and keeping house is and work.'
(S4a) 'Hard work!' said the husband.	(S4b) 'Hard work!' said the husband.
(S5a) 'You don't know what hard work is!	(S5b) 'You don't know what hard work is!
(S6a) 'You should try cutting wood!	(S6b) You should try cutting wood!'
(S7a) 'I'd be glad to,' said the wife.	(S7b) 'I'll be glad to,' said the wife.
(S8a) 'Why don't you do my work some day?	(S8b) 'Why don't you . . . Why don't you do my work so . . . some day?
(S9a) 'I'll stay home and keep house,' said the woodman.	(S9b) I'll start house and keeping house,' said the woodman.
(S10a) 'If you stay home to do my work, you'll have to make butter, carry water from the well, wash the clothes, clean the house, and look after the baby,' said the wife.	(S10b) 'If you start house . . . If you start home to do my work, well you'll have to make bread, carry . . . carry water from the well, wash the clothes, clean the house, and look after the baby,' said the wife.
(S11a) 'I can do all that,' replied the husband.	(S11b) 'I can do that . . . I can do all that,' replied the husband.
(S12a) 'We'll do it tomorrow!'	(S12b) 'Well you do it tomorrow!'
(S13a) So the next morning the wife went off to the forest.	(S13b) So the next day the wife went off to the forest.
(S14a) The husband stayed home and began to do his wife's work.	(S14b) The husband stayed home and began to do his wife's job.

Peggy's performance allows us to see a language user as a functional psycholinguist. Peggy's example is not unusual; what she does is also done by other readers. She processes graphic information: many of her miscues show a graphic relationship between the expected and observed response. She processes syntactic information: she substitutes noun for noun, verb for verb, noun phrase for noun phrase, verb phrase for verb phrase. She transforms: she omits an intensifier, changes a dependent clause to an independent clause, shifts a 'wh-' question sentence to a declarative sentence. She draws on her conceptual background and struggles toward meaning, repeating, correcting, and reprocessing as necessary. She predicts grammar and meaning and monitors her own success. She builds and uses psycholinguistic strategies as she reads. In short, her miscues are far from random.

From such data one can build and test theories of syntax, semantics, cognition, comprehension, memory, language development, linguistic competence, and linguistic performance. In oral reading all the phenomena of other language processes are present or have their counterparts, but in oral reading they are accessible. The data are not controlled and clean in the experimental sense. Even young readers are not always very considerate. They do complex things for which we may be unprepared; and, not having studied the latest theories, they do not always produce confirming evidence. But they are language users in action.

Miscues and comprehension

If we understand that the brain is the organ of human information processing, that the brain is not a prisoner of the senses but that it controls the sensory organs and selectively uses their input, then we should not be surprised that what the mouth reports in oral reading is not what the eye has seen but what the brain has generated for the mouth to report. The text is what the brain responds to; the oral output reflects the underlying competence and the psycholinguistic processes that have generated it. When expected and observed responses match, we get little insight into this process. When they do not match and a miscue results, the researcher has a window on the reading process.

Just as psycholinguists have been able to learn about the development of oral-language competence by observing the errors of young children, so we can gain insights into the development of reading competence and the control of the underlying psycholinguistic process by studying reading miscues. We assumed that both expected and unexpected oral responses to printed texts are produced through the same process. Thus, just as a three-year-old reveals the use of a rule for generating past tense by producing 'throwed' for 'threw,' so Peggy reveals her control of the reading process through her miscues.

We use two measures of readers' proficiency: *comprehending* which shows the readers' concern for meaning as expressed through their miscues, and *retelling*, which shows the readers' retention of meaning. Proficient readers can usually retell a great deal of a story, and they produce miscues that do not interfere with gaining meaning. Except for S3, S8, and S9, all of Peggy's miscues produced fully acceptable sentences or were self-corrected. This suggests that Peggy's usual concern was to make sense as she read. In contrast, many nonproficient readers produce miscues that interfere with getting meaning from the story. In a real sense, then, a goal of reading instruction is not to eliminate miscues but to help readers produce the kind of miscues that characterize proficient reading.

Miscues reflect the degree to which a reader is understanding and seeking meaning. Insight can be gained into the reader's development of meaning and the reading process as a whole if miscues are examined and researchers ask: 'Why did the reader make this miscue and to what extent is it like the language of the author?'

Miscue analysis requires several conditions. The written material must be new to the readers and complete with a beginning, middle, and end. The text needs to be long and difficult enough to produce a sufficient number of miscues. In addition, readers must receive no help, probe, or intrusion from the researcher. At most, if readers hesitate for more than thirty seconds, they are urged to guess, and only if hesitation continues are they told to keep reading even if it means skipping a word or phrase. Miscue analysis, in short, requires as natural a reading situation as possible.

Depending on the purpose of the research, subjects often have been provided with more than one reading task. Various fiction and nonfiction reading materials have been used, including stories and articles from basal readers, textbooks, trade books, and magazines. Subjects have been drawn from various levels in elementary, secondary, and adult populations and from a wide range of racial, linguistic, and national backgrounds. Studies have been concluded in languages other than English: Yiddish (Hodes, 1976), Polish (Romatowski, 1972), and American Sign Language (Ewoldt, 1977). Studies in German and Spanish are in progress.

The open-ended retellings used in miscue analysis are an index of comprehension. They also provide an opportunity for the researcher or teacher to gain insight into how concepts and language are actively used and developed in reading. Rather than asking direct questions that would give cues to the reader about what is significant in the story, we ask for unaided retelling. Information on the readers' understanding of the text emerges from the organization they use in retelling the story, from whether they use the author's language or their own, and from the conceptions or misconceptions they reveal. Here is the first segment of Peggy's retelling:

um . . . it was about this woodman and um . . . when he . . . he thought that he um . . . he had harder work to do than his wife. So he went home and he told his wife, 'What have you been doing all day.' And then his wife told him. And then, um . . . and then, he thought that it was easy work. And so . . . so . . . so his wife, so his wife, so she um . . . so the wife said, 'well so you have to keep,' no . . . the husband says that you have to go to the woods and cut . . . and have to go out in the forest and cut wood and I'll stay home. And the next day they did that.

By comparing the story with Peggy's retelling and her miscues, researchers may interpret how much learning occurs as Peggy and the author interact. For example, although the story frequently uses 'woodman' and 'to cut wood,' the noun used to refer to setting, 'forest,' is used just twice. Not only did Peggy provide evidence in her retelling that she knew that 'woods' and 'forest' are synonymous, but she also indicated that she knew the author's choice was 'forest.' The maze she worked through until she came to the author's term suggests that she was searching for the author's language. Although in much of the work on oral-language analysis mazes are not analyzed, their careful study may provide insight into oral self-correction and the speaker's intention.

There is more evidence of Peggy's awareness of the author's language. In the story the woodman is referred to as 'woodman' and 'husband' eight times each and as 'man' four times; the wife is referred to only as 'wife.' Otherwise pronouns are used to refer to the husband and wife. In the retelling Peggy used 'husband' and 'woodman' six times and 'man' only once; she called the wife only 'wife.' Peggy always used appropriate pronouns in referring to the husband and wife. However, when cow was the antecedent, she substituted 'he' for 'she' twice. (What does Peggy know about the sex of cattle?)

Comparing Peggy's miscues with her retelling gives us more information about her language processes. In reading, Peggy indicated twice that 'said' suggested to her that a declarative statement should follow: One such miscue was presented above (see S2); the other occurred at the end of the story and is recorded below.

text	*transcript*
(S66a) Never again did the wood-man say to his wife, 'What did you do all day?'	*(S66b) Never again did the wood-man say to his wife, 'That he . . . what did you do all day?'*

In both instances she corrected the miscues. In the retelling she indicated that after 'said' she could produce a question: 'And then, from then on, the husband did . . . did the cutting and he never said, "What have you been doing all day?" ' Even though she had difficulty with the 'wh-' question structure in her reading, she was able to develop the language knowledge necessary to produce such a structure in her retelling.

It has puzzled teachers for a long time how a reader can know something in one context but not know it in another context. Such confusion comes from the belief that reading is word recognition; on the contrary, words in different syntactic and semantic contexts become different entities for readers, and Peggy's response to 'keep house' suggests this. In S3, where the clauses 'I keep house' and later 'and keeping house' occur for the first time, Peggy produced the appropriate responses but repeated each several times. In S9 she produced 'stay home and keep house' as 'start house and keeping house,' and she read the first phrase in S10 as 'If you start home to do my work.' The phrase 'keep house' is a complex one. First, to a nine-year-old, 'keep' is a verb that means being able to hold on to or take care of something small. Although 'keeping pets' is still used to mean taking care of, 'keeping house' is no longer a common idiom in American or Canadian English. When 'stay home' is added to the phrase 'keep house,' additional complexities arise. Used with different verbs and different function words, 'home' and 'house' are sometimes synonyms and sometimes not. The transitive and intransitive nature of the verbs as well as the infinitive structure, which is not in the surface of a sentence, add to the complexity of the verb phrases.

Peggy, in her search for meaning and her interaction with the print, continued to develop strategies to handle these complex problems. In S14 she produced 'stayed home'; however, in S35 she encountered difficulty with 'keeping house' once again and read 'perhaps keeping house . . . home and . . . is . . . hard work.' She was still not happy with 'keeping house.' She read the phrase as written and then abandoned her correct response. Throughout the story 'home' appears seven times and 'house' appears ten times. Peggy read them correctly in every context except in the patterns 'staying home' and 'keeping house.' Yet she continued to work on these phrases through her interaction with the text until she could finally handle the structure and could either self-correct successfully or produce a semantically acceptable sentence. Thus Peggy's miscues and retelling reveal the dynamic interaction between a reader and written language.

[. . .]

Parts and wholes

We believe that too much research on language and language learning has dealt with isolated sounds, letters, word parts, words, and even sentences. Such fragmentation, although it simplifies research design and the complexity of the phenomena under study, seriously distorts processes, tasks, cue values, interactions, and realities. Fortunately, there is now a strong trend toward use of full, natural linguistic text in psycholinguistic research. Kintsch (1974. p. 2) notes:

> Psycholinguistics is changing its character. . . . The 1950's were still dominated by the nonsense syllables . . . the 1960's were characterized by the use of word lists, while the present decade is witnessing a shift to even more complex learning materials. At present, we have reached the point where lists of sentences are being substituted for word lists in studies of recall recognition. Hopefully, this will not be the end-point of this development, and we shall soon see psychologists handle effectively the problems posed by the analysis of connected texts.

Through miscue analysis we have learned an important lesson: other things being equal, short language sequences are harder to comprehend than long ones. Sentences are easier than words, paragraphs easier than sentences, pages easier than paragraphs, and stories easier than pages. We see two reasons for this. First, it takes some familiarity with the style and general semantic thrust of a text's language for the reader to make successful predictions. Style is largely a matter of an author's syntactic preferences; the semantic, context develops over the entire text. Short texts provide limited cues for readers to build a sense of either style or meaning. Second, the disruptive effect of particular miscues on meaning is much greater in short texts. Longer texts offer redundant opportunities to recover and self-correct. This suggests why findings from studies of words, sentences, and short passages produce different results from those that involve whole texts. It also raises a major issue about research using standardized tests, which utilize words, phrases, sentences, and very short texts to assess reading proficiency.

We believe that reading involves the interrelationship of all the language systems. All readers use graphic information to various degrees. Our research demonstrates that low readers in the sixth, eighth, and tenth grades use graphic information more than high readers. Readers also produce substitution miscues similar to the phonemic patterns of text words. Although such phonemic miscues occur less frequently than graphic miscues, they show a similar pattern. This suggests that readers call on their knowledge of the graphophonic systems (symbol–sound relationships). Yet the use of these systems cannot explain why Peggy would produce a substitution such as 'day' for 'morning' or 'job' for 'work' (S13). She is clearly showing her use of the syntactic system and her ability to retain the grammatical function and morphemic constraints of the expected response. But the graphophonic and syntactic systems alone cannot explain why Peggy could seemingly understand words such as 'house,' 'home,' 'ground,' and 'cream' in certain contexts in her reading but in other settings seemed to have difficulty. To understand these aspects of reading, one must examine the semantic system.

Miscue analysis shows that readers like Peggy use the interrelationships among the grammatical, graphophonic, and semantic systems. All three systems are used in an integrated fashion in order for reading to take place. Miscue analysis provides evidence that readers integrate cue systems from the earlier stages of reading. Readers sample and make judgments about which cues from each system will provide the most useful information in making predictions that will get them to meaning. S2 in Peggy's excerpt provides insight into this phenomenon. Peggy read the sentence as follows: 'One evening when h . . . he came home from work he said to his wife I want you [two second pause] do . . . all day [twelve second pause].' After the second pause, Peggy regressed to the beginning of the direct quote and read, 'What do you do all day when I am always cutting wood?' Peggy's pauses and regression indicate that she was saying to herself: 'This doesn't sound like language' (syntactically unacceptable); 'this doesn't make sense' (semantically unacceptable). She continued slowly and hesitatingly, finally stopping altogether. She was disconfirming her prediction and rejecting it. Since it did not make sense, she decided that she must regress and pick up new cues from which to make new predictions.

In producing the unacceptable language segment 'I want you do all day,' Peggy was using graphic cues from 'what' to predict 'want.' She was picking up the syntactic cues from 'he said,' which suggested that the woodman would use a declarative statement to start his conversation. From the situational context and her awareness of role relationships, she might have believed that, since the husband was returning home from working hard all day, he would be initially demanding to his wife. When this segment did not make sense to Peggy, she corrected herself. She read the last part of the sentence, 'when I am always cutting wood,' confidently and without hesitation. She was probably unaware that 'when' and 'always' are her own encodings of the meaning. She had made use of all three of the cue systems; her words fit well into the developing meaning of the story; therefore, she did not need to correct her miscues. We believe that both children and adults are constantly involved in this process during their silent reading but are unaware that it is taking place.

There are many times when the developing meaning of a story is so strong that it is inefficient to focus on the distinctive graphic cues of each letter or each word. As long as the phrase and clause structure are kept intact and meaning is being constructed, the reader has little reason to be overly concerned with graphic cues. Peggy read 'day' for 'morning' in S13 and 'job' for 'work' in S14. These miscues have a highly synonymous relationship to the text sentence, but they are based on minimal or no graphic cues. In S38 Peggy indicated to an even greater extent her ability to use minimal graphic cues. Her prediction was strong enough; and she was developing such a clear meaning of the situation that 'in a flash' was an acceptable alternative to 'in a few minutes,' although she caught her miscue and corrected it.

Another phenomenon that exemplifies the interrelationships among the cueing systems is the associations readers develop between pairs of words. Any reader, regardless of age or ability, may substitute 'the' for 'a.' Many readers also substitute 'then' for 'when,' 'that' for 'what,' and 'was' for 'saw' in certain contexts. What causes these associations is not simply the words' look-alike quality. Most of these miscues occur with words of similar grammatical function in positions where the resulting sentence is syntactically acceptable. Differences in proficiency are reflected in the ways readers react to these miscues: the more proficient reader corrects when necessary; the less proficient reader, being less concerned with making sense or less able to do so, allows an unacceptable sentence to go uncorrected. This process can only be understood if researchers focus on how readers employ all the cues available to them. For too long the research emphasis on discrete parts of language has kept us from appreciating how readers interrelate all aspects of language as they read.

Sooner or later all attempts to understand language — its development and its function as the medium of human communication — must confront linguistic reality. Theories, models, grammars, and research paradigms must predict and explain what people do when they use language and what makes it possible for them to do so. Researchers have contrived ingenious ways to make a small bit of linguistic or psycholinguistic reality available for examination. But then what they see is often out of focus, distorted by the design. Our approach makes fully available the reality of the miscues readers produce as they orally read whole, natural, and meaningful texts.

Huey (1968, p. 6) once said:

> And so to completely analyze what we do when we read would almost be the acme of a psychologist's achievements, for it would be to describe very many of the most intricate workings of the human mind, as well as to unravel the tangled story of the most remarkable specific performance that civilization has learned in all its history.

To this we add: oral reading miscues are the windows on the reading process at work.

References

Ewoldt, C. (1977) 'Psycholinguistic Research in the Reading of Deaf Children', unpublished doctoral dissertation, Wayne State University.

Hodes, P. (1976) 'A Psycholinguistic Study of Reading Miscues of Yiddish-English Bilingual Children', Unpublished doctoral dissertation, Wayne State University.

Huey, E. B. (1968) *The Psychology and Pedagogy of Reading*, MIT Press (originally published 1908).

Kintsch, W. (1974) *The Representation of Meaning in Memory*, Hillsdale, N. J., Erlbaum Associates.

'The man who kept house' (1964) in J. McInnes, M. Gerrard and J. Ryckman (eds), *Magic and Make Believe*, Don Mills, Ont., Nelson.

Romatowski, J. (1972) 'A Psycholinguistic Description of Miscues Generated by Selected Bilingual Subjects during the Oral Reading of Instructional Reading Material as Presented in Polish Readers and in English Basal Readers', unpublished doctoral dissertation, Wayne State University.

3.5 W.H.I.C.H. Parental Involvement in Reading Scheme?
A Guide for Practitioners

Keith Topping

Source: Edited version of Topping, K. (1986) 'W.H.I.C.H. parental involvement in reading scheme? A guide for practitioners'. In *Reading* **20** No. 3, 148–156.

Developing parental involvement in children's reading is arguably one of the most explosive current areas of growth in education. Although many parents have always helped their children with reading at home, it is only really in the 1980's that attention has been paid to cultivating this habit in a large number of families, and to the precise nature of the advice which should be given to parents. Some schools are still reluctant to involve parents in this area, and yet the work in Inner London at the beginning of the decade showed quite clearly that whether parents hear their children read at home is the largest factor in children's reading progress, irrespective of socioeconomic status.

Since this seminal work, a great variety of different approaches to and techniques of parental involvement in children's reading have developed in a very short space of time. Given the rapid expansion of the area, it was inevitable that some débris would be sucked in by the slipstream. In education, "good ideas" are often seized upon before they have been properly evaluated. Furthermore, teachers are idiosyncratic, and like to leave their own personal stamp on their work. This sometimes means that a variation on, or individually customised version of, a tried and tested technique is used in preference to the original — from the outset. Where this occurs without careful evaluation, the teaching profession is rapidly beset by confusion over terminology, short-lived fads and fashions, and whole movements can lose credibility because of the failures of the few. The field of parental involvement in reading currently faces this danger — death by dilution. This guide may help to clarify the situation for practitioners, not least by making clear which techniques have been well evaluated and which have not.

Parent Listening

This technique is undoubtedly the simplest, consisting largely of rather more structured than usual attempts to encourage parents to "hear their children read", often from reading scheme books, and sometimes with a list of "dos and don'ts", and occasionally with a demonstration of good practice. Launching meetings are usual, books are commonly supplied and a simple recording system is likely to be used. Haringey and Belfield are the two best known projects which have used this method. Research indicates that the children usually progress at about twice normal rates (assuming normal progress to be one month of reading age in one calendar month). There is solid evaluative evidence from control group studies, e.g. Tizard *et al.* (1982) and Swinson (in Topping and Wolfendale, 1985).

Paired Reading — pure form

True paired reading was invented by Roger Morgan in the mid-seventies. It consists of training parents and children in (a) Reading Together, with a correction procedure, and (b) the child·signalling for Reading Alone,[1] with a correction and support procedure. Training is by verbal and written input, demonstration, practice and feedback. Children have a completely free choice of reading material. The evidence from research reports is that Paired Readers progress at about three times normal rates in Reading Accuracy and about five times normal rates in Reading Comprehension. There is now massive evidence from 100 published studies including baseline, control and follow-up data. Nor are these results confined to well resourced research projects, as in one Local Authority the technique has been used widely by over a third of the schools, and in a sample of 1,200 children average gains of 3.5 in Accuracy and 5 times normal in Comprehension have been found (Topping, 1986).

However, a variety of variants on this technique have been developed.

Paired Reading — Bryans *et al.* variant

This technique consists of the parent reading a passage from a book of controlled readability, the parent and child reading the same passage together with the parent supplying any error words, followed by the child re-reading the passage alone with the parent correcting error words. Evaluation results showed that reading Accuracy increased markedly but Comprehension less so. Spelling skills were found to improve, but not phonic skills. Three small-scale studies have been reported, including baseline data (Bryans *et al.* in Topping and Wolfendale, 1985).

Paired Reading — Young and Tyre variant

In this variation, the parent talks about the passage with the child, the parent reads the same passage to the child, the parent and child then read the passage together, the parent and child then read the passage together with the parent delaying on easy words for the child to say word first, and finally the child reads the passage aloud with the parent supplying error words. The readability of books is controlled. Only one study involving thirty children has been published. This showed twice normal rates of progress to be sustained over a whole year for both 'dyslexic' and 'remedial' children, who benefited equally in a controlled study. However, the effect of other inputs such as extra spelling and writing work and 'holiday schools' was not partialled out.

Paired Reading — Gillham variant

The parent and child talk about a short book, and then read it together with any error words repeated by the parent but not by the child. As the child becomes more confident, the parent lowers their voice and fades out, joining back in wherever the child encounters difficulty. This variation is intended for beginning readers, and is designed to be used with a published series of books of controlled readability, which are to be read and re-read up to eight times. This technique is clearly very different from the original form of Paired Reading even though the associated series of commercially produced books have Paired Reading prominent on the front cover. There is no adequate published evidence of the effectiveness of this technique.

Prepared Reading

The parent talks about the book, the parent reads to the child from the book, the child reads the same passage silently, asking about difficult words, and finally the child reads the passage aloud with prompting as necessary from the parent. This method was used by Young and Tyre (1983) as an extension to their variant of Paired Reading in their original project. However there is no published evidence on the effectiveness of the technique other than as a component of the work previously mentioned, and then only for some children.

Associated with the original form of Paired Reading are two quite different techniques known as Shared Reading.

Shared Reading — original version

Originating from Cleveland and intended to be a simpler form of involvement which might be particularly suitable for younger children, this technique merely consists of the parent talking about a book with the child, followed by the parent and child reading the book together. No correction procedure is specified, and the children are encouraged to read a wide range of books. The technique has now been used in a number of schools in its home area, but limited outcome data have been published. Nevertheless, evidence of substantial gains in reading accuracy is available for 125 children. Given the simplicity of the technique and its low requirement for intensive monitoring and follow-up, this represents a high degree of cost-effectiveness.

Shared Reading — Young and Tyre version

This technique is quite different to the original version, consisting of the parent reading a book to the child, followed by the parent reading a book to the child but stopping occasionally for the child to supply a contextually relevant word unaided, with the parent supplying the word if the child cannot. Described by Young and Tyre in a recent book (1985), there is as yet no published evidence on its effectiveness. Readers should note that neither of these techniques bears much relationship to Don Holdaway's class-based "Shared Reading" concept, using giant books for reading and language stimulation.

Relaxed Reading

The intention here is primarily to reduce parental anxiety, rather than to focus on any specific technique. The child reads aloud to the parent, with the parent supplying error words as necessary. At training meetings, individualised advice is given to parents, with much emphasis on devising methods which suit the interaction styles of individual families, within the context of a relaxed and positive atmosphere. A pilot study of twenty children indicated that Relaxed Reading can be as effective as Paired Reading, but replicatory research is needed before definite conclusions can be drawn. Further details will be found in Lindsay and Evans (1985).

Pause, Prompt and Praise

Originating from New Zealand, this technique consists of the child reading aloud to the parent from texts of controlled readability, with the parent pausing at error words to allow the child to self-correct. In the absence of self-correction, the parent gives a discriminatory prompt related to the nature of the error (semantic, visual or contextual). Praise is much emphasised. Training is by verbal and written instruction, practice and prompting. Children have been found to progress at about 2.5 times normal rates, on average. There are several well-structured research studies incorporating baseline data. The technique has demonstrated effectiveness used by peer tutors (Wheldall and Mettem, 1985), while the use of the technique with parents is reported by Ted Glynn in Topping and Wolfendale (1985).

Workshops

The series of workshops for parents run at the Fox Hill First School in Sheffield have been widely reported (e.g. by Smith and Marsh in Topping and Wolfendale, 1985). Parents come into school to make teaching materials suitable for use at home, to observe demonstrations of these in use and to practise with their own child. Parents are steeped in restricted aspects of the school's reading curriculum. There is a great deal of evidence of high take-up rates and considerable parental and teacher enthusiasm, but little more substantial research evidence of objective outcomes.

Family Reading Groups

Much more orientated to raising appreciation of literature than to developing reading skills, these groups are intended for parents and children to meet regularly to discuss and mutually review books that they have read. Favourites are recommended to others, and written reviews may be produced. There is no published evidence on effectiveness, although again take-up rates and participant enthusiasm tend to be high. Procedures are well described by Obrist (1978) in the U.K.R.A. pamphlet on the subject.

Token Reinforcement

These procedures were first developed in the early seventies for use with children with very severe reading problems. The child would read single words and/or sentences on flash cards to the parent and receive a point or token for each success. Points were subsequently exchanged for rewards or treats according to a pre-arranged 'menu'. Up to four times normal gains in reading accuracy have been found to accrue, but the gains tend not to continue when reinforcement ends, and the effect on comprehension is lesser. There are several studies with baseline and reversal data, e.g. Fry in Topping and Wolfendale (1985).

Precision Teaching

Precision teaching is an approach to evaluating the effectiveness of educational input rather than a method of teaching itself. Individualised behavioural objectives in reading are set for each child, and parents check performance on the prescribed tasks daily, charting the children's improvement in correctness and speed of response. Given that programmes are individualised, overall results are extremely difficult to summarise, but many case studies indicate effectiveness for children with difficulties. A large scale project is well described by Solity and Reeve in Topping and Wolfendale

(1985). Jordan (1985) summarises data on reading age gains showing children made three times normal gains in the short run with continued acceleration at five-month and eight-month follow-up, irrespective of whether they experienced Precision Teaching with their parents or with qualified teachers.

Direct Instruction

Direct Instruction procedures are characterised by highly structured scripted materials (e.g. D.I.S.T.A.R.), used in a prescribed sequence of 'lessons', involving rapid-paced interaction and much oral responding from the children. Practice and generalisation exercises are incorporated into the teaching sequence. Placement tests ensure children are started on the programme from "where they are at". Although the use of this material is not yet widespread in the United Kingdom, except in some special schools, it has been shown that parents can learn to use the procedures and kits. Indeed, a D.I. manual for parents has been produced in the United States, although it is not available in the UK as yet. Limited research evidence on its effectiveness when used by parents is available, but what there is suggests that gains of up to 2 times normal rates of progress are noted for children with severe reading difficulty. However, the numbers involved are often small and the D.I. component effects not well partialled out. Holdsworth (in Topping and Wolfendale, 1985) offers some data, but much further work is needed.

[. . .]

Teacher's Guide

Best Buy   — Paired Reading — Pure Form
Good Value   — Parent Listening
                  Pause, Prompt and Praise
                  Shared Reading — Original Version
Worth   — Token Reinforcement ⎫ for some children with
Considering   Precision Teaching   ⎬ particular difficulties
                  Direct Instruction   ⎭
                  Paired Reading — Bryans variant ⎫ for accelerating
                  Paired Reading — Young and Tyre ⎬ reading *accuracy*
                        variant   ⎭

All the other methods referred to in this guide need further methodical research study before any large-scale adoption by the teaching profession. Any practitioners who do experiment with them should evaluate the effects with care. At this stage of development of the field of parental involvement in children's reading, there is little point in inventing yet further techniques until we are clear about the effectiveness of the existing ones. Those determined to experiment could turn their attention to the relative effectiveness of different ways of *organizing* P.I.R. projects irrespective of technique.

Readers should note that it would be foolish in the extreme to attempt to establish a project solely on the basis of the very brief accounts of techniques given here. A great deal more background reading and careful preparation is required. Further information on a wide range of techniques and details of availability of kits and materials and other resources will be found in Topping and Wolfendale (1985), while the Paired Reading Training Pack and the Paired Reading Bulletins are available from the Paired Reading Project, Psychological Service, Oldgate House, Huddersfield HD1 6QW, West Yorkshire.

Note

1 'Signalling' — through the use of some agreed non-verbal sign, the child indicates to the adult that they feel able to continue reading aloud on their own [ed].

References

Gillham, B. (1986) Paired Reading in Perspective. *Child Education* **63**, 6, 8–9.

Jordan, A. (1985) *Parental Precision Teaching Project — Summary*. London. Department of Psychology, North East London Polytechnic.

Lindsay, G and Evans, A. (1985) Paired Reading and Relaxed Reading: A Comparison. *British Journal of Educational Psychology* **55**, 3, 304–9.

McCullagh, S. (1985) *Puddle Lane Reading Programme*. Loughborough. Ladybird books.

Obrist, C. (1978) *How to Run Family Reading Groups*. Ormskirk, United Kingdom Reading Association.

Tizard, J., *et al.* (1982) Collaboration between Teachers and Parents in Assisting Children's Reading. *British Journal of Educational Psychology* **52**, 1–15.

Topping, K. (1986) Kirklees Paired Reading Project: Second Annual Report. *Paired Reading Bulletin* No. 2, Spring 1986.

Topping, K. and Wolfendale, S. (eds.) (1985) *Parental Involvement in Children's Reading*. London, Croom Helm.

Wheldall, K. and Mettem, B. (1985) Behavioural Peer Tutoring: training 16-year-old tutors to employ the 'Pause, Prompt and Praise' method with 12-year-old remedial readers. *Educational Psychology* **5**, 1, 27–44.

Young, P and Tyre, C. (1983) *Dyslexia or Illiteracy? Realizing the Right to Read*. Milton Keynes. Open University Press.

Young, P and Tyre, C. (1985) *Teach Your Child to Read*. London, Fontana.

3.6 Leslie: A Reading Failure talks about Failing

Tony Martin

Source: Edited version of Martin, T. (1986) 'Leslie: a reading failure talks about failing'. *Reading*, **20**, No. 1, 43–52.

". . . our pupils' views of what learning to read means may have very little in common with our own." (Margaret Meek, Achieving Literacy)

In September 1982 a nine-year-old boy, I will call him Leslie, arrived at a middle school. He was unable to read. Now nearly three years later Leslie is on the verge of becoming an independent reader. He can manage the most difficult 'graded' books and many of the 'ordinary' paperbacks. (He has read Roald Dahl's 'The Magic Finger' and Joan Aiken's 'A Necklace of Raindrops' among others.) He is now attempting to bridge the gulf which separates him from other novels aimed at his age group and is reading Gene Kemp's 'The Turbulent Term of Tyke Tyler' to me. He is managing — with help.

In three years Leslie has changed from a boy who cried in lessons, 'couldn't do' any of the tasks asked of him, had nightmares about school (according to his mother) and had been diagnosed by a psychologist as 'worthy' of a place in Special School to a lively, cheerful twelve-year-old who sings in the school choir, puts a tremendous amount of effort into his school work and contributes well to life in the classroom.

The purpose of this article is not to chart Leslie's progress or to advocate any particular teaching approach to such children. Rather the aim is twofold.

Firstly it is to try and indicate what was actually going on inside the mind of a reading 'failure' as he failed. Leslie is now very articulate and agreed to talk on tape about what he remembered of his time at First School as he failed to learn to read. Most of the article is a transcript of that tape. While it is to be hoped that teachers have reasons for doing what they do when they 'teach' reading, we should remember that young children will also develop a view of the tasks they have to undertake. Most, of course, learn to read so quickly and automatically that they have little time to ponder, and worry, but the failure must surely wonder 'why?'

Secondly the comments of teachers taken from Leslie's record cards are given as an indication of the 'official' position. These are permanent statements which remain with Leslie for years. However when set against the real Leslie, thinking and feeling about what happened to him at

school they are shown to be (as are most such records?) somewhat inadequate and even misleading.

★   ★   ★

Firstly we read the summaries of Leslie's teachers. Under the heading
'Language' on his First School record cards is written:

September 1978 C.A. 5 +
Leslie enjoys participating in class discussions. He copies under the
teacher's writing and has made slow progress with reading probably due
to lack of concentration.

September 1979 C.A. 6 +
Leslie enjoys talking. He has begun to write a sentence or two of his own,
but with difficulty. We had to go back to the beginning of the reading
scheme earlier this year as Leslie had forgotten previous work. He is now
doing quite well with Ladybird 3b.

September 1980 C.A. 7 +
Ladybird 3b. Free writing is almost absent. 'Read, Write and Remember'
comprehension 2. Poor spelling — tries to be tidy. Contributes warmly
to class talks.

September 1981 C.A. 8 +
Leslie is still "struggling" with reading. He has finished 5a with a great
deal of help and has been transferred to Griffin Pirates to see if he can
achieve a little more success with these. He is very neat and can write a
page of free writing but this is lacking in interest. (Leslie actually spent
the last two years in the same class with the same teacher. He had been
considered too poor to manage in the top class.)

I do not intend commenting upon these statements. The layout of most
record cards demands brevity on the part of teachers and I will do no
more here than 'question their value.' The transcript which follows displays how little they tell us about Leslie, his problems and how best he
could be helped.

Question	Can you remember what your first day at school was like?
Leslie	Horrible — I was really scared — and — and the teacher asked me a question and I couldn't answer it and another kid put up his hand and he could and it made me go all funny — inside — and I was thinking 'oh I couldn't do that and he could'.
Q	What do you remember about reading?
L	They kept giving you books over — like — when you went onto a book, right, and you finish it and then you go onto another one the teacher would say if you can't read that one go back onto the other one — well I've read it again, so that's a bit boring — she never gave, you know, a different book,

a smaller one but a different story — she's just keeping giving you the same books.

Q   The same books over and over?

L   Yeah, till you got it right.

Q   How long did it take you sometimes to get it right?

L   Half a term! (laughs) Yeah because some of the words are hard see — she never gave me no easy ones. Like the pirate, the blue pirate and the red pirate, books like that — that's how it was — really scary.

Q   Why was it really scary?

L   Well the teacher — and you come in to school (laughs) . . .

Q   But the pirate books are quite hard. What were you reading before them?

L   I weren't reading anything — just words — on cards — only the words — letters and words — she used to put them up and you had to say it — and you had to say your alphabet and that —.

Q   So can you remember what the first book was you ever had?

L   (Pause) Peter and Jane. That was the first one I ever had. Peter and Jane and then I went onto the pirate ones.

Q   How many Peter and Jane books did you read?

L   (Pause) Twenty? About twenty. And this kid right, some kids had thick books and there's me with the book this thin (laughs) — really shy and every-thing — it's funny — and then I started to pick up and then I lost it again.

Q   What happened?

L   I stopped reading — like you say 'don't stop reading' well I stopped reading.

Q   Why?

L   Because I liked, I liked, I'd rather do drawing — because I do that lots at home — and I stopped reading.

Q   So you stopped reading at school and you just did drawing at school?

L   Not just — we did have to do a bit of reading.

Q   To yourself, to another child, to the teacher?

L   To the teacher most of the time — never by yourself — they never let you have a chance — they think, oh no, let's listen to him.

Q   Why didn't you ever read on your own do you think? Did the other children read on their own?

L   Yeah — and they just — and my brother has to read to the teacher as well — he has trouble with reading.

Q   So the ones who weren't very good read to the teacher a lot?

L   Yeah.

Q   So did you ever read on your own?

L   I did at home. We took the books home.

Q   Did you read to your Mum?

L   Teacher said read a page on your own, right, and read it over again to your Mum.

Q   So why did you stop reading?

L   It was boring just reading the same books.

Q   How good were you then?

L   Medium.

Q   So there *were* children worse than you?

L   Yeah — a few — a bit worse — that's what made me happy.

Q   But you came up here as just about *the* worst. So what went wrong?

L   *The* worst?!

Q   Well who was worse than you?

L   (Pause) Well, I'll tell you what happened. I was in this class, right, and I was moving up to the top class but they kept me in that same class. So I was in with the young ones. I was in that one class. I wasn't brainy enough to go up to the other classes.

Q   But you said you were in the middle so why didn't they put you up?
L   I dunno. That's what made me think. It was just the same — with the books and everything — I was two years in that class.
Q   And did that teacher do different work with you?
L   Yes — different work.
Q   And how did you do?
L   I did all right but then I just dropped down.
Q   Why?
L   (Pause) I can't think . . . Why did I drop down? Cos I didn't try.
Q   Why not?
L   Cos I didn't think I'd learn.
Q   What do you mean?
L   Well, I could read, but I wouldn't be able to do writing and spelling and that — so I just dropped down.
Q   So your reading was good enough for you to say you could read?
L   Well I was bad but they were easy books. They were easier.
Q   Did you think you'd be able to read hard books?
L   No! Not like the ones we read now — Dr. Dolittle — no, I never thought I'd be able to read one of those. So I had to go on with the easy ones.
Q   Were there children in your class reading the harder books then?
L   Yeah — pretty hard — *they* used to have library books and *I* used to have them little books from outside and I used to go out and pick them.
Q   Was that good, going out to get your books?
L   Yeah — cos some like me used to be out there as well, see, I can't remember their names and they just picked up. And there's me (laughs) — there'd be green and blue and red and I was always on orange . . . that's me.

*   *   *

Q   So you'd sit down to read and you'd come to a word that you couldn't read. Why couldn't you read it?
L   (Pause) That's a difficult thing!
Q   I know!
L   Why couldn't I read the word? I couldn't — I wouldn't — well, you know the alphabet, say u or v, well I'd say y or v — I wouldn't really know what those letters are — so I couldn't read it.
Q   But what about the teacher holding up the letter cards?
L   Cos all the class used to say it. And I used to join in with that — if they'd start to say 'cu' I'd say 'cu' really quickly (laughs).
Q   So she didn't do this work just with you ever?
L   No. Well there was sometimes three or two of us — and they'd say 'cu' and I'd say 'cu' (laughs).
Q   So you knew you didn't know it. Why didn't you tell the teacher?
L   She'd tell me off. I was scared — cos I didn't know that word.
Q   So you thought that if you knew your letters of the alphabet you'd be able to read?
L   Yeah. That's what I kept doing — trying on the letters — oh if I could get this alphabet I could read all the words. But I didn't — I couldn't read all the words.

Q	Even when you knew the alphabet?
L	Yeah.
Q	Why not?
L	Well, you know like 'ch' — you see, then I couldn't put them together — like 'eat' or 'home'. I couldn't put the letters together to make that word. So even when I learnt the alphabet I couldn't do it. Funny aint it really. (laughs)
Q	So what did you do then? Is that when you gave up or did you do something else?
L	I (pause) did something else. Learn the words. You know, if I was stuck on a word, teacher used to give us a book and we'd write it in and take it home to learn.
Q	Learn that one word?
L	Yeah.
Q	Did she give you any words like it? A pattern — cat, bat, sat?
L	Just that one word.
Q	So you had long lists of words to take home?
L	Yes.
Q	Did you find you could recognize them when they came up in the book?
L	Sometimes . . . Sometimes not.

*   *   *

Q	Why did you think you were learning to read?
L	Cos everybody else was. And when you grew up it would help you get a good job. So I could get a good job.
Q	Did you like books?
L	Yeah.
Q	Even though you found it difficult?
L	Yeah.
Q	Did you used to worry about your reading getting nowhere?
L	Yeah — if I went to visit a place — and someone might say 'read that to me' and you'd be scared and have to say 'I can't read it'. (laughs)
Q	Why couldn't you read it?
L	. . . it was smaller and I thought that's really hard cos they're smaller — and I thought I can't read that cos they're smaller — it made me think after a bit — they used to give us books with big words in and then the teacher gave me a book with smaller words in and I thought that was harder. Like in the newspapers — really small. (laughs) And the teacher gave it me and I took it home and I couldn't read it — so my Mum read it to me — so I took it back to school and told the teacher I couldn't read it and she heard me a bit and said I'd better go back to the little books — Peter and Jane. (laughs)
Q	Were they exciting books — Peter and Jane?
L	No — they like, went to the park! But there was this brilliant one which I read over and over again — when they went to the seaside.
Q	And you could read that?
L	No! My Mum told me some words and then I looked at the pictures — and then I got to know it and could read it over and over again . . . that's another thing — if a book didn't have pictures in I'd think, oh that's hard cos it's got no pictures in — it's all writing — no pictures to help me — cos that's how I used to do it — I used to look at the pictures first and then the

word — always the picture first cos I thought it would help me — sometimes it did but sometimes it didn't — like if in the picture they're playing
I'd see a word beginning with 'p' and I'd say 'playing'.

Q   What if you were wrong?
L   Then the teacher would tell me to write it in my book and take it home to learn.
            [...]

What Leslie was able to express on tape contains many ideas and feelings which could be discussed. I believe there are a few major points to be made.

Firstly some of what Leslie remembers is perhaps muddled and his teachers might object that it does not adequately reflect what they were trying to do. This would be perfectly correct but it does not invalidate the fact that this is how Leslie viewed the situation, muddled as it may be.

Secondly Leslie's *feelings* are shown to be so important. He was both bored and scared at different times (and no doubt pleased when he did achieve something). Indeed it appears to have been boredom associated with lack of success that resulted in him giving up.

Thirdly Leslie shows how young children constantly compare themselves with their peers. Leslie knew his books were 'easier' than those read by his classmates and knew that he was failing to progress. Was this a good or a bad thing? Can anything be done about it?

Most important of all though is the way in which Leslie fastened on to the teaching strategies employed in the classroom as he searched for a method of learning to read. This, I presume, is how most people would react. He could not read, the teacher was helping him in particular ways, so these ways must surely provide the key to his problem. He was tested on his letters and so tried to learn the alphabet — then he would be able to read. Words were broken into sounds — so learn the sounds and blends. Words he could not read were written in a book — learn these for success. Of course none of these on their own provided the answer. Reading does not work like that. So Leslie failed.

Lastly the transcript indicates so clearly how Leslie most certainly *was thinking* about his reading. He was not a blank slate on which the teachers could work but was trying to make sense of what was happening to him. In the end he could not do so, and therefore gave up.

It has taken three years to get Leslie going — to rebuild what had been knocked down. He has made exceptional progress, more so than some others who have been given similar help. Of course, the key is time; time with an interested, sympathetic adult and a good book. At the middle school we were able to provide such time (half an hour per day for Leslie plus back up work in class) and so he made progress. What a pity he could not have been given such 'time' earlier on. [...]

3.7 Comprehension: Bringing It Back Alive

Bob Moy and Mike Raleigh

Source: Moy, B. and Raleigh, M. (1980). 'Comprehension: bringing it back alive'. *The English Magazine*, Autumn, pp. 29–37.

PART ONE

Comprehension work of the passage-plus-questions kind holds a prominent place in examinations in English at 16. It has the majority of course books for English in an iron grip. In many schools it accounts for a substantial amount of the time spent in secondary English. But that is only a beginning. Passage-plus-questions is a regular primary school activity; and most secondary school worksheets and textbooks in all subjects fall under its spell sooner rather than later. Indeed some of its strongest advocates are enlightened Science or Humanities specialists, well into advanced curriculum development in other ways, inventive teachers with a sensitive feel for how children learn, but who, when they want their pupils to quarry written information, tend to see an individually worked comprehension exercise as the only way that things can happen.

Do-oodle-oo

Under such circumstances the children's response is interesting. In the more formal set-ups they rule their margins, put the date, get their heads down, and then chug steadily on in an orderly and tidy isolation. Or if it is one of those classrooms where children are encouraged to discuss things, they discuss, sometimes with passion, last night's TV or the merits of the latest style of boots while separately and competently transferring from worksheet to exercise book those bits of information which, if they have carried out properly the minor surgery required, will prove to their teacher that they have grasped the workings and significance of the Arkwright loom. Look at the books a week later and you can't help but be impressed by the industry of children and teacher alike; by and large, the majority of the class have got three ticks for every cross.

But what have they understood? And how did they feel about what they were doing? Talk with them about it and the second question is soon answered: they were quietly and acceptably bored. They are not pressing for any changes, for they like the certainly of an undemanding regime they understand; but almost without exception you'll be lucky to find a single child prepared to enthuse about what they've been doing. And the moment you begin to discuss the answers they've written you discover that many of those marked 'wrong' were merely badly expressed, while many of those marked 'right' merely involved the deft fielding and return of formulations borrowed from the original that fall apart and reveal major misconceptions when you talk them through. The whole slow-burning, time-consuming exercise seems simply to have enervated the pupil while misinforming the teacher; it has allowed another piece of schoolwork to become a half-hearted ritual, one in which the pupil satisfies not a personal curiosity but an institutional call to produce. David, a second year boy, put it this way after completing a passage-plus-questions stint in Geography:

> I just wanted to put anything down . . . because I wanted to finish . . . It was not exactly boring, it was quite good, but . . . still boring. When you're on your own you go . . . you go . . . you look at the thing and you say "Oh I've done that — doodle-oodle-oo — put any answer — doodle-oodle-oo."

Comprehension exercises are not biting; most pupils toss them off with a minimum of commitment. The Doodle-oodle-oo Technique rules.

The pupils' prime concern (keeping a low profile and meeting the quota) is also the teacher's. But the teacher often has another major concern: getting full sentence answers. As he or she tours the classroom a single teaching point is repeated again and again: 'Never start an answer with "because".' There is no certainty, however often the message is repeated, that it will be acted upon. What is certain is that it will take the best part of an hour for the average pupil to answer 10 fairly simple questions on a passage of a few hundred words. The emphasis on a formal precision of reply will ensure that only undemanding questions can be. posed, and the choice of writing as the medium of exchange will mean that few questions can be put and that any feedback as to how they have been managed will be minimal, delayed for anything up to a week, and usually given in the pupils' absence.

The Glombots

But perhaps all this doesn't matter: perhaps it works. The children do seem slowly to learn things. But do they learn anywhere near as much as they might? To what extent are comprehension exercises responsible for the learning that does go on? Is the information picked up integrated fruitfully with what is already known? To answer these questions try this history comprehension exercise for size. It's a short passage on the Glombots. You won't have heard of them before, because we've made them up. That puts you where the pupils are when they are expected to break a bit of new ground. [. . .] Write careful answers to the questions set. Aim for a distinction. Don't start an answer with because. You'll know you haven't understood a thing, and you'll know that we'd know it too, but play your cards right and we think you'll be able to fix it so that, whatever you know we'd know, you'll know we'd have to give you full marks. Then try it on a range of your pupils. Mark their scripts. We think you'll get a whole range of scores and we think you'll suspect that you and all of them understood equally little of what it was all about. So where are the differentials coming from? And how often is something of the same kind happening as we use comprehension exercises to settle the rank order of our classes for their ability to understand what's there in a piece of writing?

By 1740 Glombots were bardoodling fludgerlistically throughout the scallerbars. Though some were oddlebug, the glotterest couldn't read or write. Muchupper, being petergustic murds, they seemed unable plesterly to dunk the likely modalbags of their mastions. On the other hand, despite their quite understit astulance for motropping violence, the glotterest wished to estocate only peaceful changes through moldergustic tropartion and breadalbation. In 1742 the murds squinched the strink in one of the most flugelbar and antimoldergustic dinkums that history has ever seen.

1. What were the Glombots doing in 1740 and where were they concentrating their attentions?
2. How well were they succeeding? Were people right to give them an astulance for motropping violence?
3. Mention one thing all Glombots had in common and two ways in which some Glombots were different from others.
4. Late in 1740 a full assembly of all Glombots voted on whether they favoured achieving change by detropartion. What do you think their decision was?
5. Ordinary men would have dunked the modalbags of their mastions. Why didn't the Glombots?
6. Which of the following statements are true?
   (i) Most Glombots approved of tropartion.
   (ii) When Glombots bardoodled they almost always fludged it.
   (iii) The average Glombot was petergustic and oddlebug.
   (iv) The Glombots were wrong to dunk the modalbags of their mastions.
7. Imagine you are a Glombot. Write a few sentences telling us in your own words what you can about yourself and what you do.

The traditional model of comprehension

We were cheating a bit with the Glombots. But how much? Some parts of some standard comprehension exercises may offer helpful reading experiences to some of our pupils some of the time. But how many and how often? Is the unreal busy-work element which underlies even the best-designed of these exercises ever really transcended? We doubt it. Because at their heart there lies a false and unhelpful model of what reading, learning and knowing is all about.

This model assumes that knowledge has an objective existence of its own: that, given proper skills on both sides of the transmission a person who has it can transmit it intact and unchanged to any number of others, while a third person can, from a distant vantage point, set up, supervise and assess the transmission. It further supposes that an effective medium for this transmission and for rendering proof of its reception is the written word. It suggests that the written messages concerned are self-sufficient and canonical encapsulations of meaning, and that they are therefore best transmitted and received by writers, readers and assessors working alone.

To put it in more everyday terms: this model assumes it reasonable to expect young readers to work alone to get meaning from texts, answering in writing written questions set in advance by an unknown adult and marked later in the reader's absence by a teacher, one of whose prime concerns in assessing the response will be to receive a fully-formed reply, properly constructed, properly punctuated and spelled, and neatly handwritten against the clock.

[. . .]

Formulating meaning

The case against this traditional model of comprehension should by now be old hat. It bears repeating simply because the evidence is that the practice which the traditional model gives rise to is still widespread. We can begin the case against with a reminder that, as the Bullock report has it, 'it is a confusion of everyday thought to regard knowledge as something that exists independently of someone who knows' or to think that 'learning begins and ends with instruction'. In other words, those holy texts, alone with which the young reader is to be locked, are inert, empty and meaningless 'until brought to life afresh within the knower by his own efforts.' Bringing them alive is 'a formulating process and language is its ordinary means'; and every 'formulation' is a unique affair even when the same person is regenerating it from one occasion to the next. This is what forges a mass of disparate facts into an item of 'comprehension' (etymologically a 'grasping together'). The range of legitimate meanings that can be built around a text, not to mention a young reader's ability to build them, is potentially endless — providing that the quality of the exploration is high. What can be expected to ensure that? In the words of Bullock again: 'In order to accept what is offered we have to find an individual context for a new piece of information and forge the links that will give it meaning . . . Something approximating to "finding out for ourselves" needs therefore to take place if we are to be successfully "told" . . . This is a task that we customarily tackle by talking with other people.'

Objection: *Well what you've just said in the last paragraph sounds all very fine,* *but really it's a bit heavy as a description of what you have to do when you read a simple sentence like: 'By 1740 Glombots were campaigning ineffectually throughout the conurbations.' There's a couple of words there which might cause problems; but providing you know the words, the sentence carries a clear meaning. You just read it: you don't agonize over 'formulating' it.*

Well . . . any description of what goes on in a reader's head — like any description of a complex mental process — sounds a bit heavy set against the speed and facility with which an accomplished reader manages to comprehend. [. . .] A small experiment: monitor your own mental behaviour as you read the next paragraph: what do you actually *do.*

Most recent researchers into reading would stand with Bransford, Barclay and Franks in denying that 'sentences carry meanings'. Instead they would insist that 'people carry meanings and linguistic inputs merely act as queues which people can use to recreate and modify their previous knowledge of the world.' As Husserl says, the reader's mind is needed to 'give shape to the interaction foreshadowed by the sentences.' Thus statements 'only take on their full existence in the reader' (Poulet) and 'the same utterance may be understood differently as a function of the different cognitive contributions that different listeners make' (Bransford and McCarrell). This of course reflects the inevitable situation in cognition and perception in general: 'To perceive, a beholder must create his own experience; without an act of recreation the object is not perceived' (Dewey). But it applies with particular force to the perception of meanings symbolized at several removes through printed laundry. Iser postulates the existence in every piece of writing of two different notional parts: the 'written' text (i.e. everything that is there 'in the print') and the 'unwritten' text (what the current reader must be able to provide from a personal store of past experience and previous understanding). Until these two are brought together, even the simplest 'text' ('The Glombots sat on the mat and reconsidered their strategy') does not exist except as marks on a paper sheet; as each unique marriage of written and unwritten text is accomplished, the piece of writing becomes meaningfully extant for a while.

If we're right, we think that you conducted a lightning-quick conversation with yourself to make sense of that last paragraph, that you made a *route* out of the signposts on the page, using your prior knowledge and your expectations of what was likely. So that last paragraph lives (briefly) in your head, not on the page. Otherwise, (among other things) how is it that it 'makes sense' despite the fact that mis-prints offer to make complete non-sense of two sentences? To do this job of making sense you performed a series of extremely complex and sophisticated mental operations which are quite impossible to track — and quite impossible to replicate (you couldn't read the same text again).

It is also likely that you're not quite sure that all the ends are tied up in that paragraph (the quotation from Husserl, for example — does that mean . . .?). You might worry, that is, about the comprehensiveness and the coherence of the meaning you have built. Most of the time we put up with that kind of worry. If we're bothered about it, we tend to have another go at building the meaning, this time making the 'conversation' slower and more deliberate. A natural extension of that process is to talk to others who have read the same text. That is mere commonsense. The commonsense hunch is that the text that several readers build together has every chance of being so much richer, fuller and more 'accurate' than the text which each would build alone.

The implications of commonsense

Unfortunately commonsense tends to desert us all faced with an hour with the 3rd year, and with a feeling that we ought to be doing something about their reading. What are the implications of commonsense for work in the classroom when we explicitly focus on the business of comprehension? Some obvious reforms spring at once to mind. First, for the pupils, a real shift in where they feel the initiative to be, from a position where they must tackle alone someone else's questions, for external assessment by a third person and at a later date, to one where pupils generate their own queries and evaluate their own solutions collaboratively and on the spot. Second, for the teacher, a radical shift of role, from one of puppeteer and assessor to one of consultant on call. Third, for the writer of the text, a radical shift of status, from that of distant transmitter to perfect and holy messages to that of a provider of raw material which can give no more than implicit hints about how it might be processed or about the answers that might legitimately be arrived at. Altogether, a shift from teachers interrogating pupils to pupils interrogating texts.

But for this they need the tools — which means a shift in the kind of language use we are prepared to encourage in our classrooms when doing comprehension work. From a premature insistence on the 'hard' language of the 'finished' written answer we need to shift to making generous preliminary houseroom for the 'soft' language of the tentative, unfinished, oral speculation. The formulating process feeds on an untidy, often 'incorrect', shy kind of language which we have traditionally shooed out of our rooms whenever serious work is in hand. But for children — as for us much of the time — the interior monologue of thought must be fed by the external dialogue of talking. The necessity of chat should be celebrated and undress forms of language given an honest educational name. Classrooms ought to be the safest place in the world to make a mistake, as the HMI survey *Aspects of Secondary Education in England* points out in its own stately way:

> In discussion with teachers and with heads, it was clear that at the centre of many difficulties and differences of view there lies a confusion between two functions of language — the first as a communication of what has been learned and the second as part of the activity of learning itself. Concentration on the first of these at the expense of the second, which is often more important, may obscure stages of misunderstanding, approximation and correction through which the learner often needs to pass and also may reduce the pupils' engagement with learning. For those

who find the art of abstraction difficult (and even for some who do not) the use of language to explore an experience often reveals what can be discovered in on other way. A change of emphasis from language as evidence of learning achieved to one used in the process of learning is needed ... At present talking and listening by pupils are not fully exploited. They need more experience as participants in genuine discussion, in which they attend to the contributions of others, learn to discriminate between the relevant and the irrelevant and to expand, qualify and range in and around a subject.

What the HMI's have to say about the pupils' need to become 'participants in genuine discussion' in which they 'range in and around a subject' applies to school learning in general; but it also brings up another difference of assumption between the old model of comprehension and what would need to be the new. The old model assumes that for those with the requisite reading skill the single proper meaning of a text could be neatly peeled off by any number of readers, like so many exact copies humming from the master sheet on a duplicating machine. Comprehension is seen as a right or wrong, once and for all affair: you've either got it or you haven't. The new model, on the other hand, would see comprehension as an ever-sharpening process of emergent understanding. The metaphor would not be the single pass through a duplicating machine but (borrowing from Jimmy Britton) a prolonged stay in the developing tray, where first a few key highlights might be brought up and then, as the work continued, more and more detail and interconnections made manifest. As understandings 'emerged' the look of things could be expected to change quite radically; far from being failures many early distortions and false emphases would be necessary steps on the road to eventual fullness and clarity. Meanings, then, would need to be built over a period of time and to be built piecemeal.

Back down the tunnel: three new ways

Dissatisfaction with passage-plus-questions work — what you might call the 'authorized version' — is of course not new. Its shortcomings were seen long ago and a number of attempts have been made to do something about them. These attempts at reform — new ways, as it were, for teachers to interrogate pupils rather than a determination to help pupils to interrogate texts — have resulted in three kinds of 'revised version': (1) MCT, i.e. multiple-choice technique; (2) 'the Box' (or 'Reading Laboratory'); (3) 'the Hierarchy', i.e. systematized exercises to give structured practice along a planned route through the labyrinths of various taxonomies of reading purposes and strategies. It is our belief that although these three forms of the revised version may look to be something new (especially when they are combined, as they sometimes are) they are no more than mutton dressed as lamb. To some pupils they may come as a welcome relief from the authorized version, but their early promise soon proves illusory; and this is because they are based on the same false model of what comprehension involves as the straightforward passage-plus-questions version. Perhaps a closer look at each of them would reveal why.

Multiple choice

Multiple choice is not without its strength. It does at least have the grace not to equate understanding texts with the ability to write full sentence answers not beginning with 'because'. Pupils are thus spared the indignities of the written-elocution exercise, and a lot more comprehending can be tackled in a given time. What's more, many pupils find its puzzle-game element motivating — at least for a while. But that's about it. The case against is quite simple: MCT runs against the grain of all natural reading practices. The central fact in all real reading is that readers have the freedom and responsibility for generating their own understanding; in multiple-choice exercises a third person elbows the reader out of the driving seat. In the sentence-answer version readers are at least free to shape their own answers; here even this minor initiative is taken away and they are left with is a forced choice from a handful of prefabricated responses which they know to have been engineered so that only one is allowable. The rules do not countenance participation. Again, real reading involves a process (however rapid) of emergent understanding, one in which the embedded ideas 'come up' differentially at their own rate and as a shifting web of interrelationships forms. In multiple-choice exercises possible meanings have no natural seniority: they leap full-grown and simultaneously, the unnatural progeny of the examining mind; one among them is the true prince. This puts readers to unnatural troubles: the unnatural trouble of having to eliminate false possibilities that would never have occurred to them in the normal way; and the unnatural trouble of shedding silly readings seductively phrased with which they would not have ensnared themselves. Under the circumstances readers do what they can: they develop strategies to bring success, but these strategies have precious little to do with reading in the normal sense. They include, for example, sleuthing: establishing that a given answer must be right because the others are wrong.

The last two snags are even more important. Even more than with the authorized version, multiple-choice lends itself to a nit-picking focus on vocabulary items, the exact meaning of knotty phrases and the checking up on minor items of formal logic. What it resists is application to the broader, more complex, more comprehensive issues that make the passage as a whole cohere and are what a real understanding of it would have to be about. Finally, multiple-choice presents the central problem of all traditional comprehension exercises writ large: it doesn't build reader ease and confidence by encouraging a symmetrical social relationship between readers and texts. Instead it spreads suspicion and distrust: the readers know they are on test; that attempts are being made to queer their view of things; that appearances are going to be deceptive; that watchfulness rather than engagement is what is required.

The box

The second form of the revised version is the box of reading cards, also known for some reason as a 'Reading Laboratory' or 'Workshop'. This system stands or falls by some simple, well-meant and misguided notions, principal among them being the idea that comprehension work should be 'individualized' and 'self-scored'. To solve the classroom management problems that this involves the texts have to be bland and lacking any rich but awkward resonance, while the scoring system must be reduced to a rigid right-or-wrong polarity. Thus what the pupils are given to comprehend is mostly a Readers Digest type of non-fiction prose, and the way they do it is often through multiple choice. Into the bargain they will spend about two-thirds of their time on busy-work ('working with words' and so on) which sometimes has nothing to do with the passage and always has nothing to do with comprehension. Not only this: the box, stepping neatly between the teacher and the pupils, deskills the teacher on the spot, leaving him or her merely running errands for the teacher-in-the-box. The real teacher scurries about, sustaining morale when 'working with words' gets really arcane, making sure that the disillusioned don't cheat, cheering up the disgruntled (who dispute the answer-sheet), and worrying about those gong-hunting record-breakers and their increasingly inflated views of their own powers as they race at breakneck speed through material which the Box's scientific placement test insists is at their proper level.

This is unfair: for the Box is nothing more than passage-plus-questions-plus-multiple-choice (plus-working-with-words) in a box. But it is the year of the Box: in 1979 *The Effective Use of Reading* reckoned to have demonstrated that reading labs do work, using a most disarming circular argument. That is, they work provided you use them for something like 50 of your available English lessons in the Autumn term, and provided that you measure progress by individually-worked sentence-answer comprehension tests (i.e. tests with the same questionable view of reading as the Box). To be obvious: suppose the control group, instead of having none of the extra reading lessons which the SRA group had, had spent the same time reading and discussing the little library of real books which the small fortune needed to purchase a Box would have paid for. And suppose, by way of a test at the end, the pupils in each group had been asked to chat informally about the reading they'd done and what they'd gathered from it. (There must be a reason why heavyweight reading research is always undertaken by pre-test/post-test methods originally designed for investigating grain yields at an agricultural research station.)

But is there nothing than might come of the high hopes that first encounters with a Box can induce in pupils and teachers alike? For the initial reaction of most children is positive. We believe that this is because — and this is sobering — compared with most classroom activities working from a reading lab at least gets a live teacher off their backs and out of their hair. Though nothing has really changed, the initiative feels as if its passed to them and it looks as if someone is paying them the compliment of trusting them to work by themselves. This aspect of working from a reading lab, however illusory it will turn out in the end, is worth remembering and worth trying to establish for real.

The hierarchy

The Box shares with multiple choice and the authorized version the same answer to the question: what is progress in comprehension? The answer they propose is that progress means the reader is able to handle longer passages, with more difficult argument and bigger words; the proof of progress is the ability to answer more ticklish questions or make more ticklish choices. But how do you actually get from Red to Brown, from Book 1 to Book 5, from the 200 words in largish print on 'Spending Your Pocket Money' to the 800 words in smallish print on 'Violence on Television'? The 'O' level passage is the high tide mark — but you can't see the sea rise. The comprehension-in-stages books are no help either: after mastering the last passage in Stage 3 (on the growth in popularity of budgerigars as pets, with a paragraph on how to keep them), you're faced with the first passage in Stage 4 where the class is expected to untangle a chunk of Siegfried Sassoon's diary. (You can't blame it all on the summer holidays: they just don't seem to have made the leap.)

The Hierarchy offers some hope here. It is particularly attractive to those who feel that somehow readers are allowed to get away with it once they have been awarded the decoding ribbon, once they have topped the scheme and been allowed to read books. The Bullock report called attention to the need to focus on what it calls 'higher order reading skills'. This was a cue for a sudden rush of professionalism which makes the old business of any old passage and any old questions seem primitive. The sources are mainly American. Comprehension is newly mapped. Barrett's taxonomy of reading skills is photocopied and becomes popular: literal understanding, inference, evaluation and appreciation (with sub-divisions). New techniques are found especially useful for dealing with factual and discontinuous material: surveying, skimming, scanning, attending to signal words, location skills, extracting, reciting, summarising, recording (and, all together now, SQ3R). We have attention to varieties of forms of rhetoric and modes of presentation. We have materials here for what Bullock calls (and calls for) 'advanced reading qualifications'; comprehension is technicized, just as learning to read has been. And materials also for a programme of reading instruction: a Hierarchy (indeed a matrix) of separable, teachable skills calling for development work at different stages, individually tailored for the individual reader.

This gives, en passant, new life to the Box; new laboratories are envisaged (and some old ones relabelled) to take readers all the way up one spiral or another. But there are also new Books (10 new series since 1976 for example; we hope to look more closely at some of them in Part 3 of this article) which aim to teach 'the skills of literal comprehension, deduction, evaluation etc' or to enable pupils 'to study and to practise the more advanced skills they require for independent reading'.

The problem is that the teaching approach which this kind of mapping of comprehension implies just leads us back down the tunnel of the authorized version by another route. Whatever value there may be in classifying comprehension in these ways, they wouldn't seem to tell us how readers learn to do these things. But there is another reason why the technicization should be resisted. Here, whatever harm *The Effective Use of Reading* did in giving an unwarranted puff to reading labs is redeemed by the hard look they took at the attractive 'modern' notion that comprehension is an agglomeration of separately drillable sub-skills in a neat and structured hierarchy. As the Project team explain, they began with a belief in just this notion and expected their research to prove it correct. In the event it did the opposite:

> We conclude that individual differences in reading comprehension should not be thought of in terms of a multiplicity of specialized aptitudes. To all intents and purposes such differences reflect only one general aptitude: this being the pupil's ability and willingness to reflect on whatever it is he is reading.

If comprehension cannot in fact be broken down into a multiplicity of separate skills, then to set up a teaching programme, however well-intentioned and well-designed, which assumes that it can, will only distort and overcomplicate the job. The Hierarchy, that is, gets in the way.

The old and new models: a summary

Some kind of summary at this point would be helpful. We compare below the answers which our two models of comprehension — the old (which includes the three forms of the revised version, MCT, the Box and the hierarchy) and the new — might be expected to adopt to some key questions about the reader and the text.

1. What can be hoped for when the comprehension process is successful?
Old Model: A quick, neat, accurate transfer of information.
New Model: A slow and awkward emergence of understanding.
2. What is the proper way to work?
Old Model: Alone.

New Model: Collaboratively.

3. How do readers see their situation?

Old Model: They are on test.

New Model: They are involved in a dialogue — one with another and all with the writer.

4. What is the key ability required?

Old Model: Skill in writing 'correct' and fully finished formal answers.

New Model: The knack of sensitive and intelligent oral speculation.

5. What is the proper use for half-formed intuitions?

Old Model: Keep them in your head till they are either eliminated or properly 'finished'.

New Model: Offer them raw to the group for sifting, refining and extension.

6. What will credit be given for?

Old Model: Simply for what finished conclusions you arrive at.

New Model: To some extent for the finished conclusions you arrive at but much more for the thoroughness and quality of your exploration.

7. What is the proper attitude to 'wrong' answers?

Old Model: They are useless and unacceptable; keep them under your hat if you can.

New Model: Not easy to see what would be meant by such a term. At the very least they could have a fruitful short or medium term use in opening up new possibilities. Bring them out unblushingly.

8. Whose meanings are they and where will they be found?

Old Model: The author's, and in the text; a single meaning, fixed at the point of writing, which can be got out in the same state by all readers with developed skills. The cleverer two readers are the more their interpretations will be likely to converge.

New Model: The readers, and in their heads; a range of possible meanings to be built anew each time in response to the constraints signalled in the print and according to the thinking of each new reader. The cleverer two readers are the more likely their interpretations may fruitfully diverge.

9. What are the social relationships involved?

Old Model: Assymmetrical — a writer and testing teacher in charge, pupil under interrogation.

New Model: Symmetrical; writer, teacher and readers working on equal terms to generate 'thinking under the influence of print'.

10. Who legitimates your efforts and when?

Old Model: The examining teacher after the work is over.

New Model: Your fellow readers as you go along — an easier response to assimilate and available on the run to help you trim your meanings as you go.

PART TWO

We outlined in the preceding section the features of the new model of comprehension and their implications in general for classroom work. The next section is concerned with three things: first, the kinds of texts which classroom work might focus explicitly on; second, with the issue of how much time explicit classroom work on comprehension might usefully take up; and third, with practical classroom strategies for comprehension work.

Blurring distinctions

Before thinking about a programme of classroom work on comprehension it may be useful to blur some old distinctions. There are three distinctions we would want to avoid: first, between 'learning to read' and 'reading'; second, between 'reading' and 'comprehension'; and, third, between 'comprehension of literature' and 'comprehension of non-literary material'. These old distinctions, we would say, tend to over-complicate teachers' attitudes to both the readers and the texts; our reasons for saying so arise from the general points about comprehension made earlier. [. . .]

The first point to establish about reading in school is that there should be a lot of it — and that means, in most schools and in most subjects, a great deal more than is allowed for now. The children need — above all — to be put into more situations in all subjects which expand their idea of what reading is about and what it is good for.

The second point is that most reading in school should be fast, trusting and uninterrupted. The danger with heady descriptions of how 'comprehension' brings itself into being is that they have a tendency to tempt us into imagining comprehension always to be a slower and more self-conscious process than it actually is; most of the time understanding (however complex the process) comes instantaneously and is not explicitly worked for. The vast majority of the texts offered in school should be ones which are so readily comprehend that they are hardly noticed as texts at all. Reading is a means to an end, not an end in itself, and the more transparent the print becomes the better. It's easy to become hooked on deliberate, 'reflective' reading, the overt weighing of pros and cons, the pondering, the doubling back, the careful enumeration of ideas. We read to find out what happens next. A proper school reading diet would be perhaps 90% extensive, unsupported and largely unmonitored reading in well-written content-rich texts at a technically undemanding level.

That leaves 10%: a small amount of well-supported intensive reading of rich and relevant texts that produce reading difficulties against which one can pit one's wits in company with one's peers. We should emphasize here that the words 'rich' and 'relevant' will necessarily drive a wedge between the words 'comprehension' and 'exercise'.

There is clearly no point in wasting the 10% on texts which carry a low load; they need to be dense enough to fuel the formulating process with some power; they need to be interesting enough to make it seem worthwhile to the readers to summon the effort that deliberate reflection requires; they need to be 'generous' enough to *invite* the reader to stop and reflect.

There are many different kinds of text (i.e. texts with different functions) which might fit this bill. But it is here that literary texts may come into their own — and not only in English. It is not that the reading of literary texts involves unique comprehension processes, but that they involve the comprehension processes uniquely well. They require all the work that more purely informational texts do — but more so. They make a virtue of the fact that different readers are necessarily reading 'different' texts by generously inviting different interpretations. And while literary texts are more 'demanding' in that they require more comprehending the paradox is that when properly chosen (and that depends, obviously, on the age, experience and interests of the group) they are also more accessible into the bargain. This may be precisely because they don't 'go' anywhere, they have no strings attached: the reader's purpose is, most clearly here, to find out what happens next. That means you don't normally have to justify their use to most children. English clearly has the advantage here over other subjects. But it is an advantage which needs careful nursing. It needs to be protected first against the disease of one-off-ery, that lurching from one discrete lesson to the next, which permits pupils no opportunity for developing their thinking through a sequence of work. But it needs also to be protected from the stiffening of the limbs that comes from the mechanical pursuit of a theme or topic, where texts have life only in the mind of some ghostly syllabus or coursebook. [. . .]

Talking about texts

So much for the choice of texts for the 10%. But what do you actually *do* with them? What kind of activity can we use to replace the answering in writing of somebody else's questions?

Pat D'Arcy (in *Reading for Meaning Vol II: The Reader's Response*, 1973) suggests that 'reading response at the post-decoding stage can best be developed by the provision of a wide range of literature combined with the encouragement of plenty of non-directed discussion.' Plenty of non-directed discussion (i.e. pupil-directed discussion) is certainly what we would aim for, and it's certainly also what we would want to start with. But there is plenty of evidence to suggest that pupils, given a text without questions following it and without a demand to answer them in writing, may be at a loss initially to know where and how to begin a discussion. Worse: their experience in some other subjects may continue to confirm that their past experience of comprehension in English remains the generally accepted one.

You may be lucky: you may have classes who know how to take the initiative or who quickly learn how to do so. In any case explain what it's about and what you're trying to do. Explain the benefits. If possible get hold of (or make) a tape and/or transcript of a group of older children which is using its own resources to understand a text. Emphasize the *ways* of getting under-standing rather than the achievement of particular kinds of understanding.

Objection: *I've always encouraged whole class discussion about comprehension, talking through the questions before asking for written answers, or stopping half-way through a short story to discuss what has happened. So what's new?*

Well . . . we're certainly not knocking whole class discussion which really shares views about what's important, and which really gives a class a sense of working together to crack a problem. But whole class discussion of texts is always difficult to manage, it usually doesn't involve many pupils actively, it is invariably directed solely by the teacher, and it is frequently plain gluey. Whole class discussion of packaged questions is especially so, an institution-alized guessing game which most pupils are very keen to see the end of. We see the value of class discussion as a final forum to which views are presented *after* pupils have had a chance to formulate them. The trying-out stage is best undertaken in a more intimate and safer arena: pairs is a safe way to start; more than 4 and it starts to get complicated and unwieldy.

Some techniques for getting it going

But how do you turn on the ignition for a pair (or a three) who look blankly at a text and at one another? Or suppose they get into gear the first time out and then stall the second time out?

Some frameworks (or scaffolds) may help here to give the discussion a defined shape and direction. Some of the possibilities are described below. Some caveats first. There is nothing magical about these devices; they are not new[1], they do not carry a copper-bottomed guarantee; they do not represent a *system* for developing comprehension. They are merely instrumental to the business of getting pupils *working together* to process a text — and that needs explaining to pupils. They might very well get in the way for some pupils in some discussions some of the time by seeming to over-complicate or to distract attention from the job in hand: don't invest too much in them, or allow them to become the thing that's being done (i.e. a new kind of exercise).

These are important caveats about the use of these techniques [. . .]. For the moment, here is a selection of some of the possibilities. The order is not all that significant, but it does go roughly according to the sophistication of what they ask the pupil to do. But it isn't really a hierarchy of difficulty because that is raised or lowered for any given text by the reader's prior know-ledge of the subject matter, the complexity of the linguistic surface, the way the material is organized, and so on. [. . .]

Wide-angle questions

This is a safe start for pupils in pairs. Give them, say, three questions to discuss on the passage, poem or short story. They must be questions to which there is no obvious single right answer, and of a kind which will encourage a

ranging over the text as a whole. Try and make the questions a bit eccentric.
So, for example:

> 'is this the right title for the passage?';
> 'what kind of book do you think this extract comes from?';
> 'can you think of anything the writer has left out here?';
> 'what idea of the writer (like age, sex . . .) do you get from this piece?'

Give them a time-limit; no written answers, but a quick report-back session
involving the whole class is useful.

Responding to statements

This is a superior version of multiple choice, and a fairly painless way of
focussing discussion on critical issues in, say, a short story. Make up a short
list of statements (some controversial and/or contradictory; perhaps one or
two to do with the writer's intentions) which can stand as overall comments
about the piece. Ask your pairs to work through them and decide which two
or three they consider to be most important/appropriate. A simple 'prioritiz-
ing' system can then show the consensus of opinion in the class as a whole; a
class discussion can start with those who chose unpopular statements justifying their decisions.

Question-setting

Turn the usual procedure around by asking the pupils to themselves make up
a small number of questions to which they would really like answers. It's
more difficult than it sounds to put this across, and pupils will usually tend to
go for questions of the banal kind to which they are accustomed. Making
distinctions between questions to which the answers are (a) on the lines
(b) between the lines (c) beyond the lines may provide a useful temporary
crutch. There are two possible routes after they've worked out their questions. One is to pass one pair's questions on to another pair to see if they can
answer them. The other is to collect all the questions in and get a couple of
bright sparks to make a list of the five questions most often asked. Then, next
lesson, discuss those as a class.

Marking the text

This is a simple idea as old as schools. It just involves asking the pupils to
underline (or indicate in the margin in some way) bits of the text that deal
with one thing rather than another, or to identify patterns and connections
that seem to be there.

The physical marking is a prop for close attention and the chat involved is a
preparation for whatever broader discussion is to come.

Deletion (1): single words

Give the pupils a copy of the text from which some single words have been
deleted (tippexing a photocopy is the easiest way). Take out words (but not
too many) which are in some way critical to the meaning. Ask your pairs to

agree replacements for the missing words which are syntactically and semantically (and possibly stylistically) apt. The idea is for the pupils to have an
interesting discussion, and to justify their decisions, rather than to guess the
right word. Compare pupils' insertions with the original passage.

Deletion (2): leaving only a skeleton

Give the pupils, for example, the first and last paragraphs of a passage and ask
them to read the relics and then comment on what they think the missing
pieces are about. This can be a useful technique to prepare for the reading of
the passage as a whole.

Selective substitutions

Give the pupils a text telling them that some of the words/phrases/sections
have been replaced by less good alternatives. The reader's job is to look
through and recast any parts in any way they feel would help. The range of
possible strategies for substitution — semantic, aesthetic, syntactic, logical,
surrealist — are considerable.

Prediction

This takes deleting all but the skeleton one step further. Divide the passage or
short story into instalments (choosing the stopping place with care) and give
them out one at a time. Ask your groups to work out what they think is going
to be in the next instalment by thinking about what has happened in the one
they've got. The important question to ask about a particular prediction is:
where is the evidence for it? Then compare predictions with what actually
happens. (This works best with texts with a strong narrative line.)

Sequencing

This involves serious doctoring of the text. Make copies of it and cut them
into pieces (perhaps paragraphs or half-paragraphs or stanzas). Don't make
too many pieces, otherwise it can become tricky to organize. Then give all the
bits to your pairs and ask them to assemble the bits into an order which makes
sense to them. The idea is to focus discussion on the structure of the text.
(N.B. Draughts play havoc with this game.)

Finding boundaries

This is sequencing the other way round. Ask the pupils to divide the text into
what they think are its sections, describing what makes one section different
from the next. It's made easier if you tell them at the beginning the number of
sections you think there are, and let them work from there. (It's possible to
use this technique to work on a single paragraph, though that is usually a
more demanding application of it.)

Drawings and diagrams

This just means asking the pupils to present some of the information in a text
in some visual form (e.g. a drawing, a flow-chart, a table, or a network). This

technique could be used, for example, to focus attention on the relationship between characters in a story, or their points of similarity and difference. It may also be useful for re-assembling ideas in an information text, as a way of preparing for note-taking of various kinds.

Role-playing and other extensions
Here the written material (or some of it) is re-presented in verbal form through role-play, interview or improvised 'sketch'. For example: characters in a short story, can be 'interviewed' about their motives and feelings; or two characters who don't in fact meet or talk in the story can be projected into a scene where they do.

Paraphrasing and summary
Here the written material (or some of it) is re-presented by the pupils in their own writing, possibly after earlier work with some of the techniques mentioned above. For example, an extended narrative or descriptive piece might be condensed and 'translated' into a news bulletin or short newspaper article; a piece with an unsuitable verbal surface might be rewritten to mesh more comfortably with the needs of a given target audience; or characters from the text might be asked to justify their actions or outlook in a short written statement.

The description of these techniques has necessarily been very spare — and that tends to make them sound complicated to operate. At this stage it may be useful to illustrate how these devices can be adapted to provide simple ways into a close study of a text. The selection of a particular technique, and its adaptation, will obviously depend jointly on the nature of the text, on the focus which the teacher wishes to encourage, and on the experience of the pupils in working in this way; here three different techniques are used in combination. The text we offer here is a short and deceptively simple one by Carl Sandburg, 'Remember the Chameleon'. It is preceded by the working instructions for the pupils. (The follow-up would start with the difficulties they encounter.)

REMEMBER THE CHAMELEON

Things to do:

1. Underline (with a straight line) all the phrases you consider to be complimentary to the chameleon.
2. Underline (with a squiggly line) all the phrases you consider to be critical of the chameleon.
3. Decide together what you think about the following statements. Write down in order the letters for each so that the one you agree with most is at one end and the one you agree with least is at the other.
   (a) A true hero (b) A real twit (c) An example to us all
   (d) An average guy (e) A solid citizen (f) A victim of fate
   (g) Someone who never stopped trying (h) A slave to instinct
   (i) A noble fool (j) Someone who failed to adapt (k) Someone who failed to grow up.

4. Present the meaning of 'Remember the chameleon' as a diagram or in some other visual form.

Remember the chameleon. He was a well-behaved chameleon and nothing could be brought against his record. As a chameleon he had done the things he should have done. And left undone the things that should have been left undone. He was a first-class, unimpeachable chameleon and nobody had anything on him. But he came to a Scotch plaid and tried to cross it. In order to cross it he had to imitate six different yarn colours, first one, then another and back to the first or second. He was a brave chameleon and died at the crossroads true to his chameleon instincts.

The techniques: some objections

1. *This doesn't seem a very systematic approach.*
   It isn't. It's useful to bear in mind what Frank Smith suggests: that you can't teach comprehension, you can only encourage it.
2. *How will I know if they're getting better?*
   Not by tests certainly. It is very difficult to say what progress in comprehension is because it lives mainly in the head, it isn't a steady discernible thing, and it depends so much on the intentions and the circumstances of the reader. Asking the pupils how they think they're doing is a good start; otherwise watch and listen and trust your nose.
3. *Actually I use individually worked comprehension exercises (or the Box) to keep them solidly occupied once a week (so I can have a rest/talk to individuals/ keep the noise down). This comprehension business of yours isn't going to fill that hole.*
   Your honesty is admirable: all but a few self-righteous souls would admit same. You're probably right about the noise; but you may be surprised about how much time pupils can spend discussing a text without whining for something to *do*; they may be surprised by how relaxed *and* involved they can be. Still we know what you mean: there are times . . . There are other hole-fillers: like silent independent reading for pleasure from a bookbox or from home; like a journal for light personal writing; like word-games (in absolute silence of course).
4. *I quite like the idea of your new model but all I've got for my class is 27 copies of 'Comprehension in Stages Step 2'/a set of Twitchin's 'Multiple-Choice tests'/an SRA box. (And don't tell me about photocopying because it's illegal/ we haven't got one.)*
   Well, you could do your 10% on your class reader or a short story if you like. There may also be odd passages in the books you've got which you can use without bothering with the questions. If you've only got an SRA box at least get the pupils to do the cards in pairs: it's better than nothing.
5. *This sounds like the kind of thing that might work with good readers, but what about the strugglers?*

The strugglers aren't helped by having to write down answers in individually worked comprehension exercises: what they need, more than anyone else, is to read more and to talk more; you might be pleasantly surprised.

6. *What about public examinations at 16? They use the old model (either standard passage-plus-questions or multiple-choice or both) and the kids need to get used to the idea, whatever I think of their value. (And don't talk to me about mode 3 schemes).*

A cogent point. *Some* practice in the particular form of the brass-bound exam comprehension paper is obviously necessary, just so the pupils can get used to the format and so you can teach them the wheezes. But we think the new model does work, and that should improve performance in exam papers, however daft. It certainly can't do any *worse* than the old-style formal comprehension lessons. Some research by L.A.T.E. in 1951–52 showed that lessons of this kind had no effect on above average readers and a tiny effect (if any) on the below average (and that was probably due to their lack of reading experience of any other kind). Try this if you want to do some research yourself: when the 5th year mocks come round, give the same comprehension paper to a similarly constituted group in the 4th year and in the 3rd year, and get someone else to mark them all. The results may not be statistically significant but they will be interesting — especially if you get someone in the department to give you odds that the 3rd year will come out bottom (they probably won't).

[. . .]

A checklist

To end this section here are some things to bear in mind as you try some (or some more) new things to take the place of the standard comprehension routine.

1. Are you doing too much intensive work on reading or making too much of a fuss about it?
2. Are you choosing texts to hang about on (for your 10%) that are really worth the bother?
3. How are you making explicit to the pupils that this work is not just an exercise to be done for its practice value, but that (a) there are useful connections with other work in hand, *or* that (b) there are honourable ulterior motives (e.g. the text's springboard value or its intrinsic richness).
4. Are you getting in the way by
   — unhelpful pre-digestion or spoonfeeding?
   — short-circuiting the formulating process?
5. Are you in any way suggesting that there is only one proper meaning to a given text or that 'wrong' answers and false trails are not to be welcomed and shared?
6. Are you making it clear by the way you work that the way to derive rich meaning and full understanding from a text is to process, first through speech and in company, the early meanings you begin to build around a textual offering, before finally focussing these alone and in writing?

[. . .]

Notes

1 Some of them have been used in classrooms, in one form or another, for a very long time. Descriptions of some of the individual procedures on the list — and of the principles that underlie their classroom use — have appeared, e.g. in Stauffer and Cramer's *Teaching Critical Reading at the Primary Level* (1968), in Christopher Walker's *Reading Development and Extension* (1974), and in course material from the O.U. reading team. *The Effective Use of Reading* (1979) reported substantial trials of some of the procedures, and work on them has been extended in a second Schools Council Project on reading based at the University of Nottingham, 'Reading for Learning in the Secondary School'. This Project calls comprehension activities of this type 'D.A.R.T.S.': 'directed activities related to texts'. Teachers in five ILEA schools have been involved, along with teachers in other areas, in trying out and developing further various 'D.A.R.T.S.' We are indebted here to the expertise and experience of those teachers and of the Project team. The list [provided] is our synthesis of a wide range of different possible activities — and is by no means exhaustive.

SECTION IV

Teaching Writing

Introduction

Although, like reading, writing has a well-established place in the school language curriculum, the development of children's ability to write, and how writing is taught, have been given much less attention by researchers than reading development and reading instruction. With the recent establishment of major curriculum development projects in Britain (the National Writing Project) and in the USA (e.g. the Bay Area Writing Project), it now seems that writing is coming to the fore. This is, therefore, a very suitable time to take stock of the ways that writing development and instruction have been defined and explored. In the first article, Janet Emig provides a broad review of the ways writing has been studied and taught.

Each of the two articles which follow consider aspects of teaching and learning to write in relation to specific age groups of children. Thorogood and Raban describe an investigation into the effects of a 'sense of audience' on the writing of British eight-year-olds, while Freedman and Pringle's study considers why, in the opinions of many of their teachers, American children in the seventh and eighth grades (13–15 year-olds) 'can't write arguments'.

4.1 Writing, Composition and Rhetoric

Janet Emig

Source: Edited version of Emig, J. (1982) 'Writing, composition and rhetoric'. In Mitzel, H.E. (ed.) *Encyclopedia of Educational Research*, 4. New York, The Free Press.

This [article] begins, necessarily, with definitions of the three key terms. First, all three have been assigned, in ordinary language as in the language of education, such various, conflicting, and at times pejorative meanings that apt characterizations are needed for historical, conceptual, and even political clarity. The commonplace "That's just rhetoric," for example, suggests a surface formulation, one divorced from substance and integrity — a definition far from its classical roots as a piece of discourse scrupulously wrought to persuade a given audience of an ethical point of view. Writing, even at this late moment in curriculum history, is defined by some administrators, teachers, and even researchers as handwriting, the physical act of putting words on paper, rather than as a process inevitably involving cognition. For many, composition still has the connotation of a child's simple, algorithmic response to a set, stale, teacher-made task, an activity occurring, say, for twenty minutes on a Friday afternoon when there is nothing better for either student or teacher to do.

Second, defining is an act both of marking the boundaries and establishing the acreage of a field. Full definitions will reveal that this entry describes a new or at least a substantially reinvented field (Freedman & Pringle, 1980). Indeed, it can be persuasively argued that writing, rhetoric, and composition represent a dramatic and possibly unique instance, for only since 1969 has this field come into being; only within the past twelve to fifteen years have these processes become the subjects and objects of wide and systematic inquiry.

How, then, will writing be defined? Moffett (1979) distinguishes usefully among four definitions in common use: writing as (1) handwriting: the physical act of placing words on a page; (2) taking dictation and copying: recording graphically one's own words, or, more frequently, the words of others; (3) crafting: fashioning lexical, syntactic, and rhetorical units of discourse into meaningful patterns; and (4) authoring: elaborating inner speech into outer discourse for a specific purpose and a specific audience. Writing in this entry will have only the latter two meanings; handwriting, spelling, punctuation, and matters of usage will be viewed not as autonomous and discrete skills but as support systems in a developmental sequence. Writing will be regarded as a continuous, coordinated performance and a process of immense perceptual, linguistic, and cognitive complexity. In this reinvented rhetoric, the writing process will be seen as a creative process in which meanings are made through the active and continued involvement of the writer with the unfolding text (Freedman & Pringle, 1980). When writing is viewed in this way, false or trivial distinctions fall away: if *all* writing is a creative process, setting apart and calling one segment "creative writing" is at minimum redundant, if not illogical. Also, focus on text reminds one that the response of a reader or audience must be included in any full consideration of the writing process.

Regarding writing as a field of inquiry, the account in the previous edition of this encyclopedia accurately reflects the state of the non-art, or the non-state of the art, just thirteen years ago. Before 1968 the field could be characterized, extending Thomas Kuhn's well-known term, as pre-pre-paradigmatic: essentially a-empirical and a-theoretical, undergirded by no adequate treatment of human or of rhetorical development, nor by an explicit or even a tacit intellectual tradition. Rather, the subtopics discussed — environmental factors, grammar, vocabulary, instruction — seem a grab bag of discrete components, rather like a kit for a yet-to-be assembled system. In 1969 linguistics alone among the allied disciplines was regarded as a potential base for theory building and curricular practice. Noam Chomsky (1968), the leading figure in the linguistics revolution of the sixties, stated that he saw no direct application from the theoretical examination of transformational-generative (t-g) grammar to the teaching of writing. Nevertheless, ambitious school systems and districts launched linguistically based curricula in which the tenets of t-g grammar were presented to students as early as the second and third grade. Subsequent empirical studies such as those by Bateman and Zidonis (1966) and by Mellon (1969) showed at best conflicting findings about the values of this direct grammar study for improving the quality of writing among the seventh- to tenth-grade subjects studied.

[. . .]

To talk about the recent history of writing as a field is to describe a paradigm shift. Freedman and Pringle (1980a) describe this history as the rejection of the "current-traditional rhetoric paradigm" by the paradigm of the "reinvented rhetoric." What is it in the immediate past and the tradition of composition teaching of the past century that the new, the reinvented rhetoric rejects? Young (1980) and Emig (in press) have both noted the differences between the current-traditional rhetoric and the reinvented rhetoric: Young, by specifically contrasting the work of Genung (1982; 1901) and of Rohmann (1964); Emig, by more generally contrasting what she calls, after Piaget, the tenets of magical thinking represented by the current traditional rhetoric and the tenets of nonmagical thinking [. . .] Emig sets the tenets of the two side by side to highlight their differences:

"Magical" composition teaching (current-traditional)	*"Nonmagical" composition teaching (new or re-invented)*
Writing is a product to be evaluated.	Writing is a process to be experienced.
Writing is predominantly taught	Writing is predominantly learned

rather than learned.	rather than taught.
Students must be taught atomistically, from parts to whole. Children must be taught to write words before they write sentences before they can be allowed to write paragraphs before they can be permitted to attempt whole pieces of discourse.	Writers of all ages as frequently work from wholes to parts as from parts to wholes. In writing, there is a complex interplay between focal and global concerns: from an interest in what word comes next to a concern with the shape of the total piece.
There is essentially one process of writing that serves all writers for all aims, modes, intents, and audiences.	There is no monolithic process of writing. There are processes of writing that differ because of differing aims, intents, modes, and audiences. Although there are shared features in the ways we write, there are also individual, even idiosyncratic, features.
That process is linear: all planning precedes all writing, as all writing precedes all revising.	The processes of writing do not proceed in a linear sequence; rather, they are recursive. We not only plan, then write, then revise, but we also revise, then plan, then write.
That process is also almost exclusively conscious: as evidence, a full plan or outline can be drawn up and adhered to for any piece of writing in any mode. The requirement to produce an outline also assumes that writing is transcribing; since it can be so totally prefigured, thought must exist fully formed prior to any linguistic formulation.	Writing is as often an unconscious or a preconscious roaming as it is a planned and conscious rendering of information and events.

"Magical" composition teaching (current-traditional)	*"Nonmagical" composition teaching (new or reinvented)*
Perhaps because writing is conscious, it can be done swiftly and on order.	The rhythms of writing are uneven, indeed erratic. The pace of writing can be very slow, particularly if the writing represents significant learning. Writing is also slow since it involves what Vygotsky (1962) calls "elaborating the web of meaning," supplying the explicit links to transform lexical, syntactic, and rhetorical pieces into organic wholes.

There is no community or collaboration in writing: it is exclusively a
silent and solitary activity.

The processes of writing can be
enhanced by working in, and with,
a group of other writers, perhaps
especially a teacher, who gives vital
response, including advice.

Efforts to find or redefine an appropriate heritage have been twofold:
extensions of two of the five arts of classical rhetoric (invention and style); and
efforts to discern an intellectual tradition within the contemporary milieu of
the twentieth century.

Classical rhetoric
Classical rhetoric is divided into the five arts of invention, arrangement,
style, memory, and delivery. Within the past fifteen years rhetoricians have
focused primarily upon invention and secondarily upon style, while essentially ignoring the other three arts. Indeed, invention emerges as "a central
focus, almost as our chief focus of interest, in theory, in research and in
pedagogy" (Freedman & Pringle, 1980). When Young (1976) surveyed the
field, he found four major approaches to invention: a revived interest in
classical invention itself; Burke's dramatistic method (1945), with its emphasis upon the pentad; Rohman's prewriting method (1964); and Pike's
tagmemic invention (1967; Young, Becker, & Pike, 1970; Lauer, 1967). To
these can be added Moffett's use of meditation techniques (1981). In another
essay Young (1980) has divided contemporary theorists into romanticists and
classicists. What distinguishes the classicists from the romanticists is a belief
in heuristics, which he defines as "explicit strategies for effective guessing,"
a mode of invention.

A fresh consideration of style has also intrigued some contemporary
theorists. A notable effort here has been the concerted and extensive work
involving sentence combining. Unsophisticated forms of sentence-
combining activities appear in the very earliest composition textbooks of
American imprint (Walker, 1808), with students encouraged to combine
series of short, uninteresting sentences into longer, more interesting ones.
The activity continues as a steady pedagogical exercise into today's most
widely reprinted handbooks, such as those of Harbrace and Warriner.

Only with the formulations of transformational-generative grammar did
the practice find a system, a sequence, and a theoretical justification. Stotsky
(1975) and Corbett (1980) have reviewed this work. Corbett attributes to
Ohmann (1964; 1966) an early use of t-g grammar as an analytical tool for
exploring the structure of existing sentences and accounting for how these
sentences came to be the way they were. Despite the unequivocal claims on
the part of proponents, findings from empirical studies — say, with college
students — have been mixed. Ney (1976), in an experiment conducted with
thirteen sections of freshman students at Arizona State University over an
eleven-week period, found that the exercises in sentence combining did not
enhance students' syntactic fluency and may even have retarded it.

Morenberg, Daiker, and Kerek (1978) conducted an experiment in sentence combining at Miami University in Oxford, Ohio. They claimed that the reason the students in the Ney experiment did not show gains was that they spent only ten minutes each in twenty-seven class periods practicing sentence combining, for a total of only four and a half hours. Subjects in the experimental Miami group, in contrast, engaged in sentence-combining exercises during every class of a semester. When contrasted with subjects in a comparison group at Miami who took the regular freshman composition course that contained no work in sentence combining, the experimental group scored higher in a posttest on two indices of syntactic maturity — clause length and t-unit length (Hunt, 1965); in addition, compositions written on a common theme at the end of the semester by the experimental subjects were adjudged superior in quality to those by comparison subjects. Maimon and Nodine (1978) achieved similar results with freshman students at Beaver College in Pennsylvania.

Intellectual tradition

Theorists are also finding roots for the new rhetoric (the metaphor was originally Fogarty's; see Fogarty, 1959) in the multidisciplinary tradition of the twentieth century with its emphasis on process: Weschler (1978) notes that in the twentieth century science, like art, "has begun to recognize the relationship of perceiver and objective reality." Emig, for example (1980), suggests that the field of writing is devolving from a tacit tradition composed of thinkers from philosophy (Cassirer, Dewey, Langer); psychology (Luria, Kelly, Piaget, Vygotsky); literary and reading theory (Rosenblatt, F. Smith, Y. and K. Goodman); the history of science (Kuhn, Polanyi); and now neural science (Eccles, Epstein, Milner, Young). What the members of this tradition share, despite their disciplinary diversity, are their beliefs in the learner as an active construer of meaning; their sense of learning as a transaction between knower (subjective perceiver) and known (objective reality); and their commitment to a developmental view of experience and of education.

Four specific events occurring from 1966 to 1971 contributed to the renaissance in the field: (1) the Anglo-American Seminar on the Teaching of English, held in the summer of 1966 at Dartmouth, more commonly known in the profession as the Dartmouth conference; (2) the publication of *Teaching the Universe of Discourse* and *A Student-centered Language Arts Curriculum* by James Moffett; (3) the publication of the first documents from the [British] Schools Council Project, by the team of James Britton, Nancy Martin, and Harold Rosen; and (4) the shift in research emphasis from product to process, with the publication of *The Composing Processes of Twelfth-graders*, by the [U.S.A.] National Council of Teachers of English (NCTE).

The Dartmouth conference

Fifty educators from the major English-speaking nations met in the late summer of 1966 to participate in the Anglo-American Seminar on the Teaching of English, described by Herbert J. Muller, one of its two official historians, as "the first large-scale international conference on this basic subject" (Muller, 1967). The seminar was organized by James Squire following a meeting with Boris Ford at the National Council of Teachers of English convention in Cleveland in 1965. The seminar participants swiftly found that they could not even agree on a definition of what "English" is. For the British, English was a child-centered process, and their goal was the intellectual, social, and emotional growth of the child; for the Americans, English was a subject-centered product, and their explicit concern was the learning and teaching of the formal structure of the disciplines of literature and linguistics. The differences in beliefs and practices concerning the learning and teaching of writing reflected the basic differences concerning the learning and teaching of English generically. For the Americans, writing was a skill subsidiary to the learning of language and literature; for the British, writing was a primary process supported by literature and by language study through which the child discovered meaning and constructed reality.

If the seminar can be regarded as a debate, all oral and written accounts confirm that the British won the day. Many of the Americans present realized that in contrast to the documents the British were producing, the curriculum materials developed earlier in the sixties through the Project English centers were as partial, and philosophically dubious, as they had been expensive (one center had been given $60,000 to write an eighth-grade unit on *Hiawatha*).

Moffett's study

One of the many American participants profoundly affected by the Dartmouth seminar was James Moffett, who in 1964 had been given a grant from the Carnegie Foundation to write a book of theory and practice in which he set out his integrated theory and curriculum for the teaching of English. *Teaching the Universe of Discourse* (1968) was the first major theoretical text in the profession to regard cognitive psychology as a base discipline. Drawing from the theories especially of Piaget and Luria, Moffett developed his thesis that "the psychological development of the child is the backbone of the English curriculum," While at the same time mapping a sequence of rhetorical development consonant with his view of human growth. Writing, in Moffett's theory, was clearly a primary mode for personal as well as intellectual growth.

The London group

Two other events of consequence occurred at almost the same time: one in England, one in the United States. In 1966 the Schools Council gave Britton, Martin, and Rosen of the Institute of Education at the University of London a grant to examine the status of writing in United Kingdom schools. The team collected 2,122 pieces of writing, or scripts, from 500 students between the ages of 11 and 18, and examined them for the mode in which they were written and the audience toward which they were directed. The team found it necessary to devise their own category systems for analysis both of mode and audience. Britton published schemas now in wide use. Writing, he claimed, initially emanates from an expressive need that may then transform itself into either the poetic or the transactional mode, the poetic being writing that is an aesthetic end in itself and the transactional being writing that gets work done in the world. The empirical findings were that as British students moved up the forms in school from first to sixth, they wrote more and more in the transactional mode and less and less in the poetical mode, until, by the sixth form, well over four-fifths of the writing they did for school subjects was transactional. [. . .]

Process emphasis

In his introduction to Emig's *The Composing Processes of Twelfth-graders*, Buxton noted that the monograph (using case studies) "describes an expedition into new territory, an investigation of the writing process," whereas "researchers in written composition . . . by and large have focused their attention upon the *written product*" (p. v). This shift in emphasis from product to process represented a significant change in research for the field. To the characterizations of the process (Perl, 1978; Matsuhashi, 1979) have been added telling characterizations of the writer (Graves, 1975; Kaufman, 1981) and of the interrelationships among process, product, and writer (Pianko, 1977). Like Emig, most of the investigators into process have elected-case study as their primary mode of inquiry.

Modes of inquiry

[. . .]

Since writing, as Gardner (1975) notes, represents one of the most complex and mutifaceted human activities, which, it seems, is impaired by trauma to any portion of either hemisphere of the brain, it is not unexpected that the process should intrigue epistemologists and neural scientists alike. Indeed, one of the most massive speculative contributions relevant to the field is *The Self and Its Brain*, a dialogue between the philosopher Popper and the biologist Eccles (1977). In the first experimental study from a neural perspective (Glassner, 1981), thirty male and female community college students wrote briefly on two topics — "Describe a process that interests you," and "Describe a deeply felt personal experience" — while encephalograms (EEGs) were being made. Although Glassner's initial hypothesis that given modes of discourse emanated predominatly from given spheres of the brain (exposition and argument, dominant hemisphere; description and narration, minor hemisphere) was not substantiated, another equally intriguing generalization tentatively emerged. When the brain waves were divided according to a program that indicated right and left hemisphere distribution, first and fresh formulations, initial explorations of a topic, proved to be minor hemisphere activities, whereas re-contemplation and reformulation proved activities of the dominant hemisphere. In classical terms, the minor hemisphere seemed to govern invention (*inventio*), whereas the dominant sphere governed rehearsal and reformulation.

Studies emanating from a cognitive psychological base and concerned with ages, stages, and levels of sophistication may be the most swiftly growing interdisciplinary branch of research into writing. Many of these studies attempt to delineate the linguistic and rhetorical maturity in students of given chronological ages (for example, Graves, 1978; Pianko, 1977; King & Rentel, 1979; M. Smith, 1980; Kroll, 1980).

[. . .]

Growing more numerous and significant are ethnographies, both intranational and international (cross-cultural) inquiries into who writes what to whom and for what purposes. Heath (1981) used ethnographic methods to identify needs for writing in the out-of-school lives of black and white high school boys in North and South Carolina. Writing instruction, it seems, proceeds most effectively when the school writing tasks deal with actual functions of writing that students discern in meaningful, real-life situations rather than with artificial, decontextualized exercises and what Britton (1978) calls "dummy runs."

Scribner and Cole (1981) investigated the uses of literacy among the tri-literate Vai, a tribe in northwest Liberia. [. . .] Scribner and Cole asked themselves if there were any cognitive consequences to letter writing among the Vai, their major mode of literacy (with no connection to formal schooling); they constructed two ingenious tests to obtain responses to their question. The studies indicated that their experience with reading and writing does have psychological consequences. The significance of this cross-cultural, contextually framed inquiry seems clear. Only if we acknowledge the true range of diversity in literacy practices in cultures other than our own can we make sensible, accurate, and nonparochial statements about the relations of language and learning and about the unique values of given modes — say, exposition — for cognitive growth.

[. . .]

Writing, listening, talking, and reading

Writing as a process of language cannot sensibly be treated wholly apart from the three other verbal processes of listening, talking, and reading, since in literate societies we tend to orchestrate the four in our daily lives. How researchers elect to relate these processes makes a logical, conceptual, and even political difference for the conduct of inquiry. In the literature can be found various ways of categorizing the likenesses and differences among these processes. Some writers posit a distinction between the receptive (listening and reading) and the productive (talking and writing) functions. Some refer to encoding (speaking and writing) and decoding (listening and reading). Some claim that talking and writing are active processes, whereas listening and reading are passive. Linguists distinguish first — order symbolic systems (talking and listening) from second — order systems (writing and reading).

Some of these characterizations are obviously more useful and more accurate than others. "Passive," for example, has a connotation of inactivity or nonactivity not substantiated by any sustained observation of, or introspection into, the processes of listening and reading. Most contemporary researchers and theorists would claim, rather, that all four processes are active, selective, and creative, or at least re-creative.

As regards research that compares writing to another process, the studies concerning deaf and partial-hearing children regularly report a deficit or time-lag in their writing abilities when set against the abilities of hearing children of like chronological age (Bloom & Lahey, 1978). In the United Kingdom, though not in the United States, infants are tested for aural acuity shortly after birth, with those revealing any hearing loss immediately fitted with hearing aids. An interesting cross-cultural study would be a comparison of these two groups of English-speaking children as later writers.

In the considerable research on the relation between talking and writing there are two strands with distinct, even opposing, sets of assumptions. In one, writing is viewed as emanating developmentally from talking; a commonplace feature identifying this view is that writing, initially, is talk written down. In the other, talking and writing are viewed as emanating from different somatic bases — literally from different portions of the brain. Otherwise quite distinct inquiries can share an assumption about this relationship. Zoellner (1969) examined from a behaviorist perspective the way in which training students to talk systematically about their writing could enhance their abilities to write; Britton (1978) and other members of the London group have frequently asserted that writing, developmentally, could usefully be viewed as talk written down. However, such major figures as Vygotsky and Luria have maintained that talking and writing are neurally distinct: as evidence here are persons who can talk but not write after certain types of brain damage and trauma. Groff, in his review of the research on the relation between writing and talking (1979), concludes that the idea that pupils' written language in the middle grades is based on oral language needs to be qualified. Talking in groups as a prelude to individual writing seems, however, a well-substantiated phenomenon (Elbow, 1973). Obviously, the nature of this relationship requires far more extensive and profound exploration.

One theme in this entry is the dominance of reading over writing for public and professional valuing and for allotment of instructional time, particularly in the elementary school (Graves, 1980).

[. . .]

Perhaps the imbalance of reading and writing is in part responsible for the curious situation that obtains in the literature whereby the two processes of literacy are seldom treated together. Among the studies that treat both reading and writing are those of Page (1975) and Read (1975).

[. . .]

The situation is curious, because developmentally the two processes have common origins but writing rather than reading is the process to develop earlier (Graves, 1980). What, ontogenetically and phylogenetically, are the origins of writing and of reading? Gesture has been seen as the origin, a view shared by such otherwise disparate thinkers as Huey (1908), Mead (1934), and Vygotsky (1962). Vygotsky presents the fullest case, claiming that the gesture is "the initial visual sign that contains the child's future writing as an acorn contains the future oak." Gestures are writing in air, and written signs frequently are simply gestures that have been fixed. Early on, children shuttle between actual gestures and scribbles on paper that supplement this gestural representation. In fact, Vygotsky regards the child's first marks on paper developmentally as recorded gestures rather than as drawing in any true sense of that word. These marks on paper go through a series of evolutionary changes, from undifferentiated marks through indicatory signs and symbolizing marks and scribbles to the drawing of little figures and pictures (pictographs), until the moment when the child realizes that one can draw not only things but speech. This recognition makes possible the transformation of writing from a first-order symbolic act to a second-order symbolic act, from the mnemotechnic stage to the stage where one can deal with disembodied signs and symbols — to the stage, that is, of symbolic maturity. (Vygotsky also makes the case for symbolic play as the second link between gesture and written language.)

A second strand of these developmental inquiries is being conducted by Y. Goodman and K. Goodman (1978), Harste and Burke (1980), and DeFord (1980) under the rubric "print awareness," which they define as the ability of children to distinguish the salient features of written discourse from those of oral discourse. In these experimental studies children as young as age 2 reveal abilities to produce written records and to demonstrate print awareness by discerning differences between oral and written discourse.

A third strand of these inquiries into origins of literacy is that into children's "invented spelling." Read (1975) was the first researcher to examine the highly regular developmental sequence children aged 3, 4, and 5 follow as they invent and then modify a system of phonological rules that comes to approximate the system of standard American English orthography. Subsequent confirmation of his findings appear in the work of Bissex (1981), Calkins (1979), Graves (1979), and Milz (1980).

The fourth strand is the research on children's sense of story. As with the prior three, the generalization that obtains is that children's sense of story occurs far earlier than researchers had previously thought. Halliday (1975), reviewing functions of language in his case study of his son "Nigel" (pseudonym), states: "The child also uses language for creating a universe of his own, a world initially of pure sound, but which gradually turns into one of story and make-believe and let's pretend, and ultimately into the realm of poetry and imaginative writing" (Applebee, 1977, p. 343). As Applebee notes (1977), "Nigel has begun this progression by the age of 15 months when he is still in what Halliday calls 'Phase I' of language development. (This is a phase that *precedes* the acquisition of the lexicogrammatical system usually identified as the beginning of speech.)" (p. 343).

[. . .]

Writing Across the Curriculum (WAC)

Perhaps the most pervasive curricular movement in writing, particularly in higher education, concerns how and why students write to learn, not only for their English classes but also for other classes and disciplines. This movement has been dubbed "writing across the curriculum," and is also known by the acronym WAC. Systematic concern with the role of writing across the curriculum, by this designation, can be traced to the work of the [British] Schools Council project in the late 1960s — notably, to the efforts of the London team led by Britton *et al.* (1975).

As appendix to *Language, the Learner, and the School* (1971) by Barnes, Britton, and Rosen, the first document of consequence treating the WAC issues, Rosen set forth a language policy that proceeded from the assumption that all teachers of all subjects regard themselves as teachers of writing and that together they develop a coherent policy for the assignment and evaluation of all written schoolwork. [. . .]

In 1977 Emig, in an essay, "Writing as a Mode of Learning," presented the argument, synthesized from the work of such psychologists as Vygotsky, Piaget, and Bruner, that writing may well be a unique way to learn since the process inherently demands acts of analysis and synthesis that mark higher-order intellectual functioning. Some experiments have been conducted to test that hypothesis. In a study involving 178 undergraduate and graduate students and 5 college instructors, Weiss (1980) attempted to determine whether subject-related writing tasks assigned in college courses increased the amount and clarity of student learning, led to improved student writing performance, and changed levels of student apprehension about writing. Although differences in apprehension and in writing performance were not significant, the greatest significance occurred in contrasting clarity of concept learned by writing and clarity of concepts learned without writing: students assigned writing tasks had significantly higher gains in learning content subject area.

[. . .]

For learning and teaching writing and the other language arts cannot sensibly be regarded discretely and in isolation from one another. Reading impinges on writing, which in turn is transformed by listening and talking. Sponsorship of wholly autonomous research inquiries and curricular ventures into any one of the four language processes is now theoretically and empirically suspect.

An integrated approach, however, will not preclude indepth studies of persons as writers. What is the interplay of level of cognitive abilities with linguistic and rhetorical abilities? What are the interconnections of personality with cognitive and conceptual styles and writing? What insights can contemporary psychoanalytic theory proffer to writing? How can Vygotsky's "zone of proximal development" be generatively interpreted for the learning and teaching of writing?

Through writing, as through other symbolic activities, like mathematics, brain becomes mind. To comprehend the full scope of this transformation is an ultimate research task.

References

Applebee, A. A sense of story. *Theory into Practice*, 1977, **16**, 342–347.

Barnes, D., Britton, J. & Rosen, H. *Language, the Learner, and the School*. Baltimore: Penguin Books, 1971.

Bateman, D.R. & Zidonis, F.J. *The Effect of a Study of Transformational Grammar on the Writing of Ninth and Tenth Graders* (NCTE Research Report No. 6). Urbana, Ill.: National Council of Teachers of English, 1966.

Bissex, G. *Gnys at Wrk*. Cambridge, Mass.: Harvard University Press, 1981.

Bloom, L. & Lahey, M. *Language Development and Language Disorders*. New York: Wiley, 1978.

Britton, J. The composing processes and the functions of writing. In C. Cooper and L. Odell (eds.) *Research on Composing*. Urbana, Ill.: National Council of Teachers of English, 1978.

Burke, K. *A Grammar of Motives*. Englewood Cliffs, N.J.: Prentice-Hall, 1945.

Calkins, L.M. Andrea learns to make writing hard. *Language Arts*, 1979, **56**, 569–576.

Chomsky, N. *Language and Mind*. New York: Harcourt Brace Jovanovich, 1968.

Corbett, E.P.J. Ventures in style. In A. Freedman & I. Pringle (eds.), *Reinventing the Rhetorical Tradition*. Toronto: Canadian Council of Teachers of English (L&S Books), 1980.

DeFord, D. Young children and their writing. *Theory into Practice*, 1980, **19**, 157–162.

Eccles, J. & Popper, K. *The Self and Its Brain*. New York: Springer International, 1977.

Elbow, P. *Writing without Teachers*. New York: Oxford University Press, 1973.

Emig, J. Writing as a mode of learning. *College Composition and Communication*, 1977, **28**, 122–128.

Emig, J. The tacit tradition: the inevitability of a multi-disciplinary approach to writing research. In A. Freedman and I. Pringle (eds), *Reinventing the Rhetorical Tradition*, Toronto: Canadian Council of Teachers of English, 1980.

Emig, J. Inquiry paradigms and writing. *College Composition and Communication*, in press.

Fogarty, D. *Roots for a New Rhetoric*. New York: Columbia University, Teachers College, 1959.

Freedman, A. & Pringle, I. (eds.). *Reinventing the Rhetorical Tradition*. Toronto: Canadian Council of Teachers of English (L&S Books), 1980.

Gardner, H. *The Shattered Mind: The Person after Brain Damage*. New York: Random House, 1975.

Genung, J.F. *The Practical Elements of Rhetoric*. Boston: Ginn, 1892.

Genung, J.F. *The Working Principles of Rhetoric*. Boston: Ginn, 1901.

Glassner, B. *Lateral Specialization of the Modes of Composing*. Unpublished doctoral dissertation, Rutgers University, 1981.

Goodman, K., & Goodman, Y. *Learning to Read Is Natural*. Paper presented at the Conference on Theory and Practice of Beginning Reading Instruction, Pittsburgh, April 13, 1978.

Graves, D. An examination of the writing process of seven-year-old children. Research in Teaching of English, 1975, **9**, 227–241.

Graves, D. *Balance the Basics: Let Them Write.* New York: Ford Foundation, 1978.

Graves, D. *The Growth and Development of First-grade Writers.* Paper presented at the annual meeting of the Canadian Council of Teachers of English, Ottawa, May 10, 1979.

Graves, D. Research update: A new look at writing research. *Language Arts,* 1980, **57,** 913–918.

Groff, P. The effects of talking on writing. *English in Education,* 1979, **13,** 33–37.

Halliday, M.A.K. *Learning How to Mean: Explorations in the Development of Language.* London: Edward Arnold, 1975.

Harste, J.C. & Burke, C.L. Examining instructional assumptions: The child as informant. *Theory into Practice,* 1980, **19,** 170–178.

Heath, S.B. Toward an ethnohistory of writing in American education. In M.F. Whiteman (ed.), *Variations in Writing: Functional and Linguistic Cultural Differences* (Vol. 1). Hillsdale, N.J.: Lawrence Erlbaum Associates, 1981.

Huey, E.B. *The Psychology and Pedagogy of Reading.* Cambridge, Mass.: MIT Press, 1968. (First published in 1908)

Hunt, K.W. *Grammatical Structures Written at Three Grade Levels* (Research Report No. 3). Urbana, Ill.: National Council of Teachers of English, 1965.

Kaufman, S. *Conceptual Styles and Composition.* Unpublished doctoral dissertation, Rutgers University, 1981.

King, M.L. & Rentel, V. Toward a theory of early writing development. *Research in Teaching of English,* 1979, **13,** 243–253.

Kroll, B. Developmental perspectives and the teaching of composition. *College English,* 1980, **41,** 741–752.

Lauer, J. *Invention in Contemporary Rhetoric: Heuristic Procedures.* Unpublished doctoral dissertation, University of Michigan, 1967.

Maimon, E.P. & Nodine, B.F. Measuring syntactic growth: Errors and expectations in sentence-combining practice with college freshmen. *Research in the Teaching of English,* 1978, **12,** 233–244.

Matsuhashi, A. *Producing Written Discourse: A Theory-based Description of the Temporal Characteristics of Three Discourse Types from Four Competent Grade 12 Writers.* Unpublished doctoral dissertation, State University of New York at Buffalo, 1979.

Mead, G.H. *Mind, Self, and Society.* Chicago: University of Chicago Press, 1934.

Mellon, J.C. *Transformational Sentence-combining: A Method for Enhancing the Development of Syntactic Fluency in English Composition.* Urbana, Ill.: National Council of Teachers of English, 1969.

Milz, V. First graders can write: Focus on communication. *Theory into Practice,* 1980, **19,** 185.

Moffett, J. *Teaching the Universe of Discourse.* Boston: Houghton Mifflin, 1968.

Moffett, J. Integrity in the teaching of writing. *Phi Delta Kappan,* 1979, **61,** 276–279.

Moffett, J. Writing, inner speech, and meditation. In J. Moffett (ed.), *Coming on Center.* Clifton, Va.: Boynton & Associates, 1981.

Morenberg, M., Daiker, D., & Kerek, A. Sentence combining at the college level: An experimental study. *Research in the Teaching of English,* 1978, **12,** 245–256.

Muller, H.J. The Uses of English: guidelines for the teaching of English From the Anglo-American Conference at Dartmouth College, New York: Holt, Rinehart and Winston, 1967.

Ney, J.W. The hazards of the course: Sentence-combining in freshman English. *English Record,* 1976, **27,** 70–77.

Ohmann, R. Generative grammars and the concept of literary style. *Word.* 1964, **20,** 423–439.

Ohmann, R. Literature as sentences. *College English,* 1966, **27,** 261–267.

Page, W. (ed.) *Help for the Reading Teacher: new directions in research.* Urbana, Ill.: National Council of Teachers of English, 1975.

Perl, S. *Five Writers Writing: Case Studies of the Composing Processes of Unskilled College*

Writers. Unpublished doctoral dissertation, New York University, 1978.

Pianko, S. *The Composing Acts of College Freshmen.* Unpublished doctoral dissertation, Rutgers University, 1977.

Pike, K.L. *Language in Relation to a Unified Theory of the Structure of Human Behavior.* The Hauge: Mouton, 1967.

Read, C. *Children's Categorization of Speech Sounds in English* (Research Report No. 17). Urbana, Ill.: National Council of Teachers of English, 1975.

Rohman, D.C. & Wiecke, A.O. *Pre-writing: The Construction and Application of Models for Concept Formation to Writing* (USOE Cooperative Research Project No. 2174). Washington, D.C.: U.S. Office of Education, 1964.

Scribner, S. & Cole, M. Unpackaging literacy. In M.F. Whiteman (ed.), *Variation in Writing: Functional and Linguistic Cultural Differences* (Vol. 1). Hillsdale, N.J.: Lawrence Erlbaum Associates, 1981.

Smith, M. *Aspects of Verbal Behavior in Written Composition: contrasts between formal and non-formal thinkers of college age.* Unpublished doctoral dissertation, Rutgers University, U.S.A., 1980.

Vygotsky, L.S. *Thought and Language.* Cambridge, Mass.: MIT Press, 1962.

Walker, J. *The Teacher's Assistant in English Composition.* Carlisle: Printed by George Kline, 1808.

Weiss, R.H. & Walters, S.A. *Writing to Learn.* Paper presented at the annual meeting of the American Educational Research Association, Boston, April 7–11, 1980.

Weschler, J. (ed.). *Essays in the Aesthetics of Science.* Cambridge, Mass.: MIT Press, 1978.

Young, R. Invention: A topographical survey in teaching composition. In G. Tate (ed.), *Ten Bibliographic Essays.* Fort Worth: Texas Christian University Press, 1976.

Young, R.E. Arts, crafts, gifts, and knacks: Some disharmonies in the new rhetoric. *Visible Language,* 1980, **14**, 341–350.

Young, R.E., Becker, A.L. & Pike, K.L. Rhetoric: *Discovery and Change.* New York: Harcourt, Brace & World, 1970.

Zoellner, R. A behavioral approach to writing. *College English,* 1969, **30**, 267–320.

4.2 Fostering Development in the Writing of Eight-Year-Olds

Lynne Thorogood and Bridie Raban

Source: Edited version of Thorogood, L. and Raban, B. (1985) 'Fostering development in the writing of eight-year-olds'. *Reading* **19**, No. 2, 100–109.

Research suggests that children writing for an audience are more likely to be able to produce good writing. With this in mind a study was planned to investigate the relationship between a sense of audience and the improvement of writing quality, and whether any gains achieved could be sustained and would remain evident in a more mundane writing task in an everyday classroom environment.

In the investigation described below, an activity was devised which involved older children (8-year-olds) writing stories for younger children (3–5-year-olds) in their own school. The project was carried out over one term and was conducted as follows:

Week 1
The class of thirty 8-year-old children were asked to think about what they would need to do if they were going to write a story for the children in the nursery or reception classes. Their responses fell into the following categories:
Neatness: 'Be neat so they can read it.' 'Do your very best handwriting.' 'Make it look tidy so it can go in a book.'
Imagination: 'Make it a nice story.' 'It should be the kind of thing they like reading.' 'You've got to think of something they haven't heard before.'
Spelling, Punctuation, Grammar: 'You must spell everything properly or else the little children will learn to do mistakes.' 'And put full stops and capital letters.' 'You shouldn't put things like "we was" when you write something.' 'You should make it be like a proper book, with commas and everything.'
Illustration: 'Make it look nice and put pictures in.' 'It should be colourful and nice to look at.'
Vocabulary: 'Don't use too many hard words.' 'We can read words they can't, so you should remember to make it easy or else they won't be able to read it.'

After this discussion the children were asked to write their story for younger children, taking as much time as they felt they needed. They were provided with rough paper, and lined paper for the final copy. At the end of the day all the children had completed their work. The stories were later read by two teachers who selected ten children as being especially fluent and imaginative writers. These children were divided into two groups of five, one group to be introduced to the writing project, the others to be taken as a group for practical maths work once a week. If there were any differences between these two groups with respect to their ultimate writing development, then it could not be due to the extra attention alone.

Week 2

Five children were taken for extra maths work and this continued in every subsequent week. The other five children were introduced to the writing project. This latter group first discussed the kinds of books they themselves like reading and what attracted them to a book. Next the children visited the nursery and reception classes and looked at the books available for the children to pick up and look at, one girl taking particular note of the degree of 'well-thumbedness' of different types of books. They also looked through the teachers' bookshelves of story books to read aloud to the class. They talked to the younger children about what their favourite books were, and whether they preferred being read to aloud or reading things for themselves. After the visit, decisions were made about whether to write their stories for the nursery class, in which case the story would be read aloud to the younger children, or for the reception class children to read for themselves. Four children opted for the former as they considered quite appropriately that the latter option would restrict vocabulary which would cause them difficulties. Only one chose this option.

Week 3

At this stage the children visited the nursery unit (four children) and the reception class (one child). In the nursery the children read aloud to groups of three and four year olds, and the one who visited the reception class heard some of the children read. On their return the children discussed their findings, and it appeared from their comments that they were beginning to gain insights into the problems of producing children's books and into the reading processes of the younger children. One girl remarked that it was hard to believe that she had once had to struggle like that to get through her reading pages. Her companion compared the younger children's reading with his own efforts to read the sports report in his father's *Daily Telegraph* that morning, 'You're trying so hard to read the words you forget what it's about.'

After a little more discussion on the criteria for producing 'listenable' or readable stories the first roughing-out of ideas was started.

Week 4

The girl who was writing for the reception class requested word lists of the first books of the reading scheme in order to remind her of the vocabulary limitations. Writing continued, and at the end of the session the first drafts of four stories were completed.

Week 5

All the first drafts were completed and the children exchanged work and read each other's stories, then offered comments and suggestions on how to improve, simplify or correct their efforts. An altered intermediate version was then read aloud by each author to the rest of the group and further suggestions on grammar and modification of story structure were made.

Week 6
The final versions were produced and the design of the 'book form' was started. The reception class story was tried out using two children as 'guinea-pigs. Help was given with spelling and grammar in the final versions.

Week 7
The children began producing illustrations for their books, and brought in friends to help them with this.

Week 8
The illustrations were completed and handed, with the final copy of the stories in 'book form', to the printers. Older children from a nearby sixth form who had been assisting throughout this project helped to prepare the books in final form.

Weeks 9 and 10
Printing in progress.

Week 11
The completed books were returned to the children, and they were taken to the nursery and reception classes and used with the younger children there, the authors reading aloud to groups or hearing reception class children reading to them.

Week 12
The whole class of thirty children were asked again to write a story suitable for younger children — the suggestion was that it could be used as part of a nursery or reception class assembly.

Results and discussion of findings

Many of these children could already write well, but writing to some purpose other than to please the teacher was seen as beneficial for their writing development. If children know that their writing is going to entertain and interest others, they are more likely to take care and pride in good presentation. Children seemed to understand the need for correct spelling and punctuation, particularly if the finished effort is to be read by the younger ones. The constraints involved, for example, the limitations of language, vocabulary, and the like, were seen as a challenge to the children's writing ability rather than as drawbacks. The activity was also seen as being beneficial in a more social way, of giving the older children a feeling of responsibility and achievement, and the younger children a new kind of support in the early stages of their reading development.

During class activity of week 1, all but three children completed their story during the session before playtime. These three were slower, poorer writers rather than the better ones. Only four children used the rough paper which was provided, and they only did so to try out spellings they were unsure of. There was little real evidence of the planning stages. The 'conception' and 'incubation' stages described by Britton (1975) seemed to run concurrent with writing, although there was some premeditation time available at the beginning of the session as the children discussed the things they would need to remember when writing for a younger group. It is interesting to note, however, that several of the better writers spent the first five to ten minutes of writing time finding and sharpening pencils, visiting the cloakroom to fetch handkerchiefs and writing the sentence 'Once upon a time', which they later rubbed out. This could indicate that a kind of planning was taking place, with children finding various activities to fill their 'thinking time' so as not to be accused by the teacher of time-wasting.

This description offers an interesting contrast with the final class activity after the selected group had spent several weeks producing stories for younger children. There was a short discussion time, as on the previous occasion, and then the children were asked to write their story. Most of the class, including the maths group, expanded or contracted the task to fit the available time, exactly as before, leaving a few spare minutes at the end for drawing or reading. The project group, however, spent the first few minutes alternately doodling and jotting down notes on the rough paper and staring into space. Not until later had every child started to write their story, and again three of them had not completed their work by playtime. On this occasion the three were from the writing project group, who came back during lunchtime to complete the first copy of their stories. All five children from the writing group suggested rewriting their story in their 'best writing' and checking spellings, one child offering to do this at home in his own time.

The analysis of the children's work was based on a study of Menig-Peterson and McCabe (1978). Although the method of analysis was used by them to assess spoken stories it was felt that it could equally well be applied to those which had been written, and would be more appropriate than the possible alternatives of counting words, types of words, sentence length and the like. The writing was scored according to their criteria in the categories Who, Where, What, When, How and Why, with a maximum possible score of 13:

Measure of Writing

1. Who　　0 No reference to participants
　　　　　　1 use of indefinite pronoun only
　　　　　　2 adequate specification
　　　　　　3 full specification, including the writer's relationship to the participants

2. Where   0 Specification absent or confused
             1 partial specification; where some but not all of the events took place
             2 adequate but incomplete specification
             3 full specification

3. What   0 Specification inadequate or confused
             1 partial specification; use of indefinite pronoun
             2 naming all objects

4. When   0 Time reference absent or confused
             1 adequate time reference but incomplete
             2 full time reference

5. How   0 Confused
             1 incomplete
             2 complete

6. Why   0 Absence of causality
             1 presence of causality

The work of the five children who completed the writing project and the five children who completed the maths project was analysed, together with the work of five other children chosen at random from the class. Work from the first and the final week was analysed as well as the completed project work. A comparison of the children's mean scores can be seen in Table 1.

It was clear that the children involved with the project benefitted in several ways from their experience. In all but one case the work completed in the activity which took place in the last week of the study scored one or more points higher than the first week's work. In no case was it lower. This can be contrasted with the work of the maths group and that of the rest of the class, which in only two cases was higher and in the case of five children was lower on the final activity.

The work of all but one child which was produced for the project was of a higher standard than their efforts at either of the whole class activities. This child, who scored one point lower on her project work, was very inhibited by the fact that she was writing for the children in the reception class and had planned to produce something for them to read themselves, using almost exclusively vocabulary of the first few books of the reading scheme. She set herself a difficult task, and despite her slightly low score was in many ways very successful in achieving her own aims.

Table 1 Comparison of Mean Scores from Writing of 3 groups

	Mean Scores		
N = 5	1st week story	Project story	Final week story
Project group	9.4	11.2	10.8
Maths group	7	—	5.2
Class group	6	—	5.6

Although several children in the maths group and in the rest of the class seemed to have deteriorated when judged on their final score, other factors indicate that this may not be the case. Many children wrote much longer stories and had improved in both spelling and grammar, none of which was considered in the method of assessment used here. However, this was also true of the project group, and served to enhance their scores even further by comparison with the other children in the class.

Conclusions

Despite the fact that there were some difficulties and problems involved with organizing this activity it was felt to have been worthwhile and of benefit to both the writers and their audience. The writers were already writing well in a spontaneous, creative manner, but were reaching a point where they were ready to try new techniques, having achieved possibly as much as they could without further prompting. The gains made by the project group and their increased concern for the planning, appearance and presentation of their work due to their having a 'sense of audience' seem sufficiently worthwhile for this kind of project to be carried out with many more children.

References

Britton, J. (1975) *The Development of Writing Abilities* 11–18. Macmillan/Schools Council.
Menig-Peterson, C.L. and A. McCabe (1978) 'Children's orientation of a listener to the context of their narratives'. *Developmental Psychology*, **14**, No. 6.

Appendix

Elizabeth's stories written during the project.

Week 1 story: 'Mr. Teddy-bear Kind-heart'
One day a horrible boy called David started throwing his toys about. That night the toys came to life and they talked. There was a teddy-bear called Kind-heart and a baby teddy-bear called Soft-heart and they planned to run away then they got back in the toy cupboard and went to sleep. In the morning they were again tossed around. So that night off they ran. Then they looked at their map of jangillo (which is where they lived) and they rushed off down peculiarness avenue. Half way down the avenue they found a hospital and went in and Kind-heart found out that Soft-heart had broken his arm in three places. The nurse said to Kind-heart Soft-heart will be in here three weeks so when Soft-heart was mended they went on there way. They wandered on for days eating wild berries and at last they came to a house. They knocked on the door a little girl opened it and she really loved them so they stayed with her and lived happily after.

Project story: 'Milly-Jane's Dinosaur' ·

1. Once there lived a little girl called Milly-Jane Smith. Milly-Jane lived on a farm which was called Riverside Farm because it was beside the River Tinkle. One fine summer morning she decided to take her toys Teddy and Dolly for a walk by the river. (Picture of M-J + toys)
2. A few minutes later she was sitting by the river watching the ducks swim by. Suddenly she noticed a thing like an egg lying in the marshy ground by the edge of the water. She picked it up and saw that it was a strange looking egg, very big and dark brown. (Picture of M-J holding egg)
3. She took it home and asked her mummy if she could put the egg under Mrs. Warm the broody hen. Her mummy said 'Yes', because she did not think the egg would hatch, but three weeks later it did hatch. Out of the egg came a strange looking animal, a bit like a lizard. Milly-Jane was pleased with her new pet. She called it Rosie.
4. Big picture of the baby dinosaur.
5. Rosie followed Mrs. Warm around the farm, and ate dandelions and grew and grew. Farmer Smith, Milly-Jane's Father noticed Rosie, and he said, 'Your new pet is starting to look like a dinosaur.' That is just what Rosie grew into. She was a friendly dinosaur who only ate plants. She liked to paddle in the River Tinkle with Mrs. Warm and Milly-Jane on her back. (Picture of paddling dinosaur)
6. After about one year farmer Smith was getting cross because Rosie was eating his corn and barley and she was really big by then so she ate a lot. He said Rosie would have to go and live in the zoo, so that is where they took her, and the zoo manager was very pleased because he could have the only dinosaur in the world. He said Milly-Jane could visit Rosie any time, and get in the zoo without paying, so everyone was pleased and they all lived happily ever after.
7. Picture of zoo.

Final week story: 'Rude Jan and unselfish toys'

In a town a long way from here there was a house called happy home and it was a happy all except for Jan. She was very rude. Her mother told her to go and get some potatoes and she said no I shan't go and get them I wo'nt and Jan got sent up to bed. That night Jan's mother sat and cryed in the nursery. Jan's toys heard her and they were so upset. That night when Jan's mother had gone out of the nursery the toys started to move and whisper. 'Twelve o'clock then', said Teddy yes they all whispered. So at twelve o'clock the toys all came into Jans bedroom and they had a party a small one Jan woke up and said 'oh toys I am very pleased to see you are'nt you pleased to see me'. 'Not very' said the toys. 'You should be kind to your mother, you say those things to her. You should change' 'I wo'nt! Jan snapped. So the toys ran away thinking Jan has hurt µs and torn us we will go to poor children who will mend us and look after us. So off they went and they went to a childrens home where the children did look after them and not long after they had settled in they heard that Jan had changed and she was not rude any more. So being kindhearted and forgiving they bought her new toys and she was never rude any more.

Scoring procedure: completeness of context

The writing pieces are assessed in terms of adequacy with respect to each of the following and given an appropriate score as follows:

1. WHO
Four degrees of specification of the participants are possible, with scores ranging from 0 to 3:

(a) There is no reference to the participants at all; this receives a score of 0.
(b) The participants are referred to with an indefinite pronoun, 1.
(c) The participants are adequately sepecified, with the child providing at least the first names of all of the participants (e.g. 'I played with Sally'), although the child has not specified his or her relationship to that person. In addition, this category includes unspecified pronouns whose identity is easily inferred because of our shared assumptions about the world. For example, if a child writes 'we went to the hospital in the middle of the night' one can assume that the parents took him or her, 2.
(d) The participants are fully specified, with the child embedding all of the participants in the context of their relationship with the child, for example, 'my neighbour, Bonnie', 3.

The entire piece must be at or above a certain level to get that level's score. Thus, a child who fully specified four participants but referred to the fifth with an indefinite pronoun receives a score of 1.

2. WHERE
Four levels of specification are possible with scores ranging from 0 to 3:

(a) No specification or a confused specification of where receives a score of 0.
(b) Partial specification includes a description of where some but not all of the events took place, 1.
(c) Adequate specification provides part of the 'where' information, but is incomplete. For example, 'I was at Gail's' is adequately specified, although it specifies neither Gail's relationship to the writer nor her geographical location, 2.
(d) Full specification provides either a geographical location ('I went to the Town Hall') or, in the case in which the child is describing a visit to somebody, a specification of that person's relationship to the writer ('I went to visit my Aunt Joan'), 3.

3. WHAT
Three degrees of specification of the objects involved are possible, scoring 0 to 2:

(a) No specification or a confused specification of objects that are necessarily present is given a score of 0.

(b) Partial specification includes referring to an object with the indefinite pronoun 'it' and receives a score of 1.

(c) Full specification includes naming all of the objects and receives a score of 2.

If no objects are mentioned and none are obligatory, the writing piece is not scored for 'what'.

4. WHEN

It is possible to orient with respect to both relative time and absolute time. The proportion of narratives that provide a relative time orientation averages about 27% for all ages and is not considered here. For absolute time (calendar and clock time), the following three levels of specification are possible, with scores ranging from 0 to 2:

(a) There is no time reference, or a confused one, 0.

(b) There is an adequate time reference that specifies part of the time information but not all, for example, 'it was night-time' without mentioning how long ago that night was, 1.

(c) There is full time reference, for example, 'last Easter' or 'when I was just 4 years old', 2.

If it is possible to infer the time even though it is not overtly stated, such as in a writing piece about visiting Santa Claus, the piece is scored as adequately referenced with respect to 'when'.

5. HOW

Each writing piece is scored as:

(a) Confused such that the reader cannot understand what occurs, 0.

(b) Incomplete, or missing important information in terms of the actions that occur, 1.

(c) Complete or fully comprehensible to the reader, 2.

The scores range from 0 to 2.

6. WHY

Two types of causation are possible. The child could be explicit concerning why the events occur, or could imply the causal relationship without overtly writing it down.

The example 'he started crying because I hit him' overtly states the causal relationship; 'I hit him and then he started crying' gives the sequential progression of the events and implies the cause for the crying, but does not explicitly state it.

No clear justification can be made for considering one type of causal relationship as superior to the other, so the writing can be scored only with respect to the presence or absence of 'why'.

4.3 Why Students Can't Write Arguments

Aviva Freedman and Ian Pringle

Source: Freedman, A. and Pringle, I. (1984) 'Why Students Can't Write Arguments'. *English in Education* **18**, no. 2, 73–84.

We know relatively little about how well students succeed in mastering different modes or genres in their writing. There are a limited number of research studies which focus on very specific aspects of the writing — syntactic complexity, in particular — but most of our evidence comes from impressionistic comments made by teachers or markers (or even, in times like the present, by politicians or newspaper editorialists). A typical teacher's complaint about student writing in the intermediate grades, for example, is that students can write stories well enough, but 'they just can't write arguments'. Precisely what it is that students cannot do in argumentation or can do in narration, however, is never defined.

In a recent study, therefore, we tried to find out what the real problem is.

Subjects

The subjects of our study were 500 students in the Carleton Board of Education, a suburban Ottawa school board. These 500 students constituted the entire population of 17 grade seven and eight classes; only those who were absent for one or another of the two writing assignments were excluded from the study. Each student produced two pieces of writing, one a narrative and the other an argument, so that we had 1000 scripts to work with. Originally this writing had been elicited as part of a holistic scoring experiment conducted by other researchers which was designed to train teachers in holistic evaluation and to correlate holistic grades with the students' in-class performance. Once that experiment was completed, we were given both scripts for our own analysis, as well as the holistic marks for each piece of writing — that is, the combined holistic score of four independent ratings by classroom teachers. We were thus able to correlate the results of our own analysis with these holistic scores.

Ottawa is, in general, an upper middle class city, a 'government town', with no heavy industry and very little poverty. The average educational level of the population is very high, and the students studied perform at an extraordinarily high level — on average well beyond the norms reported for the high achievers in other jurisdictions at the same grade levels. All in all then, the weaknesses that teachers perceive in the students' argumentative writing are not due to sócio–economic factors, different cultural expectations or rhetorical patterns, or deficits in overall language ability.

The analysis

When asked to verbalize and analyse the reasons for their dissatisfaction with their pupils' attempts at persuasion, teachers typically respond: 'They just don't seem to be able to organize their ideas. Their essays have no form or structure.'

Our own reading of the student writing, both their stories and their arguments, suggested that the issue of 'structure' might indeed be crucial, although not perhaps in the usual sense, and for this reason we decided to compare the degree to which the stories and arguments respectively were able to incorporate the classical schema or conventional structure for those genres. In other words, we wanted to see how well the stories accorded with the formal pattern for narrative preferred in our culture and how well the arguments realized the formal properties and pattern of argumentation. To do this, we developed two instruments, one defining the basic features of story structure, the second, the essential characteristics of argumentation.

Our instrument specified that in order to 'succeed as a story', that is, to realize the conventional schema for the genre, a piece of writing had to include some setting information and at least one complete episode.[1]

As to the instrument evaluating arguments, since there is no comtemporary 'grammar' of argumentative structure as there is for story structure, we turned to the centuries-long tradition, beginning before Aristotle, which has attempted to formulate and codify rules for persuasive discourse. On the basis of contemporary and classical rhetorical analyses, we defined the following features as essential to argumentation. First, the whole piece of discourse must be unified by either an implicit or (more commonly) an explicitly stated single restricted thesis; that is, the whole must be so unified that each point and each illustration either directly substantiates the thesis or is a link in a chain of reasoning which supports that thesis. Secondly, the individual points and illustrations must be integrated within a hierarchic structure so that each proposition is logically linked not only to the preceeding and succeeding propositions but also to the central thesis and indeed to every proposition within the whole text. Although a series of other studies (which are reported elsewhere) examined different aspects of all the scripts, for this particular study we restricted our analysis to a random subsample of 112 (11 per cent).

Findings

All the narratives analysed contain some setting information, and 98.25 per cent include at least one complete episode. In other words, over 98 per cent of the narratives incorporate the classical schema for story structure. This is especially interesting in light of our findings in another research study where, in a comparable group of grade 5 student narratives, over one third did not realize these minimal criteria for story structure.

Furthermore, the crudeness of our measure does not reveal the sophistication of these grade 7 and 8 students in their handling of story structure. Setting information, for example, is not presented baldly and separately at the beginning of the story in the manner of many typical fairy tales: 'Once upon a time, in a far away land, there lived a good king, his beautiful queen, and their daughter Princess Cordelia' (as quoted in Rumelhart 1975, p. 213). Instead, the setting information is presented indirectly and subtly, as part of the presentation of the action. In the same way, these student writers display impressive control of episode structure; not only do their narratives incorporate such structure, but the writers seem able to play with that structure at will, to use it to make psychological points, to tease the reader and reverse his expectations. Examine, for example, the following narrative, which was in fact judged holistically by the teachers to be below average.

> The nerves in my stomach were jiggling around like butterflies. Today was the big game and *I* was starting! When the coach told me I was starting centre, I couldn't believe it! At first I tried to convince him to start Elsa but he wouldn't listen. I implored him 'Don't you want to win? Don't you want to be state champions?' He nodded. 'Then why start me?' Coach Brown looked shocked at my tone.
>
> 'Listen Connie, I'm coach and what I say goes!' How well I remembered those words. Even though it didn't seem so, I cherished the thought of starting centre.
>
> 'Hey Connie!' It was Elsa, our star player. I turned around, not wanting to face her. Would she be mad or jealous or maybe she would be just plain sarcastic, her knowing that she out-ranked me as a player. 'Connie, wait up! Let's go and get changed into our uniforms. You're starting you know.' I couldn't tell if there was any sarcasm in her voice. Oh well, I thought to myself, maybe if I am seen with Elsa, people would notice me. It was Elsa, not I, who got all the guys. It was Elsa, not I, who got elected to all the offices and who won the awards. Elsa was somebody and I was nobody. I hurried to catch up with her, but her six foot body had already reached the locker room. As I opened the door the loud voices of our John Leer College Basketball Team were blasting out our school cheer.
>
> > Go John Leer Go!
> > Beat'em!
> > Bust'em!
> > That's our custom!
> > Go John Leer Go!
>
> It was hardly appropriate for basketball but we loved it.
>
> The team rushed out on the court. The starting girls set up for the jump. I missed it, as usual on the very first whistle. I was taken off for Elsa. As the game progressed it was very close. Finally, with one minute to go, it was tied, 24 all. The coach called a sub and put me in for Elsa. I decided then and there to win the game. I got the ball and dribbled as I have never dribbled before. I went up for a lay up and scored! I was filled with joy until I noticed the grim faces of my team mates. I glanced up at the scoreboard. Two points went up — for the other team! I scored on the wrong basket! Tears sprang to my

> eyes as I met the angry stares of my friends. Then Elsa came up and said 'You played a great game!' Then I knew why everyone liked her. She cared.

The writer builds up a conventional climax, reverses that in what has itself become a stock twist of the plot, though a considerably sophisticated one, and only then makes the real point — Elsa's reaction to the direct consequence. Such manipulation of the elements of story structure reveal a sense of complete ease with the genre.

The analysis of the arguments, however, revealed a sharp contrast. Only 30.4 per cent contained either an explicit or implicit thesis, and only another 23.3 per cent were judged to be marginal. And as to their ability to organize the individual points within a hierarchic logical superstructure, only 12.5 per cent were judged to satisfy this criterion, and a further 10.6 per cent were marginal. In total, then, only 12.5 per cent are able to realize the minimal criteria specified for argumentation.

As to the remaining 82.5 per cent, they fall into two groups which we categorized on the basis of the kind of organizing patterns and consequent thinking strategies implied: these we named 'focal' (28.6 per cent of the scripts) and 'associational' (50 per cent of the scripts). A focal essay is one in which each point individually relates back to a central focus (the topic or, in some cases, the thesis) although the points themselves are not logically related to each other, as in the following essay:

> Young teenagers have a tendency to get into trouble that would require some punishment but I can think of many more reasonable punishments besides physical such as being confined to barracks, getting extra chores, staying inside all weekend, etc.
> Teenagers that get into trouble with the law should be maybe if necessary be physically punished by a slap along with chores. Otherwise I think teenagers should be physically punished because when they get older any physical punishment they received might cause child abuse to their children.
> If a parent physically punishes a boy or especially a girl around 13 they might seriously injure them for that is around the age of puberty.
> If serious physical punishment is received by a young teenager it would most likely disturb them which would cause problems at home and at school.
> The young teenager might get into fights to protect his or her parents reputation.
> So that's why I think physical punishment to a young teenager is absolutely unheard of.

Associational writing, on the other hand, begins with some statement regarding the topic. Each succeeding argument or proposition relates to the one immediately preceding, but is in no way tied to a central argument. The development resembles stream of consciousness somewhat; the connection between adjacent points is not necessarily logical, and the individual points are not themselves interrelated within some hierarchic superstructure. Consider for example, the following essay:

> I think it really depends on the reason or need for the punishment. If the young teenager lied to the parent and the parent found out then I feel that talking out the issue would be best. And if the teenager hit the younger sister or brother, the parent should ask if the teenager would like it. The average teenager would most likely say, 'Yes, I

wouldn't mind' because they feel if they said 'No' you may think they were a chicken. So maybe you should hit them but not very hard. Ask the question over and over. I would say as a young teenager with a younger sister I would never dream of hitting her again. I would personally never hit any young child, then you are teaching them that it is all right to hit someone.

My opinion is to, whether you use it or not, talk the problem out and agree of a punishment.

To sum up then, while over 98 per cent of the students were able to embody narrative structure in their stories, only 12.5 per cent of these same students were able to realize the classical argumentative pattern. These findings may explain the teachers' intuitions concerning their students' writing of argumentation and narration. What the teachers seem to be responding to is the difference in the degree to which students can realize the conventional 'form', the classical pattern or structure for the genre.

And indeed, when we correlated the holistic scores with a series of distinct features of the writing — with syntactic complexity, for example, and with mechanical correctness — we found only one correlation of any strength: that between the holistic scores and the degree of realization of the classical argumentative pattern.

Discussion

The conventional analysis given by teachers for their students' difficulties with argumentation is thus misleading. It is not the case that 'these students just can't organize', that they have 'no sense of form or structure yet'. These student writers proved to be extraordinarily adept at organizing — narrative material. Their difficulty is more specific, the organization of argumentation.

Why? A number of reasons suggest themselves. First, students are exposed to, even inundated with, material embodying narrative structure from an early age. What they first read tends largely to be narrative, and more significantly, what they first hear read is narrative. What they see in films and on television also usually follows the same basic structure.

Nor is it only in literature or drama that children are exposed to story structure. Even more significantly, they hear narratives or stories as part of normal daily conversation. James Britton long ago pointed out the relationship between gossip and literature (Britton 1970); we all tell the stories of our days and of our lives, and children listen to their mothers, fathers, caretakers, and siblings tell these stories to each other from the time they first understand language. In attending to these stories, the children gain an insight into the nature of narrative structure from a very different vantage point: not only do they hear stories which embody that structure, but they see how that kind of structure is imposed on the formless material of life itself. For life does not come to us as a story; story structure must imposed upon material that is itself formless, diffuse, inchoate. When a little girl, say, shares with her father the experience of an afternoon and then hears him select from his experiences,

connecting 'and heightening those selected in particular culturally determined ways in order to tell her mother an anecdote based on the afternoon's
experiences, she learns an important lesson not just about the surface features
of story structure, but about the process whereby it is created. And she thus
learns to tell her own stories too.

With argumentation, however, there is no such early training ground. Our
children don't read arguments early, nor are arguments what they hear read.
They do, of course, hear oral arguments, and they participate in them as well.
But there is an important difference: oral arguments differ radically from
written arguments in a way that oral stories do not from written. There are
two important points here then. Firstly, children do not have the early
exposure to written argumentative structure that they have to story structure.
And secondly, the oral skills that children develop in telling stories can be
transferred to their writing of narratives, whereas in order to move from oral
to written argumentation children need to develop a new set of cognitive and
rhetorical strategies.

Carl Bereiter and Marlene Scardamalia (1982) present a very penetrating
analysis of the cognitive difficulties involved in the shift from 'conversation
to composition', and by extending their analysis we can understand a great
deal about the difference between narration and argumentation. As Bereiter
and Scardamalia point out, the rules of oral discourse allow each person only
a specified length of time (or words) for each conversational turn. Consequently when they first begin to write, children tend to produce material that
is equivalent to one conversational turn. Samples of student argumentative
writing by ten and twelve-year-old children show exactly this phenomenon; in
each case, the children produce one or perhaps two points concerning a
specific topic, not because they don't know any more about it (for when they
are asked to produce more, they do so readily), but because they are con-
forming to the rules for language production that they have already learned
— the rules for producing spoken discourse.

One cognitive ability, then, that must be acquired in learning to write is the
capacity to continue, to produce more text. However narration is an exception. When one tells a story, one is granted conversational permission to
continue beyond the usual length allotted for a single utterance. The ability
to generate extended discourse for written narratives, then, has already been
acquired in the production of oral narratives.

Equally important is the fact that telling a story is a solo, whereas having an
argument is necessarily a duet at least. The production of a story is entirely
the work of one individual: although the story teller relies on the hearers'
feedback in order to determine how well they understand the story, he or she
receives no help from the audience in the generating of the story material, nor
in imposing a structure upon that material.

In an oral argument, in contrast, all the speakers share in the generation of
the material, and this sharing involves more than simply the parcelling out of
different tasks, with each person assigned the responsibility for generating
ideas on a particular subtopic. The generation itself is shared: each new idea is

produced in response to the immediately preceding point. In other words, in presenting a new idea, each speaker is also prompting their partner and prodding his or her memory, aiding thus in the generation of the next point. However, when the argumentative task is a written one, the writer must acquire a new solitary, ability — the ability to scan one's own memory to retrieve all the relevant material. And beyond this, there is a different ability required as well. An argument does not consist merely of a series of points relating to a central topic. To produce a successful piece of argumentation, the writer must be able to hold all the points generated in mind (or on paper) and to find some way of organizing them according to the appropriate structure.

Again, the organizational structure of oral argument provides no model. The pattern of oral argumentation is that of a tennis match where each shot is parried by one's partner, and each shot may change the direction of the argument so that the end may be played on very different territory. There is no requirement (and little likelihood) of internal logical consistency or patterning. Thus in learning to write argumentation, the novice writer must acquire another new skill — the ability to discover and/or create a rigorously logical structure which will unify and order the individual points generated.

It is this ability, we would argue, which is particularly difficult to acquire; because at bottom what is required in order to structure argument appropriately is an ability to abstract and conceptualize. To say this is not to make the obvious point that the basic units of narrative are specific concrete events while the basic units of argumentation are generalizations. What we are arguing is that in order to incorporate the conventional pattern required in argumentation, in order to produce a unified and logically structured piece of persuasive discourse, one must first be able to abstract and to conceptualize; the very ordering of the material implies the power to abstract and conceptualize, in precisely the sense that Vygotsky uses the terms in his chapter on concept formation in *Thought and Language* (1962).

Vygotsky specified the individual cognitive steps in the process of the progress towards true concept formation. One must first be able to perceive objective bonds that bind similar objects; then, one must be able to analyse that similiarity in order to determine the common element(s), which are necessarily abstract; subsequently, one must be able to formulate what is common in language, that is, to verbalize the concept; and then one must show such a mastery of that concept as to be able to apply it to other experiential configurations and finally to interrelate it with other such abstract formulations.

This is precisely what we must do in order to find a unifying thesis and an organizing pattern for an essay. Having generated a series of separate points all relating to the central topic, we must group together those that are like, that is first perceive their similarity, then analyse that similarity in order to discover the abstract common bond, formulate that commonality in language, and then interrelate that formulation with other such abstract formulations derived from other similar groupings: an extraordinarily complex conceptual task, which becomes still more difficult as the number of individual points and groupings of such points increase. In the light of the enormous complexity of the task, our students' failure are more understandable, and indeed predictable in the light of Vygotsky's finding that the ability to form concepts seems to be acquired only about puberty.

Moreover, Vygotsky's analysis of the progress towards the stage of true concept formation is particularly illuminating in the context of the student writing we examined. He distinguishes three distinct stages in the progress towards the ability to conceptualize and further discriminates several types of thinking characteristic of each stage; two of these, typical of his second stage, have very close parallels with the kinds of organizing strategies we found represented in our students' argumentative writing.

The second stage as a whole he calls 'thinking in complexes'. At this stage children are able to recognize objective concrete and factual common bonds, but not abstract or logical ones. This is analogous to the strategy employed by our student writers which we called 'focal', in which each of the individual points presented related to the central topic, though none of the points related to each other.

A second pattern that Vygotsky identified is thinking in chains. There is no common bond uniting the chain as a whole at all, no internal structure. This Vygotsky identifies as the archetypal pattern of thinking in complexes, and its analogy with our associational writing, the strategy of 50 per cent of the 12 and 13-year-old students, is striking.

The implication is, then, that the majority of these students, are still thinking at the level of complexes and not yet able to attain to true concepts. Their failure in argumentation may thus be attributed precisely to this fact, that they have not yet acquired the ability to abstract and conceptualize which argumentative structure requires. Presumably once these students have reached that stage in early adolescence when the cognitive processes mature to the point that they can form true concepts, they should also become able to incorporate classical argumentative form in their writing.

Vygotsky's discussion of concept formation may also cast some light on a different phenomenon, noted by a number of researchers in the writing of much older students. Susan Miller (1980), for example, has described how her students had demonstrated their ability to write effective arguments on a series of tasks; however, when confronted with a more intellectually or morally demanding assignment, they showed a sudden breakdown in their rhetorical skills — they could no longer write effectively structured argumentative pieces.

If the ability to discover and create the formal pattern of argumentation involves the process of forming true concepts, as defined by Vygotsky, that task may be made more difficult by changing the nature of the data. For example, the common bonds, the likenesses between the items may be more subtle and difficult to discern. Or there may simply be more data to take into account. Or more difficult still, writers may have to go up several rungs on the ladder of abstraction: that is, they may have to formulate the common abstract bonds uniting several different groupings, then once again find common groupings among those abstracted concepts in order to formulate their similarities in conceptual form, and so on. In each case, the task, which is fundamentally that required for the appropriate presentation of argumentative material in the classical formal pattern, becomes more taxing. This may explain as well — at least in part — the phenomenon acknowledged by all of us who write: Writing never becomes easy.

One major reason for this is that the constant growth in our experience as humans necessitates new representations of reality in language, as John Dixon (1967) explains in his penetrating gloss of T.S. Eliot's powerful statement on this subject in East Coker.

However, in the writing of argumentation, there may be a further cause as well. As the intellectual challenge of the task becomes more demanding in the ways specified above, the imposition of the mind's logical pattern upon one's data may become increasingly difficult. As Lloyd-Jones writes: 'As one's intellectual reach is extended, one's once-adequate writing is no longer sufficient. . . . To some extent, confusing prose is a sign of active engagement with new ideas as opposed to routine regurgitation through the pen of what is stuffed into the ear. What little we know about writing suggests that it is *not* an activity which one masters once and for all' (1977, p. 220).

Implications for teaching

The moral for teachers. First, if we wish our students to be able to succeed at this particular genre (and given how central argumentative writing is to the academic concern, there are good reasons for desiring to cultivate such a skill), then we must first ensure that they have sufficient exposure to the genre in their reading, remembering that not all transactional writing is argumentative but rather that the argumentative mode is a special sub-category.

And the second lesson for teachers (and evaluators) is — patience. If success in written argumentation requires cognitive maturation, then we ought not to expect our students to succeed before that maturation has been achieved. This is not to say that pupils should not be encouraged to write in this mode before puberty; on the contrary, they should be offered ample opportunities for argumentative writing, provided opportunity is understood as just that, and not as assignment. For if they are encouraged to state their views on subjects they feel strongly about, their 'intention' to write, as Britton points out, may very well allow them to achieve cognitively what had seemed beyond them when measured by experimental tests. Moreover, the task of concept-formation may be more or less difficult depending on the nature of the primary data; where similarities are more subtle and difficult to discern, where there is simply more data or more groupings to be made, the task may be considerably more taxing. It is not always easy for a teacher to gauge the conceptual difficulty of a particular topic for a specific student.

The trick is therefore to rely on the students' own responses as indications of what and how much they can deal with, and to allow them to go in the direction they are straining towards.

Note

1 Although Stein and Glenn (1979) specify the criteria for a complete episode, they do not use these criteria as a way of measuring relative success in incorporating the schema for the genre in the way that we have done. What encouraged us to use these criteria in this way was our pilot work evaluating the work of professional writers according to such an instrument. We found that our minimal criteria of success (the inclusion of some setting information and at least one complete episode) were satisfied by the stories analysed.

References

Bereiter, C. and Scardamalia, M. (1982) From Conversation to Composition: The Role of Instruction in a Developmental Process, in R. Glaser (ed.), *Advances in Instructional Psychology* (vol. 2). Hillsdale, N.J.: Erlbaum.

Britton, J.N. (1970) *Language and Learning*. London: Penguin.

Dixon, John (1967) *Growth Through English*. Reading, England: National Association for the Teaching of English.

Lloyd-Jones, R. (1977) The Politics of Research into the Teaching of Composition. *College Composition and Communication* **28**, pp. 218–22.

Miller, Susan (1980) Rhetorical Maturity: Definition and Development, in A. Freedman and I. Pringle (eds.). *Reinventing the Rhetorical Tradition*. (Conway, Ark.: L&S Books for the C.C.T.E.), pp. 119–27.

Rumelhart, D.E. (1975) Notes on a Schema for Stories, in D.G. Brown and A. Collins (eds.), *Representation and Understanding: Studies in Cognitive Science*. New York: Academic Press.

Stein, N.L. and Glenn, C.L. (1979) An Analysis of Story Comprehension in Elementary School Children, in R. Freedle (ed.), *New Directions in Discourse Processing* (vol. 2). Norwood, N.J.: Ablex.

Vygotsky, L.S. (1962) *Thought and Language,* edited and translated by E. Hanfmann and G. Vakar. Cambridge, Mass.: M.I.T. Press.

SECTION V

Monitoring and Assessment

Introduction

This section is made up of a diverse collection of readings on what is a very broad area of educational activity. A consideration of 'monitoring and assessment' of language and literacy in schools must properly include everything from the most formal, general and impersonal surveys of the linguistic behaviour of whole populations of schoolchildren, to the most informal, individualized and responsive judgements made by teachers about the language capabilities and performances of the children in their care. One area of assessment in which these two extremes may come together is the *assessment of reading*, in which formal tests of reading are commonly employed by classroom teachers to supplement more informal assessments. In the first article, Peter Johnston provides a comparative, historical review of ways reading has commonly been assessed.

The next article takes us to the level of national surveys of performance, for it consists of extracts from the influential first report of the survey of the language performance of children in English, Welsh, and Northern Irish primary schools by the Assessment of Performance Unit of the Department of Education and Science. The brief extracts which have been chosen focus on the assessment of the *reading and writing* of eleven-year-olds, but our hope is that this reading will also provide some useful insights into how the APU functions, the scope of its surveys and the kinds of methods that have been developed and employed in the course of its activities.

Some educationalists have welcomed the introduction of formal monitoring by the APU, regarding it as an endeavour well-founded on linguistic theory which will provide a better quality of information about children's abilities (see, for example, Thornton, 1986). Others, however, have expressed strong concern — not only about the validity of these monitoring exercises, but also about the political purposes which might implicitly inform the whole of the APU's monitoring programme. One of the most direct criticisms of this kind came, in 1982, from Harold Rosen, in which he focused on the APU survey report from which the previous reading was taken. An edited version of Rosen's critique is included as the third reading in this section. (Direct references by Rosen to parts of the previous reading are indicated thus: [para 2.79].)

Children's oral language has traditionally been given much less attention by assessors than has their literacy. However, now that 'oracy' has been discovered, the balance is shifting. The writer of the fourth article, Margaret

MacLure, was involved in the early development of the APU's programme of assessment of oral language. Her article provides an up-to-date review of this rapidly developing field.

The final article in this section provides an unusual, and informative, perspective on assessment practices in school. In it, Barry Stierer tries to relate his own activities as a researcher investigating assessment practices to those of the teachers and children he observed.

Reference

Thornton, G. (1986) *APU Language Testing 1979–1983: an independent appraisal of the findings.* London, Department of Education and Science.

5.1 Assessment in Reading

Peter H. Johnston

Source: Extracts from Johnston, P. H. (1986) 'Assessment in reading'. In Pearson, P. D. (ed.) *Handbook of Reading Research*. New York, Longman.

This chapter[1] examines the development and current status of the assessment of reading. While reading assessment is "as old as the first mother or teacher who questioned and observed a child reading" (Farr & Tone, in press), its documented development goes back only a short distance into the last century. [. . .]

The chapter provides historical overview in which it is claimed that certain early developments set up a paradigm that all but determined our current assessment practices. As Haney (1981) comments, ". . .standardized tests appear to be social artifacts as much as scientific instruments" (p. 1030).

[. . .]

Some history

The beginnings of reading assessment

The formal assessment of reading as a cognitive activity probably originated in the Leipzig psychological laboratory of Wilhelm Wundt around 1880. James McKeen Cattell was Wundt's research assistant in his attempts to measure the speed and nature of mental events. While reading *per se* was not the focus of this work, Cattell was concerned with word and letter perception and the standardization of tasks with which to measure this perception (Cattell, 1886). Around the same time, Javal (1879, cited in Anderson & Dearborn, 1952) was relating eye movements to the reading process. Javal simply watched readers' eyes and described how the eyes moved "par saccades." By making a small hole in the middle of a page, Miles and Segal (1929) observed eye movements as a clinical assessment method. This technique was later developed as an assessment device called the Ophthalm-O-Graph (American Optical Company, 1936). The corneal reflection method, first used by Dodge and Cline (1901), is still in use in the investigation of dyslexia (Pavlidis, 1981). [. . .]

Before the turn of the century, Binet (1895, cited in Freeman, 1926) had also made some initial progress in developing reading comprehension tests, though his motivation was to use these comprehension tests as an element in his attempts to assess intelligence. This relationship between reading and intelligence was echoed by Edward Thorndike (1917), who, in trying to measure reading, concluded that "reading is reasoning." Indeed, for a considerable period of time, it was difficult to tell apart intelligence tests and reading tests. For example, the following item is drawn from an early intelligence test (L.L. Thurstone, n.d.).

> "Every one of us, whatever our speculative opinions, know better than he practices, and recognizes a better law than he obeys" (Froude.) Check two of the following statements with the same meaning as the quotation above:
> — To know right is to do right.
> — Our speculative opinions determine our actions.
> — Our deeds fall short of the actions we approve.
> — Our ideas are in advance of our every day behavior.

The item could easily have come from a reading test. Interestingly, a good proportion of the people developing reading tests were also producing intelligence tests. The difficulties of this (reading-reasoning) relationship have persisted to the present time (cf. Johnston, 1983; Tuinman, 1979).

The measurement of reading as an educational achievement (as opposed to a psychological process) was brought to America by Rice, who had also studied at Leipzig. He developed the notion of assessing instructional effectiveness with specific tests. He began in 1894 with a comparative assessment of spelling performance that, along with his other suggestions, was received with derision at the 1897 meeting of the Department of Superintendence of the National Education Association. By 1914, however, Rice's ideas had gained general acceptance, and large-scale surveys of educational progress were well under way (Ayers, 1918), developing full momentum in the 1920s and never really looking back.

Two driving forces were behind the testing movement. One of these was the intention to make psychology worthy of the term *science*, and this seemed entirely dependent on quantification and "objectivity." The second motivating factor was the rapidly increasing number of children enrolled in education programs and the press for educational accountability. Immigration and population growth in the two decades on either side of the turn of the century caused part of the increase. But the problems were exacerbated by the growth of compulsory schooling and child labor laws (Landes & Solomon, 1972; Resnick, 1982), and by increased societal expectations for literacy. The high failure rate in schools meant that one in six were retained in first grade; by eighth grade, one in two were behind their age peers (Ayers, 1909, 1918). To monitor this problem, school surveys were instituted. This group testing movement, already institutionalized, had its future ensured in 1935 when the IBM 805 was introduced to score tests, the effect being to reduce the cost of testing by about a factor of ten (Downey, 1965; Resnick, 1982).

Educational testing initially served a gatekeeping function between school grades (a function to which it has recently returned). Although it pointed to some difficulties with curriculum and instruction, the major function of educational testing did not turn out to be assisting teachers in their instructional planning. Indeed, there was considerable opposition from teachers to the testing. Support for comparative testing initially came from school administrators, who were particularly pleased about the accountability function of the tests (Resnick, 1982).

This group focus, along with the silent reading emphasis, which had also reached a peak [. . .], produced a climate in which a certain kind of test would survive. Thus, while diverse approaches were developed initially, the fittest in terms of efficiency soon surfaced. Reading tests came to consist of the silent reading of a passage, followed by the solving of brief, generally text-related, problems; usually questions. Thorndike, in developing his 1917 prototypical test, might be considered the father of modern group tests of reading. Parenthetically, Thorndike's influence did not stop with the form of the test. He was also the father of modern reliability theory, which forms the basis of test evaluation. In his 1904 text, he comments that "we measure the unreliability of any obtained measure by its probable divergence from the true measure" (p. 136). While this theory has formed the basis of psychometrics for three-quarters of a century, it is fundamentally flawed in several ways (Lumsden, 1976). Nonetheless, it pervades all reading tests that report statistical data.

By the time Gertrude Hildreth published her *Bibliography of Mental Tests and Rating Scales* (1933), most of the tests available were of silent reading. The proliferation of silent reading group tests is also attested to by Gray (1938), who commented: "During 1914–1915 two thirds of the (reading) studies reported dealt with the organization, standardization, and application of silent reading tests" (p. 102). Clearly, mainstream reading measurement has been heavily oriented toward the group assessment of silent reading. Consequently, the theory surrounding the group silent reading test has developed to a highly sophisticated level. Few question the scientific nature of psychometrics; this was, after all, one of the major reasons for its existence.

Methodology
With the increased interest in reading and its assessment, the first two decades of this century saw considerable diversity in approaches to the problem of measuring reading performance systematically. The most labor-intensive approach was probably that of scoring verbatim free recalls. Several methods of accomplishing this were proposed. Courtis (1914) advocated counting the number of idea units reproduced and interpreting it in terms of the number of units possible. This method was also supported by Brown (1914), and it is a primitive version of current propositional-analysis techniques (e.g. Kintsch & van Dijk, 1978; Turner & Greene, 1977).

Starch (1915) used a timed reading with free recall. Thirty seconds' reading time was allowed, and unlimited recall time. He suggested using the ratio of "relevant words" to the total number of words. This simpler measure was calculated by deleting "wrong" and "irrelevant" words and repetitions to leave the relevant words, a procedure not unlike that currently used in experimental studies of children's summarizing strategies (Winograd, 1982). Gray (1917) supplemented this scoring procedure with ten questions for each passage to provide greater validity. These scores were averaged to increase the reliability. The use of oral recalls represented an improvement in terms of the validity of the test for less able writers.

[. . .]

The "reproduction" approach began to fall into disrepute early because, as Kelly (1916) pointed out:

> It is generally agreed, I think, that the ability to reproduce is quite a separate ability from the ability to get meaning, and, therefore, the ability to get meaning which involves a minimum of reproduction (p. 64).

While the approach survived in the Silent Reading subtest of the *Durrell Analysis of Reading Difficulty* (Durrell, 1937, 1955), it was generally dropped until Goodman and Burke (1970) revived it in a slightly different form called the "retelling." Retellings were not to be verbatim, were prompted, and were scored according to a "story grammar" model (e.g. Mandler & Johnson, 1977; Stein & Trabasso, 1982) adapted by awarding points for character analysis, theme, plot, events, and additional information. The procedure is very time-consuming and is not commonly used.

Kelly (1916) proceeded to develop the Kansas Silent Reading Test in which students were allowed five minutes to complete as many as possible of 16 exercises. Each exercise consisted of a brief paragraph forming a very simple task such as modified cloze, verbal logic problems, or convoluted instructions to follow. A similar technique of brief paragraphs each followed by single responses was used by Monroe (1918), although the requisite response was the underlining of a word that answered a question. Haggerty (1919) used sentence and paragraph comprehension with yes-no questions to assess reading ability. The format was not unlike that still found in the Stanford (Karlsen, Madden, & Gardner, 1976), though the response requires the selection of one of four words to complete a sentence. Courtis (1917) also developed a unique test in which the reader had three minutes to read as much as possible of a two-page story, followed by five minutes with the same passage broken into paragraphs each with five yes–no questions. As an assessment technique, this seems to have been a terminal evolutionary line.

Chapman's (1924) task of detecting erroneous words in the second half of paragraphs fell into disuse until recently. [. . .] Interest has recently been renewed in the technique in a research context (Markman, 1977; Winograd & Johnston, 1982) and in an early reading context (Clay, 1979). Clay uses the approach to test children's knowledge of letter order and line order.

In describing "devices for guiding and measuring comprehension," Gates (1937) describes a number of alternative devices for the assessment of reading. He lists:

1. the selection of the best illustration to describe a paragraph.
2. pupil illustrating the paragraph.
3. marking parts of a picture either with an X or so as to complete it to represent the paragraph.
4. making titles for an illustration with respect to the paragraph.
5. executing directions given in the text.
6. questions — multiple choice — true/false statements — true and nonsense statements — completion.

The completion task that Gates suggests is the cloze task. Currently a common assessment technique, this was popularized by Taylor (1953), but its roots go back to the completion tasks used by Ebbinghaus in 1897 in his efforts to find a measure of mental fatigue. Though Ebbinghaus found it unsatisfactory for this purpose, he noted its excellence as a measure of intellectual ability (Freeman, 1926; Webb & Shotwell, 1932). Gates's "execution task" was often a picture accompanied by a paragraph describing what marks to draw on it. For example, the May Ayres Burgess Scale for Measuring Ability in Silent Reading (Burgess, 1921) required such performances as putting a woman's shoe on by blackening her foot in the picture, or drawing smoke coming from a man's pipe and billowing in a particular direction.

The number and length (roughly inversely related) of texts used in tests over the years has varied considerably. Gray (1917) used three relatively long texts, each child reading but one. Starch (1915) had each child read two lengthy texts. One, on the reader's grade placement, was read on the first day, and on the second day an easier one was read. Kelly (1916) used 16 very brief paragraphs, and some of those used by Thorndike (1917) were only a sentence long. Currently, while there is some variability in this, the texts used in reading comprehension tests tend to be many and brief.

Further early developments in the field of reading assessment were noted by Gates (1937), who stated:

> A survey of published standardized tests for grades IV to VIII shows a large number and great variety. Among the tests located, twenty-seven measure *speed* of reading materials of uniform difficulty and five of these measure both *speed* and *accuracy*, and twenty-three measure *level* or *power* of comprehension. Fourteen tests of vocabulary or word knowledge were found. It is apparent, moreover, that there is an increased tendency to produce series, or batteries, of tests which include measures of several phases or types of reading. . .(pp. 382–383).

The increase in the number of available batteries was driven by the dual emphases on diagnosis and standardized development.

Oral reading errors were also used in assessment, but they drew little comment in the literature of the first two decades of the century. Oral reading had fallen into disrepute by the end of the first decade of this century. Complaints generally revolved around oral reading not dealing with understanding and not being the most important kind of reading. Nonetheless, such tests continued to be developed, if slowly.

Gray's (1917) Standardized Oral Reading Paragraphs consisted of a graded series of paragraphs to be read aloud for the examiner to code errors and reading time. Norms for reading time were provided, and error types included omissions or additions (of sounds or words), substitutions, mispronunciations, repetitions, self-corrections, words given assistance on, and the ignoring of punctuation. The recording procedures became more refined with Gates (1937) adding the error of hesitation and not coding self-corrections as errors. The latter advance was ignored until 1970 when Goodman and Burke produced their Reading Miscue Inventory. This fact is indicative of the manner in which reading errors were interpreted. They were basically considered faults to be corrected. While descriptive and comparative studies of errors increased in frequency (e.g. Daw, 1938; Duffy & Durrell, 1935; Madden & Pratt, 1941), there were few attempts to use errors to model the processes, knowledge, and misunderstandings that produced them. Goodman and Burke's scoring method developed this element in the assessment literature. Their scoring system was comprehensive and systematic, and their analysis of error patterns ("miscues") was directed toward discovering the nature and balance of strategies used by the reader. This approach was suggested much earlier, for example by Gates (1937). However, it does not seem to have held great appeal at the outset.

A conceptual shift occurred with Durrell's (1937) use of error rates to describe task difficulty rather than reader ability. He stated: ". . . we assume that one error in twenty running words is the maximal difficulty of material for this grade . . ." (p. 335). Betts (1946) developed this concept further. If the error rate was 1 per cent, the material was at the reader's independent level. Material read with a 2 to 5 per cent error rate was at the reader's instructional level, and material with a greater than 5 per cent error rate was "frustration" level. Corresponding levels of accuracy at answering questions were suggested as 90, 75, and 50 per cent. Unfortunately, these scoring criteria were developed using only fourth-graders who preread the text. Arguments over the adequacy of these criteria adorn the literature without resolution (Fuchs, Fuchs, & Deno, 1982; Powell, 1970; Weber, 1968).

These arguments notwithstanding, the development of oral reading assessment has been painfully slow. Even the problems involved in one-to-one oral reading have been slow to surface. For example, the fact that an oral reading diagnosis is in a sense "negotiated" by the examiner and examinee via their verbal and nonverbal interaction has been a recent realization (McGill-Franzen & McDermott, 1978; Mehan, 1978). Note, too, that statistical evaluation procedures have not generally been applied to oral reading techniques. For example, while considerable statistical effort has been devoted to examinations of the multi-dimensionality of group tests (e.g. Davis, 1944, 1972; Drahozal & Hanna, 1978; Spearitt, 1972), similar statistical effort has been applied to oral reading errors only recently (e.g. Haupt & Goldsmith, 1982). This slow development is unusual considering the early start that the field had on other disciplines. Only recently has mathematics been highly involved in the analysis of arithmetic error patterns as indicators of underlying misconceptions or information deficits (e.g. Brown & Burton, 1978). The reason informal oral reading tests were downplayed was probably partly because of their lack of "objectivity." "Subjectivity" is generally frowned upon.

The major approach to the assessment of reading that is currently in use (largely group silent reading tests) seems to have been the result of an ideological thrust that favored ease of use over all else. The reasoning is probably best captured by Anderson and Dearborn (1952):

If the reader will now ask himself this double-headed question as to (1) just how he is going to find out how much and how well the individual pupils in a class understand or comprehend what they have read silently, and (2) just how he is going to make it easy for the teacher or tester to score the findings in terms of age and grade norms, he will come to understand why the tests of silent reading are as and what they are, and why they have so many shortcomings or limitations (p. 301).

From the brief historical account presented here, it can be seen that the current situation exists largely through accident rather than design and that it has been maintained more through societal press than scientific process. [. . .]

Notes

1. I am indebted to my colleagues Dick Allington, Peter Mosenthal, Fred Ohnmacht, David Pearson, and Jaap Tuinman for helpful comments on an earlier version of this paper, and particularly to David Pearson for getting me involved in it in the first place.

References

American Optical Company, Southbridge, Mass. Manufacturer of the Ophthalm-O-Graph, 1936.

Anderson, I. H. & Dearborn, W. F. *The Psychology of Teaching Reading.* New York: Ronald Press, 1952.

Ayers, L. P. *Laggards in Our Schools: A study of retardation and elimination in city school systems.* New York: Russell Sage Foundation, 1909.

Ayers, L. P. History and present status of educational measurements. In *Seventeenth Yearbook of the National Society for the Study of Education.* Bloomington, Ill.: Public School Publishing, 1918.

Betts, E. *Foundations of Reading Instruction.* New York: American Book, 1946.

Brown, H. A. The measurement of efficiency in instruction in reading. *Elementary School Teacher,* 1914, *14*, 477–490.

Brown, J. S. & Burton, R. R. Diagnostic models for procedural bugs in basic mathematical skills. *Cognitive Science,* 1978, **2**, 155–192.

Burgess, M. A. *A Scale for Measuring Ability in Silent Reading.* New York: Russell Sage Foundation, 1921.

Cattell, J M. The time it takes to see and name objects. *Mind,* 1886, **11**, 63–65.

Chapman, J. C. *Chapman Unspeeded Reading-comprehension Test.* Minneapolis: Educational Test Bureau, 1924.

Clay, M. M. *The Early Detection of Reading Difficulties: A diagnostic survey with recovery procedures* (2nd ed.). Auckland, New Zealand: Heinemann, 1979.

Courtis, S. A. Standard tests in English. *Elementary School Teacher.* 1914, **14**, 374–392.

Davis, F. B. Fundamental factors of comprehension in reading. *Psychometrika,* 1944, **9**, 185–197.

Daw, S. E. The persistence of errors in oral reading in grades four and five. *Journal of Educational Research,* 1938, **32**, 81–90.

Dodge, R. & Cline, T. S. The angle velocity of eye-movements. *Psychological Review,* 1901, **8**, 145–157.

Downey, M. T. *Ben D. Wood, Educational Reformer.* Princeton, N. J.: Educational Testing Service, 1965.

Drahozal, E. D. & Hanna, G. S. Reading comprehension subscores: Pretty bottles for ordinary wine. *Journal of Reading,* 1978, **21**, 416–420.

Duffy, G. B. & Durrell, D. D. Third grade difficulties in oral reading. *Education,* 1935, **56**, 37–40.

Durkin, D. *Teaching Young Children to Read* (2nd ed.). Boston: Allyn & Bacon, 1976.

Durrell, D. D. Individual differences and their implications with respect to instruction in reading. In *The Teaching of Reading: A second report* (Thirty-sixth Yearbook of the National Society for Studies in Education, Part 1). Bloomington, Ill.: Public School Publishing, 1937.

Durrell, D. D. *Durrell Analysis of Reading Difficulty.* New York: Harcourt, Brace & World, 1937, 1955.

Farr, R. and Tone, B. Text analysis and validated modelling for the reading process (1973–81): implications for reading assessment. In R. Farr and B. Tone (eds), *Reading Comprehension from Theory to Practice.* Hillsdale, N.J.: Lawrence Erlbaum, in press.

Freeman, F. N. *Mental Tests: Their history, principles and applications.* Chicago: Houghton Mifflin, 1926.

Fuchs, L. S., Fuchs, D. & Deno, S. Reliability and validity of curriculum-based informal reading inventories. *Reading Research Quarterly,* 1982, **18**, 6–25.

Gates, A. I. The measurement and evaluation of achievement in reading. In *The Teaching of Reading: A second report* (Thirty-sixth Yearbook of the National Society for Studies in Education, Part 1). Bloomington, Ill.: Public School Publishing, 1937.

Goodman, Y. M. & Burke, C. L. *Reading Miscue Inventory Manual Procedure for Diagnosis and Evaluation.* New York: Macmillan, 1970.

Gray, W. S. *Studies of Elementary School Reading through Standardized Tests* (Supplemental Educational Monographs No. 1). Chicago: University of Chicago Press, 1917.

Gray, W. S. Contributions of research to special methods. In G. M. Whipple, (ed.), *The Scientific Movement in Education* (Thirty-seventh Yearbook of the National Society for the Study of Education). Bloomington, Ill.: Public School Publishing, 1938.

Haggerty, M. E. *Haggerty Reading Examination.* Yonkers, N.Y.: World Book, 1919.

Haney, W. Validity, vaudeville, and values: A short history of social concerns over standardized testing. *American Psychologist,* 1981, **36**, 1021–1034.

Haupt, E. J. & Goldsmith, J. S. Expanding the factorial structure of reading errors: Frequency, severity, and higher order components in reading errors. Paper presented at the annual meeting of the American Educational Research Association, New York, March 1982.

Hildreth, G. H. *A Bibliography of Mental Tests and Rating Scales.* New York: Psychological Corporation, 1933.

Johnston, P. *A Cognitive Basis for the Assessment of Reading Comprehension.* Newark, Del.: International Reading Association, 1983.

Karlsen, B., Madden, R. & Gardner, E. F. *Stanfoɪ l Diagnostic Reading Test.* New York: Harcourt Brace Jovanovich, 1976.

Kelly, E. J. The Kansas silent reading tests. *Journal of Educational Psychology,* 1916, **7**, 63–80.

Kintsch, W., & van Dijk, T. A. Toward a model of text comprehension and production. *Psychological Review,* 1978, **85**, 363–394.

Landes, W. & Solomon, L. Compulsory schooling legislation: An economic analysis of law and social changes in the nineteenth century. *Journal of Economic History,* 1972, **32**, 54–91.

Lumsden, J. Test theory. *Annual Review of Psychology,* 1976, 223–258.

McGill-Franzen, A. & McDermott, P. *Negotiating a reading diagnosis.* Paper presented at the National Reading Conference, St. Petersburg, Fla., December 1978.

Madden, M. & Pratt, M. An oral reading survey as a teaching aid. *Elementary English Review,* 1941, **18**, 122–126.

Mandler, J. M. & Johnson, N. S. Remembrance of things parsed: Story structure and recall. *Cognitive Psychology,* 1977, **9**, 111–151.

Markman, E. M. Realizing that you don't understand: A preliminary investigation. *Child Development*, 1977, **48**, 986–992.

Mehan, H. Structuring school structure. *Harvard Educational Review*, 1978, **48**, 32–64.

Miles, W. R. & Segal, D. Clinical observation of eye-movements in the rating of reading ability. *Journal of Educational Psychology*, 1929, **20**, 520–529.

Monroe, W. S. Monroe's standardized silent reading tests. Bloomington, Ill.: Public School Publishing, 1918.

Pavlidis, G.Th. Sequencing, eye movements and the early objective diagnosis of dyslexia. In G.Th. Pavlidis & T. R. Miles (eds.), *Dyslexia Research and its Applications to Education*. New York: Wiley, 1981.

Powell, W. R. Reappraising the criteria for interpreting informal reading inventories. In E. L. DeBoer (ed.), *Reading Diagnosis and Evaluation*. Newark, Del.: International Reading Association, 1970.

Resnick, D. P. & Resnick, L. The nature of literacy: An historical exploration. *Harvard Educational Review*, 1977, **47**, 370–385.

Spearitt, D. Identification of subskills of reading comprehension by maximum likelihood factor analysis. *Reading Research Quarterly*, 1972, **8**, 92–111.

Starch, D. The measurement of efficiency in reading. *Journal of Educational Psychology*, 1915, **6**, 1–24.

Stein, N. L. & Trabasso, T. What's in a story: An approach to comprehension and instruction. In R. Glaser (ed.). *Advances in the Psychology of Instruction* (Vol. 2). Hillsdale, N. I.: Erlbaum, 1982.

Taylor, W. Cloze procedure: A new tool for measuring readability. *Journalism Quarterly*, 1953, **9**, 206–223.

Thorndike, E. L. Reading as reasoning: A study of mistakes in paragraph reading. *Journal of Educational Psychology*,1917, **8**, 323–332.

Thurstone, L. L. *Psychological examination* (Test 4). Stoelting, n.d.

Tuinman, J. J. Reading is recognition — When reading is not reasoning. In J.C. Harste & R. R. Carey (eds.), *New Perspectives on Comprehension* (Monograph in Language and Reading Studies, No. 3). Bloomington Ind.: Indiana University Press, 1979.

Turner, A. & Greene, E. *The Construction of a Propositional Text Base* (Technical Report No. 63). Boulder: University of Colorado Press, April 1977.

Webb, L. W. & Shotwell, A. M. *Standard Tests In the Elementary School*. New York: Farrar & Rinehart, 1932.

Weber, R. M. The study of oral reading errors: A review of the literature. *Reading Research Quarterly*, 1968, **4**, 96–119.

Winograd, P. *An Examination of Strategic Difficulties in Summarizing Texts*. Doctoral dissertation, University of Illinois, Urbana-Champaign, January 1982.

Winograd, P. & Johnston, P. Comprehension and the error detection paradigm. *Journal of Reading Behavior*, 1982, **14**, 61–76.

5.2 Language Performance in Schools

T. P. Gorman, J. White, L. Orchard, A. Tate and B. Sexton

Source: Extracts from Gorman, T. P., White, J., Orchard, L., Tate, A. and Sexton, B. (1979) Extracts from *Language Performance in Schools: A.P.U. Primary Survey Report No. 1*. H.M.S.O., London.

[. . .]

Preliminary proposals for assessing language performance

2.10 The Bullock committee, whose report on *A language for Life* was published in 1975, reviewed the tests and procedures that have been used in previous national surveys. The Committee concluded that there was a need for tests of reading proficiency which would serve to indicate "the extent to which reading proficiency had been developed to serve personal and social needs". They proposed also that "the instruments of assessment should therefore include samples of performance considered to be important and representative of attainments". They suggested that the measures developed should also be responsive to developments in the curriculum, and they recognised that this requirement, in turn, would entail the use of instruments that incorporated the means for discarding out of date materials. The committee further proposed that monitoring should embrace teaching objectives for the entire ability range and that tests should draw on a variety of sources to ensure an extensive coverage of the area to be assessed in contrast to the inevitably narrow focus of assessment afforded by a single test. Finally, the Committee suggested that the criterion of literacy adopted should be "capable of showing whether the reading and writing abilities of children are adequate to the demands made upon them in school and likely to face them in adult life".[1]

2.11 The report of the Bullock Committee clearly established the need for a new range of measures to assess reading nationally, but a number of theoretical issues had to be investigated and a number of practical problems overcome before tests with the characteristics proposed could be devised. By what means, for example, are 'teaching objectives for the entire ability range' in language attainment to be determined; and how are the demands made upon the reading and writing abilities of pupils in school and adult life to be defined? Reading behaviour is so complex that there is no simple answer to such questions; nor indeed, is there agreement among experts as to how the structure of reading abilities should be defined. Many studies have been undertaken in which researchers have attempted to isolate factors that might be said to underlie reading and to differentiate reading 'sub-skills'; several of these are discussed in the following section. However, no model of the reading process is generally accepted to be an adequate representation of the processes by which readers comprehend what they read; and as such comprehension is as complex as thinking itself, this lack of consensus is to be expected.

2.12 The assessment of writing poses even more complex theoretical and practical problems than the assessment of reading. The Bullock Committee clearly pointed out a number of questions that needed to be asked and problems that had to be solved if any attempt was to be made to monitor standards of achievement in writing, eg "What features of writing should be assessed?"; "By what criteria can one measure them?"; "How are reliability and validity to be ensured?".

2.13 A number of these questions were considered at length by the Working Group (subsequently the Steering Group) convened by the APU to formulate an initial set of guidelines for the research team which was established in 1977. The Group comprised teachers, HMIs and Advisers and university personnel. The Steering Group drew up an initial set of proposals relating to aspects of reading and writing that it would be appropriate and desirable to assess in a monitoring programme.[2] In considering the form that tests of performance in reading and writing might take, a functional perspective was adopted, i.e. the guiding questions posed were: what do pupils read and why, and what do they write and why? This approach led to the specification of a range of tasks in both reading and writing which were similar to activities which pupils would be asked to undertake in different contexts.

2.14 In the initial proposals for reading assessment the Steering Group identified a number of reading activities which pupils at different age levels might appropriately be asked to complete. It was not assumed that the different tasks suggested required the exercise of different sub-skills in reading.

It was proposed that pupils should be asked:

1 questions about passages that could be answered with reference to explicit statements contained within the passages and

2 questions that involved the recognition of information that was implicit in what was written.

3 to interpret and evaluate the writer's assumptions and intentions.

4 to show an awareness of characteristics of different kinds of writing so that they

might, for example, be able to indicate in general terms the possible source of a passage, e.g. whether a passage was taken from a work of reference or a work of literature.

It was suggested that pupils should be asked to apply their reading skills in such activities as the following:

5   Reading to gain an overall impression of a single passage or chapter so as to be able to identify the general theme or gist.

6   Reading of different passages to select information relevant to a particular topic and to recognise information that is redundant in terms of the particular question asked.

7   Reading to expand on information previously supplied. Pupils might also be asked to amplify and re-interpret the information provided in one passage by information given in other passages, charts or diagrams.

8   Reading to follow a sequence of instructions, or to interpret a set of directions. The instructions could be such as to lead to the preparation of a diagram or chart in which information from the passage would be tabulated.

The activities referred to reflect the ways in which reading is applied in the classroom. It was envisaged that the range of activities would be extended with reference to activities undertaken by pupils of different ages when reading a variety of written materials for different purposes.

2.15 A decision was taken to assess reading and writing separately in the first instance. Some pupils are able to read but find it difficult to express their understanding of what they have read in extended written responses. However, it was recognised that both in and out of school reading is frequently preceded by discussion and followed by a form of writing activity and it was thought essential to include in the assessment programme some composite activities that involved both reading and writing.

Pupils' attitudes to reading
[. . .]
2.17 The Steering Group recognised the desire of teachers to encourage pupils to see reading as a source of enjoyment and to ensure not only that pupils can read but that they want to read. It is not possible to measure enjoyment or motivation in the same way that certain other aspects of reading attainment can be measured, but it seemed important to obtain, as part of the monitoring programme, information on the voluntary reading undertaken by pupils and their attitudes to reading in general.
   [. . .]

The preparation of the reading tests

2.28 The development of APU language tests is collaborative in the sense that arrangements are made for initial drafts of tests and other measures to be discussed with one of a number of liaison groups of teachers which have been convened by Advisers or Inspectors in different parts of the country (see Appendix 4). After pre-testing, the materials are reviewed by members of the Steering Group. In addition, head teachers whose schools participated in the initial survey were also invited to comment on the tests and on their pupils' reactions to them.

2.29 The majority of the measures developed to assess reading at Primary level take the form of short booklets each containing a story or passages relating to a common theme. The passages used are selected or adapted from textbooks, works of reference and works of literature of a kind likely to be employed or referred to by teachers of 11-year-old children. The different themes in the series of tests were chosen, and the booklets designed, in a way likely to engage the interest of most children in this age group.

[. . .]

The range of materials to be read

2.31 The materials that pupils are asked to read differ in their sources and subject matter and in their form and function or purpose. They also vary in style, in content, and in the way what is said is organised or structured. In several cases the subject matter of the booklets relates to topics that pupils might deal with in more than one area of the curriculum. While much of the material is presented in the form of related paragraphs or passages, a number of booklets contain materials in other forms such as lists, schedules, or timetables, sets of instructions and sources of information including maps, tables and diagrams, as well as extracts from longer works of different forms. An attempt has been made also to select reading materials written for different purposes. The passages are selected to cover a range of general functions such as informing, describing, narrating or directing. The functional range of the materials to be read is less diverse at primary than at secondary level, and the intention is that this should be extended at both levels as new materials are prepared.

Type of questions asked

2.32 The range of questions pupils are asked to answer varies to some degree according to the type of passage being read and the purpose or purposes for which the pupil is reading it. In devising questions, the guiding principle was that they should be questions that an experienced teacher would be likely to ask pupils, taking account of the subject matter, form and function of the passage or passages. The kinds of questions it is appropriate to ask about a short story or a poem naturally differ from the questions that would be posed about an account of an experiment or an expository passage providing information on a particular topic.

[. . .]

2.38 The texts of the reading booklets were designed to have a degree of coherence. The descriptive and explanatory passages were sequenced in such a way as to enable the reader to extend his or her knowledge of the subject by moving from general to more specialised issues; each passage expands on an aspect of the passage preceding it. In *Whales* booklet 1 [for example] the extract from a story that concludes the booklet was intended to provide both information and narrative interest. Illustrations were used on each page in this booklet to add to the children's knowledge of whales, and to make the booklet more interesting to look at and to read.

The materials were arranged in the following way:

1 An introductory page, giving facts about whales (somewhat in the style of *The Guinness book of records*) which is arranged as a sequence of sub-headings, each followed by a single sentence.

2 A general description of whales as mammals, with information about their habitat and methods of communication: 'How whales are adapted to living in the sea'.

3 A passage specifying the two main types of whale: 'Whalebone whales and toothed whales'.

4 More detailed information about 'Three species of toothed whale'.

5 A passage adapted from a reference book, which gives precise details about the physical characteristics of different species of whale: 'Six species of whale'.

6 An extract from a novel, depicting a young boy's first encounter with a group of dolphins: 'Johnny and the dolphins'.

2.39 The structure and contents of the booklet allowed a wide range of questions to be asked, including questions on specific passages or sections of passages and questions that involved children in referring from one passage to another to compare and relate different sources of information. This approach meant that children were presented with approximately 2,000 words of material organised in sections which had to be scanned or skimmed or read in detail according to the questions asked, in addition to the reading material in the answer booklet.

[. . .]

The assessment of reading performance: a summary statement

2.78 The measures used in reading attainment provided detailed information about pupils' ability to carry out a number of the reading tasks they were asked to complete or engage in and also allowed for a single 'global reading score' or ability measure to be derived for each pupil. In the first place, all pupils were asked to follow or employ the detailed instructions given in an answer booklet for the purpose of locating and interpreting information given in a reading booklet which contained six to eight related sections plus a contents page and index. The tasks ranged from exercises in which the pupils had to read and interpret single words or phrases in context to those in which the content of the booklet as a whole needed to be taken account of.

2.79 As is to be expected, pupils had least difficulty in answering questions about matters that were both clearly asserted and easy to locate in the text. Even when the scope of questions is extended to encompass paragraphs and sequences of paragraphs or passages, pupils find it relatively easy to answer questions if these two conditions are met. In *Whales* booklet 1, (discussed earlier), for example, there were a number of items with these characteristics which were answered correctly by between 90 and 97 per cent of the pupils involved.

2.80 Many questions involved the use of more complex reading skills and strategies. With reference to *Whales* booklet 1, approximately three-quarters of the pupils were able to answer correctly one or more questions that involved comparing information given in different passages for the purpose of establishing whether such information added to what was known about a topic, or whether it was a re-statement of information that had already been presented. Over two-thirds of the pupils who read the booklet gave evidence of being able to use an index efficiently to assist them in locating information given in different sections of the booklet.

[. . .]

5.31 There was no significant difference between the performance of girls and boys. As would be expected, a significant difference was apparent between the performance of pupils who spoke English as a second language and that of native speakers of English. The mean score of pupils in the Midlands was significantly below that of pupils in the other regions. The mean score of pupils in non-metropolitan areas was significantly higher than that of pupils in metropolitan counties. However, if the relative affluence of the school catchment area was taken account of there was no significant difference between the performance of children in the least affluent catchment areas, or between that of children in the most affluent areas in the two locations. In general, mean scores decreased as the proportion of pupils entitled to free school meals increased. They tended to decrease also as the pupil/teacher ratio decreased. Pupils in schools with a relatively low number of pupils in the age-group obtained higher mean scores than pupils in schools with larger numbers of pupils in the age-group.

The information provided about the relationships between performance and background variables should be interpreted with caution for the reasons stated earlier. The pattern of relationships will become clearer when the data obtained are related to the information that will be gathered in subsequent surveys.

The assessment of writing

Establishing a framework for the assessment of writing

4.1   The initial model proposed by the Language Steering Group for the assessment of writing assumes that the ability to write, like the ability to read, develops out of children's general desire and ability to communicate. It was assumed also that the ability to write includes the capacity to adjust what is written to different audiences and social relationships. As children grow older, they are increasingly capable of matching their writing to particular tasks and to particular contexts.

4.2   In developing the initial proposals for assessment, the Group identified a number of variations in task and context which, judging from the research findings then available, it was thought would be likely to influence children's performance. The proposals for assessment were also intended to reflect the range of written work that takes place in schools.

Variations in task

4.3   A number of dimensions were considered within which specific writing activities could be sampled. One dimension related to the contrast between different types of writing: narrative/descriptive on the one hand and reflective/analytical on the other. A second dimension concerned the degree of control granted to writer or assessor. At one end of the scale are tasks in which the assessor seeks to define as fully as possible both the topic and how it is to be dealt with; at the other the selection of both are left to the writer. Thirdly, the source of subject-matter was considered. Some tasks draw on the writer's first-hand experience and others on knowledge derived from elsewhere. Finally, it was acknowledged that the range of purposes for which a child might write also differs. Some tasks require a pupil to create a literary work such as a story, and others a piece of writing which sets out to inform, direct or persuade.[3]

4.4   On the basis of these considerations the Steering Group proposed a range of tasks for pupils at the two ages of monitoring. It was suggested that the writing of 11-year-olds be assessed with reference to the following categories:

1   Personal response to pictures, music, short quotations from poems or prose, or similar stimuli.
2   An autobiographical narrative or anecdote.
3   A fictional story.
4   A description or account in which the pupil is invited to reflect upon what is described and express his feelings about it.
5   An account of something the pupil has learned or read about.

6 A verifiable description or account in which the pupil is required to represent faithfully what he has observed.

7 An account of how the pupil plans to carry out a task, scheme, or project of some kind.

[. . .]

Variations in context

4.5 The social context in which writing usually takes place, and the writer's relationship with this audience, were both emphasised as important factors in writing performance. It was accordingly proposed that some realistic variety of audience be introduced into the assessment programme. To this end three possible contexts for the assessment of writing were selected:

A. Writing produced in traditional test conditions.

B. Writing produced in response to a specific task [set], on a given occasion, by a teacher to whom the child is accustomed to address writing.

C. Pieces selected by the teacher, from writing produced in the normal course of classroom work.

Most of the writing to be gathered in the surveys was thought likely to correspond to condition A. There is evidence to hand now, however, that the conditions under which writing is produced in the surveys are not generally interpreted as 'traditional' test conditions, but are more like those envisaged under condition B. Class and subject teachers are encouraged to introduce the writing tasks before the group of pupils begins writing. However, the focus of the writing is not necessarily given by the teacher. To date, the attempt to devise writing materials which make credible an address to different readers has had some success. The close analysis of children's scripts has revealed that 'test situation' notwithstanding, young writers are sensitive to the need to moderate content and style to the demands of a hypothesised reader.

It is not thought necessary, therefore, to attempt to maintain a rigid distinction between work gathered under conditions. A and B as originally proposed. Research is, however, being undertaken to determine the feasibility of obtaining written work selected by the teacher from writing produced in the normal course of classroom work.

The development of measures of writing ability

[. . .]

4.10 In deciding which specific tasks a pupil would be asked to write on, a number of factors were kept in mind: comparability of results, assessment across a pedagogically meaningful range of tasks, and ease of administration in schools. A series of ten writing booklets was designed, each booklet including four parts: a short writing task common to all booklets, one of ten different writing tasks, an editing task, and a final section comprising three short questions relating to pupils' attitudes to writing. Booklets were distributed in such a way that each school received only booklets of the same number.

Writing tasks employed in the primary survey

4.11 Pupils were asked to produce writing relating to three of the following activities, two of which (the explanation of a viewpoint and the editing task) were common to all ten writing booklets:

General purpose of writing	*Written product or outcome*
1. To describe	(a) Sustained description of person, place or object.
	(b) Description and expression of feelings towards what is described.
2. To narrate	(a) Imaginative narrative based on given characters and setting.
	(b) Original end to story selected by the pupil.
3. To record	Autobiographical account of event experienced.
4. To report	(a) Verifiable account of an event.
	(b) An account of something learned.
5. To change the reader's mind/to persuade	Informal letter to a friend.
6. To request	Letter to a person in a public institution.
7. To explain/expound	Explanation of and reflection on a convention or regulation.
8. To plan	An account of an activity to be undertaken.
9. To edit	Editing of a written account.

In all of these tasks, variation in *audience* and in the writer's control over *form* was envisaged.

[. . .]

The marking schemes and methods of marking employed

Impression marking

4.30 A panel of markers was recruited from among experienced primary teachers. 40 markers participated in the first stage of assessment in which they were asked to form a rapid impression of each pupil's writing ability on the evidence of the two tasks completed. Marks were awarded on a scale of 1 to 7. A score of 1 corresponded with the marker's judgement that the pupil was an extremely poor writer for an 11 year old, and a mark of 7 denoted that a writer was considered to be extremely good for this age group.

Each script was read by two markers. The design adopted in assigning scripts to markers was the simplest one that would allow for all markers to be linked on a common scale which reflected their relative leniency and stringency. The scripts were assembled into 80 sets and each marker dealt with four sets of scripts. After an initial training session, two sets of scripts were marked. These were then returned and each set assigned to a different marker in the team for double marking.

Analytic marking

4.31 In a second stage of assessment a random sample of 10 per cent of the essays was selected from across the complete range of booklets and the essays were marked analytically on an ascending scale of 1 to 5 with reference to the following sets of criteria:

1 Content and organisation
2 Appropriateness and style
3 Grammatical conventions
4 Orthographic conventions

Judgements relating to the first of these categories referred to the entire essay; for appropriateness and style, and grammatical conventions, markers were referred to the first 20 lines of writing; in assessing orthography, the first 10 lines of the essays were taken account of.

The following notes provide a brief account of the detailed instructions given to markers in assessing written work in relation to the analytic criteria.

Content and organisation

4.32 At primary level it has not proved feasible to separate these features, (because of the shortness of some of the scripts) though at secondary level they are to be assessed separately. Judgements relating to this category were concerned with the subject-matter of the essay or written task and the manner in which what was written was ordered or sequenced. Such judgements were topic-related and took account of the instructions given, particularly with reference to the general purpose of the writing and the suggested audience, where this was specified.

4.33 In rating the tasks, markers were also asked to take account of the fact that pupils would organise or order the information they were conveying in different ways in the various written tasks they completed. For example, the order in which events are recounted and sequenced in a narrative characteristically differs from the order of presentation that might appropriately be adopted in an essay in which the pupil is presenting and justifying a particular argument or point of view.

4.34 Markers were instructed to assign a rating of 5 to writing in which the content was in their view apt and (where appropriate) original, and in which what was said was organised coherently. Writing which was wholly inadequate in content (in terms of the task undertaken) and incoherent in structure was given a grade of 1.

Appropriateness and style

4.35 The term "style" is used in many different ways. In this case it is used to refer to the writer's choice and purposeful use of vocabulary and sentence structure and the general appropriateness of such expression with regard to the writer's subject-matter, audience and purpose, insofar as these can be determined. The writer's knowledge of rhetorical conventions associated with certain forms of writing, as in letter writing, for example, would also be taken account of in relation to this set of criteria. Markers' judgements relating to style are therefore also topic-related. In writing a story, for example, pupils may be required to relate sequences of clauses without obvious repetition of the same connectors between clauses and sentences. Writing a plan for future action poses a similar problem, with the additional stylistic demand that pupils need to maintain consistency in consecutive clauses when relating a series of future hypothetical events. In such tasks, the unvarying use of sentence connectors and, less frequently, the inappropriate use of such connectors is one feature of expression that markers would take account of, as they would of other characteristics of style involving repetition or redundancy.

4.36 One of the most common stylistic difficulties that pupils of this age encounter in writing essays involving, for example, description or exposition, stems from the fact that the writing reflects usage connected with colloquial speech. While such usage might be judged to be appropriate in a personal letter it would not necessarily be appropriate in other contexts. Markers were asked to take note of the occurrence of such usage, and of the use of words or phrases characteristic of formal or literary expression in a context in which these were inappropriate. They noted also the occurrence of words, phrases or sentences, such as clichés, that were judged to be stylistically inappropriate or infelicitous.

4.37 Markers were asked to give a rating of 5 to writing in which the choice and ordering of the wording was appropriate to the subject-matter and audience, and which gave evidence of the fact that the pupil was able to write in such a way as to achieve consciously effects such as economy of style, if this was appropriate in the context. Essays which contained a high proportion of stylistic errors in the first 20 lines of text and which, in effect, failed to take any account of the need to adapt what was said to the subject-matter and audience were given a grade of 1.

Knowledge of grammatical conventions in written English

4.38 In written English a number of conventions are observed by proficient writers which reflect, in particular, the need to represent unambiguously the relations between components of sentences, and clause relations and boundaries. In speech, these relations are indicated in part by patterns of intonation. In writing they are indicated for the most part by marks of punctuation. Markers were asked to note omissions of punctuation marks where such omission resulted in the fact that the grammatical relationship between two or more clauses or sentences was unclear or open to more than one interpretation, as in the following statement: "It was a rainy day and we were bored as usual we could not go out and play . . . " The grammatical relationship between parts of a sentence may also be misunderstood and therefore misinterpreted if, for example, commas are omitted or wrongly placed around phrases in apposition, in a succession of nouns or adjectives, or between clauses and phrases. Not infrequently, pupils introduce a comma between sentences which are linked in meaning. While such usage does not necessarily lead to misunderstanding, markers were asked to take note of it as evidence that a grammatical boundary was insufficiently defined.

4.39 Other common grammatical errors are the result of the lack of cohesion or relatedness between different parts of a sentence or between successive clauses. In this connection, markers were asked to note problems that pupils had in maintaining tense sequence in adjacent clauses, or difficulties in maintaining grammatical 'agreement' between components of a sentence where this was required.

4.40 Markers were asked not to record as grammatical errors the use of grammatical features that are characteristic of regional variants of standard English or the use of colloquial expressions or of slang. If such usage was judged to be inappropriate in a particular context it was taken account of in relation to the category of style, as was the inappropriate use of non-standard word forms e.g. "I done it".

4.41 Essays that contained no grammatical errors were given a grade of 5. Writing in which none of the sentences in the first 20 lines was grammatical in the sense defined above was given a grade of 1.

Orthographic conventions

4.42 In assigning a mark in relation to this category assessors were asked to take account of the pupils' knowledge of conventions of spelling and word division; the appropriate use of upper and lower case letters and conventions relating to capitalisation; the occurrence of errors in the use of punctuation marks that did not result in grammatical error as defined above.

4.43 A grade of 5 was given to essays which showed a complete mastery of orthographic conventions. Writing in which none of the sentences in the first ten lines could be fully deciphered on first reading because of departures from orthographic conventions (and not simply because of the type of handwriting used) was given a grade of 1.

The final stages of writing assessment

4.44 In the case of certain tasks, it was possible to apply an additional form of quantitative assessment in which specific features of writing were noted as being present or absent. Two of these tasks are reported on below. In each case the task concerned was also assessed impressionistically and analytically.

4.45 After pupils' writing had been marked analytically, all scripts relating to the topics to be released were re-read with a view to obtaining more understanding of the problems that pupils encountered in carrying out the tasks proposed, and further insight into the nature of achievement among pupils in the sample. This close reading of the scripts did not lead to the production of an additional set of ratings but supplied information needed for qualitative interpretation of pupils' performance. [. . .]

Examples and discussion of specific writing tasks

[. . .]

Discussion of the report on the sighting of a UFO

4.50 One of the writing tasks pupils were set involved the writing of a factual report addressed to a Ministry, based on a first person narrative account. The narrative told of the sighting of a strange object in the sky; it included a description of the object and of the writer's whereabouts and emotional reactions to the event. A simple sketch map accompanied the story for the purpose of clarifying essential details. Pupils were also given a set of 'guidelines' for making their report, under the title 'Advice for UFO Spotters'. The topic for writing, narrative account, map and guidelines are reproduced below:

> *Read this account of the sighting of a strange object in the sky.*
>
> It was nine o'clock on a damp, foggy November evening — November 20th 1978. I was on my way home from the youth club, walking up the dimly lighted lane that leads to our house. I was more occupied with the prospect of supper than anything else and at first hardly noticed the high pitched ringing noise.
>
> As it got louder I stopped and rubbed my ears hard. They were beginning to hurt. I stopped and stood in the road by the vicarage gate and felt my eyes growing rounder as from behind the grey outline of the church steeple emerged a blue pulsating light.
>
> The noise ceased. The church suddenly seemed to be floodlit. The lights — I could see more of them now — hovered above the steeple. The swifts that roost in the belfry rose in a cloud, shrilling out to each other in terror.
>
> I could see the object clearly. In fact, I couldn't take my eyes from it. Less than 100 yards away, up in the air above the church there was a kind of dome at least 30 feet across. It was a translucent blue and it throbbed like a beating heart. It glowed blue, lit up from within, and stood out quite clearly against the dark sky.
>
> Suddenly, before I had time to blink, the object shot upward — straight up,

further and further away — the cluster of blue lights growing smaller and smaller till they faded out among the stars.

I was still standing in the lane. The whole thing had happened in less than five minutes. I shivered, shook my head, and walked on home.

Sketch map of where I saw the object.

ADVICE FOR UFO SPOTTERS

This form is to be used by persons wishing to report sightings of UFO's to the Ministry of Defence.

The following information should be clearly recorded.

1. Date, time and how long the sighting lasted.
2. A description including shape, size, colour and brightness of the object.
3. Where you were at the time.
4. The direction in which the UFO was first seen, and how far it was away, with any landmark that might help to pinpoint the position.
5. What movements the object made, with an estimate of speed.
6. Weather conditions at the time — including details of cloud cover, mist, haze, etc.

The instructions given to the pupils were as follows:

Read the account of the sighting of a strange object in the sky. Then read the 'Advice for UFO Spotters'.

Imagine that you are the person in the story and that you wish to report your experience to the Ministry of Defence. *Following the advice given,* write a report of what you saw.

4.51 A total of 467 pupils attempted this task and their scripts were assessed in four ways. All scripts were double impression marked, a 10 per cent sub-sample was analytically marked, then the entire set was scored with reference to a check list of points derived from the suggested guidelines, 'Advice for UFO Spotters'. Finally, the scripts which had been marked analytically were then reviewed in detail by a panel of two markers working in collaboration with members of the language team. All four processes were separately phased, and offer different perspectives on the way the task was undertaken by pupils.

4.52 In their commentary on a sub-sample of scripts on this topic, the analytic markers felt that the main difficulties relating to content stemmed from pupils' interpretations of the requirements of the topic and of the presented text which together posed a complex task for 11 year olds. Plainly, any writing task based on a written source will be assessing both reading and writing skills, difficult though it is to pinpoint their interaction. A characteristic of performance on this task was that few pupils confined themselves *only* to the information contained in the given account, and very few (3 per cent) reported *all* that was suggested as being necessary. In fact, the majority of pupils (80 per cent) attempted just over half the suggested items for the report. Had there been only a limited time available for writing, the test could have been interpreted as 'speeded', but neither this writing task nor any other in the survey is subject to strict time limits. The teacher's notes on the presentation of this task had included the instruction "Please explain that the written report must be faithful to that given in the account provided. Pupils do not need to invent details or events not given in the account". However, many pupils preferred not to restrict themselves to the experience of the story teller. An analysis of both the facility values of items on the checklist and omission figures for them may serve to expand these comments, as well as to illustrate further the nature of the stylistic demands posed by the report task.

4.53 The proportion of pupils correctly reporting specific items of information ranged from 18 per cent to 73 per cent. While there is some tendency for items which are suggested later rather than earlier in the guidelines to be more frequently omitted, position in the guidelines does not emerge as a strong predictor of inclusion or omission. For example, 19 per cent of pupils omitted to refer to the duration of the sighting, 37 per cent did not report on the brightness of the object and 19 per cent gave no report on the observer's position.

4.54 The items which emerged as having the highest facility value relate to the reporting of the colour of the object (73 per cent) and the date of sighting (70 per cent). On these items the omission rate was low (6 per cent). About 25 per cent of responses on both these items were inaccurate however, reflecting the markers' commentary that numbers of pupils were not always using the facts given in the story as the basis for their report. The following two scripts are quoted by way of illustration:

The date was the 6th of January 1976 at the time of 10.15 pm. I saw strange object hovering above the sky. And it lasted for approximately 6½ minutes then flew off. The shape of the object looking sidewards was sort of ovel with a little door and I think a small window. It was quiet big in size. The colour of it was white . . .   [1]

. . . a bright shinning object moved towards me. I faintly saw the colour it looked a browny goldy colour. It looked like a big saucer. It lasted for about 3 minutes. I was quite frightened because seeing an object like that by a vicarage on a cold wintry night was'nt very nice   [2]

4.55 A group of items with facility values around 60 per cent relate to details of time, and description of the object. Thus between 60 and 65 per cent of pupils were able to report correctly the time at which the sighting took place, the duration of the sighting, the distance the object was from the observer and the object's size. Details relating to distance and size were omitted by about 20 per cent of pupils (more than omitted to give details of date and time of sighting), but the proportion of inaccurate responses was again around 20 per cent, indicating the number who chose to invent their own situation or alter the given one. Approximately 60 per cent of pupils accurately indicated the degree of brightness of the object and the general weather conditions; slightly under 60 per cent said what movements the object made. Omissions for these items respectively were 37, 26 and 30 per cent. Other items on which the figure for omissions is greater than that for inaccurate responses included the request for further details describing the UFO, namely its shape and estimated speed. The facility values for these items were 55 per cent and 51 per cent. A statement as to the position of the observer was correctly made by 55 per cent of pupils, but fewer pupils (46 per cent) specified an identifying landmark, or the direction in which the object was first seen. Under 20 per cent of pupils gave details of the weather conditions.

4.56 In all, a total of six specific items were omitted by between 27 per cent and 72 per cent of the sample. The items are not strongly connected as a group either by theme or position, either in the narrative account or outline for reporting, so no one explanation will account for their omission.

4.57 One of these items was the question concerning details of weather conditions, which perhaps seemed redundant to pupils who had already given general information about the state of the weather. There was also potential confusion over the opening statement of the story, "damp, foggy . . . evening", and the later reference to the blue lights "(fading) out among the stars". To be precise, the report would have to include information about fog *and* clear patches of sky. The request in this case was for descriptive details for which there was no single word or phrase ready to hand in the narrative. Though this item had by far the highest rate of omissions, others of perhaps the same type were also omitted. For instance, the degree of brightness of the UFO can be inferred from the word "floodlit", and the observation that "(it) stood out quite clearly from the night sky", but the narrative does not say in so many words that the object was 'very bright'.

4.58 Similarly, to form an estimate of the speed of the object an inferential reading of the remarks "before I had time to blink" and "The whole thing happened in less than five minutes", was necessary. In contrast to other items in the report this was one where an intelligent guess was all that could be expected, and possibly as a consequence the item failed to discriminate between groups of high and low performers overall. 44 per cent of pupils omitted this item; perhaps some were deterred by the fear of inaccuracy, or were simply unused to making estimates.

4.59 The problem of having to relate two separate pieces of information not consecutively presented, before making an accurate report, possibly contributed to the 30 per cent omission rate with regard to the movements made by the object; this was first observed to be hovering, then shooting upward. About 13 per cent of pupils reported this information inaccurately.

4.60 Items relating to the location of observer and object were found difficult by about half the pupils. These items involved the use of the sketch map provided, firstly, in order to establish the direction in which the UFO was first seen. 27 per cent of pupils omitted to report this, and of those who did, approximately 29 per cent were mistaken. Secondly, the map could have been used to pinpoint the observer's position: over half of the pupils offered information on this item but the error rate was again around 25 per cent. The third item which might have been clarified by reference to the map concerned the identifying landmark, although another factor here could have been that the word 'landmark' is itself unfamiliar to the 44 per cent of pupils who missed this item. (One pupil, for example, observed "The UFO was 100 yards from me the pinpoint was by the church".) Although the omission rate here is equal to that on the question concerning estimate of speed of object, the item statistics are quite different in other respects: while less than half the pupils were correct in indicating what the landmark was, the element of 'lucky guessing' is not apparent, in that the item discriminated clearly between high and low performers.

4.61 The fact that the summary terms so far discussed ('speed', 'movements', 'brightness', 'landmark') do not appear in the narrative yet are part of the language of the report guidelines, highlights a dimension of the task which evidently proved difficult to a number of pupils. What was required here was to effect a form of 'translation' between the more general term and the various particularised details offered in the narrative. Even writers who successfully noted the information required did not always escape stylistic awkwardness in their attempt to synthesise facts from the narrative, and the questions in the report guidelines. Such scripts tend to oscillate between abrupt notetaking and full but disjointed sentences:

1 November 20 1978 time 9 oclock 5 minutes
2 round shaped colour blue it was bright . . .
5 The movements of the object were hovering above the steeple and suddenly emerged at about 150 miles.

[3]

The movement that the object made was shot upward straight up further away. The estimate of the speed was 100 miles per hour.

The weather was a damp, foggy November evening

[4]

4.62 Reports which were structured as narratives, and full of detail, were not penalised provided the writing was clearly organised. Nevertheless, the analytic markers commented on the rarity, among the scripts they reviewed, of attempts to apply a detached, terse 'report style' of the kind that would have resulted if the numbered list in 'Advice to UFO spotters' had been followed. One script which was judged highly on stylistic criteria is quoted in full below:

1 The date of the sighting was November 20th 1978. The time was nine o'clock, the sighting lasted five minutes.
2 The shape of the sighting was a dome and about 30 feet across. It was translucent blue and it throbbed like a beating heart. It stood out quite clearly against the dark sky.
3 I stood in a lane by the vicarage gate.
4 The UFO was first seen in the North and it was less than 100 yards away.
5 The UFO shot upward and further and further away. It went about 75 mph.
6 It was damp and foggy at the time.

[5]

4.63 In analysing the stylistic achievements of this writer, one would want to draw attention to certain contributing factors. At best, the style is one which condenses information, so an ability to group ideas which look at first sight disparate seems essential. Obviously a report can vary in the degree to which it is the personal statement of its author; the majority of pupils writing on this topic opted for the 'I narrative'. ("I was very hungry and thinking of my supper", "I looked around for a car or a lorry", "I . . . nearly fell into the vicarage gate".) In fact, given the nature of the task instructions as well as the age of the children concerned, it was not anticipated that there would be much experimentation with impersonal modes of address. Nevertheless, the writer quoted above already displays an impressive command of the skill of detached reporting.

4.64 While it is undeniable that pupils writing reports on the sighting of the UFO faced problems relating to organisation and style which were perhaps unfamiliar, it is also apparent that the presence of a written source afforded them some support. The narrative account provided a pre-existing structure which many used as the skeleton for their report, as well as finding ready-to-hand, in the text, well-formed words and phrases which could be transferred or adapted into their own work. Though this did not always make for particularly original writing, it gave a borrowed competence to writers who might otherwise have performed less well on the criteria of grammar and orthography.

[. . .]

The assessment of writing performance: a summary statement

4.133   The assessment of writing involved the use of procedures that were in certain respects innovatory, particularly with respect to the methods used to take account of variations in the relative leniency or stringency of markers and of the relative difficulty of tasks. It was also necessary to develop a new approach to assessing written work analytically in that it was intended that the definition of the categories employed should reflect a coherent view of the process of essay writing, having regard to both the purpose and form of tasks which pupils were asked to undertake.

4.134   The subsequent review of written work with reference to the different analytic criteria supplied information needed for a quantitative interpretation of pupils' performance. It was possible to characterise variations in performance in relation to specific criteria from task to task. In the story writing exercise, for example, it was easier for pupils to obtain a high rating for content than for style; the report-writing task, based on an eye-witness account, tended to produce writing with few orthographic errors, but which was less highly rated for content. It was also possible to obtain information about the accomplishments and difficulties associated with writing for different audiences and with differing degrees of formality. Discussion of two contrasting letter-writing tasks indicated some of these difficulties. The results of the editing component can be interpreted to provide evidence of what eleven year olds generally consider to be departures from a written norm as well as information about the problems they encounter in correcting written work. In subsequent surveys it will be possible to build upon the preliminary findings reported in this connection.

4.135   In earlier sections of this chapter, discussion has highlighted a range of orthographic and grammatical conventions associated with the varieties of the written language which many 11 year olds are still in the process of mastering. Nevertheless, over 96 per cent of the pupils whose work was marked analytically were judged by the markers to have attained sufficient control of orthographic conventions (including word-division, spelling, capitalisation and certain features of punctuation) for what they wrote to be understood on first reading. Analytic marking also indicated that approximately 95 per cent of the pupils concerned had some knowledge of the conventions used to separate or relate sentences and parts of sentences in written English. The written work of approximately 12 per cent of these pupils, which received an analytic rating of 2, contained numerous errors — on average one orthographic error in each line, and one grammatical error in each three lines analysed. However, the written work of approximately the same proportion of pupils (11 and 13 per cent respectively) was assigned ratings which indicated that the work was judged to be well in command of the knowledge of orthographic and grammatical conventions used in written English. It was also the case that there were a small number of pupils who had much to learn about aspects of spelling, capitalisation and punctuation who were, nevertheless, judged by the markers to be able to produce writing that was both stylistically appropriate with regard to subject-matter, audience and purpose, and interesting and relevant in terms of content. In the majority of cases, however, writing that was judged to be excellent in terms of style and content was also judged to be proficient in terms of the other criteria applied in analytic marking, and vice-versa.

[. . .]

Pupils' performance in relation to background variables: writing

[. . .]

Summary

6.12 The results of the survey indicated that girls obtained significantly higher mean scores than boys and that this pattern of performance was apparent in each region. Pupils whose first language was English performed significantly better than pupils who spoke English as a second language and, again, this pattern of performance prevailed in each region. The mean score of pupils in the Midlands was significantly lower than that of pupils in other regions, and the mean scores of pupils in Northern Ireland significantly higher.

6.13 There were no significant differences apparent between the overall performance of pupils in schools in metropolitan and non-metropolitan counties, though a difference in performance was apparent in one sub-category if the relative affluence of the schools' catchment areas was taken account of.

6.14 Mean scores of pupils decreased as the proportion of pupils entitled to free school meals increased. They tended to decrease as the pupil/teacher ratio decreased, except in schools in which the size of the age-group fell below 30. No significant differences were apparent between the mean scores of pupils in schools in the four categories analysed with respect to the size of the age-group.

Notes

1   *A Language for Life*, HMSO, 1975.
2   The finalised set of proposals was subsequently published in the form of the pamphlet *Language Performance*, 1978.
3   These proposals are further discussed in the pamphlet issued by the APU, *Language Performance*. 1978, DES.

5.3 The Language Monitors

Harold Rosen

Source: Extracts from Rosen, H. (1982) *The Language Monitors: A Critique of the APU's Primary Survey Report 'Language Performance in Schools*, Bedford Way Paper No. 11, Institute of Education, University of London.

The Assessment of Performance Unit's Primary Survey Report, *Language Performance in Schools*,[1] is not about language performance in schools. It is about performance in a series of tests of reading and writing, or 'battery' as it is more appropriately called. It would be too much to expect that the Report would attempt to justify in general testing procedures in education, though the authors must know that testing of this kind is surrounded by bitter controversy and that the activities of the APU are the focus of suspicions, doubts and anxieties by some, and enthusiastic, insistent promotion by others. This is certainly true of the APU's testing programme (see Holt, 1981, and Carter, 1980). The compilers of this Report keep their heads down and do not meddle with the politics of their own existence. They do not place the whole Report in a relevant context. We may contrast it with the opening of a document produced by the National Association for the Teaching of English (NATE), *Assessing Children's Language* (Stibbs, 1979):

> At a time of cultural insecurity, there is a special unease about language, because language reflects social values. There are pressures on teachers — often from the least informed about language and education — to teach a narrow set of language skills and uses, and to accept teacher-free assessments which seem to measure, more accurately than teachers can, the performance of children and schools.

There is no discussion in this document of the main purposes of this huge, ever-expanding exercise.[2] Nowhere is there a calm appraisal of what are intended to be the consequences for pupils' language development, teachers' practices in language education and the political uses of their findings. To have done so would have invited a different kind of reading of this text.

As it stands it tempts the reader to become embroiled in the testers' problems rather than his own. What, in brief, is the relevance of this exercise? Ambitious claims are made in passing, but this is a very different matter from an open discussion of these claims.

We can, however, recover a little of the provenance of this particular Report by reference to another better-known one. The progenitor of the APU Report, is acknowledged in the Preface by the Joint Heads of the APU

> The Bullock Report expressed the belief that 'a monitoring system . . . must present a comprehensive picture of the various skills that constitute literacy.' The Language Steering Group of the APU was guided by this principle in devising a framework for monitoring language performances.

If that were so, then the unfortunate Steering Group would have selected a guiding principle which could only have postponed the actual testing procedures to a distant date. In the event no such 'comprehensive picture' of literacy skills emerges from this Report, nor for that matter any novel contribution to that extraordinarily ambitious goal. There is no indication in the Report that 'skills' is an inadequate concept for handling the complexities of what readers do or might do with texts, nor how a writer constructs or might construct a written text. These matters have had considerable attention in recent years and the theoretical studies all point to the difficulty of building a coherent theory of literacy which encompasses the psycho–social processes involved.[3] Such a theory would have to be linked to an understanding of the ways in which children's responses to literacy tests are embedded in the meaning of literacy in contemporary society. In spite of all this, which would not be news to some members of the Steering Committee, the Report declares its uncritical allegiance to the Bullock Committee's Utopian guiding principle — as indeed, we must suppose, it was bound to do. There are contexts within contexts. Everyone knows that the Bullock Report (HMSO, 1975) itself was commissioned at a time when 'allegations about lower standards' was appearing on the national political agenda. Small wonder that the Bullock Committee devoted a whole chapter (Ch. 3) to 'Monitoring'. It is to that chapter we should return if we wish to understand fully the promptings which lay behind the principles and procedures of the National Foundation for Educational Research.[4] Somewhat surprisingly, the Report under review does not take us back to the moment of its birth. Certain oddities emerge at once. The Bullock Report did much more than ask for a 'comprehensive picture . . . (etc.)'. It elaborated with uncharacteristic, meticulous detail the precise features of the proposed tests and they are almost entirely adopted by the APU. The whole thrust of these recommendations can be brought under the rubric of *standards*.

> . . . . we think it appropriate to complete this section on standards by setting out our conclusions on how they can be more effectively monitored. (p. 36)

and

> . . . . it seems to us beyond question that standards should be monitored and this should be done on a scale which will allow confidence in the accuracy and value of the findings. (p. 44)

The concern that a sophisticated view of language skills should be the launching pad for the tests was linked to this other concern about the credibility of the findings which needed to satisfy not only the hungry demands of the more-tests lobby but also the demands of those who might criticize the tests on the grounds that they were based on naive views of what language is and how children use it. How much that hope was justified we shall examine in due course. Meanwhile, let us repeat that the unambiguous central intention was to monitor standards, an intention which receives very muted acknowledgement in the final sentence of the Preface.

We hope this Report will help to inform the debate about standards of literacy.

It does no such thing, especially if we recall that the debate has not been about what children can do with language, but about whether they are getting better or worse at doing it. It *does* contribute a few marginal statistical items, but nowhere does it enter the debate nor suggest how its findings might contribute to it. Its authors must have known that more was expected of them.

⋆ ⋆ ⋆

Indeed, when we return to the body of the Report as distinct from the Preface, we find pretensions to something much more grandiose and yet at the same time what appears to be a retreat from expectations. There is an opening fanfare of aspirations, followed by a muted requiem. The fanfare first: the aim, we are told, is nothing less than to offer to the public the first APU contribution to '*a national picture of language development*' (our italics). That is followed by a disclaimer: the aim is 'not . . . to pronounce on whether the standards revealed by the survey are higher or lower than they should be'. Curious that, having espoused the Bullock Report, these should be announced as the goals of the Report. But even more curious when we attempt to judge whether these goals have been attained.

When did language development become part of the APU's terms of reference or, rather, its main object? The clear intention, we repeat, had always been to monitor *standards*. Had the huge, exciting investigation of language development been the aim, then, in first place, the entire operation would have had to be conducted in quite a different manner; secondly, it would have meant ignoring why the APU was set up. The language task of the APU would have become so different as to be unrecognizable. Anyone concerned with the study of language development knows what a vast and complicated operation would have to be planned. Even the study of the process of early language acquisition has proved to be more exacting than the first grammar-based studies proposed (compare, for example, Brown, Cazden and Bellugi, 1969, with Halliday, 1978, and Wells 1981) and is far from completed; and that early stage is more amenable to observation and collection of data. No reputable researcher would take seriously the proposal that language development could be studied by using the results of an annual series of tests. When we bear in mind that the development of language beyond the early years (almost unknown territory) is complicated by functional variety, cultural diversity and literacy, we know that kind of proposal would be dismissed as absurd irrelevance. A serious study of language development would require at the very least numerous detailed and longitudinal case studies of the language of children being used for genuine purposes. Needless to say, nothing faintly like that appears in the Report, not even a few in-depth case studies of some of the children who figure only as statistics or disembodied 'answers'. It is true, of course, that this Report is the first in a series, but it does not provide even a credible foundation for a language development study, especially as that would have to be based on the interaction of the different modalities of language: speaking, listening, reading and writing, the former two of which await the development of yet more tests. The truth is that the reader will search in vain for any clear statement in which the findings are pointed in the direction of language development: how, for example, they might in due course make a contribution to development during the years of secondary schooling. For that matter they will search in vain for any discussion of language development. A glance at the tepid 'Conclusion' (pp. 133–4) will show how the pretentions of the opening statement dwindle to

> ... it will be possible to relate and, in some cases, to amalgamate information in successive surveys.

A somewhat opaque promise. It is such a far cry from the earlier one that we can only conclude that the latter was no more than a genuflection to an idea which is currently in favour.[5] Between the alpha and omega of this Report is the more familiar and humdrum business of test manufacture and administration into which the energies of the authors have been poured with no nonsense about language development.

We can now turn to the equally surprising opening statement that the Report has nothing to say about rising or falling standards. Perhaps it was intended to convey no more than that, since this was the first Report in the projected series, we must await the others for pronouncements about standards. Such a straightforward statement is easily composed in the English language. Why then did the authors not choose to make it? Why else all the huge concern with the application of the Rasch model to the language tests (elaborated with full technical detail in Appendix 2). The model, we are told, is used solely to establish 'comparability of success rates' obtained in different phases of testing. It is, to say the least, disingenuous to leave the matter in the way the Report does and leave it to us to track through the pages to discover whether (a) they will be getting round to standards in due course, or (b) rising and falling standards are no longer within their purview at all. We might pass over this confusion and put it down to infelicitous language performance by the authors. However, if we turn to *Language Performance*[6] (APU, 1978), we find without cautious ifs and buts,

> The substantial quantity of rich information that would be made available would serve not only to monitor change in standards but also to provide the kind of detail on which appropriate action could be based. (p. 3)

Very clear. Those were the marching orders given to the NFER and, as far as we can tell from the outside, they were never withdrawn.

* * *

[. . .]

In the comments which follow we shall be pursuing what seems to us a difficulty which surrounds all testing of this kind. The demand for testing, vociferous and importunate, lures some people genuinely concerned with matters of educational principle to run ahead of their own competence. Having once agreed to participate in this hazardous programme, they must in the end either let pragmatism triumph over principle or simply down tools. We have already seen how the authors, having scrupulously set out the glaring deficiencies of a language testing procedure, then proceed to commit themselves to its use. There is no reason to assume that our understanding of the processes of reading and writing is so advanced that a team of testers can confidently set about monitoring standards on a national basis.[7] Nor can we assume that there is some kind of consensus about English teaching and language education which can be used to justify one procedure rather than another. It is the headlong drive for the production of simple figures which stands in the way of sober and sensitive concern for progress in children's use and reception of language. [. . .]

The APU have adopted the practice of claiming that their exercise is concerned with *language performance*. But as they themselves know this is not correct. They have until now whittled down their concerns to reading and writing and offer their explanations. However, giving priority to literacy tests can only confirm the deep-rooted assumption within the educational system that what is written and printed has no essential connection with speaking and listening and that 'back to basics' means back to pens and books. For many years there has been a determined attempt to make the spoken language an intrinsic part of school learning (Wilkinson, 1965 and Barnes *et al* 1971). It is unlikely to receive encouragement from the priorities established in this Report. Whatever we are promised for some indefinite future, there is no concession that a productive way of exploring a topic, such as that in the booklets *Whales*,[8] is to talk about it.

The APU was certainly uneasy about this. *Language Performance* (op. cit.), picking up once again from the Bullock Report and acknowledging that 'talking and listening occupy more time than either of these (i.e. reading and writing) in the life of most human beings' asks whether these activities should also be monitored (p. 3). Two objections are raised: (a) subjectivity would be too great; (b) 'it would be difficult to establish comparability across time'. However, they suggest that 'suitable monitoring instruments and economical procedures' should be developed by research. All the contradictions of national testing are concentrated in these few lines. Oral performance is of critical significance but it is difficult, if not impossible, to test in the approved 'objective' manner. Postpone the endeavour but assume a solution to be possible. Meanwhile proceed with the supposedly less subjective business of testing the testable. Subjectivity, which includes making principled value judgments on argued criteria, is perceived as an obstacle, an impediment which testers abhor. Since comparability over time is the goal, learning activities, however important, which cannot be reliably stored and compared must either be rejected or somehow or other (not forgetting 'economical procedures') be coaxed into testable format. More significantly, no indication is given of the hazards of isolating oral language from written language: it is simply taken for granted that each kind of language use must be separately assessed. Can we expect when the full testing programme goes into action statistical procedures will be devised for an even more global score? But, then, speaking is an essentially collaborative activity and collaboration in learning, to which we so often pay lip service, is the very last thing to which test constructors, steeped in individualistic ideology, give attention. And all this in spite of the fact that there is impressive evidence of what children can achieve by collaboration in learning, unembarrassed of course by the problems they are creating for anyone wishing to record individual scores. Thus talking and listening become jam tomorrow. The backwash implications are obvious.[9] In the concluding Chapter 7 of the Report we are promised that the APU will 'extend the scope of the monitoring programme to encompass the skills involved in listening and speaking' and, more positively, that this will link reading and discussion as well as writing and listening. But why are these two forms of interaction chosen? Why not, for example, discussion of first drafts of writing, or dozens of other possibilities? Somewhere or other there must be a record of the proceedings which led to these decisions. However, if we are tempted to welcome this further proliferation of the programme, we should try to imagine what this promised addition will look like compared with the committed talk of children which has emerged from a continuous context of learning and at its best is a serious engagement with the 'grammar of motives'. It might seem that there is a paradox here. On the one hand we have argued that the omission of talking and listening will have a backwash effect and on the other its inclusion will be disastrous. The paradox is, of course, only resolved by refusing to be lured into 'improving' the language performance tests and rejecting the whole operation. On the other hand, there are important studies of the performance of pupils engaged in different kinds of talk (see, for example, Barnes and Todd, 1977). What emerges from them, as we have noted for language development in general, are the theoretical difficulties of analysis and interpretation (Adelman, 1981) and deep awareness of how much more remains to be done.[10] One thing is certain: what we need now is more observation and analysis, not commando raids for the collection of monitoring samples. The APU work is a diversion of resources and attention from this kind of task.

* * *

We can now turn to the assessment of reading which is where the whole of the language performance operation began in the distant days of the setting up of the Bullock Committee.

As we have already noted the Report is nothing if not frank when it stares soberly at the task confronting it in the assessment of reading.

. . . no model of the reading process is generally accepted to be an adequate representation of the processes by which readers comprehend what they read; and as such comprehension is as complex as thinking itself, this lack of consensus is to be expected. [para 2.11]

Consensus[11] is beside the point. What should be paramount is an appraisal of the explanatory power and limitations of rival representations of the reading process. Anything less is abdication. It is nevertheless true that we do not have a perfect understanding of reading.

The process of reading is not very well understood. Researchers do not yet know enough about the developed skills of the fluent reader, the end product of the instructional process, let alone the process of acquiring these skills. But researchers are beginning to realize that reading will not be completely understood until there is an understanding of all the perceptual, cognitive, linguistic and motivational aspects not just of reading, but of living and learning in general. (Smith, 1971)

That should not unduly dismay those teachers who succeed in teaching thousands of children to read but it should be chastening to anyone seeking how to compile comprehensive tests of the *extent* to which those teachers have been successful. Nothing daunted by the lack of adequate theoretical equipment the APU pressed on. We are offered an examination of the research literature, but it is the literature of *reading assessment*. An appraisal of theories and studies of the reading process would have been a much more arduous task.[12] The one principle which was clearly enumerated for reading was the theory of context:

. . . there is always a context about which we can ask, 'Who is saying (or writing) what, to whom and why?'

and

In schools, the importance of trying to provide a context within which pupils can use language with a real purpose is not, perhaps, sufficiently recognized. (APU, 1978, p.5/6).

Context is a more complicated matter than this, but we would agree wholeheartedly with the principle. Here, as so often in the Report, the logical consequences of this principle are not frankly confronted. The context in which a child might want to seek out a book about whales (a book not a booklet of heterogeneous snippets) is utterly different from a context of responding to being tested. There is a context, no question of that, but it is a bad one. There is a 'real purpose' but it has little to do with the child's purposes.

The reading tests are based on short booklets containing passages 'selected or adapted from text-books, works of reference and works of literature of a kind likely to be employed or referred to by teachers.' It is claimed that the selection of themes and the design of the booklets were likely to engage the interest of most of the children in the age group'. Two specimen booklets are included with the Report. No doubt they are being scrutinized eagerly by publishers. Of the test questions this ambitious claim is made:

> In devising the questions, the guiding principle was that they should be questions that an experienced teacher would be likely to ask pupils. [para 2.32]

All very reassuring until we examine these comments more closely. As Carter (1980) has pointed out the snippets in the booklets bear a dismal resemblance to 'the force feeding of facts and a language curriculum which demands that young children work mechanically through endless comprehension and other 'English exercises'. As for the 'experienced teacher' and his/her 'likely' questions, that person is a figment of the testers' imagination. They must be very distant from schools to try to foist on us the notion that all experienced teachers share a common way of asking children questions or, indeed, that they would choose to ask a set of questions at all, let alone printed ones calling for written answers.

In order to pass judgment on the booklets (*Whales* 1 and 2) the questions based on them and the comments in the Report, a reader must cope with the section called *Examples of Pupils' Reading Performance* (2.37–2.68). There is no space here to show how difficult it is to make sense of this section. Suffice it to say that it requires many readings and dartings to and fro in the text for the reader to be confident of grasping the principles and procedures. There are three matters with which a reader will be concerned: (a) the reading booklets themselves; (b) the questions on them; (c) the pupils' responses.[13] Some of his difficulties will arise from the fact that national testing has inevitably to be surrounded with a security operation. We cannot therefore be given all the facts and we have to take on trust that we have been given representative examples. So it is that we are given two of the booklets (both on the same theme!) but not even the titles of the others, and that we are given only a selection of the questions asked. The selection does not include all the questions discussed in the text. Many teachers reading this Report will be keenly interested in the way in which literature was handled in the tests. Their interest will be cooled when they learn 'it is not possible to learn in detail in this Report the range of pupils' responses to the literary works or passages . . . without releasing materials needed for use in future surveys'. A test of the kind of detective work expected of a reader would be for him to attempt to answer this central question, 'What exactly would any individual pupil have to do in completing the reading tests?' He will never discover, for example, how many questions a pupil was asked, nor how long he would be given to amswer them.

Of the passages in the booklets, this much should be said. There are in many respects typical of the 'information books' which have flooded into primary classrooms. With the exception of the 'literary passages' they consist of very limited selections of items of information strung together under titles like 'Three species of toothed whale' or 'Two centuries of whale hunting' (20 lines!). [. . .] As for the questions themselves, as we might have guessed, they are multiple-choice questions. Recollect that these are supposed to be questions which, typically, a teacher might ask. So we have (p. 45),

Having read this passage, which of these words do you think best describes dolphins?

1 Foolish
2 Beautiful
3 Hideous
4 Infectious
5 Friendly

It has all been said before. Questions of this sort do not work with the grain of the reader who constructs his idea of what dolphins are like without thinking whether they are infectious or not or by running through lists in his head. It may well be that what the passage most impresses on the young is that dolphins are intelligent,[14] but then that is not one of the choices. Any one of the alternatives could be plausibly supported.

[. . .]

It would be tedious to trace in detail the shortcomings of those questions we are permitted to see and the discussion of them. It is, however, worth lingering on the way in which literature is handled. There are teachers who regard the reading of literature as central not only to reading development but to the whole development of a child. Literary passages are included in the tests and some perfunctory statements made (p. 31) about how a reader 'certainly interprets the meaning of what is written'. To be sure, 'all literature pupils are capable of understanding and appreciating some aspects of works or passages of literature, provided an appropriate selection of such passages is made'. These rather patronizing[15] statements settle nothing. Of course children can respond in delicate and perceptive ways to what they read. What is at issue is whether it is possible to test this in the style we are presented with here and whether any useful statements about the *national* significance of their responses can be made. There is too another cause for concern, namely, the selection of 'appropriate' passages. Nowhere in this Report do the authors make an attempt to come to terms with cultural diversity.[16] This is the more surprising since during the period of the preparation of this Report all the controversial and difficult issues surrounding multicultural education have been highlighted in public discussion and official statements have urged all those involved in education to take account of cultural diversity in our schools and our society. Nowhere in the testing of reading is this likely to be so salient as in the choice of literature (though it is also true of themes like whales). Of this kind of appropriateness not a word anywhere in the Report. It is as though the right hand of the DES does now know what the left hand is doing. It would be interesting to know what the Swann Committee would make of it all. 'Appropriate' assumes some kind of shared culture and patterns of feeling and meaning. It is precisely those feelings and shared meanings with which literature engages, and with which the reader negotiates with the writer.

The multiple-choice question does not begin to tap this many faceted negotiation. Much is made of handling words in context, especially metaphorical uses. The example is given of 'the line *snaked* through our hands' and 66 per cent 'recognized that the implication was that the line could be said to be more like a snake'. Many of those children could have chosen that meaning when supplied with nothing more than the isolated phrase. It is difficult to judge from this 18-line passage, but the choice of 'snaked' is likely to have been made because it adds to the sinister aspect of the whale-killing. There is more to metaphor than the discovery of a literal translation. But then what a reader responds to in a text, and how, is very different from what they can make explicit about the means by which that response was elicited. This does not deter the APU. We find on page 32 this startling information:

> . . . pupils were asked to consider the stylistic effect of the last four sentences used in the account.

Needless to say the pupils were asked to do nothing of the sort, nor should they be if the assumption is that there is one correct answer.[17]

Here is the actual question (p. 51):

> 34. What effect do the last four sentences have on the story?
>   (1) They make the mood calmer
>   (2) They show the sailors were happy
>   (3) They give us a shock
>   (4) They introduce a new mystery
>   (5) They make it more amusing

The Report tells us that 41 per cent recognized that their effect was to make the 'mood' of the story calmer. 'Recognized' is a euphemism meaning 'selected that form of words to have put in their mouths'. The comment in the Report seems to suggest that this method can produce initial evidence that 'some 11-year-olds are capable of appreciating stylistic effects of considerable subtlety'. The evidence is crude and unsatisfactory compared with what a discussion could produce when children have been moved by a work of literature. In the context it strains credulity to ask us to believe that the APU thinks it has made a discovery.[18]

The reading performance tests like the writing tests are scored on the basis of percentage of correct answers. What use can anyone make of these data when only certain questions and scores are presented to us? Firstly, distributed through the text are the percentages relating to particular questions. So we learn what percentages of pupils can identify 'the main idea or gist of a paragraph' or 'locate information' and so forth. There is no discussion of what all this fragmented and partial information might add up to, nor how it might be used by teachers or parents. Two brief paragraphs summarize the findings.

It is difficult to imagine who could cite them and expect them to be taken seriously. They run like this (a selection) [paras 2.79–2.80]:

> (a) As is to be expected, pupils had least difficulty in answering questions about matters that were clearly asserted and easy to locate in the text. . . . There were a number of items which were answered correctly by between 90 and 97 per cent of the pupils involved.
> (b) With reference to *Whales* (booklet 1) approximately three-quarters of the pupils

were able to answer correctly one or more questions that involved comparing information given in different passages . . .

(c) Over two-thirds of the pupils who read the booklet gave evidence of being able to use an index efficiently . . .

We shall pass over briefly the study of pupils' attitudes to reading. Those who have some faith in attitude testing are hardly likely to be persuaded in so short a space to change their views. The chief difficulty is that people have attitudes to their attitudes and to those who are enquiring about them. With children the difficulties are even greater for they must find some verbal formulation of unformulated feelings and ideas which are undergoing change, and therefore fraught with contradiction and tentativeness. All attitudes are potentially dynamic, but since we are here concerned with attitudes to a construct (myself as reader) which is in a formative and highly plastic state, the chances of trapping this elusive creature by the well-known tests are very small. [. . .]

We are not suggesting that the findings in this section of the Report are worthless but rather that, where they do shed light on expressed views which are of interest, invariably they are only the beginning of what we need to know.[19]

Talking about books was by far the most popular activity as a follow-up to reading. In contrast, two-thirds of the sample expressed their dislike for writing about a book after reading it.[20] (p. 81)

It is just possible that there are some who are not aware that children feel that way and may be moved towards a change of view should they chance to light on this finding. But for others it is only a spur to understanding why talking is popular and writing disliked. At best the attitude tests give us tantalizing glimpses of the answer.

One child responding to the attitude test on reading completed the sentence, 'The place I like to be when I am reading is . . .' with 'a very quiet corner in the classroom'. We all know how difficult it is to probe that invisible dialogue of the child with the book. We start asking questions on the assumption that we know what is to be understood and how it is to be understood; what, in other words, should be the nature of that dialogue right down to what the child should be feeling. Writing is in some respects quite another matter. The very motive for writing is that it should produce a removable product. We may not know much about how a mind behaved in order to produce it, but we can analyse what is in front of us in great detail.

* * *

The research team's task in studying the response to their writing tests was therefore less inevitable than for the reading tests. This section of their Report is by far the most interesting and their discussion of the scripts could form a better basis for discussion than any other. However, as we shall see, it is the tester's needs which cause the greatest problems. Let us begin by setting the investigation of children's writing into its daunting research context. Vygotsky, writing in the Thirties (Vygotsky, 1978, trans.) put it like this.

> The developmental history of written language, however, poses enormous difficulties for research. As far as we can judge from the available material, it does not follow in a single direct line in which something like a clear continuity of forms is maintained. Instead, it offers the most unexpected metamorphoses, that is, transformations of particular forms of written language into others . . . it is as much involution as evolution. This means, together with the processes of development, forward motion, and appearance of new forms, we can discern processes of curtailment, disappearance, and reverse development of old forms at each step.
>
> . . . But only a naive view of development as a purely evolutionary process involving nothing but the gradual accumulation of small changes and the gradual conversion of one form into another can conceal from us the true nature of these processes.

The question then is, 'How can this development be investigated?' The APU had to administer its entry into schools with all the usual complicated protocol and ultimately confront children with specially designed writing tasks based on certain assumptions about the nature of writing. The most surprising assumption is that at 11 years of age most pupils are able 'to adjust what is written to different audiences and social relationships' and, judging by the nine activities [para 4.11], to produce 'different types of writing'. The development of this capacity to differentiate writing according to function and to audience is very slow and many reasonably competent adult writers never achieve it fully and have little or no need to do so. Moreover, the chances of discovering the extent to which embryonic forms of these kinds of writing occur are small when performance is linked to separate tasks. In pre-adolescent children they are more likely to be observed embedded in kinds of writing which they find both easier and more congenial. Bedevilled as usual by the constricting conditions of the investigation, the APU is aware that the actual context for the writing scarcely provides genuine audience or genuine communication, i.e. to whom am I writing this and for what acceptable reasons? We are given the possibilities, A 'traditional test conditions'; B 'specific task' given by the normal teacher; and C normal class course work. Inevitably, in practice, the choice imposed by the imperatives of comparability and cost of administration dictates the choice of A. It is just possible that for some, even many, pupils the design of A might permit the pupils to treat the writing task more like B or C. Certainly the most unpromising and inappropriate stimulus can be taken up enthusiastically by someone. This can hardly be depended on to produce valid responses. There is an attempt to reassure us that there is 'evidence' and 'close analysis has revealed (etc.)'. Since we are not permitted to inspect the evidence nor appraise the analysis, we must take this on trust and readers will have to judge from the rest of the Report how far they are prepared to do this. The problem emerges very sharply when we inspect the items on the list of activities. They include an informal and a formal letter. Every child will be aware that the task is a bogus one and that the only meaning he/she can put on it is that he/she is being tested. Thus the informal 'letter to a friend' is not going to be judged by the true recipient for appropriateness. The same is true for other activities, e.g. to report (a) 'verifiable account of an event' (b) 'an account of something learned'. Why? We know it to be true that vast quantities of writing are demanded in schools which are not genuine communications. That many pupils submit to this unceasing demand to produce does not justify the replication of the practice in a prestigious series of tests. The most likely consequence is that this list will spawn thousands of composition titles calling for responses in conditions not dissimilar to those set up by the APU.

The decision was taken to use two types of marking for the compositions,[21] impression marking and analytic marking, and this decision is supported by an experimental study. Tediously, we must again draw attention to the fact that this experiment on which such a crucial matter turns is not reported. We hear what by now is a refrain in the Report, 'it would not be appropriate to summarize the findings' (not even summarize?). Indeed this whole section on marking is confusing. The analytic marking is not related to background variables since only a sub-sample was marked in this way. If they are really valid procedures their use becomes very limited. We learn, too, that the marking schemes could be applied by teachers who had undergone a period of training but we discover nothing about the training programme.[22]

The analytic marking uses four sets of criteria [para 4.31]

1. Content and organisation
2. Appropriateness and style
3. Grammatical conventions
4. Orthographic conventions

These are put before us as self-evident components of the written system which should be subjected to analytic marking. There is a common-sense rationale here but there is nothing objective in the selection. 1 and 2 are global characteristics, requiring the same order of judgement as impression marking, where both 3 and 4 examine highly specific features of the writing system. There are enormous difficulties here and they cannot be enlarged upon, but the paragraphs relating to 1 and 2 [4.32–4.3] are far too sparse to reassure us that these have been satisfactorily resolved. 'Appropriateness and style', for example, were marked on the first twenty lines of the scripts. The paragraphs [4.35–4.37] dealing with these yoked criteria reveal both a vagueness and over-specificity.

> The term 'style' . . . is used to refer to the writer's choice and purposeful use of vocabulary and sentence structure and the general appropriateness of such expression with regard to the writer's subject matter, audience and purpose, insofar as these can be determined. [para 4.35]

The criteria here, avowedly somewhat inapplicable, cover so much of what is essential to writing that it would be impossible for any marker to separate them from other criteria. There is a strong sense that the team are both laying down dubious laws in a dogmatic manner and at the same time leaving loopholes in the laws. So, dealing with colloquial language, they tell us

> While such usage might be judged appropriate in a personal letter[23] it would not
> necessarily be appropriate in other contexts.

A few lines below we find the Report speaking of 'stylistic errors' as though they had provided grounds for confident allocation of language to outer darkness. 'It would not necessarily . . .' hardly constitutes a useful guideline to a marker and, even less, does it enable a reader to perceive how this criterion would be applied.

There is no avoiding the fact that written discourse is governed by an interaction of cognitive demand and social conventions, but the conventional aspects of writing (including stylistic choices) are constantly being renegotiated by writers because their style cannot be separated from their social, ethical and ideological stance, which leads them not only to be concerned with their ideas but also the medium. The point here is to ask what kind of model of writing is in the minds of the APU team. Each one of their common-sense categories for analytic marking suggests that prior analysis of them is at a very superficial level. We might take, for example, what would seem at first blush to be an uncontroversial category, namely 'content'. This is construed, we must conjecture, as a set of propositions evaluated for their aptness. There is no way, however, of judging the aptness of content without being able to specify what the writer was supposed to transmit for his/her own purposes and by what criteria what kinds of writer need what selection of information. The focus must always be on the writer's meaning. As Dillon (1981)[24] puts it,

> If this finding and expression of meaning involves constructive activity by human
> subjects . . . then quantifying the content and measuring the efficiency of its transmis-
> sion by various sentence forms becomes an impossible and futile undertaking. (p. 163)

Grammatical and orthographic matters are in some ways, but certainly not all, much more straightforward for the observer, but how a marker decides on where to place a script on a five-point scale on the basis of twenty or ten lines of writing (why lines and not number of words?) is another matter. To put it at its simplest, how does one compare one pupil's errors which are due to ambitiousness in vocabulary and sentence structure with another who by writing with caution makes herself less accident prone. The fact that orthography and grammar were weaker in the story task than the report task is related to this difference. The Report mentions (4.91) that different tasks produce different tendencies to error but does not acknowledge that within-task differences can be significant.

*   *   *

We can now examine how the APU discusses the application of its procedures and comments on the pupils' performance in three of the tasks: 'reporting, narration, and writing to change the reader's state of mind', more specifically (a) a report on the sighting of a UFO, (b) a story based on some suggestions, (c) a letter to cheer up an absent friend (a formal letter is also discussed at this point). [This edited version of the critique examines only the first of these. *Ed.*]

The UFO report

The pupil is presented with a first-person narrative of the UFO sighting, a sketch map and a formal document setting out the items which should be included in a report to the Ministry of Defence on a UFO sighting. The task is then to read the documents and, *'Imagine you are the person in the story . . . write a report of what you saw'* (i.e. to the Ministry of Defence). Once again there is a test behind the test. Once again a fiction is created, for the pupil did *not* write the narrative, the pupil did *not* undergo the experience, and, most important of all, is *not* writing to the Ministry of Defence. And yet this mock report is to be judged by all the criteria which should be applied to a genuine report. Since we were given to understand that the language tests were all considered to be eminently suitable for eleven-year-olds, we must be left wondering how a bogus report to the Ministry of Defence fits that description. A genuine formal written report is not likely to be within the experience of most eleven-year-olds, nor does there seem to be any good reason why it should be, unless some natural compelling occasion arose.[25] The task is ingeniously devised but can only be applauded if we accept its assumptions. It is an excellent example of the kind of exercise which has been in English text books for decades, since, in fact, the arrival of 'social' English in the 1930s.

A further difficulty is commented on in the Report.

> Plainly, any writing task based on a written source will be assessing both reading and writing skills, difficult though it is to pin-point the interaction. [para 4.52]

There follows the usual indigestible detailed information about percentages of pupils who correctly reported such items of information and some thin speculation to account for the figures. But there is no return to the very point being raised. It is left floating in mid-air, as though the recognition of a difficulty in some way resolves it. We ourselves have suggested that linking reading and writing would be no bad thing, but this kind of assessment creates its own difficulties. In due course (Ch. 6) we are going to encounter mean scores for writing performance. Yet we are told here that this exercise assesses both reading and writing in a way which makes one inextricable from the other. What then is the meaning of these scores with all their air of numerical precision?

[. . .]

The chapter closes with a pyrotechnic display of selection of statistics. Since all the niceties are derived from the value judgment we have already discussed we shall make no comment on them. A summary statement at the end of the chapter gives as much attention to the development of testing methodology as to any meaning which may be attached to the results. It includes the unjustified claim that it has obtained information about writing for different audiences. Not until we have a thorough theoretical analysis from a sociolinguistic point of view of what the written system of English consists of, can we do more than scratch the surface of children's development as writers. Meanwhile in judging performance and progress, we need to examine writing produced in different kinds of school contexts and not performance on tests however artfully contrived.

The two remaining chapters (5 and 6) of research findings deal with the relationship between 'background variables' and the reading and writing results. Before we plunge into these pages of statistics, we must remind ourselves what we are looking at. As we have pointed out, we are looking at global scores for reading and writing which have been derived from diverse activities each scored separately for its 'facility value' (level of difficulty). As we have shown, standing a long way back from these figures are the procedures which give rise to specific items. In some cases decisions have been made about what constitutes a 'correct' answer and in others (e.g. analytic marking of writing) abstract qualities in a written text have given rise to hard figures of dubious validity. Once we move away from the initial processes of children's performance and testers' assumptions and practices, the whole operation consists of deriving statistics from other statistics. When we bear in mind that all these subsequent manipulations are based on the Rasch model, which has been seriously criticized, we can make some estimate of how much reliance we can place on this final statistical flurry. It is not, therefore, our intention to allow ourselves to be enticed by these tables and statistics into considering their implications. It is most important to signal that when these figures are cited in public debate they should not be treated as gospel. Some observations are, however, in order.

On page 121 [para 6.12] we note the sudden attention to speakers of English as a second language. This is a matter of most serious concern. In all the lengthy description and analysis which precedes these figures no reference has been made to such groups of pupils. Now we have thrust before us a handful of generalized statistics. It seems clear that concern for these pupils is perfunctory . . . It is ironical that the Report which in general transmits an air of high statistical expertise should base its figures on incredibly shaky foundations. To put the matter briefly, speakers of English as a second language are treated as a homogeneous group, in spite of the fact that even a passing interest in bilingualism[26] teaches us that it exists in many different forms and, more obviously, competence in the second language ranges from zero to highly fluent use. Furthermore, the information on numbers of second language speakers 'was obtained from head teachers' and we have good reason to know that this is not necessarily a reliable source. Pupils who have a native-speaker fluency in English do not necessarily make known their first language, nor do some head teachers make it their business to find out.

Given the coarse data by means of which this background variable is investigated, it cannot be wondered at if the APU arrives at findings which are already commonplaces among those concerned with bilingualism. This group of pupils has lower mean scores than first language speakers. Those who were literate in their first language[27] did better than those who were not. It must be emphasized that the language performance of second language speakers needs delicate and sophisticated study, such as that being pursued at the University of London Institute of Education by Josie Levine and teacher colleagues. Whereas the APU make frequent references to ambitious plans for expanding their work in many directions, no indication is given that they have the intention of refining this crude and very limited undertaking.

Perhaps the best comment on these sections of the Report is to be found in the text

> The information provided about relationship between performance and background variables should be interpreted with caution . . .(p. 31)

We are promised that the pattern will become clearer when more information is made available.

★ ★ ★

It will no doubt seem to some that this lengthy appraisal is hypercritical, carping and ungenerous. Certainly a general impression which comes from a reading of the Report is of huge energies conscientiously devoted to a monstrous task. More than that, it is apparent that the team have wrestled heroically with ever increasing problems as they have attempted to work with the grain of educational practice and also to stay close to the interests of the children. But a close reading of the Report is a frustrating experience requiring no little concentration if one is to penetrate its mysteries. It is, after all, only the tip of the iceberg which we are permitted to inspect. Repeatedly we are told or have to infer that more has gone on than is reported. The text has been carefully policed.

There will be many who quite properly will be envious of the resources allocated to an endeavour which has produced so little and the effects of which can so easily be harmful. For it would not be difficult to propose a study of school pupils' language development, one which we so desperately need and which could be conducted in a manner which would constitute a unique form of in-service education for teachers. We may well sympathise with the research team, but that sympathy must be tempered by a scepticism about the whole strategy in which they become involved, its political background, its long-term intentions and the use to which it will be put. Though we may see the team locked in an heroic struggle with the tiger of assessment, we must also see that they should not have ventured on the jungle safari in the first place. We said at the outset that nothing can obscure the fact that this Report is linked to a preoccupation with standards. It may make some teachers nervous; it may make some teachers shift their practices in ways which will not be helpful to children; but it is unlikely to raise standards of performance. There is an alternative; it is the active participation of teachers in assessment, teachers who are close to the children being assessed. The possibilities have already been sketched out. Stibbs (1979) calls it 'in-service training through collaborative marking':

> To join other teachers, perhaps more experienced than ourselves in assessing the course work of many pupils, helps to get a sense of what represents progress and excellence in language use, while reminding us that different pupils progress in different ways. (p. 36)

The constraints imposed on the research team by the grand design of the APU could not have permitted them to carry out the kind of investigation of children's language which could give us deep insight into language development. Language development is nevertheless inscribed boldly on the Report's programme. Here is the alternative proposed so long ago by Vygotsky (trans. 1978)

> Any investigation explores some sphere of reality. An aim of the psychological analysis of development is to describe the internal relations of the intellectual processes awakened by school learning. In this respect, such analysis will be directed inward and is analogous to the use of X-rays. If successful, it should reveal to the teacher how developmental processes stimulated by the course of school learning are carried through inside the head of each individual child. The revelation of this internal, subterranean developmental network of school subjects is a task of primary importance for psychological and educational analysis.

The APU Report does not give us x-rays but rather fuzzy aerial photographs.

Notes

1 Primary Survey Report No. 1, HMSO, 1981.
2 We are promised many further developments at various points in the text.
3 My point is not that we understand nothing of these things but rather that we have no 'comprehensive picture'. Further, what we can conclude from the rapidly mounting accumulation of studies is the need, before we rush to testing, to devote resources to this kind of work.
4. We shall continue to refer to the APU as the body responsible for Report No. 1, as indeed it is. However, the design of the tests and their implementation was farmed out to the NFER. It was, in fact, the Bullock Report which nominated the NFER for the monitoring commission, though no reasons were given for this confident patronage — such as its past performance in language testing research.
5 Publishers too have adopted this practice retaining the most conventional English courses as courses in language development.
6 This document, to which we shall refer again later, was, so to speak, the foundation stone of APU language testing. Until the appearance of the Report under review it was the only publicly available document which gave in some detail 'the stage of thinking reached by the working group set up in 1975'. The working group was set up to consider forms of assessment and specifications for the NFER research team which started work in 1977.
7 See *Achieving Literacy: a kind of evidence*, Meek, *et al.* Routledge and Kegan Paul, (1983). This is a study of five children learning to read in which the authors record and analyse their observations over four to five years. Even a cursory reading will show how much we

have learnt, and *have still to learn*, about the engagement of a young reader with a written text.

8 Most of the reading measures adopted by the APU are based on short booklets containing short passages of prose. Two of these are included with the Report, both with the same theme, *Whales*.

9 It should not be forgotten that the no-talk lobby is still a powerful one. It is epitomised in Stuart Froome's 'Note of Dissent' to the Bullock Report in which we can find the extraordinary statement, 'It is doubtful if children's talk in school does much to improve their knowledge, for free discussion as a learning procedure at any age is notoriously unproductive'. (p. 538)

10 The scope of further enquiry is outlined in *Investigating Talk*, Schools Council Language for Learning Project, University of London Institute of Education, 1981. There is a rich experience and understanding amongst teachers on which this work is being based.

11 On p. 23 we are told that the development of the language tests was collaborative. For example, liaison groups of teachers (listed in Appendix 4) were convened by Advisers and Inspectors and consulted about initial drafts. We never discover how these teachers were selected.

12 It is one of the more depressing features of reading tests that they have emanated from the psychometric community. The qualifications for the job are your credentials as a psychometrist not that you are a respected authority or even a serious student of reading. Such people are unlikely to regard semiotics as relevant to their purposes.

13 The difficulties for the reader are compounded by the fact that for some reason best known to the authors they have placed their data on 'background variables' a hundred pages away in Chapter 6 and critical details of administration in Appendix 1, p. 137 and Appendix 2, p. 146.

14 It contains '. . . We knew they were friendly, intelligent creatures' and 'The strange, un-human but intelligent head . . .' and 'it seemed to be saying to its companions, "Look at me — see how clever I am!" '

15 Illiterate pupils can do these things too if they are read to. The old confusion between decoding and responding is present here.

16 In dealing with 'background variables' towards the end of the Report some figures are set out on the performance of speakers of English as a second language. This is another matter, though clearly connected with the question of culture.

17 It would be interesting to ask a number of outstanding literary critics of the different schools of thought what they thought the stylistic effect (not effects, notice) of the last four sentences was and then present them with the APU's multiple-choice question. One would not need to go to such extremes. A group of English teachers would do very well.

18 There are many disquieting features of the comments on the literature tests. Discussing the pupils' answers to questions on Walter de la Mare's poem *The Horseman*, the authors tell us that less than 10 per cent judged it to be a description of a 'real' horseman. Though they do not say so, this was presumably scored as incorrect. Why? And what do these children *mean* when they say that? Contrast this with the lengthy and refined statistical analysis.

19 The Report tells us that the research team is affected in attitudes-to-reading investigation by 'immediate economics which prevent large-scale investigation of pupils by the research team'. (p. 55) Who does the sums? Suppose large-scale observation were to *replace* some of the other research work and were carried out in collaboration with LEAs and groups of teachers?

20 Interesting to note the contrast here with the claim that children enjoyed writing on the booklets. However that claim was not backed up by an attitude test.

21 We shall not refer to children's writing as 'essays', though the Report repeatedly does so. It is a significant habit in certain quarters to use this misleading term. The belles-lettrist

essay model has for a long time hampered the development of composition work in school. It can only be applied with absurdity to task 2, 'imaginative narrative . . .' ·

22 The present writer was a member of the team which tested out the method of multiple impression marking. The work is cited in the Report (Britton *et al.*, 1966). Since that time he has been troubled by the fact that the method depends for its reliability on a tendency for there to develop amongst teachers, especially teachers of English, an invisible consensus on what constitutes good writing. Training will reinforce and extend this tendency. The problem is ideological not psychometric.

23 It is difficult to know how anyone other than the recipient could consider anything inappropriate in a personal letter. As we have pointed out the recipient in the test context is, however, a fiction for the examiner.

24 Dillon's book *Constructing Texts,* develops this argument much more fully and persuasively. The work is worth citing here because it constitutes a marked contrast with the APU's model of writing and its general argument is that the way we respond to writing or value it cannot be quantified.

25 The difficulties of what looks like a simple task will be appreciated by those who have had to fill in a claim for car accident insurance. The Report tells us, as though we should be surprised, that, 'the analytic markers commented on the rarity . . . of attempts to apply a detached "report-style" ' [4.62]. In a comment in a later paragraph [4.64], the Report confesses that the pupils were confronted with unfamiliar problems. Instead of being honestly self-critical it fudges the issue by claiming that the printed material gave support ('borrowed competence'). Further, 'It was not anticipated that there would be much experimentation with impersonal modes of address' [4.63]. It is interesting to have this tantalising glimpse of the APU's 'anticipations'. What were the others?

26 See, for example, Simoes, A. *The Bilingual Child,* Academic Press, 1976. The title is selected arbitrarily. The APU team would not have found it difficult to assemble for themselves a bibliography in an area which has received international attention and more recently is being studied in the English context (see Rosen and Burgess, 1980).

27 Another obscurity : how was this information obtained?

References

Adelman, C. (ed.) (1981) *Uttering and Muttering*. Grant McIntyre.

Assessment of Performance Unit (1978) *Language Performance*. Department of Education and Science.

Barnes, D., Britton, J. and Rosen, H. (1971) *Language, the Learner and the School*. Revised edn, Penguin.

Barnes, D. and Todd, F. (1977) *Communication and Learning in Small Groups*. Routledge and Kegan Paul.

Britton, J., Martin, N. C. and Rosen, H. (1966) *The Multiple Marking of English Compositions*. HMSO.

Brown, R., Cazden, C. and Bellugi, U. (1969) 'The Child's Grammar from I to III'. In J. Hill (ed.), *Minnesota Symposia on Child Psychology*, Vol II. University of Minnesota Press.

Carter, D. (1980) 'APU Tests a Mistake'. *The Times Educational Supplement*, 27 June.

—— (1981) 'Bogus Objectivity'. *The Times Educational Supplement*, 2 October.

Chatman, S. (1978) *Story and Discourse*. Cornell University Press.

Department of Education and Science (1975) *A Language for Life*. (Bullock Report). HMSO.

Department of Education and Science/HM Inspectorate (1978) *Primary Education in England: a survey by HM Inspectors*. HMSO.

—— (1979) *Aspects of Secondary Education in England: a survey by HM Inspectors*. HMSO.

Dillon, G. L. (1981) *Constructing Texts*. Indiana University Press.

Ginette, G. (1980) *Narrative Discourse*. Basil Blackwell.

Halliday, M. A. K. (1975) *Learning How to Mean*. Arnold.

Holt, M. (1981) *Evaluating the Evaluators*. Hodder and Stoughton.

Meek, M. (1981) *The Cool Web*. Bodley Head.

Meek, M. *et al.* (1983) *Achieving Literacy: a kind of evidence*. Routledge and Kegan Paul.

Rosen, H. and Burgess, T. (1980) *Languages and Dialects of London School children: an investigation*. Ward Lock.

Schools Council Language for Learning Project (1981) *Investigating Talk*. English Department, University of London Institute of Education.

Simoes, A. (1976) *The Bilingual Child*. Academic Press.

Smith, F. (1971) *Understanding Reading*. Holt, Reinhart and Winston.

Start, K. B. and Wells, B. K. (1972) *The Trend of Reading Standards*. NFER-Nelson.

Stibbs, A. (1979) *Assessing Children's Language Performance*. Ward Lock/National Association for the Teaching of English.

Vygotsky, L. (1978) *Mind in Society*. Harvard University Press.

Wells, G. (1981) *Learning through Interaction*. Cambridge University Press.

Wilkinson, A. (1965) *Spoken English, Educational Review*. Occasional Publications 2.

5.4 Assessing Spoken Language: Testing Times for Talk

Margaret MacLure

In the not-so-distant past, talk in schools was largely invisible. Language education was mainly concerned with reading and writing, and very little attention had been given to classroom talk and the opportunities it provides — or perhaps fails to provide — for children's development, both as communicators and as learners. The last two decades have seen a gradually strengthening movement to make talk visible in schools: to make classrooms places where children can extend their spoken as well as their written language resources, and use these resources as a means of directing and shaping their own learning. In recent years these arguments for the importance of talk in school seem to have borne fruit. 'Oracy' has finally taken its place alongside literacy on the language curriculum, and teachers are now being enjoined to take a major responsibility for children's spoken language development beyond the pre-school years. The recent documents on the English curriculum by Her Majesty's Inspectorate, for instance, give speaking and listening equal priority with reading and writing amongst the central concerns of English teaching (DES, 1984; 1986). And, in 1987, a National Oracy Project has been set up in England and Wales to generate and co-ordinate initiatives in curriculum development.

Inevitably, this contemporary interest in the development of oracy has been accompanied by increased concern about its assessment. New initiatives have been taking place throughout the education system: in the national programme which monitors standards of performance in curriculum subjects, in the public examinations system, within Local Education Authorities, and in individual schools and classrooms. At the national level the earliest of these initiatives came from the Assessment of Performance Unit (APU) within the Department of Education and Science, which in 1982 carried out the first ever large scale surveys in England, Wales and Northern Ireland of pupils' performance in oracy at age 11 and 15 (APU, 1984a; 1984b). Oral assessment is also now compulsory for all students taking the English exams in the General Certificate of Secondary Education (GCSE) at sixteen-plus;[1] and Local Education Authorities are using a variety of assessment schedules in the profiling and Records of Achievement schemes which are used to chart children's progress in school and provide information at the point of transfer from primary to secondary.

At both the national and local levels, therefore, the assessment of children's spoken language is already well under way. Indeed in terms of national policy and public expenditure, assessment initiatives seem to have got off the ground in *advance* of widespread curriculum debate and development, or at least at a faster rate than we might have expected given the comparatively recent arrival of spoken language on the educational agenda.

One outcome of this state of affairs is that the development of assessment procedures has been in large part a 'bootstrapping' exercise. As the APU language team acknowledge in their first report to include oracy, until recently there has been no shared educational vocabulary for talking about progress and achievement in spoken language, in contrast to reading and writing; nor can we look to linguistics or other disciplines for a complete theory of oral communication that would establish stages of development and provide definitions of competence (APU, 1984a: ch. 2). Indeed it is only fairly recently that linguists have begun to study genuine communication between real speakers, rather than the grammar or semantics of invented (written) sentences (cf. Stubbs, 1983); and although a great deal of interesting work is now being done, linguists would be the first to acknowledge that we are still a long way from a comprehensive theory of spoken language and its development.

Test constructors and assessors have also had to confront the well-known difficulties of assessing children's spoken language without distorting perceptions of their competence through the artificiality of the test situation. Since talk is always bound up with the social situations in which it occurs, there is always the risk that what children say, and how they say it, will reflect their interpretation of the test situation, and of the motives and intentions of the assessor rather than more general aspects of their competence as communicators (see for example Barnes, 1980 and Labov, 1969).

Problems such as these had led the Bullock Committee to conclude in 1975, despite its strong advocacy of the development of oracy in schools, that national monitoring was not a feasible enterprise (DES, 1975:41). By 1980 however the APU had begun developmental work towards the monitoring of oracy, arguing that this was warranted by the demand from teachers and educationalists for more information about children's spoken language abilities (APU, 1984a:17).[2]

Those who have been involved in producing assessment procedures — whether they are members of the national monitoring programme, language advisers in LEAs, English panels in Examining Groups, or individual teachers trying to trace their own pupils' progress — have inevitably been forced therefore to try to fill in the gaps in current understandings of how talk 'works', how it develops over time, and how it varies according to the situations in which it is embedded. They have been obliged in other words to construct — whether explicitly or implicitly — a *theory of competence* in spoken language at the same time as a machinery for assessing it.

This is not only a vastly complex, but also a high-risk enterprise. The history of assessment in other subjects does not encourage us to be optimistic about the models of competence which have been reflected in test procedures, where the scope of assessment has often been guided more by what it is easiest to count or measure than by what it is important for children to accomplish. In the case of oracy the dangers of such an outcome are particularly severe. We know from the work of sociolinguists and ethnographers that spoken language is closely linked to speakers' personal and social identity, and the values and practices of their communities and cultures. We know too that judgements about competence in spoken language, or about the difference between 'good' and 'bad' talk are notoriously difficult to dissociate from strongly-held but often unacknowledged assumptions and attitudes, which may have little to do with intrinsic qualities of the language itself (see, for example, Trudgill, 1974). Because the rapid spread of assessment of children's spoken language is of necessity generating — or at least augmenting — definitions of their competence, those who are developing assessment techniques bear a heavy responsibility to ensure that these definitions do not overlook aspects of children's communication which may be less easily quantified, or inadvertently reward the competence of some groups of children at the expense of others.

This is all the more important since trends in the assessment of oracy are likely to exert a strong influence on the language curriculum itself. Indeed there are signs that this is already happening. HM Inspectorate, in their discussion document towards a new English curriculum from 5 to 16, recommend to the attention of teachers the APU's language tests, stating that these, 'particularly in the case of oracy, point to ways in which practice may be improved' (DES, 1984:16). This view is elaborated in an appraisal of the APU's work by a former member of its language Steering Group (Thornton, 1986).[3] It is inevitable too that the assessment procedures established for the examining of Oral Communication in the GCSE English exams will strongly influence what gets taught in English classes.

It seems timely therefore to review current approaches to the assessment of oracy. In the remainder of this paper I shall outline what seem to me to be key notions in the schemes which are in use at present, and consider what has been achieved and the problems and issues which remain to be tackled. The discussion will focus primarily on the work of the APU, since by virtue of its early appearance on the scene and the public endorsement which it has received, the APU approach seems to have played a prominent part in setting the agenda for the assessment of oracy.[4] I shall also refer however to some aspects of other assessment schemes, such as those used in GCSE English syllabuses.

Current approaches to assessment: general principles

The central notion which recurs in contemporary formulations of the aims of assessment is that of *communicative effectiveness*, in which priority is given to children's ability to use language for different purposes in diverse situations.

The first primary oracy report by the APU states that 'we would . . . wish to emphasise that we are primarily interested in the communicative effectiveness of pupils' spoken language skills: that is, the extent to which they are able to achieve a range of communicative purposes' (APU, 1984a:18). HM Inspectorate state this principle in very similar terms: 'whatever the task, the main criterion for assessing pupils' competence in speaking is the communicative effectiveness of what they have said. Different tasks make different demands. What needs to be assessed therefore is the pupil's success in achieving the purposes for which he or she is speaking' (DES, 1984:18). In the National Criteria for English, to which all GCSE English syllabuses must conform, the first aim of all English courses is that they should 'seek to develop the ability of students to . . . communicate accurately, appropriately and effectively in speech and writing' (SEC, 1984:1), though we might note in passing that this formulation could be read as giving accuracy priority over effectiveness.

The notion of communicative effectiveness is not without its problems — noticeably that it begs the question of how we might define effectiveness, and whose definitions are likely to prevail. But as a general principle it allows for a generous view of what is involved in successful communication. It places speakers' meanings and purposes in the forefront of attention, and recognises that the demands of communication vary according to situation and circumstance.

This view of communication would reject some of the narrow views of competence which have been reflected in previous attempts to assess spoken language. For instance it would be impossible to contemplate assessing children's spoken language by means of a single test. The emphasis on meaningful communication would rule out the testing of speaking and listening as separate skills, and especially the use of listening comprehension tests, which in the past have required children to listen for no particular purpose, in order to recall facts for which they have no particular use (cf APU, 1984a: 15–16). It would also argue against a framework which restricted its scope to the formal and rather artificial tasks which were common in CSE English oral examinations, such as giving a prepared talk, holding a 'conversation' with a teacher or assessor, and reading aloud from a passage of prose (cf Barnes, 1980).

The notion of communicative effectiveness rejects, too, ideas of competence which focus on grammar or vocabulary as primary indicators of ability, since it implies that children's choice of words, and the grammatical structures they use, must be considered in terms of the purposes for which they are speaking and the goals that they are trying to achieve. There is no good reason to assume for instance that successful communication necessarily depends on maintaining a high 'count' for grammatical complexity across all situations; nor would there be much point in trying to help pupils to brush up on their grammatical structures. As Barnes (1987) points out, we are not usually aware of the structure of our own utterances, focussing as we do on the meanings and messages that we want to convey rather than the technical resources for doing this. (A similar point is argued in APU, 1984a:19.)

At the level of general principles of assessment, then, the notion of communicative effectiveness appears to offer a broad view of competence, which recognises the diversity of language use according to speakers' purposes, and the communicative versatility which is needed to meet the demands of different situations. It does not follow of course that the aspirations codified in statements of principle will necessarily be realised in actuality, and we need also to look at how assessment schemes work in practice. I shall turn now to the work of the APU, with these issues in mind.

The work of the Assessment of Performance Unit

In the APU framework the notion of communicative effectiveness is expressed in a functional model, in which linguistic structure and organisation are understood in terms of the different functions which language serves. Each function, or 'communicative purpose' as these are called in the APU model, is exemplified in one or more tasks, and it is these tasks on which pupils are assessed. Figure 1 shows the functions and tasks which have been included in the oracy surveys to date. (The numbers 11 and 15 in parentheses indicate whether the task in question was included in the primary surveys at age 11 or in the secondary surveys at age 15.)

Figure 1   Examples of oracy tasks used in APU surveys

General purpose	Task	Audience*
Describing and specifying	Describing pictures for identification. (11,15)	P
	Description of a place and explanation of interest. (15)	P/A
	Description of a sequence of pictures. (11)	P
Informing/ expounding	Interpretation of an account of a process (with diagrams). (11,15)	
	Exposition of the gist of the account to others. (11,15)	PP
	Interpretation of an account of an experiment. (11)	
	Exposition of the process to others. (11)	PP
Instructing/ directing	Practical interpretation of rules of a game. (11)	
	Instructing pupil to play the game. (11)	P
	Constructing a model following a sequence of instructions. (11)	A
	Instructing others how to carry out an experiment. (11)	PP
Reporting	Report of something learned and explanation of interest. (15)	P/A

Figure 1 *continued*

General purpose	Task	Audience*
	Report on a favourite book and explanation of interest. (11)	P
	Report of the results of an experiment. (11,15)	PP
Narrating	Interpretation of a story, retelling to others. (11)	PP
	Interpretation of anecdote narrating personal experience. (11)	A
	Telling a story based on a sequence of pictures. (11)	P/A
Arguing/ persuading	Interpretation of opposing arguments, restatement of gist of argument and explanation of viewpoint. (11,15)	PP
	Explanation of choice of career — argument/ justification of point of view. (11,15)	P
Focussed questioning	Several tasks required this, e.g. in obtaining further information about an object described or a process outlined. (11,15)	PP
Collaborative discussion/ evaluation of evidence	Interpretation and discussion of evidence to decide on proposed action. (11,15)	PP
	Interpretation and discussion of arguments to reach a consensus. (15)	PP
	Interpretation and discussion to reach agreement. (11,15)	PP
Speculating/ advancing hypothesis	Speculating on the reasons for an experimental finding. (11,15)	P/A
	Speculating on the characteristics of a hidden object and production of a diagram. (15)	P

(From Gorman, 1986: 24–25)

*Key: P Pupil's friend   PP Other pupils   A Assessor

There are precedents for functional models of language in research on early child language development (e.g. Halliday, 1975; Tough, 1977) and on writing development (Britton *et al.*, 1975). The APU's taxonomy is a fairly eclectic collection: some of the purposes (e.g. informing, instructing, questioning) are similar to the communicative acts defined in speech act theory (e.g. Searle 1969); some invoke cognitive strategies (e.g. speculating/ advancing hypotheses), while others seem closer to the idea of genres of speech (e.g. narrating, arguing/persuading). We might also question whether collaborative discussion should be considered a function of language in the same sense as the others in the list, as a discussion might include within it several of the other functions, such as describing, persuading, informing or speculating (see Barnes and Todd, 1977).

I am not too concerned here with the internal, theoretical respectability of the APU model in strictly linguistic terms. However, the overlap and inconsistency in the list of functions probably reflects the lack of an adequate theory of language which would specify the different dimensions and levels of language (eg utterance/function/situation/role/genre etc) and how these interrelate (see Sweetman, 1987).

Nevertheless the framework attempts to get to grips with the ways in which characteristics of spoken language vary according to purpose and audience, and to this extent it could contribute to a critical vocabulary for talking about talk, which teachers and children might use as a starting point for reflecting on the range of language experiences that could be provided in the classroom, and the requirements of different kinds of tasks.

Certainly the list as a whole reflects a much wider range of oral activities than had been contemplated in preceding attempts to assess spoken language. We can note that it recognises the 'informal' language of narrative and anecdote[5] as well as the more formal kinds of speech required in tasks such as reporting back and summarising; and that the tasks are broadly cross-curricular in their subject matter.

The APU approach also tries to minimise the 'communicative stress' that can arise in formal testing: children take part in friendship pairs, and often interact with one another rather than with the adult assessor. This avoids putting children into the anomalous position of having to tell an adult assessor what s/he already knows (APU, 1984a: 22–23). In this respect, as in its emphasis on assessing talk which is meaningful to the participants, the APU model gives priority to validity over reliability in its strictest and most restrictive sense (cf Gorman, 1986: 40).

Assessment criteria

Two forms of marking are used on the tapes of children's performance collected during the surveys. The first, impression or holistic marking, need not concern us here, since rapid subjective judgements of talk do not tell us much about the implicit criteria which are being applied by the markers.[6] The second form of marking — analytic assessment — 'breaks down' the talk on each task into a number of separate categories or dimensions, broadly definable as content, sequential or discourse structure, lexico-grammar and 'performance features' such as hesitation, tempo etc. (MacLure and Hargreaves, 1986:13). The first two of these categories are task-specific, since the criteria for evaluating the content and organisation of what is said must depend on the particular tasks that speakers are attempting and the purpose of their talk. Thus stories for instance are assessed in terms of the discourse structures associated with narratives.

Space precludes a detailed discussion of the APU analytic categories. The framework has the merit of trying to stay close to the details of the talk itself, rather than relying on vague and often value-laden notions such as 'fluency', 'clarity' etc. The APU team attempted to derive their assessment categories inductively, by listening to tapes of children carrying out the various activities and generating descriptions of competence which reflected what the children actually said, in response to the demands of the task in question. This has enabled them to capture some of the complexity of the linguistic and interpretive resources that children bring to bear on specific tasks.

The APU analytic framework tries therefore to go beyond global judgements about 'good' talk by tackling empirically the question of what children have to do to achieve success on particular tasks, and by attempting to capture the multi-dimensional nature of that competence. If nothing else therefore it has promoted an attitude towards the assessment or evaluation of children's spoken language which insists that we must look closely at what children actually say and do, and try to understand this in the context of the purposes for which they are speaking and the tasks they are trying to accomplish.

Some unresolved problems in the APU model

There are however some continuing problems in the APU approach to the assessment of children's spoken language. Some of these are associated, I think, with the particular constraints of national monitoring, such as the requirement to standardize procedures over large populations of children, and the 'one-off' nature of the encounter between the assessor and the assessed. These problems need not necessarily arise in more informal kinds of classroom-based assessment. There are other problems however which may be more deep-seated, and which arise also in other forms of assessment which are in use at present.

Effects of the assessment situation

The APU approach can reasonably claim to have mitigated some of the more obvious and intrusive effects of formal testing by working with children in pairs, and advising assessors on ways of creating an informal atmosphere. (1984a:21–22). It is doubtful, however, whether these steps are — or indeed could be — enough to overturn the inherent dynamics of the assessment situation. The decision to use 'scripts' for administering the tasks, undertaken with reluctance in the attempt to ensure that each child would receive roughly the same kind of 'input' from each assessor, is obviously an unsatisfactory capitulation to the imperatives of reliability and standardisation. As the first APU Primary Survey Report acknowledges in a critique of one task (paper folding: 1984a:44–46), the pre-scripted encounter overrides the contingency and moment-to-moment responsiveness which characterises spontaneous interaction between speakers.

Even more problematic than this however is the question of whether it is *possible* to 'control' for the ways in which different children will interpret and respond to any given situation. As Barnes (1980) and others have pointed out, and as the APU surveys acknowledge (MacLure and Hargreaves, 1986), the ways in which we 'read' situations and formulate strategies for action or response depend on what we bring to that situation: on how we make sense of the occasion in terms of our previous experiences and cultural expectations, and the motives and intentions that we ascribe to the other participants in the light of these expectations.

The APU's brief contains no provision for exploring the nature of these expectations, or for finding out how children's previous experiences — both in their classrooms and in their wider culture — influence their perception of what is required of them as participants in the APU tasks. The APU surveys are forced to proceed therefore on the implicit assumption that all children see the world in the same way and ascribe the same significance to the communicative tasks they are asked to take part in. I shall suggest below that this has serious implications for the criteria which are used to judge children's performance.

Task and purpose

One of the strengths of the APU approach, at least in comparison with the kinds of oral assessment which had preceded it, is its commitment to the principle that assessment must reflect the abilities that are needed in *meaningful communication*. The first primary survey states the aspiration to provide 'a more varied range of communicative tasks which approximate more closely to the range of purposes for which pupils need to use talk in their real life situations' (1984a:14). This is a worthwhile, and indeed a centrally important, aspiration. We need to ask, however, whether it has been achieved in practice.

Some of the tasks used in the surveys seem of doubtful validity under the above definition: for example, describing pictures of two bridges so that the listener can distinguish these from four very similar bridges; listening to a tape about the structures of the brain and then relating this information to others; explaining what is involved in a particular job (e.g. librarian, doctor etc); giving a report of something which was learned recently. The problem is not so much that speakers would never do such things, but more that they would seldom do them in the carefully structured and compartmentalised ways required in the surveys, and that the decision whether or not to do them would be a matter of choice or particular circumstance. If particularly inspired by a TV or radio programme about the brain, we might want to tell others about it. We might get into an exposition of the demands of a particular job in the context of a wider, real-life discussion. And we might (though probably very occasionally) feel the need to describe something we have seen in great detail. One could imagine an experienced bird-watcher doing this to instruct a novice, though unlike the children in the surveys, the speaker would be doing this on the basis of personal expertise and a genuine wish or need to communicate. Moreover in all these hypothetical examples it would be this genuine desire to communicate, with the particular people involved, which determined the speaker's choices about what to mention and what to leave out, how best to get their point of view or information across to their listeners.

One of the central dilemmas in the APU surveys (cf Rosen 1982 and previous article) is that pre-set tasks and make-believe purposes for speaking have to be substituted for the genuine purposes which arise out of speakers' everyday lives and their engagement with others.

Assessment criteria
The APU reports devote a great deal of space to the discussion of the nature of pupils' performance on each task, as revealed in the analytic assessment categories. This has strengths, as we have seen, in highlighting some of the ways in which talk varies according to task and purpose. However this scrutiny of the structure and content of particular tasks often yields insights which may be of little general interest or wider applicability. In the tasks which required children to describe two bridges for instance, the task-specific category of 'Criterial Features' involved a detailed analysis of the constructional and geometrical characteristics of each bridge, as conveyed by the children (APU, 1984b: 33). This does not give us much information about children's strategies for describing which could be applied to descriptive tasks which did not involve bridges.

One of the outcomes of this close scrutiny of the demands of particular tasks is that it has tended to divert attention away from wider questions about the criteria themselves. There is very little discussion for example of cultural diversity in children's responses to the tasks, and the extent to which the assessment criteria recognize this diversity. Indeed the reports tend to assume a cultural homogeneity in their definitions of competence, apart from the recognition and acceptance of diversity of accent and dialect (APU 1984b: 199). One partial exception to this occurs in a short discussion of possible gender biasses in those (few) secondary survey tasks on which girls received significantly lower scores than boys (1984b:77). Here the report considers the possibility that the subject matter may have been uncongenial to girls, and that the criteria for one task (arguing for a pay-rise) favoured a confrontational style of argumentation which girls may be less likely than boys to adopt (cf Coates, 1986).

Elsewhere in the reports, however, there is very little critical reflection about the cultural or social assumptions that might be embodied in the tasks set or the assessment criteria employed, although the team is critical of other aspects of its own methodology. Mercer *et al.* (1987) point out for instance that the criteria used in one of the APU primary oracy tasks, which required children to make up a story based on four pictures, are predicated on a model of narrative which is essentially literate, and which rewards pupils who are able to reproduce the structures and stylistic features associated with a particular genre of stories written for children. This model would fail to recognise the cultural meanings and the textual structuring of stories from children who might be working within an oral narrative tradition which diverges from this pattern (cf Heath, 1983).

Similar issues could be raised in relation to other tasks. One task required pairs of children each to choose one from a list of ten jobs, preferably one they knew something about, and then to tell one another about it. The commentary on the task notes that pupils who chose one of the professional jobs on the list (e.g. doctor, vet, pilot) gained higher mean scores that those who chose non-professional ones such as hairdresser or ambulance driver (APU, 1987:115). Although there is some discussion of the possibility that children's knowledge of jobs may be influenced by what they are told by their parents, the commentary does not raise — and indeed could not answer — the question of whether those children who opted to describe professional jobs tended to be those with professional parents, and whether the marking might therefore have reflected a social class bias in favour of children from professional families.

It is important therefore that the criteria used to assess children's spoken language should be the subject of continuing review and discussion by teachers and students, since it is these criteria which will establish the parameters of what is to count as success or failure in communication. This applies of course not only to the APU's work, but to any assessment framework. For example, we might ask what kind of criteria are being invoked in the following commentary on the performance of two sixteen year old students who have been asked to enact the roles of disgruntled customer and car dealer:

> The manager does not present a very convincing interpretation of the role, and his performance is not helped by his repetition of 'I don't know'/'I mean' and mannerisms, such as rubbing his face. He seems indecisive and uncertain in his approach and somewhat uninvolved in the whole business. One suspects that he would not long survive in a real-life, competitive situation, though he does engender a certain degree of sympathy from the audience. He paid out the refund far too easily, without even securing a receipt!
> The customer, on the other hand, has a sure and precise grasp of essentials and a perhaps surprising knowledge of technical details, and altogether displays a confident, articulate and persuasive attitude.
> *Marks*: Angela (customer) 8 [out of 9];   Steven (Manager) 4
> London and East Anglian Examining Group, 1987)

This commentary is taken from the notes accompanying a video tape issued by one of the GCSE Examining Groups to familiarize English teachers with the kinds of tasks that might be set, and the assessment criteria to be used in the coursework (i.e. continuously assessed) component of the Oral Communication syllabus. It raises several questions about what is being assessed in this task, and the criteria which are being applied in the marks given to each participant. Is Steven being penalised for failing to show promise as a car dealer; or for a lack of competitive ethos; or for being 'uninvolved in the whole business'? Or are both speakers being judged in terms of their acting ability? In either case, we might ask whether these qualities are a legitimate concern of *oracy* assessment. The comments also seem to penalise the use of colloquialisms and 'mannerisms', which are pervasive and unexceptional features in informal speech, while favouring Angela's expertise in technical vocabulary and her 'articulateness'.

The commentary indicates a number of assumptions about 'good talk', therefore, which are not spelled out in the general instructions to teacher-assessors. There is also an unresolved tension between evaluation in terms of what one might expect of a 'real' car dealer (e.g. a combative stance towards the customer) as opposed to a dramatic performance for an audience, and this is further compounded by judgements which seem to invoke a-contextual criteria such as confidence and articulateness. It would be surprising in view of this if the students themselves were aware of the criteria that would be applied in assessing their performance, and what they should aspire to in order to do well on this task.

Simulation and role play activities share some of the limitations of the APU tasks discussed above, in a more extreme form. Children are required to assume the imagined or imaginary purposes of the role-play scenario, and to attempt a creditable 'performance' in encounters of which they have no real experience (cf Barnes, 1987). However, such activities are being widely recommended in GCSE syllabuses as examples of the kind of oral work which teachers might include in their courses.

Describing development

So far I have been considering assessment in terms of children's spoken language at particular ages. For many teachers however the main function and rationale of assessment would be to illuminate *progress* in children's communicative abilities over time. Assessment at discrete ages, as in the APU surveys at 11 and 15, might in principle shed some light on progress, since it seeks to characterise the communicative 'repertoires' that are typical of children in each of the two age groups. In practice though, the APU in their review of the first two years of monitoring in oracy (1987:176) are unable to reach any firm conclusions about trends across the two age groups.

In any case, assessment of this kind could not tell us *how* children got from one stage of attainment to another. What is needed here is a theory of development over time in children's spoken language abilities. Again however we come up against our lack of a comprehensive picture of this development. Much of the research into children's spoken language development has concentrated, for a variety of reasons, on the first five years of their lives (see, for example, Willes, 1983), and although later language development is now being studied in more detail, it is still by no means clear what this development looks like and whether it follows a 'natural' course which is invariant for all children. HM Inspectorate provide a broad sketch of the likely course of children's development beyond the pre-school years in terms of:

> an increase in the range and variety of purposes for which pupils can understand and use language; correspondingly, an increase in the range and variety of appropriate forms, techniques and styles of language which they can respond to and use.
>
> (DES, 1984:2)

This formulation is intuitively acceptable as a general statement of what

Suffolk Record of Language Achievement

LANGUAGE FIELDS	LEVEL 1	LEVEL 2	LEVEL 3	LEVEL 4	LEVEL 5	LEVEL 6
O 1 LISTENING SKILLS	Can listen for a short while e.g. whilst identifying everyday sounds	Can listen attentively to a short story	Can listen attentively to a taped story or radio programme	Can listen with sustained concentration, awareness, and anticipation		
O 2 SPEAKING SKILLS	Speaks hesitantly, putting ideas into words only with difficulty	Speaks clearly and audibly but with little fluency or expression	Can speak clearly and expressively	Speaks confidently, using appropriate vocabulary		
O 3 LISTENING AND RESPONDING EFFECTIVELY	Can respond correctly to a simple oral instruction	Is able to follow a sequence of oral instructions	Can explain what s/he has been told	Can identify points in an argument	Can make reasoned comparisons between oral statements	Can interpret and carefully evaluate what s/he hears
O 4 SPEAKING INFORMATIVELY	Can relay a simple message	Can give expression to needs and problems	Can give a simple account of work done	Can report and explain work done	Can give both prepared talks and informal reports, with some skill	Can present information skilfully and confidently e.g. in interview situation
O 5 LISTENING AND RESPONDING SENSITIVELY	Can understand simple songs and poems	Can respond with understanding to heard stories and poetry	Can enjoy humour, suspense, speech rhythms and rhymes	Can distinguish between different styles and presentations	Often shows sympathetic understanding and some critical ability	Can appreciate and criticise various styles and presentations
O 6 SPEAKING EXPRESSIVELY	Can communicate feelings adequately	Can communicate feelings effectively	Can engage the interest of others in the telling of a story	Can communicate his/her own ideas and feelings	Communicates imaginatively, taking account of the listener's needs	Can express appropriately a range of ideas and feelings, in a variety of contexts
O 7 COMMUNICATING SOCIALLY	Can listen and respond to others in conversation	Can listen and contribute to a group discussion	Can take an active part in group discussion and decision making	Co-operates effectively with others in group projects	Co-operates effectively in group work and responds helpfully in more formal situations	Can converse successfully, even in formal and unfamiliar situations

Source: (Suffolk County Council, 1987).

children still have to learn about communicating after they start school, and it fits in with current work on children's language development. But it is very difficult to fill in the details of this broad trajectory.

The magnitude of the task can be glimpsed in the excerpt in Fig. 2 from a Record of Language Achievement scheme which is being tried out in one Local Education Authority, as a way of charting children's progress from their entry to school at 4/5 to the end of compulsory schooling at 16. The oral component of the scheme contains seven 'fields', each divided into six levels of achievement.

One of the main problems with this scheme is that it conflates and confuses different dimensions of spoken communication. For example, each of the six levels in language Field 3 — Listening and Responding Effectively — seems to relate to different aspects of spoken language rather than to a developmental progression within one area. Following instructions (level 2) is a quite different kind of activity from explaining (level 3), identifying points in an argument (level 4), making reasoned comparisons (level 5), and interpreting and evaluating (level 6). It is hard to envisage how one level might lead on to the next. Similar problems arise with the various levels within Field 4, Speaking Informatively.

Several problems arise in the definitions of the levels within the field of Speaking Expressively, which progresses through communicating ideas 'adequately', 'effectively', 'imaginatively' towards the final stage of expressing ideas and feelings 'appropriately' in a variety of contexts. Firstly there is the question of whether teachers would feel able to reach a consensual definition of 'adequacy', 'effectiveness' and so on. Secondly, the placing of each of these activities within a developmental sequence seems to imply that children replace adequacy, first with effectiveness, then with imaginativeness and finally with appropriateness; or at least that they don't attain the latter before they have acquired the former. This does not accord with our informal knowledge of what children are capable of as communicators. Children of age 5 and below are usually adept at communicating imaginatively and taking account of the listener's needs (level 5); indeed this is one of the strengths and the impressive achievements of young children's language (cf Garvey, 1984). And even a three-year old ought to be able to attain level 4 — communicating his/her own ideas and feelings.

It is not my intention to be over-critical or dismissive of the effort and reflection which has been devoted to a scheme such as this, nor to devalue the urgent search for ways of understanding children's development as communicators. As with many of the other issues which have been raised in the preceding pages, the scheme reflects the considerable obstacles which teachers and children and test constructors alike are facing in their attempts to understand what progress and achievement in spoken language looks like.

Conclusion

Developments in the field of oracy assessment are taking place very rapidly, and it is difficult to anticipate the possible outcomes of these developments. The assessment schemes which have emerged in recent years are considerably more sophisticated and informed than might have been anticipated five or six years ago, and they have begun to contribute to a critical vocabulary for describing progress and achievement in spoken language which captures some of the complexity of children's oral communication.

However, the condensed timetable which has been imposed on the development of viable assessment procedures has pre-empted discussion and debate amongst teachers, test developers and children about aims and methods of assessment. This means that a number of important issues remain to be tackled. Perhaps the most urgent of these is the question of how we can illuminate children's progress and their achievements without requiring them to take part in decontextualised activities which disengage language from its anchor in the real-life purposes, relationships and struggles of those who use it.

Notes

1 The testing of spoken English had been carried out from the 1960s in CSE English exams.
2 There may of course be wider wider-reasons why the national monitoring of oracy came to be seen as 'feasible' around the start of the 1980s. Barnes (1987) develops an argument which places the current endorsement of 'oracy' by policy-makers and government in the context of the ideologies of the 'Radical right' and the New Vocationalism.
3 The APU is itself actively promoting discussion of the curricular implications of its surveys. Copies have been made available to teachers centres and schools of language 'kits' containing examples of APU tests and assessment criteria. The Unit has also organised regional seminars for advisory staff and others who might be interested in exploring the potential of the APU approach in the school context.
4 The APU approach to assessment is also the one with which I am most familiar, as a former member of the Language Monitoring team. The views expressed in this paper could not therefore aspire to be 'objective': whether or not outsiders see more of the game, it is certain that the vision of insiders is coloured by their membership of the institution, the brief they are given by their employers etc. It should be stressed too that in those places where I present a critical view of the APU's work, I do not exempt myself from those criticisms.
5 It is questionable though whether such personal uses of language as anecdote ought to be assessed. Although it is illuminating to discover how skillfully constructed children's anecdotes can be, it is difficult to justify assigning 'grades' to them.
6 The APU reports state that there was an acceptable degree of inter-marker agreement in the grading of tapes. However as Rosen (1982: 48) points out *a propos* the APU writing surveys, agreement amongst markers may simply reflect, and through training consolidate, an 'invisible consensus' amongst teachers.

References

Assessment of Performance Unit (1984a) *Language Performance in Schools*. 1982 Primary Survey Report. London: DES.

Assessment of Performance Unit (1984b) *Language Performance in Schools*. 1982 Secondary Survey Report. London: DES.

Assessment of Performance Unit (1987) *Language Performance in Schools: Review of Language Monitoring 1979–1983*. London: DES.

Barnes, D. (1980) Situated speech strategies: aspects of the monitoring of oracy. *Educational Review* 32, 2: 123–131.

Barnes, D. (1987) The politics of oracy. Paper presented to the International Oracy Convention, University of East Anglia, April 1987.

Barnes, D. and Todd, F. (1977) *Communication and Learning in Small Groups*. London: Routledge and Kegan Paul.

Britton, J. Burgess, T. Martin, N. McLeod, A. and Rosen, H. (1975) *The Development of Writing Abilities (11–18)*. London: Macmillan.

Coates, J. (1986) *Women, Men and Language*. London: Longman.

Department of Education and Science (1975) *A Language for Life*. Report of the Bullock Committee. London: HMSO.

Department of Education and Science (1984) *English from 5 to 16*. London: HMSO.

Department of Education and Science (1986) *English from 5 to 16. The responses to Curriculum Matters 1*. London: HMSO.

Garvey, C. (1984) *Children's Talk*. London: Fontana.

Gorman, T. (1986) *The Framework for the Assessment of Language*. (APU) Windsor: NFER-Nelson.

Halliday, M. A. K. (1975) *Learning How to Mean*. London: Edward Arnold.

Heath, S. B. (1983) *Ways with Words*. Cambridge: Cambridge University Press.

Labov, W. (1969) The Logic of Non-Standard English. *Georgetown Monographs on Language and Linguistics*, Georgetown.

London and East Anglian Examining Group (LEAG) (1987) *English: Oral Communication. Guide to Coursework Videotape*. London: LEAG.

MacLure, M. and Hargreaves, M. (1985) *Speaking and Listening. Assessment at Age 11* (APU). Windsor: NFER-Nelson.

Mercer, N. Edwards, D. and Maybin, J. (1987) Putting context into oracy: the construction of shared knowledge through classroom discourse. Paper presented to the International Oracy Convention, University of East Anglia, April 1987.

Rosen, H. (1982) *The Language Monitors*. Bedford Way Papers 11. London: Institute of Education.

Searle, J. (1969) *Speech Acts*. Cambridge: Cambridge University Press.

Secondary Examinations Council (1984) The National Criteria for English.

Stubbs, M. (1983) *Discourse Analysis*. Oxford: Blackwell.

Suffolk County Council (1986) Record of Language Achievement.

Sweetman, J. (1987) Towards a radical teaching or oracy. Paper presented to the International Oracy Convention, University of East Anglia, April 1987.

Thornton, G. (1986) *APU Language Testing 1979–1983. An Independent Appraisal of the Findings*. London: DES.

Tough, J. (1977) *The Development of Meaning*. London: Allen & Unwin.

Trudgill, P. (1974) *Sociolinguistics*. Harmondsworth: Penguin.

Willes, M. (1983) *Children Into Pupils*. London: Routledge and Kegan Paul.

5.5 A Researcher Reading Teachers Reading Children Reading: Notes on the Task of Making Sense of Reading Assessment in the Classroom

Barry Stierer

Source: Stierer, B. (1983) 'A Researcher Reading Teachers Reading Children Reading: Notes on the task of making sense of reading assessment in the classroom.' In Meek, M. (ed.) *Opening Moves*, Bedford Way Papers 17, Institute of Education, University of London.

. . .the social scientist of necessity draws upon the same sorts of skills as those whose conduct he seeks to analyse in order to describe it. . .
Anthony Giddens, *New Rules of Sociological Method* (1976, p. 155).
. . .anyone concerned with the interaction of groups and individuals may find in the act of reading the basic principles that govern the human activities he studies; for reading ever so curiously mingles person and thing and person and person.
Norman Holland, *Five Readers Reading* (1975, p. xiii).

In 1981–82 I spent two terms carrying out participant/observation research in three first-year junior classes. My brief was to collect as much detailed 'data' as possible related to teachers' everyday practices for evaluating children's reading in the classroom. I worked closely with the three teachers, studying the complex process by which they came to 'know' their pupils as readers: what they looked for; when, where and how they looked; why they looked for certain things at certain times; what kinds of judgements they formed about children as readers; and what actions they took on the basis of these judgements. Ultimately I wanted to see what kind of relationship emerged between teachers' assessment practices and their teaching of reading.

With the field work in schools finished, the collection of 'data' just referred to fell into two categories. The first category was the tangible, documentary record, consisting of: field notes taken during observations of teachers and children working right across the range of school activity; many hours of tape-recorded classroom talk; and the notes and tape-recordings arising from many discussions with the classroom teachers. The second category of the data consisted of my own personal 'feel' for the events recorded in the documentary record, which was the result of my having been an active participant within them. This second, unofficial record is what Charles Hull (1981) calls the 'black market record': the 'understandings built up over time and carried in [the researcher's] head' (p. 1). The tangible record — the notes and tapes — are evocative of those classroom events which the researcher observed and took part in, but fall short of 'telling the story': of conveying the meanings which the researcher became party to as the project progressed. The unofficial record, based on the researcher's familiarity with the unique lore of the three classrooms, is the corpus of evidence which transforms the first record into a living story, but which is too personal to be easily verifiable or even communicated to others.

The starting point for this paper, then, is the dilemma facing the researcher attempting to resolve the tension between these two categories of data. With the more reliable, but two-dimensional, documents of the first record on the one hand, and the highly personal and intuitive, but undocumented, second record on the other, what strategy should the researcher adopt to produce the fullest and yet the most valid account and analysis?

I shall present a piece of evidence from the documentary record of my classroom research project, and then go on to explore some of the ways in which the interplay between the documentary record and the unofficial record within the research process actually mirrors the dynamics of each of the two classroom processes being investigated in the research — children reading and teachers evaluating their reading.

This piece of evidence is an excerpt from a transcript of a tape-recording made in a first-year junior class. The event this transcript relates to is a fairly routine (for this class) reading session: children are reading quietly from their reading books at their tables and queueing up to the teacher at her desk either for help with difficult words or to be 'checked' on a book they have finished in order to be given their next book. The excerpt begins when the session has been formally in progress for about three minutes: most children have settled to their books, a queue has formed and the teacher is finishing up some administrative business before dealing with Colin[1] who stands at the head of the queue with his finished reading book.[2]

Ms Harvey:	*Has Julie gone?*
several pupils at once:	Yes . . . Yes.
Ms Harvey:	Oh, well, in that case Patrick would you like to take that clock back to Mrs Arthur and say Ms Harvey says 'thank you'?
Patrick:	Yes.
Ms Harvey:	*(after pause) Right.* Now . . . You *should* be reading your reading book . . .
pupil:	*(barely audible)* I'm not.
Ms Harvey:	*(after pause of six seconds)* If I heard a person say 'I'm not' I want to know the reason why.
Colin:	*(after long pause, begins reading)* Brasilia . . .
Ms Harvey:	No, from here please.
Colin:	*(begins again)* The people of Brazil nearly all lived along the sea coast. The new city was built far // island *(miscues* 'inland') // inland *(self-corrects)* on a road // ha // ha //

Lucie:	(*interrupting*) My finger hurts.
Ms Harvey:	Oh, *tough*. Would you like me to chop if off?
Colin:	(*trying to continue reading*) ha // ha
Lucie:	No.
Ms Harvey:	Can't do anything about it, other than chop it off. (*To Colin, as prompt*) . . . road? . . .
Colin:	ha // ha //
Ms Harvey:	Well, pretend that's a 'b' . . . what would it say?
Colin:	back.
Ms Harvey:	Right. Now, change it to an 'h'.
Colin:	hack.
Ms Harvey:	hack? . . .
Colin:	hacked through the steaming jungle. It is a city of-of concrete and marble and glass. There are no traffic lights, for every crossroads (*miscues* 'crossroad') is a flyover or an underpass. There are great blocks of — There are great blocks of . . .
Ms Harvey:	(*whispering to another pupil*) Oh, thanks very much.
Colin:	well painted (*miscues* 'planned') offices. There is a cathedral. There are churches and schools and shopping centres free from traffic. There are green // lawns and bright, tropical flowers, — and there are people. Thousands and thousands of men, women and children have flocked to (*inserts* 'see') the country's new capital. They have come from poor, dusty villages and crowded // seaports. They have found homes and work and friends. They have brought life to Brasilia.
Ms Harvey:	Right. Now, that's fine. Now, have you picked out a story from that?
Colin:	Uh, no.
Ms Harvey:	Pick out a story that you particularly enjoyed and just write a brief account of it for me please. All right?
Colin:	Can I do this one, 'cos I . . .
Ms Harvey:	Well, if you, if you want to, but don't copy it will you? (*To Thomas, next child in queue*) Yes?

How can the researcher go about achieving an understanding of 'what happened' in this scene? How can he be certain that the meaning he does manage to extract from (or read into!) this short fragment does not merely reflect 'the pattern of the researcher's head' (Willis, 1976, p. 136)? And how can he communicate his analysis to those who did not participate in the event being examined, while still preserving both the authority of the 'documentary record' as well as the immediacy of the 'unofficial record'?

Layers of evidence

These questions become critical when applied specifically to the task of analysing this classroom scene in terms of its significance for the assessment of reading. What counts as reading assessment here, and how can it be interpreted? What reading assessment there *is* going on seems so deeply embedded in the fabric of meaning in the classroom that it is difficult to tease out its particular significance.

We can begin an analysis of this scene by looking at the first part of the 'documentary' record — the transcript of the tape-recording. The story which the transcript tells only breaks the surface of the layers of meaning operating here: 'teacher finishes administrative business; teacher reinforces the instruction which defines the terms of the lesson; teacher listens to pupil's oral reading; pupil is interrupted by another pupil who is dealt with by the teacher; pupil continues reading; teacher intervenes when pupil encounters difficulty; teacher closes interaction with pupil and issues writing assignment.' Of course there is much more we can glean from the transcript by careful scrutiny. We can gain a sense of the rules which govern the various interactions between teacher and pupils; we can see that those rules are formally mediated by the teacher; we can gain a sense of the acceptable level of sarcasm permitted in the classroom; we can observe the teacher's techniques for coping with conflicting demands on her time; and we can formulate hypotheses about what the teacher is 'doing' as she listens to Colin's reading.

The transcript, however, is only the starting point of an analysis of what reading assessment transpires between Ms Harvey and Colin. From the transcript we can consult the other part of the documentary record, the observation notes. The notes 'show' that Ms Harvey and Colin are holding the book together; that Ms Harvey uses Colin's Reading Record as a marker, moving it down line-by-line as Colin reads; that Ms Harvey occasionally points to words in Colin's book with her pen as a silent prompt, which of course is not picked up on the tape; that the queue builds up, as Colin reads, to as many as six or seven children; that a parent volunteer enters the room while Colin is reading, sets herself up in one corner of the classroom, and proceeds to call the first child on the list of children whom she hears read on a weekly basis; that the head teacher has come into the room and is standing at Ms Harvey's desk waiting for an opportunity to speak to her.

But of course the researcher's notes taken during the event are by no means an objective record or account of 'what happened'; neither do they really 'speak for themselves'. They are the outcome of a highly selective and interpretative process, shaped to a large extent by the researcher's prior knowledge of the teacher and the pupils, by his own relationships with them and by his accumulated understanding of what he might expect to have happened in the event recorded in the observation notes. The notes are also shaped by the researcher's own idea of what a researcher's observation notes ought to look like. They are therefore in one sense a crude record of his own experience of the event.

It is, however, only when we begin to consult the 'black market record' — the researcher's own personal understanding of the meanings operating in this scene — that we begin to 'know' what is happening. The 'black market record' suggests that this lesson has a familiar and well-defined structure, and that Ms Harvey's reinforcement, 'You *should* be reading your reading book', is sufficient to signify to the class that this structure has taken effect; that Ms Harvey considers Colin to be a technically fluent but uninspired reader; that Ms Harvey and Colin know that permission to move on to the next reading book is contingent on (i) an oral rendition by Colin of part of the final chapter in the reading book, during which he should not get 'stuck' too often, and (ii) the completion of the short piece of writing she assigns him; and that the likely object of the head teacher's visit is to follow up a complaint Ms Harvey had made to him that morning. These 'black market' aspects of the event are either entirely absent from the transcript or only remotely implied within it, and yet the researcher will be vividly aware of them as he 'reads' the transcript. Furthermore, his analysis of this event, months after it happened, will draw on the knowledge and relationships which he built up in the classroom subsequent to the event, as well as on the working environment in which that later analysis is carried out. To what extent, for example, will his analysis of the scene's significance for reading assessment be shaped by his knowledge in hindsight of Ms Harvey's more recent views about Colin's reading, expressed to the researcher, or indeed by the pressures brought to bear on the researcher to report his findings impersonally? None of these are explicit aspects of the documentary record, but they are almost impossible to exclude from an analysis of the event.

The text and situation of data

One possible exit from this quandary is provided by socioinguists in their analysis of the relationship between language and the setting in which language is used. Michael Halliday, for example, develops the concepts of 'text' and 'situation'. He defines 'text' as 'the instances of linguistic interaction in which people actually engage: whatever is said, or written, in an operational context' (1978, pp. 108–9). Elsewhere (1976, p. 123) he writes that the term 'text'

> covers both speech and writing, and is quite neutral as regards style and content: it may be language in action, conversation, telephone talk, debate, dramatic dialogue, narrative fiction, poetry, prayer, inscriptions, public notices, legal proceedings, communicating with animals, intimate monologue or anything else.

'Situation' on the other hand is seen as 'the environment in which the text comes to life' (1978, p. 109). Although to Halliday it is possible to identify *types* of situations governed by rules of communication derived from wider social and cultural structures, Edwards and Furlong (1978) warn (pp. 55–6).

> . . . that context should not be used as an ill-defined and static dumping ground for what the participants are supposed to know about that part of their social world. The relevant context changes rapidly.

Sociolinguists agree, however, that text and situation are part of all language and are inseparable features of all language.

Sociolinguistic theories of text and situation provided an extremely useful model for describing the relationship between the 'documentary record' and the 'unofficial record' in my research on reading assessment. The more tangible kinds of evidence — the observation notes, the tapes, the transcripts

— are all examples of language in operational contexts and therefore qualify as 'texts'. The inexplicit element of the text — the researcher's familiarity with the structure and meaning of the social situation in which the text was produced — is an example of Halliday's notion of 'situation'. Halliday writes:

> If it is true that a hearer, given the right information, can make sensible guesses about what the speaker is going to mean — and this seems a necessary assumption seeing that communication does take place — then this 'right information' is what we mean by the social context. *It consists of those general properties of the situation which collectively function as the determinants of text.* (1978, p. 110) (my italic)

If we replace 'hearer' and 'speaker' with 'language producer' and 'language receiver' — and this is justifiable since 'text' embraces written as well as spoken language — this passage provides a serviceable description of the analytic process in case-study research. Tapes and field notes, for example, however revealing as texts, are unabled to convey the 'general properties of the situation which collectively function as the determinants of text'. The type of interaction between Ms Harvey and Colin on the tape transcript may be recognizable as 'teacher hearing pupil read' but only those with an intimate familiarity with this classroom would be able to describe the special structure and significance of the lesson which Ms Harvey inaugurates with the words, '*Right*. Now . . . You *should* be reading your reading book.' This unofficial data is the 'right information' which renders a text intelligible. Similarly, the researcher's observation notes, of the interaction between Colin and Ms Harvey, are ultimately texts communicated by the researcher to himself for reading at a later date. In order for the 'communication to take place' — in order for the 'hearer' to make 'sensible guesses about what the speaker is going to mean' — 'and in order for the researcher to make sense of his own observation notes, he must make use of the 'right information': his familiarity with the social context which is absent from the observation notes but which can be provided by the researcher's own experience of the event.

Expressing the relationship between the documentary record and the unofficial record in sociolinguistic terms helps to forge an image of analysis in classroom research as an active and creative process involving the reconstruction of meaning by the researcher as he re-works the data in the light of his experience. Rob Walker writes that:

> the task of research is to make sense of what we know. The investigator dismantles and reassembles conventional or common-sense meanings, altering the balance between what seems strange and what seems familiar, striving to find new ways of looking at the world (1980, p. 224).
> . . . Significance has to be won from the chaotic patterns: 'meaning' does not naturally fall out of the data, sense has to be made of it (1980, p. 234).

As soon as the documentary record in case-study research is seen as potentially-meaningful language, rather than merely as facts, the unofficial record becomes an indispensable component of the data, and the analysis of that record perforce becomes a personal interpretative activity. And because this method of analysis is explicitly interpretative it is in a real sense far less of a 'fiction' than traditional quantitative research methods which 'give no clues as to the actual process of discovery, to the ways conventional wisdom has had to be stretched and squeezed' (Walker, 1980, p. 228).

Research as reading

Anyone familiar with the writings of psycholinguists on the subject of children's reading will react to all this talk of 'sensible guesses' and 'context', of 'constructing meaning' and 'making sense', with a strong sense of *déjà vu*. We've heard this before somewhere. Consider Margaret Meek's description of the act of reading, bearing in mind what I have suggested so far about the process of analysis/interpretation in case-study research:

> In the act of reading what someone has written, we enter into a kind of social relationship with the writer who has something to tell us or something to make with words and language. The reader takes on this relationship, which may feel like listening, but is in fact different in that it is more active. He recreates the meaning by processing the text at his own speed and in his own way. As he brings the text to life, he casts back and forth in his head for connections between what he is reading and what he already knows. His eyes scan forward or jump backwards. He pauses, rushes on, selects from his memory whatever relates the meaning to his experience or his earlier reading, in a rich and complex system of to-ing and fro-ing in his head, storing, reworking, understanding or being puzzled. Some successful readers say that they feel they are helping to create the work *with* the author. (1982, pp. 20–1)

This eloquent account of the reading act, which celebrates the active, personal and interpretative response to a text by a reader, can clearly be read as an extended metaphor of the act of analysis in case-study research. This is not entirely a coincidence, since both psycholinguistics and case-study research share an emphasis on the *meaning* which individuals make of their experience, and a rejection of mechanistic views of social action. In this sense both disciplines are broadly phenemenological in their theoretical orientation.

So, what can the case-study researcher learn from the psycholinguistic view of reading? The insight into the research process provided by sociolinguistics, which helped to support a view of data as text, and of analysis as active contextualization, can now be further extended by psycholinguistics by suggesting that the interplay between the documentary record and the researcher's experience approximates a 'reading' of the data. And the 'meaning' of the researcher's data is no more intrinsic to the words of the tape transcript than the 'meaning' of a reader's text is intrinsic to the words on the page. Whatever 'meaning' there is in the transcript is the product of an interaction between the words and the researcher's inside knowledge, or as I.A. Richards puts it (1943, p. 94):

> ... the proper meaning of a passage (what it really means) is a kind of scholastic ghost with very much less in it than a good reader will rightly find there.

Reading as reseach

The analogy is not one-way, however. Formulations of the reading act may shed light on the task of analysis in research, but at the same time much can be learned about the task of reading from descriptions of the research process. Although psycholinguistics supports a vision of research analysis as an active, personal and interpretative response to the data by a researcher, recall that this was only part of the solution to the problematic relationship between the documentary record and the unofficial record. There was a significant sociolinguistic element to the picture as well. For Halliday a text is not merely part of a specific communication between individual speakers and hearers (or, for the reading act, writers and readers). Text is also located within a complex network of social structures and relationships.

Text — whether it be a researcher's tape transcripts and observation notes, or a child's book — is produced within an elaborate social context which is 'entered into' and 'recreated' by the researcher/analyst or by the child/reader when the text is received. But at the same time, written text of any kind is *received* within an elaborate social context which is almost certainly different from the situation within which the text was *produced*. This receiving-end context is, too, an integral part of the interaction between written text and reading situation. The researcher 'receives' the text of his own documentary record within a social context quite unlike the social context within which he 'produced' it. The classroom where the data were collected differs markedly from the academic environment in which the analysis is carried out, but both contexts will influence the sense he makes of the data. Similarly, for a child in school, the social context in which he or she 'receives' the text of a book probably bears no relation to the social context from which the text came. The act of reading a text in the classroom is, for a child, inextricably bound up with the social structures and relationships operating there, and the sense he or she makes of the text will be influenced by that context at least as much as by the context in which the text was produced. Angela Hale has observed that 'what counts as reading varies according to the demands of the social situation' (1980, p. 25) and that, in school, this social situation embraces relationships between teachers and pupils, definitions of reading and literacy, and structures of knowledge and power, which will combine to shape the meaning of reading acts (Hale, 1979 and 1980). How, for example, can we separate Colin's 'reading' of the text on Brasilia either from the immediate classroom business surrounding the interaction between Colin and Ms Harvey or from the structural significance which the event of reading aloud has for both Colin and his teachers?

Psycholinguists point to the importance of the 'kind of social relationship with the writer' which the reader 'enters into' as he or she engaged with the text. Sociolinguists, on the other hand, can provide the basis for a more structural description of the task of reading at school, which involves the entering into a social relationship of a very different kind — the more immediate interaction with teachers and peers in a classroom context. A reading of a text, whether by a researcher or pupil, is a social and cultural activity, and as such it will be affected by and in turn have its own influence upon the social structures and relationships within which that reading of the text takes place.

Assessment as sense-making

What then can be learned from this about the classroom teacher faced with the task of evaluating pupils' reading? My argument so far, that the act of research analysis and the act of reading are analogous *kinds* of tasks, applies equally to classroom assessment. Coming to 'know' a reader is, after all, a case of making meaning within a complex social context. Just as for research and reading, a sociolinguistic emphasis makes explicit two vital aspects of reading assessment. First, it reinforces the sense-making nature of assessment, in contrast with the widely-held belief that it is an unambiguous mechanical operation. Second, it locates the assessment process within (to use Halliday's term once again) a 'situation' which comprises a complex network of social structures and relationships.

And yet, however much a sociolinguistic perspective may facilitate research analysis by legitimizing the 'unofficial' dimension of the research-er's data, it also magnifies the central methodological difficulty in 'making sense' of teachers' reading assessment practices in the classroom. I began by recognizing that the reading assessment taking place between Colin and his teacher seemed so embedded in the fabric of meaning in the classroom that it was difficult to tease out its particular significance. Despite the insights about that scene afforded by the inclusion of the 'black market record', this central problem of 'embeddedness' is not greatly overcome. In what sense can we say that Ms Harvey is *assessing* Colin's reading, on the basis of (official as well as unofficial) evidence available to us?

Does the scene's significance for reading assessment derive from the information about Colin as a reader, which is 'available' to Ms Harvey in Colin's oral reading? Does it derive from the fact that Colin's 'promotion', to the next reading book in the scheme, was 'at stake' here? Does it derive from the fact that Colin was ultimately allowed to exchange his reading book for the 'next one up' in the reading scheme? Does it derive from the possibility that Ms Harvey may draw on her perceptions about Colin's reading during this episode when later required to communicate her appraisal of Colin as a reader to parents, other teachers, and so on? Does it derive from the fact that Ms Harvey has reported in interview that she bases her judgements of chil-dren's reading on their oral reading fluency? Or does it derive from the extent to which Colin and Ms Harvey *behave* as though Colin's reading is being assessed? It all depends on our definition of 'reading assessment', a term which is generally taken to stand for practices with a self-evident existence but which for a researcher are very difficult to identify and describe. If the classroom observer defines 'reading assessment' as *the formation of judgements, by teachers, about children with respect to their competence as readers*, he is attempting to identify a process which is by definition hidden (i.e. inside the teacher's head) and therefore unavailable for inspection. He can describe the *sources* from which information about children's reading may have been gathered ('texts'). He can describe the *settings* within which that information was available ('situations'). And he can describe words and actions which appear to be the *outcomes* of reading assessment. He cannot, however, infer from either the sources and settings, or the outcomes, that the *process* of reading assessment has necessarily taken place. So long as he defines reading assessment as a judgement-making process rather than an observable form of behaviour, the nearest he can get is by carefully describing *all* possible manifestations of reading assessment, and by building up a picture which is the composite of these varied and sometimes contradictory representations.

Of cource, gaining access to hidden processes is not a problem which only concerns researchers of classroom reading assessment. The reading process itself is widely held to be a hidden process (i.e. it happens inside the reader's head) and is therefore unavailable for inspection. Differing definitions of reading have generated different approaches to gaining access to it, but these approaches invariably render (private) reading public by means of a product or outcome of reading. If reading really is a hidden process then these products and outcomes are only 'the visible tip of far less accessible behaviour' (Pugh, 1978, p. 89), in which case close attention to those aspects of reading which are closest to the reader, i.e. the 'text' and 'situation' of a reading act, are probably more reliable indicators of the quality of a reader's experience. Building up a picture of readers based on all possible manifestations of reading, whether they corroborate each other or not, is probably the nearest we can get. This is what Margaret Spencer calls for when she writes that 'we should do well to move our feet and eyes and try to see what the learning looks like from where the learner stands, his book in hand' (1980, p. 61). Teachers often have this kind of intuitive sense of how their pupils experience reading. If assessment is a sense-making, rather than a technical, exercise, this 'black market record' will form an indispensable context against which other, more outcome-based, assessments will be made sense of. Recovering the process by which that 'unofficial record' is produced may be an impossible research task, but its existence and legitimacy should not be questioned.

Conclusion

Rob Walker writes that 'the subject being studied can impose its own authority on the sense that is made of it by the investigator' (1980, p. 224). In the present project the subjects being studied did more than impose their own authority on the sense I made of them: they provided living examples of sense-making activities which reinforced the foundation for an interpretative methodology. By the same token an approach to research, which made explicit its dependence on social interaction and relationships for access to the meaning of classroom events, helped to highlight the inseparability of children's reading, or teachers' assessment practices, from the context of background knowledge and social interaction through which they occur. For me, the recognition that the teacher assessing reading, the child reading a text, and myself studying teachers' practices, were all in a real sense engaged in analogous kinds of sense-making activities, sharpened my understanding of all three tasks.

Notes

1. Pseudonyms are used throughout for persons' names.
2. The following notation is used in the transcription of Colin's reading:

//	indicates pause;
(*miscues 'inland'*)	indicates that the word preceding the brackets is a miscue of the word in brackets;
(*self-corrects*)	indicates that pupil corrects own miscue without audible prompt;
'of-of'	indicates repetition;
(*inserts* 'see')	indicates that word in brackets was vocalized by pupil but does not appear in text.

The text Colin reads in the transcript is pp. 119–20 of Flowerdew, P. (1972) *New Interest: Book Two*. Edinburgh: Oliver and Boyd.

References

Edwards, A. D. and Furlong, V. J. (1978) *The Language of Teaching*. London: Heinemann Educational Books.

Giddens, A. (1976) *New Rules of Sociological Method*. London: Hutchinson.

Hale, A. (1979) 'Hearing children read: a sociological analysis of the definition of reading implicit in a routine teaching activity.' Unpublished Ph. D. thesis, University of Manchester.

—— (1980) 'The social relationships implicit in approaches to reading.' *Reading* **14**, 1, July.

Halliday, M. A. K. (1976) *Learning How to Mean*. London: Edward Arnold.

—— (1978) *Language as Social Semiotic*. Routledge and Kegan Paul.

Holland, N. N. (1975) *Five Readers Reading*. London: Routledge and Kegan Paul.

Hull, C. (1981) 'Between the lines: data analysis as an exact art.' Paper presented to the 1981 conference of the British Educational Research Association.

Meek, M. (1982) *Learning to Read*. London: The Bodley Head.

Pugh, A. K. (1978) *Silent Reading: An introduction to its study and teaching*. London: Heinemann Educational Books.

Richards, I. A. (1943) *How to Read a Page*. London: Routledge and Kegan Paul.

Spencer, M. (1980) 'Handing down the magic.' in Salmon, P. (ed.), *Coming to Know*. London: Routledge and Kegan Paul.

Walker, R. (1980) 'Making sense and losing meaning: problems of selection in doing case study,' in Simons, H. (ed.), *Towards a Science of the Singular: Essays about case-study research and evaluation*. Norwich: Centre for Applied Research in Education, University of East Anglia.
Willis, P. (1976) 'The man in the iron cage: notes on method.' *Working Papers in Cultural Studies*. Centre for Contemporary Cultural Studies, University of Birmingham, pp. 135–43.

Index